ACROSS THE COLOR LINE

# ACROSS THE COLOR LINE

*REPORTING 25 YEARS IN BLACK CINCINNATI*

Mark Curnutte

University of
CINCINNATI | PRESS

About the University of Cincinnati Press

The University of Cincinnati Press is committed to publishing rigorous, peer reviewed, leading scholarship accessibly to stimulate dialog between the academy, public intellectuals and lay practitioners. The Press endeavors to erase disciplinary boundaries in order to cast fresh light on common problems in our global community. Building on the university's longstanding tradition of social responsibility to the citizens of Cincinnati, state of Ohio, and the world, the press publishes books on topics which expose and resolve disparities at every level of society and have local, national and global impact.

The University of Cincinnati Press, Cincinnati 45221

Library of Congress Cataloging-in-Publication Data
Names: Curnutte, Mark, author.
Title: Across the color line : reporting 25 years in Black Cincinnati / Mark Curnutte.
Other titles: Cincinnati enquirer.
Description: Cincinnati : University of Cincinnati Press, 2018. | Includes
bibliographical references and index. |
Identifiers: LCCN 2019002197 (print) | LCCN 2019007702 (ebook) | ISBN
9781947602021 (eBook, PDF) | ISBN 9781947602038 (eBook, EPUB) | ISBN
9781947602014 | ISBN 9781947602014(hardback) | ISBN
9781947602021(e-book :PDF) | ISBN 9781947602038(e-book :EPUB)
Subjects: LCSH: Cincinnati (Ohio)--Race relations. | African
Americans--Ohio--Cincinnati--Social conditions. | Curnutte, Mark.
Classification: LCC F499.C59 (ebook) | LCC F499.C59 N4232 2018 (print) | DDC
305.896/073077178--dc23
LC record available at https://lccn.loc.gov/2019002197

ISBN 978-1-947602-01-4 (hardback)
ISBN 978-1-947602-02-1 (e-book, PDF)
ISBN 978-1-947602-03-8 (e-book, EPUB)

Designed and produced for UC Press by Bryce Schimanski
Typeset in: Scala Regular
Printed in the United States of America

Newspaper stories published from 1993 through 2018 in *The Cincinnati Enquirer* used by permission with photographs courtesy of *The Cincinnati Enquirer*.

First Printing

# ON THE COVER

TOP LEFT

"Avondale Heroes" mural by ArtWorks Cincinnati © 2018

ArtWorks is a non-profit organization dedicated to teaching Cincinnati's youth artistic and life skills, and producing transforming art around the city. To date, Artworks' Youth Apprentices and artists have created 132 public murals in Cincinnati and surrounding areas. This particular mural is located at 3371 Reading Road, Cincinnati, Ohio 45229.

Lead designer: James Pate

Project Manager: Brandon Hawkins

Teaching Artist: Tiara Harmon

Youth Apprentices: Shalaisjah Cason, Aiden Cobb, Noor Essakalli, Fiona Harrell-DuChaine, Theresa Johnson, and Mattie Masrorocco

Photograph by Nicholas Scarpelli

TOP RIGHT AND BOTTOM RIGHT

Images of Avondale in 2018.

Photographs by Nicholas Scarpelli. Nicholas Scarpelli is a photographer from New York, now based in Cincinnati. His website is https://www.nickscphoto.com/.

BOTTOM RIGHT

Author photograph by Cara Owsley. Cara Owsley is Director of Photography at *The Cincinnati Enquirer* and for USA Today Network news organizations throughout Ohio. She led the visuals team on the Enquirer's 2017 "Seven Days of Heroin" project, winner of the Pulitzer Prize for Local Reporting.

All images throughout the book originally ran in *The Cincinnati Enquirer* from 1993-2018. The photographer for each image, if known, is named in the credit line.

In Memoriam:
Elizabeth A. Curnutte (1929–2006)
John T. Curnutte (1923–2003)
Victoria Lara (1928–2014)
Alphonse Lara (1924–2014)

Dedicado a la reina de mi corazón, mi esposa, Diana.

# TABLE OF CONTENTS

# ACKNOWLEDGMENTS

In addition to my gratitude to the people herein who opened their lives to me, I thank the following people:

"Across the Color Line" collaborators Tom Callinan, the Hon. Nathaniel R. Jones, and Cara Owsley, and everyone at University of Cincinnati Press.

*The Cincinnati Enquirer* executive editors who saw value in this work and allowed me to pursue it: Larry Beaupre, Ward Bushee, Tom Callinan, Carolyn Washburn, Peter Bhatia, and Beryl Love.

*Enquirer* copy editors and photojournalists and my many assigning editors, most notably Bill Cieslewicz and Randy Essex. Teammates all.

Retired *Enquirer* reporters Allen Howard and Ben Kaufman, who guided me and shared their sources with me in 1993; former writing coach Michael Roberts; and *Enquirer* colleagues Michael McCarter, Byron McCauley, and Carol Motsinger.

Journalism, literature, and poetry teachers who showed me the beauty and power of the written word: David Abrahams at the Dixon (Illinois) *Evening Telegraph*, and Jack Dempsey at Dixon High School; and Donald Daiker, Frank Jordan, Hugh Morgan, and Marilyn Throne at Miami University, Oxford, Ohio.

Byron E. Logan, Miami University, a geographer who opened the world to me and helped me appreciate its many cultures.

And Donna Jones Baker, Eli J. Bortz, Ozie Davis III, Milton Hinton, Beverly Lathan, the Rev. Damon Lynch Jr., Dr. Olugbenga Olowokure, Iris Roley, Carl B. Westmoreland, the Rev. Mr. Royce Winters, and Michele Young.

All my love to my brothers and sisters: John, Paul, Joan, Barb, Lucy, and Spencer; my wife, Diana; and children Peter, Matthew, Emma, and Alexa and son-in-law Josh.

# FOREWORD

The various lenses through which Mark Curnutte has observed unfolding events in the nation, and particularly the Cincinnati community, as a journalist, enrich this narrative, and are an invaluable contribution to those thirsting to learn about the amazing (yet incomplete) societal transformation that is occurring here. Included in the transformation are the periods in which staid institutions are challenged to change, and longstanding customs are being reformed as persons are forced to look into mirrors and note realistically how sectors of the community live.

What strikes me as particularly useful is the degree to which the author was able to win and sustain the trust and confidence of a wide range of people, recognizing the different components of interests that make up what we call the "black community."

In writing *Across the Color Line*, and, in particular, his introduction, "Into the Marvelous Light," Curnutte generously opens the curtains on the stages of his life to share with readers insights into the experiences he honestly exposes himself to and what he learned in pursuing his journalistic career. His technical skills were honed by his experience as a beat reporter and a sports writer. Even more impressive, however, are his unique humanitarian qualities, including those displayed during his time spent in Haiti immersing himself in the culture and documenting the lives of impoverished families. Yet the sharing is only a part of this rich story, a gift that Curnutte offers his readers. The full appreciation of what the author brought to this task as a white man being trusted and accepted into the inner councils of Cincinnati's varied black communities says much about the good faith, sensitivity, and awareness of Mark Curnutte, which all enabled him to navigate the perilous shoals of American racism.

The National Advisory Committee on Civil Disorders (Kerner Commission: 1968), in its monumental report on the disturbances that threatened to rip this nation apart, analyzed the role of the media in precipitating disorders, as well as misrepresenting to the public the social and economic injustices that created the dry rot that the disorders ignited.

In Curnutte's brilliant reporting and clear writing, we see a fully formed and gifted journalist who personifies what the Kerner Commission prescribed as necessary to get at the misinformation on race that our segregated institutions have historically perpetuated.

The nature of the challenge that Curnutte confronted in Cincinnati, and his successful address to that challenge, is apparent in the acceptance of him and his writing on race matters by both black and white readerships of the storied newspaper, the Cincinnati *Enquirer*. To make the point, the Kerner Report included a statement from an interview that highlighted the lack of trust that was typical of many black readers of what they regarded as the "white press:"

> The average black person couldn't give less of a damn about what the media say. The intelligent black person is resentful at what he considers to be totally false portrayal of what goes on in the ghetto. Most black people see the newspapers as mouthpieces of the "power structure."

Readers will be moved by Curnutte's descriptions of the emotions that overwhelmed him, whose faith had been formed as a white Catholic in the German tradition, as he was taken into the bosom of the predominantly black Church of the Resurrection located deep in the heart of Bond Hill, a largely segregated community that had long since served as a destination point for black "refugees" of urban change. The music and warmth of the service extended to him as a white Catholic in the black Catholic parish drew from him this reaction: "I feel free to express myself and literally let the spirit move me." Some serious surgeries that had "badly broken" him physically also led him to the point that he could feel himself breaking psychologically. But now, he writes, "I was in a church where people openly admitted their brokenness and joyously praised the God who helps to put them back together."

The "restoration" process he underwent strengthened him, and otherwise provided him with the intellectual and moral armor to go forward and seek facts as a journalist throughout the black community about the social conditions stemming from racism with an authenticity to report on them – with a credibility that few journalists could claim.

A reading of Curnutte's remarkable book, *Across the Color Line*, convinces in no uncertain terms that the uniqueness of his qualities and the clarity of his insight elevate him far above the pedestrian class of journalists that the Kerner Report cited. To the contrary, Mark Curnutte gives journalism a good name.

**The Hon. Nathaniel R. Jones**
Retired, U.S. Court of Appeals for the 6th Circuit
Cincinnati, Ohio
Jan. 31, 2018

# PROLOGUE

# A Race through Time

*Originally published November 14–19, 1993*
*Updated July 24, 2018*

Notable events in Cincinnati's history that have helped shape present-day racial attitudes:

1787: The Northwest Ordinance prohibits slavery in the region that will become Ohio, Michigan, Indiana, Illinois, and Wisconsin.

1788: Whites settle Cincinnati.

1794: First blacks arrive.

1800: Black population is confined to segregated Bucktown, an area bordered by present-day Main, Broadway, Sixth, and Seventh streets. Northwest Territory Gov. Arthur St. Clair decides that the anti-slavery passage does not apply to slaves brought into the territory before 1787. Blacks can neither vote nor sit on a jury.

1804: A year after its founding, Ohio enacts an "anti-immigration law" to regulate the population of "black or mulatto persons" in the state. A later ruling requires blacks to pay $500 for residency and to carry citizenship papers at all times.

1829: Ohio passes "An Act to Provide for the Support and Better Regulation of Common Schools." The law bars black children from attending public schools, although Cincinnati's black property owners pay taxes that support them.

1829: Fearing that blacks will threaten their job security, a group of whites living near the river marches on Bucktown, pelting homes and businesses with rocks. Blacks defend their property, killing one white. Seven whites and ten blacks are arrested. City officials fine each white $700 and rule that blacks acted in self-defense.

1830: Cincinnati becomes a prominent stop on the Underground Railroad. But local businessmen, because of their strong economic, cultural, and social ties to the South, oppose any cause that might offend their neighbors on the other side of the Ohio River.

1836: Pro-slavery whites storm the office of publisher James G. Birney, whose weekly *Philanthropist* advocates black equality, throwing parts of his press into the river.

1840: James P. Ball along with brother Tom opened one of the largest photo galleries/studios in the heart of Cincinnati, "Ball's Great Daguerrean Gallery of the West," quite a feat for a black man in the 1840s.

1842: A street brawl between blacks and Irish immigrants causes city officials to declare martial law and vow to uphold Black Laws designed to "control the Negro."

1842: The Ohio Supreme Court rules that it is illegal for public funds to be used to educate black children.

1844: Six blacks-only schools operate in Cincinnati with private funds.

1850: Legislation passed by the Ohio General Assembly improves opportunities for blacks, who establish successful barrel-making, tailoring, pickling, grocery, and construction businesses in Cincinnati.

1851: Although a state law establishes black public schools to be funded by taxes collected from black property owners, Cincinnati refuses to release any of the tax money because black school trustees were not elected officials and therefore could not drain funds from the city treasury.

1853: The Ohio Legislature creates a segregated black school system to be funded by both white and black taxes but still governed by a white school board.

1856: The white school board returns control of Cincinnati's public schools to a board of six black trustees to be elected annually by black male voters.

1861: Having acted to prevent persons of mixed white and "African" blood from voting, the Ohio Legislature then declares that "it shall be unlawful for persons of pure white blood to intermarry with or have illicit carnal intercourse with any negro (sic), or person having a distinct and visible admixture of African blood."

1862: Blacks previously ignored as Civil War recruits are enlisted as the "Black Brigade" to build Ft. Mitchell in Kentucky.

1869: When Congress submits the Fifteenth Amendment (black suffrage) to the states for ratification, Ohio quickly refuses. The state later ratifies the amendment only when the legislature realizes it will pass nationally regardless of its objection.

1870: Poor Irish and German immigrants settle in and around Bucktown, but most eventually move out, leaving only the poorest whites to live in an uneasy peace with economically trapped blacks. About 500 blacks live in Walnut Hills, recently annexed by Cincinnati, and work as domestics in the nearby hillside homes of affluent whites.

1871: The Ohio Supreme Court challenges the federal bill of rights given to blacks by ruling that "Equality of rights does not involve the necessity of educating white and colored persons in the same school." The ruling also eliminates Cincinnati's black school board and returns control of black schools to the white board.

1887: The Arnett bill repeals the last of Ohio's Black Laws, including ones calling for segregated schools, but it prescribes no means for enforcement. Blacks begin attending the city's three main high schools – Walnut Hills, Hughes, and Woodward – but as more blacks enroll, black schools close and black teachers are fired. Not until 1948 would the Cincinnati Board of Education allow blacks to teach white students.

1910: Forty-four percent of the city's black population lives in the West End, in "tenements and apartments of different, though generally lesser, degrees of quality," David A. Gerber writes in *Black Ohio and the Color Line 1860-1915*. In Walnut Hills, home to a fifth of the city's blacks, "there were an ample number of affluent black homeowners." Small clusters of blacks were developing in the central hilltop communities of Clifton and Avondale, near where blacks worked as domestics.

1914: Blacks fill manufacturing jobs vacated by white Cincinnatians fighting in World War I. Blacks are displaced, however, when whites return at war's end.

1925: A period of dramatic growth in Cincinnati's black population ends with an "acceleration of trends already underway: huddled together in increasingly large concentrations in decaying, congested neighborhoods, suffering from disease, low wages, periodic or chronic unemployment, discrimination, and the dislocations of resettlement. At the same time, the growing presence of the southern migrants severely strained the limits of an already weakened white tolerance," Gerber writes in *Black Ohio*. The "Official City Plan for Cincinnati, Ohio" cites the shortage of adequate housing as the city's primary problem, which would unavoidably continue because of the "unusual influx of colored people."

1931: Frank A. B. Hall is the first black elected to Cincinnati City Council.

1933: Ohio is the first state to enact federal housing legislation, and the Cincinnati Metropolitan Housing Authority (CMHA) is created and enters into a contract with the Ohio Board of Housing to provide low-income housing in Cincinnati, Columbia, Springfield, and Sycamore townships.

1935: Cincinnati Metropolitan Housing Authority decides its top three priorities will be a slum clearance project for whites in the West End, a vacant land project for whites on Este Avenue and a vacant land project for blacks on land north of Lockland (Lincoln Heights). The black project would provide housing for blacks displaced in the West End and would, according to CMHA, "help prevent the scattering by negroes in the various residential areas of the city."

1937: The February flood, worst in the city's history, exacerbates the need for low-income housing. CMHA writes President Roosevelt and asks for additional federal funds for an additional black housing project because "it has been the desire of the community to see the proposed Laurel Homes project in its present location be occupied by white tenants." CMHA formalizes its decision to exclude blacks from Laurel Homes because they "could not pay the rent."

1938: The Suburban Division of the United States Resettlement Administration completes planning for the white suburb of Greenhills that includes golf courses, parks, and woods. A planned black suburb, Lincoln Heights, however, calls for no paved streets, gutters or sidewalks, and no connections are secured for utility lines.

1939: Pressure from the federal government requires that blacks be allowed to live in 1,039-unit Laurel Homes. Although 700 black families were displaced by Laurel Homes construction, only 302 units are allowed for blacks, 737 for whites.

1950: Laurel Homes is converted to "Negro occupancy," and 85 percent of the city's black population now lives in the Basin, almost all of them in the 2,318 units of public housing constructed by CMHA or in apartments rented by white landlords who had been encouraged to concentrate the black population there. CMHA promises to find "suitable" housing for whites displaced by the development of the black ghetto. The Cincinnati Board of Education cooperates in the "ghettoization" by building a "new Negro" elementary-high school in the area.

1951: Black students in Cincinnati Public Schools are allowed to swim in pools with white students. Previously, blacks were not allowed to swim or were allowed to swim only on Friday afternoons, after which time policy stated the pool must be drained and cleaned.

1953: Porter-Hays school opens. Its student body is 95 percent black.

1954: The U.S. Supreme Court, in *Brown vs. Board of Education of Topeka, Kan.*, rules unanimously that racial segregation in schools is unconstitutional. Black teachers are assigned to only eight of the 86 Cincinnati Public Schools, each one with a black student population in excess of more than 70 percent. These schools are located in the West End, which is 85 percent black.

1963: Nine years after the *Brown* decision made school segregation illegal, the Cincinnati chapter of the National Association for the Advancement of Colored People (NAACP) lawsuit alleges that the Cincinnati Board of Education practiced racially segregated intact busing between schools. Also, the first blacks are elected to the Cincinnati Board of Education and City Council since the repeal of proportional representation, a method of ranking choices for council.

1965: Cincinnati Human Relations Commission is formed.

1966: Cincinnati approves new regulations to assure equal opportunities in city construction. Meanwhile, more than 1,000 blacks and whites participate in Home Visit Sunday, when families invite people of another race into their home for the afternoon.

1967: Four days of rioting in Avondale result in 107 arrests, 40 fires, 12 serious injuries and $3 million in property damage. Blacks had met to protest the arrest of a black protester and the unequal enforcement of the city's anti-loitering ordinance.

1968: Four days after the assassination of Martin Luther King Jr., a memorial service spills into rioting in Avondale. One the evening of April 8, two die, 220 are arrested, and $3 million worth of property is damaged.

1968: The University of Cincinnati agrees to an eight-point plan that will broaden the involvement of blacks in campus courses, employment, and policies. The leader of the United Black Association of students is Dwight Tillery, who 23 years later will be the first black mayor of Cincinnati elected by popular vote.

1969: Blacks boycott the city's major department stores over the lack of black Santas. Shillito's promises to have black Santas for Christmas 1970.

1970: Race-related fights and violence close several Greater Cincinnati high schools – including Withrow and North College Hill – for several days at a time.

1973: Black students become the majority in Cincinnati Public Schools.

1974: NAACP lawyers file the *Bronson vs. The Cincinnati Board of Education* suit that seeks complete desegregation of the city's schools.

1979: The practice of prohibiting the sale of homes to blacks is stopped. More than 1,000 deeds in Hamilton County still carry such covenants.

1981: A sales manager at the Westin Hotel distributes an internal memo to hotel executives saying that employees can expect loud guests, drug dealing, and poor tipping during the 20th annual Kool Jazz Festival, which attracts a predominantly black audience of 60,000 to

Riverfront Stadium over two nights. A banquet honoring former Cincinnati Mayor Theodore Berry scheduled for the Westin is moved to the Netherland Plaza.

1982: A white fraternity at the University of Cincinnati, Sigma Alpha Epsilon, holds a "Martin Luther King Trash Day" party, which promotes negative stereotypes of blacks. The SAEs are placed on probation by UC President Henry Winkler.

1984: After weeks of intense negotiations, Cincinnati Public Schools and the plaintiffs in the *Bronson* case reach a consent decree that calls for a federal court to oversee nine areas within the system.

1987: A neo-Nazi group of white youths called White American Skin Heads (WASH) begins recruiting in Corryville and places an ad with Warner Cable. Black business owners call for the ad to be removed.

1988: A judge orders Covington's Glass Menagerie to stop discriminating against blacks who have been prevented from entering the lounge and dance club.

1989: Twelve arts organizations – including the Cincinnati Symphony, Cincinnati Art Museum, and Taft Museum – receive a more than 300-percent increase in funding from the city but are told to begin opening their boards, staffs, and committees to "people of diverse backgrounds" and to create programs that reflect the "rich, multifaceted culture here."

1991: The Buenger Commission, a critical private-industry assessment of the Cincinnati Public Schools, calls for a major overhaul to the system by reducing administration costs and wasteful business practices. Its release is meet with criticism from black leaders who say its all-white membership from the business establishment made no effort to include blacks or other minorities.

1991: Cincinnati Public Schools are released from seven of nine areas of supervision under the *Bronson* agreement. Only discipline and performance in low-achieving schools will remain under watch.

1991: A study by the Federal Reserve Board finds that Greater Cincinnati banks are two times more likely to deny black applicants mortgage loans than white applicants.

1992: Former Cincinnati Reds controller Tim Sabo files a wrongful-firing suit against Reds President and CEO Marge Schott in Hamilton County Common Pleas Court. Sabo claims Schott called former Reds outfielders Eric Davis and Dave Parker her "million-dollar niggers."

1995: A coalition led by the Cincinnati NAACP demands the firing of three Cincinnati Police officers involved in the arrest of a black teenager, Pharon Crosby, that was captured on video by a local television station. The year also marks the beginning of a seven-year period during which 14 African-Americans, 13 men and one male child, are killed in conflicts with Cincinnati officers. At least two of the suspects had fired first at officers.

2000: Protesters picket eight downtown restaurants that closed for the weekend in late July during two high-profile events that draw tens of thousands of African-Americans to Cincinnati, the Coors Light Jazz Festival and Ujima Cinci-Bration.

2001: In March, the American Civil Liberties Union joined the Cincinnati Black United Front in filing a lawsuit accusing the Cincinnati Police Department of 30 years of illegally targeting and harassing blacks based on race.

2001: Three weeks later, in early April, an unarmed black man, Timothy Thomas, 19, who had a record of minor offenses, mostly traffic-related, tries to run from police. He is shot and killed in an alley in Over-the-Rhine by a white police officer. His death touches off weeks of rioting and social unrest and a declaration of martial law.

2002: The Collaborative Agreement is signed and changes the way the Cincinnati Police Department does its job. Changes in use of force, accountability, data collection, bias-free policing, and community-oriented policing become policies. The goal is to increase trust between the department and the city's black community.

2003: The Cincinnati Bengals hire their first African-American head coach, Marvin Lewis, amid an NFL-wide effort to increase minorities in top coaching and front office ranks.

2008: The Cincinnati Reds hire their first African-American manager, Dusty Baker. The team had previously hired a popular Cuban-American manager, popular former Reds player Tony Perez, who was fired just 44 games into the 1993 season.

2011: For the first time, a majority of African-Americans is elected to the nine seats on Cincinnati City Council.

2012: After an election recount, Tracie Hunter wins a contested race and becomes the first African-American Juvenile Court judge in Hamilton County. Two years later, she is convicted by a jury of one felony charge for giving confidential records to her brother, a juvenile court employee. The case divides the city and county racially.

2014: The Urban League National Meeting is held in Cincinnati. The century-old civil rights organization had pulled its convention from Cincinnati in 2002, honoring a boycott established by African-American leaders in the wake of the 2001 Timothy Thomas shooting.

2015: A white University of Cincinnati police officer, Ray Tensing, shoots and kills unarmed black motorist Sam DuBose during a traffic stop in Mount Auburn. Tensing faces two murder trials, which end in hung juries, in 2016 and 2017. The case further polarizes a polarized community along racial lines.

2015: The Urban League of Greater Southwestern Ohio publishes a 164-page book titled *State of Black Cincinnati 2015: Two Cities.* Its findings reveal pervasive racial division in inequality:

- Seventy-six percent of the 14,000 families who lived in poverty in the city of Cincinnati from 2005 through 2009 were African-American.

- Life expectancy of black men in Cincinnati, 63.8 years, was exactly 10 years less than life expectancy for white men.

- The rate of home ownership in 15-county Greater Cincinnati was 33.1 percent for African-Americans but 74.5 percent for whites.

- Three of every four black children in Cincinnati lived in poverty.

- Ohio's prison population was 45 percent African-American, though African-Americans made up just 12.5 percent of the state's overall population.

2017: The Sentinel Police Association, an advocacy group of black Cincinnati Police officers, unanimously votes that it has no confidence in Sgt. Dan Hils, the white president of the police union.

2018: Two racial incidents occur within weeks in Warren County. A white female Mason Middle School teacher tells a 13-year-old African-American student that he will be lynched by classmates if he does not get back on task. White players on a youth basketball team take the court in jerseys bearing the names "Knee-Grow" and "Coon" across the back.

Were we ever to arrive at knowing the other as the same pulsing
compassion would break the most orthodox heart.

Claudia Rankine
"Coherence in Consequence" (2001)

ACROSS THE COLOR LINE

# INTRODUCTION

# INTO THE MARVELOUS LIGHT

April 12, 2015. Early Sunday afternoon.

I reached down to lift the kneeler and sat back in my pew. My third Mass at this church neared its end. I had received Communion and prayed for God's grace to help me make sense of life on the other side of stage III colorectal cancer.

On Christmas night 2014, I needed six hours of emergency surgery. I experienced a significant drop in blood pressure. Septic shock, doctors said. They feared stroke or organ failure were next. I had to be fed through a line in my chest. After a month in the hospital, nurses told me what to expect physically. No one told me how surviving cancer would mess with my head: the mood swings, the intensity of emotions that could dart from tearful gratitude to punch-a-door anger.

The cancer journey became a film in my mind's eye. It premiered in spring 2015 and replayed some of the most harrowing scenes from my treatment. At times, the visuals would trigger sensations of physical pain. A cold IV line stuck in the back of my hand. Nerve damage in my feet and fingers. The flashbacks rolled across the screen. A stab in my upper chest. "Chemo Lamaze," said the nurse, reminding me to breathe, before she poked the needle through the skin and into the metal port. The liquid drug flowed through that gateway into a large vein near my heart; a few hours later I'd taste hot metal on my tongue.

I sat up, straightened my back, gripped the front edge of the pew bench, closed my eyes and inhaled, pulling air in through my nose to the count of eight. "Breathe, like the nurse said," I told myself. "Pray. Give it all to God."

The acoustic piano and drums introduced another hymn. I looked up to see choir members in black robes and gold sashes swaying in unison. Like many songs in the African-American worship tradition, this one started slowly and softly then built to a spiritual epiphany. One of the women in the choir stood out front with a microphone. She sounded as if she were wailing with pain and grief yet opening a communal wound to healing and hope.

I had not heard this song before. One lyric opened me.

*When I think about what God has done for me.*

Suddenly, I had to lock my jaw and shut my eyes again to try to maintain my composure. That's what I was taught by my family and what we white Catholics, especially ones of German ancestry, like me, did during Mass if the need ever arose. Suppress emotion. Remain stoic. Or walk out swiftly with a purpose, like you had to use the restroom, or your baby was crying and disturbing people around you. Yet here, in the predominantly black Church of the Resurrection in the urban Cincinnati neighborhood of Bond Hill, that time-tested method of restraint did not work. Besides, for the first time at Mass as a lifelong Catholic, I felt free to express myself and, literally, let the spirit move me. I had been badly broken physically and could feel myself breaking psychologically. Now, I was in a church where the priests and deacon and parishioners openly admitted their brokenness and joyously praised the God who helps to put them back together time and time again.

I fell to my knees and buried my face in my hands. My tears broke loose. That hymn, "Jesus Christ is the Way," swirled to its crescendo, the choir taking it high into the altar and then straight into me. The emotional and physical trauma and fear and anxiety of the 16 months since my diagnosis seemed to compress into a single moment.

*I will open up my heart to ev'ryone I see.*

The tears kept coming. I couldn't stop them. Then, I felt a hand on my shoulder. I looked up and saw the African-American woman who sat to my right. Even through my blurry eyes, swollen with hot tears, I could see a face filled with compassion and empathy. She held out a small package of tissues. I sniffled. I didn't know her and had not spoken to her before, other than to greet her with a handshake a few minutes earlier during the sign of peace.

"I'm sorry," I said, choking on my words. "I had cancer. I don't know why I . . . " I couldn't finish my sentence.

"It's okay," she said. She stretched left her arm across my shoulders. I felt another hand gently patting my back as if to comfort a hurting child. I turned to see an elderly woman sitting in the pew behind me.

"Let it out, it's okay," the first woman said in a reassuring whisper, as if she knew – or could feel – the whole scope of my story and the reason for me breaking down.

"You're safe here," she said.

For the first time in a long time, I believed I was.

\* \* \*

The Resurrection community become my home within my adopted hometown of the past 25 years. I accepted a reporting job in 1993 at the *Cincinnati Enquirer* and moved into the urban affairs beat.

My first summer as a Resurrection member, 2015, became a turning point. I realized that what had started as an academic and professional interest in African-American culture and history and the city's black community had become personal. My comfort at Resurrection – I experienced the inner peace of knowing I was where I was supposed to be – caused me to reflect on the previous 22 years and what led me there. My job.

I started to read profiles and issue and news stories I'd clipped and saved about African-Americans and the neighborhoods in which they lived. Most of the stories I'd written even during nine seasons on the *Enquirer*'s NFL/Cincinnati Bengals beat featured black players and coaches. I started to sort the stories by subject matter. This book began to take shape. A handful of stories formed "The NFL Beat" chapter. One of the most memorable looked at the relationship of Bengals defensive back Madieu Williams and his younger brother, Mike, who was in middle school when their mother died. Madieu became Mike's guardian. Mike moved from Maryland. I nurtured the idea with Madieu for a year before he agreed to the story.

I had written several dozen featured obituaries, which the *Enquirer* labels as "Lives Remembered." These were summaries of lives well-lived, many detailing how black men and women who died in their 80s and 90s had overcome segregation and discrimination. But not without personal cost. Activist Nannie Hinkston fought for residents of Over-the-Rhine when it was the city's repository for the poor, black, and homeless. Bennett Cooper Sr. became the first African-American director of a state prison system in 1972. This chapter would provide natural closure to the collective story I now wanted to tell of the people and places I'd come to know over a quarter of a century in black Cincinnati.

The chapters are organized by topic, and the stories within each chapter are dated and sequenced chronologically.

Most of the people in these stories were everyday citizens who formed the heartbeat of their community, yet their stories had been relegated to the underbrush of Cincinnati's history. They were the nameless, faceless, and anonymous whose primary neighborhood, the West End, was bisected by construction of Interstate 75 and the clearance of the Kenyon-Barr neighborhood. A few years later, the building of Interstate 71 to the east carved a lifeless concrete gulch through Avondale, Walnut Hills, and the very heart of Evanston. With resilience, the city's African-American residents moved forward, struggling under the weight of institutional and personal oppression yet all the while forgiving their oppressors and believing change would come.

These were black men and women who served with distinction in the U.S. military in World War II, Korea, and Vietnam, believing their sacrifice and love of country would level the playing field when they returned home. It didn't. That theme runs through several stories I'd reported about Cincinnati's African-American veterans in a chapter titled "Military." I wonder, even today, in an era when NFL and Major League Baseball games come with jingoistic sideshows, do we honor African-American veterans and active-duty military, police, and fire personnel with the same apparent fervor we do whites?

During a three-year stint from 1996 through 1998 in the *Enquirer's* full-fledged features section, Tempo, I'd kept my focus on the black community while being assigned and developing many other kinds of stories. I profiled community elders for a Black History Month series in 1998.

Looking back, I see that I benefitted from the gift of time and place. I'd worked in three states at three newspapers over the first nine years of my career. The *Enquirer* would become my newspaper home for 25 years. Editors allowed me to create three distinct bodies of work based out of our nineteenth-floor newsroom at Third and Elm streets. I have had three stints as a reporter in local news, commonly known as Metro, separated by long runs in Tempo and Sports. African-Americans and their stories are the common thread.

For this book, I've chosen some stories that I think capture the essence of the black experience in a specific time. An example is the advance essay I wrote for the NAACP's national convention, "These are no ordinary times," held in July 2016 in Cincinnati. In it, I quoted a black mother, Nicole Taylor, gazing at her cherubic 9-year-old son, Jordan Stephens, and saying, "In a few years, he is going to be a young black man and looked at as a threat."

Other stories, I hope, have a timelessness to them, in that they're as relevant today as when I reported them. I assembled a string of stories about the community's bedrock institutions – the church, barbershop, newspaper, and radio station – into another chapter. The message was clear: for all our societal attempts to integrate racially, we still live in and retreat largely to two separate communities. Health disparities between African-Americans and the larger white society are a historical problem that persist. Urban violence grows out of the hopelessness of race-based poverty. Where some outsiders see only chaos from a distance, I saw order and protocol in predominantly black neighborhoods, even down to the street code of revenge and retribution among low-level drug dealers and gunrunners.

I became part of these varied communities and reported on perspectives and experiences that were and remain every bit as diverse as those in the white community.

I went there. Often and with intentionality. I invested large chunks of time reporting from the ground up in predominantly black neighborhoods. Residents there, not politicians nor the police downtown, set my agenda. Community members provided most of my story ideas.

The stories are written in Associated Press style, with shorter paragraphs than readers are accustomed to seeing in books. For a time in the late 1990s, our newspaper style was to use courtesy titles such as *Mr.* or *Mrs.* Featured obituaries always take those titles. The pieces published before 2012 benefitted from multiple layers of editing by my assigning supervisors and the dearly departed unsung heroes of the newspaper industry, members of the copy desk. I deeply miss their occasional 9:30 p.m. calls to check a spelling, statistic, or awkward sentence structure. That beloved safety net helped to reduce the 2 a.m. panic sweats that I'd made a factual error. I explore the changes in our industry over my *Enquirer* years in the Author's Postscript.

What does this book mean to me? I am a father and a husband and a son and a brother; I've volunteered for 25 years through the Catholic Church to raise money for infrastructure and human development in Haiti. I've written extensively about Central American immigrants. I am part of a Pulitzer Prize–winning team that reported for the *Enquirer* on the heroin scourge in 2017. Yet my personal investment through my newspaper work in Cincinnati's black community means more to me than the Pulitzer or any other award I've received. Cross-racial understanding is the legacy I hope to leave. I sense that the work chose me, though. I didn't choose it. To paraphrase Lincoln, I didn't shape the times or the place. They shaped me.

In having the opportunity and good fortune to revisit these past 25 years through these newspaper stories, reliving the happiness and heartbreak and – above all – our common humanity, I sense myself saying to the reader or people who haven't spent time in these neighborhoods, "Come with me."

That message is the sum of these stories.

In this book, I am handing you, the reader, this invitation: "Meet me downtown at the *Enquirer* building, hop in my car and ride with me to Avondale or Bond Hill or Evanston. We can even walk to the north end of Over-the-Rhine or over to the West End. Let's get dressed up and attend 11 a.m. Sunday service at New Jerusalem Baptist Church in Carthage and hear the Rev. Damon Lynch Jr. preach. Let's spend an evening at a community meeting about police-community relations at New Prospect Baptist Church in Roselawn. Let's walk Ridgeway Avenue in Avondale or hear black teens talk about the challenges they face growing up and in high school. You ought to hear the spoken-word poets perform; their rhymes teem with insight. There's so many people to meet. Let's say hello as we pass on sidewalks or go into the shops, soul food restaurants, barbershops or community centers. We're invited into private homes. Hear the personal stories. Listen. Learn this history from the inside out, not from the outside in. It's our shared history as Cincinnatians and, in a larger sense, as Americans. Come with me across the color line."

To the African-Americans who allowed me into their communities and lives and entrusted me with both small and large pieces of their personal and collective story, I say, simply, thank you. I want these stories to be accurate snapshots that add up to a larger telling of the events and personalities of our times.

My deepest gratitude extends to the people I've come to know as friends and fellow members of the Catholic Church of the Resurrection in Bond Hill. In an era of increased racial tension and hostility, you did the extraordinary. You welcomed a cancer-ravaged white man into your midst as one of your own.

* * *

I first walked through those heavy, weathered, and oversized wooden doors into Resurrection as a reporter. Now I walk in as a member. My decision to join had nothing to do with getting a story or developing sources. Resurrection feels permanent. The relationship is bigger than me, one that has built over time. There I am embraced and appreciated and loved, allowed to embrace and appreciate and love in return without hesitation or explanation.

The person who embodies the character of Resurrection is the woman who comforted me when I broke down at Mass. Shahidah Akbar, retired from the U.S. Postal Service, grew up in Bond Hill. She came to Mass every Sunday morning at 11. She sat in the same pew with her father, James Brown, whom I had interviewed in 2012 for a neighborhood profile. Mr. Brown was 99 when he died in March 2017. I was recovering from major surgery to address another post-cancer complication. I sent Shahidah a message from my hospital bed and apologized for not being able to attend her father's funeral. "I understand," she responded. "Just get better and come back. We miss you."

On a hot Sunday morning in May 2018, I made sure to arrive at Mass before Shahidah and placed a long-overdue gesture of gratitude, three yellow roses, in her pew. And, finally, I asked her a question I'd wanted to ask her for three years: "Why? Why were you so kind to me? A white guy . . . you didn't even know." I choked up. I stopped speaking.

Tears quickly filled her eyes, too. "You looked like you needed someone to put their arm around you and tell you that no matter what you were going through you would be okay and that we were here for you," she said.

The answer Shahidah gave me aligns with what African-American theologians and clergy have told me when I asked about the warmth afforded me at Resurrection – not to mention the welcome I've received as a white man and reporter in dozens of other black churches of many denominations throughout Cincinnati.

"A nurturing tradition" is how Adam Clark describes what I experience, most notably at Resurrection. He is African-American and an associate professor of theology at Xavier University in Cincinnati. "African-Americans, especially black women, are wounded healers. They do ministry out of their own woundedness," he said. "Black people deal with tragedy their whole lives. They have experience with it. It's not uncommon. When you enter that space with a black person, they know what to do. They're not scared of it."

My time at Resurrection has reduced my own fear and increased my faith. The community helped me overcome post-traumatic stress disorder. I had not planned to routinely worship there or eventually join the community as a member. My wife, Diana, whose first language is Spanish, and I had belonged to a Spanish-language parish nearby in the Cincinnati neighborhood of Carthage. San Carlos Borromeo is home to a couple of thousand Mexican and Central American immigrants. I'd fallen away during my cancer treatment.

Then, as winter turned to spring in 2015, I woke one Sunday morning – Palm Sunday – and told Diana that I needed to hear the Mass again in English. I was going to Resurrection.

"I think there's something there for me," I said.

Why Resurrection? Easy. Every experience I'd had there for work was warm. Community members were kind and helpful. Or as the church's music minister, the late Deborah Shipps, had said to me when I told her how much I loved the choir and was moved by the music, "It's no coincidence. The Holy Spirit brought you here."

I'd have to agree.

* * *

I first visited the church in 1993. It had a different name then, St. Agnes. I went to interview its white pastor, the Rev. Giles Pater. At the time, his church was one of the only racially integrated faith communities in the Cincinnati Archdiocese. I talked with him for a story on how 11 o'clock Sunday morning was the most segregated hour in American life. We talked about how Christianity in the United States had largely failed to capitalize on the shared beliefs of whites, blacks, and Latinos to close racial and ethnic gaps, fault lines that have only continued to widen.

Father Pater, who died in November 2017, spoke candidly to me about the need for interracial worship. "I have heard my colleagues, other priests, say, 'We don't have a race problem because we have no other races,' to which I say, 'That's exactly why you have a problem,'" he said.

That story would be part of a sprawling six-part series on race relations in Greater Cincinnati, titled "A Polite Silence." We showed how the region's preoccupation with a false, mannered front created the illusion that few racial problems existed and prevented it from doing the hard work of discussing race. It's still true today.

In Cincinnati, now as then, even the suggestion that a race problem exists – let alone the use of the term "white privilege" – often draws an angry response from many white people. What too many whites don't realize is that they, too, though to a much lesser degree, lose from their racial privilege. Crossing the color line in a region like Greater Cincinnati requires a degree of intentionality. The metropolitan area, which includes southwest Ohio, northern Kentucky, and southeast Indiana, is the fifth-most racially segregated region in the country, according to a 2016 analysis by 24/7 Wall St. (a Delaware-based financial news and opinion content provider).

I prefer not to think about what I would have missed if I had lived a segregated life, comfortable in a suburb, surrounded by people with similar incomes, educations, and, of course, complexions. My newspaper work opened the door to a more fulfilling life.

And it all started with the "Polite Silence" series. I've since immersed myself in the city's African-American community, culture, and history. Cincinnati has a proud abolitionist legacy that included the opening, in 1830, of a local law office by Salmon P. Chase. The future Chief Justice of the U.S. Supreme Court passionately defended runaway slaves, freed black men, and white abolitionists and would later help to shape the Fourteenth and Fifteenth Amendments, which define U.S. citizenship and bar racial limits on the right to vote.

The story of the local black church matches that in any other American city. Cincinnati's first black congregation, Union Baptist, founded in 1831 in the West End, provided sanctuary to fugitive slaves and gave them food and clothing and taught many to read and write. One hundred years after the Civil War, another Cincinnati-based black church, Zion Baptist, led by its pastor, the Rev. L. Vanchael Booth, would reshape the religious landscape. Booth helped found the Progressive National Baptist Convention, giving a young Alabama-based preacher, the Rev. Martin Luther King Jr., and another 2.5 million people a denominational home. Locally, Booth led a movement to use the financial autonomy of the black church to spur housing and business development in the black community.

Black Cincinnati, though not known as a national black city like Detroit, Chicago, Atlanta, or Newark, was and remains significant, with many of the same afflictions and assets. Greater Cincinnati's black and oftentimes suburban middle class mirrors other major cities, just on a smaller scale. Poverty, violence, and educational and economic inequality are all here. So are problems with police-community relations. So are solutions. Cincinnati rioted in 2001 after a white police officer shot and killed an unarmed black man. City leaders then crafted nationally acclaimed police reforms in 2002 in what's known as the Collaborative Agreement. Thousands of residents of predominantly black neighborhoods in Cincinnati, like those in other major U.S. cities, continue to be displaced by white gentrification – just as they were in post-war America by federal interstate construction and urban renewal projects that novelist James Baldwin dubbed "Negro Clearance."

Black resilience and achievement in Cincinnati – in business, medicine and the other sciences, education, politics and public service, the military, and arts and athletics – defeated Jim Crow.

I became witness to racial intersections that were as frequently hostile as they were harmonious.

I've given voice to no one. I've gone into communities of color and listened to the strong voices there and recorded the tales of tragedy and triumph. Black Cincinnati matters.

Residents have welcomed me into the all-black suburbs of Lincoln Heights, Lockland, and Forest Park and the Cincinnati neighborhoods of Bond Hill, Avondale, Evanston, the West End, and Over-the-Rhine – the latter before it was gentrified. I like the sense of equilibrium and purpose I experience when I am there. Most of all, I like the people the job introduced me to, people I'd otherwise not likely have known. Those days are my happiest.

My hardest days would begin in late 2013.

My year of cancer care – 28 radiation treatments, 852 hours of chemotherapy, 90 hours in a hyperbaric oxygen tent, and at least 11 trips to the operating room; I count everything – made me start to wonder if there were something more to life and work than being a newspaper reporter.

In November 2014, I accepted a corporate buyout. I declined to reapply for a job I'd done and, according to my annual performance reviews, done well for 30 years. I'd grown increasingly interested in civil rights work. I spent most of 2015 as the vice president of communication, marketing, and key initiatives at the Urban League of Greater Southwestern Ohio. I'd reported and written about the local Urban League affiliate off and on since I got to town.

The highlight of my eight months working there was editing and managing the 164-page "State of Black Cincinnati 2015: Two Cities" report. It told of the racial disparities across the city and region in the areas of education, employment, housing and the relationship to police and the justice system.

Even though I could write as much as I liked on the league's website — including an opinion piece, "A Meditation on White Privilege," that the *Enquirer* published in August 2015 as an op-ed column on its Cincinnati.com website — I went back to newspaper work in January 2016. I wasn't done being a reporter. I had thought I was. I missed the frenetic pace. I missed the sense of being involved and in the know. I also learned in that year away that I wasn't cut out to be an executive and spend much of my day in meetings.

Yet my eight months working at the Urban League provided lessons and experiences available nowhere else. I was the only white male in a workplace of about 60 people.

Summer 2015 was eventful. On July 20, during a break from the senior staff meeting, an African-American colleague, Angela Williams, was despondent, almost lifeless, far less engaged in the conversation than normal. I asked her why.

She brought up the shooting death that had occurred the previous evening nearby in the Mount Auburn neighborhood. An unarmed black motorist, Sam DuBose, had been shot at close range through the head during a traffic stop for a missing front license plate. The shooter was a white University of Cincinnati police officer, Ray Tensing, who would later testify in two trials that DuBose was trying to run over him with his car. Both of Tensing's murder trials would end in hung juries. (I would help to cover them for the *Enquirer*.)

A month before DuBose's death – on June 17 – an avowed white supremacist, 21-year-old Dylann Roof, shot and killed nine African-Americans during a prayer service at Emanuel African Methodist Episcopal Church in Charleston, South Carolina. He later admitted to the nine murders and said he had hoped to start a race war.

Angela, whose deceased father was a longtime local Baptist church pastor, the Rev. Anderson Culbreath, connected the two shootings and their toll on the black psyche.

"I was just starting to get over Charleston," she said. "You hope it doesn't happen again, but as a black person, you're always waiting for the next shoe to drop. It dropped last night."

Like the relationships with my Urban League colleagues, conversations with the agency's program participants did not stay on the surface. With little pretense, they most often went deep quickly. Maybe that honesty was the result of me being the minority and African-Americans being the majority. My friends and co-workers there generally gave me a lot of themselves. And they expected the same in return. Few if any games were played. It's the same at Resurrection.

You have to show up and contribute. Going through the motions is not an option. If you hold back, you are likely to be asked why or called out – both of which have happened to me.

Despite my belief in the Urban League mission and feeling a bit torn about leaving, I looked forward to getting back to newspaper work. I handed my written two-week notice to the president and chief executive, Donna Jones Baker, the Friday before Christmas. I'd received an offer to return to the *Enquirer*. I knew the move was the right one for me at the time, yet I'd only worked at the league for a short time. I greatly respect and like Donna, who was a trusted newspaper source for many years before she became my supervisor. I hated to disappoint her. I handed her the folded letter.

"Oh, no," she said. She breathed deep and stepped forward to hug me. I was expecting her to be angry.

Instead, she said, "I hope you felt nurtured here. You've been through so much."

I had talked privately with her about the challenges of my cancer recovery. I updated her on the progress I was making in therapy. She encouraged me to continue and said not to worry if I needed to leave work for it.

She said a second time, "I hope you felt nurtured here."

I said that I had. I thanked her for the opportunity and for trusting me with the "State of Black Cincinnati" report. I told her I just needed to go back to newspaper work.

"I understand," she said. "I'm disappointed to lose you, but I understand."

\* \* \*

My eight months at the Urban League became a key part of my personal timeline in black Cincinnati. Renewed and reenergized and back in the *Enquirer* newsroom, I could see those old-school paper files I maintained in my desk or my stories in the newspaper's electronic library as adding up to something bigger. And I had a model.

A chronicle of newspaper stories about black Cincinnati does have precedent. Almost a century ago, in 1926, black newspaper publisher Wendell P. Dabney released *Cincinnati's Colored Citizens*.

Carrying an ambitious subtitle, "Historical, Sociological and Biographical," Dabney's volume sought to document black life in the early 1900s in Cincinnati by providing portraits and sketches of some of Cincinnati's influential black citizens and black institutions. Beginning in 1902, he published the *Ohio Enterprise*, the forerunner of the *Union*, which he published from 1907 until his death in 1952, using his weekly paper to champion the cause of African-Americans and their struggle against prejudice. I kept a copy of Dabney's book on my desk.

The 440 pages of *Colored Citizens* include some material Dabney had published for the previous 25 years in his newspapers. The September 1927 edition of the *American Journal of Sociology* reviewed Dabney's book as having gathered "the local traditions of the colored people of Cincinnati" and that it "has historical significance."

I hope for the same for this collection of my material from the *Enquirer*, gathered over roughly the same number of years as Dabney's a century earlier. What you see in this book is not an exhaustive or definitive history of black Cincinnati for these 25 years. Far from it. These are snapshots of the black people, black institutions, and black events I reported and wrote about. One white reporter's journey across the color line.

The first milepost is 1993.

I accepted a permanent job at the *Enquirer* as a general assignment news reporter that May. (I'd worked at papers in Lafayette, Indiana; Rockford, Illinois; and Raleigh, North Carolina; before coming back to Cincinnati, where I'd had a sports reporting internship in 1984.)

I'd only been full-time at the *Enquirer* a month when I received the race series assignment. Executive editor Larry Beaupre called me into a conference room to meet with a half-dozen editors, who explained how they wanted me — new to town and unaffiliated with any sources — to get to know African-Americans in Cincinnati in broader, deeper ways. Go to events and meetings in the neighborhoods, get familiar with the city's racial history, interview leaders and citizens from all races, and come back to them with a fresh set of story ideas. Though initially overwhelmed, I recognized the terrific opportunity.

Larry told me I had the background for the project because I'd had nine years of experience writing news and human-interest stories and had been an editor. He also said he could tell from a few of my application clippings that I was comfortable writing about race.

Despite my earnestness, I stumbled more than once. I interviewed a couple of hundred African-Americans for the series. Marie E. Michel-Tucker had worked at Procter & Gamble Co. and moved on to a position as field marketing manager at the Coca-Cola Company in Cincinnati. She also was president of the local chapter of the National Black MBA Association.

She asked me how long I'd been at the *Enquirer*. I said about a month and that I had come from the *News & Observer* in Raleigh. She said she'd gone to college in Durham, which I assumed meant she had graduated from North Carolina Central University, a historically black state school.

"No," she said, "I went to Duke."

Marie graciously accepted my apology and, later on in the reporting process, contributed key insights to a round-table discussion on race and race relations that wrapped up the series.

I still cringe at the memory.

* * *

What I didn't know then was how the five-month "Polite Silence" experience would change the direction of my career and change me as a person. Three of those stories form this book's first chapter.

Early in the reporting process, I went through a brief but painful week of coming to terms with the unearned privileges I knew I had as a white man in America but had not fully confronted. I came out the other side feeling liberated. Age 31 and father of two preschool-aged sons, I had enough maturity to understand what was beginning to happen. I started to see the world differently – through the black-and-white lens of race and my distorted racial advantages – and to understand the singular nature of the African-American experience. I read and studied a dozen books on race and black culture. I learned how to be "the other" in settings in which I was the only white or among a small minority and how to carry the weight of representing my race.

That collection of stories from '93 won a handful of national citations, most notably the Unity Award from Lincoln University of Missouri. My passion lit, I just kept on covering urban affairs. I reported and wrote – either solo or as part of a small team – from the city's black community and learned that there was no such thing as a singular African-American perspective. Opinions and personalities in the mythically monolithic black community were every bit as divergent as they were among whites.

I wrote these stories, enthusiastically, small and big. Reporters were regularly assigned to write featured obituaries; we called them Lives Remembered. Instead of scouring the paid obituary listings, filled primarily with white people, for a worthwhile person, I developed working relationships with the black-owned funeral homes that handled arrangements for most African-American families. Funeral directors from Renfro, J. C. Battle and Sons, and Thompson Hall & Jordan began calling me and saying, "I think I have a good one for you."

I seized the opportunity. Editors were pleased to have a reporter on staff who wanted to write about African-Americans. A couple of my black reporter colleagues told me they appreciated not having "the black stories" reflexively assigned to them by white editors. I covered breaking news that had racial overtones. I looked for news enterprise, feature stories, and profiles of African-Americans. The story ideas started to come to me from community members.

One such reader tip led to meeting with a group of African-American World War II veterans, Tuskegee Airmen, who organized and were still fighting for equality and recognition almost 50 years later. The story of one of the airmen, John Leahr, plainly illustrated the systematic nature of American racism. After the war, no private airline hired black pilots – even a Tuskegee Airman with a distinguished flying record. All he ever wanted to do was fly.

"We really thought it would change when we came back," Leahr told me. "We thought we would come back to a different country. We thought this [World War II] was the big fix. We were over there, willing to die. We thought people would finally get over the race issue. We were wrong. We're still wrong."

I spent several weeks learning about the life of Michael "Spike" McCoy, a black teenager who died when he shielded and saved the life of a friend's infant during a drive-by shooting in Evanston.

Spike's father, Michael McCoy Sr., told me: "In all the chaos of that neighborhood, he provided some sanity. He was trying to take charge of his life, and he certainly took charge of his death."

Leaders of the local Nation of Islam trusted me to write about their community during the buildup to the Million Man March in 1995. I was the only white man on a bus filled with black men traveling overnight from Avondale to the National Mall in Washington. I understood why a few young African-Americans on the bus didn't like seeing a white man walk down the aisle. I didn't take their objections personally. I befriended my seatmate, a former Negro League baseball player named Sonny Webb, whom I would profile.

It was 1995, a little more than 13 years before Barack Obama's first term in the White House. Sonny Webb counted the Rev. Jesse Jackson's 1988 presidential bid among the highlights of his life as a black man living in the United States. "Some of those things were just inconceivable when I was a kid," he said.

Webb died December 30, 2007, less than a year before Barack Obama's election as the nation's first African-American president. He was 72 years old.

During the mid-1990s, I also started to view my newspaper work on race as something more than my livelihood. As a lifelong Catholic, I realized I was experiencing the formation of a vocation. When and where possible, I purposefully linked my newspaper work to the Church's teaching on social justice and the pursuit of the common good. I'd write about injustice, racial and otherwise, and the heroic efforts to overcome it. My goal – as beautifully expressed in the hymn "Prayer of Saint Francis" – was to understand, not to be understood. It's as if God had tapped me on the shoulder and redirected me.

My growing professional awareness of race and my white privilege made me regret some decisions I'd made in my personal life. I was embarrassed to live in suburban Clermont County – the population of which, still, according to the latest census estimates, is 95.3 percent white and 1.6 percent black – and grew angry with myself that I had deferred to my wife on that decision. Through the 1990s, you affixed a sticker to your license plate that spelled out in all-capital letters your county of residence. I wore it like a scarlet letter when I drove into black city neighborhoods. No one ever mentioned it, even if they did notice.

More noticeable was the racial makeup of my sons' public elementary school in West Clermont Local Schools and the larger prevailing community-wide attitude that was, at best, dismissive of African-American concerns and racial inequality. I coached my oldest son's youth baseball team for three summers. I had one nonwhite player – a Latino. I didn't want to bring up my children there or live there myself any longer. I felt like I lived in two worlds. I grew increasingly comfortable in my work world and less so away from it.

I embraced the move into Hamilton County and the racially and socially mixed Finneytown Local Schools district. It shares an almost indistinguishable border with the similarly diverse city neighborhood of College Hill.

\* \* \*

My personal life began to resemble my professional life after the move.

Black and Jewish and even some Muslim, Latino, and African immigrant families shopped at the same grocery that I did. I coached my second son's baseball team for five consecutive years, and one season we had four African-American players and another from a Pacific-Islander family originally from Los Angeles.

My young family and I were never happier than during the first couple of years in Finneytown. I found a treasure chest on the other side of the color line, filled with unimaginable perseverance that has overcome oppression, a faith that sustains, minimal pretense and maximum authenticity – in short, humanity – and a surprising lack of bitterness and vengeance, given how much wrong has been done and continues to be done to African-Americans in this, their country.

Obviously, I am not the first or only white person to discover these riches of African-American culture and to be invited to share in them. Yet, I came to understand that my position as a newspaper reporter most likely allowed me greater access into the community.

One of the people I came to know well, whom I otherwise wouldn't have met, was the Rev. Fred Shuttlesworth. My first couple of contacts with him were over the phone. One of my mentors, Allen Howard, a respected veteran African-American reporter at the *Enquirer*, suggested I meet Shuttlesworth in person. I knew he had been on the dais with the Rev. Martin

Luther King Jr. in August 1963 for the March on Washington for Jobs and Freedom. The extent of Shuttlesworth's historic importance had been a void in my formal education. Once I learned that he had a place on the civil rights movement's Mount Rushmore, I called to apologize and set up an appointment. He said he thought nothing of any perceived slight and asked me to stop by his church. Greater New Light Baptist became a regular stop on my rounds.

Shuttlesworth had led the movement to victory in the country's most viciously segregated city, Birmingham, Alabama, over one of segregation's most stubborn and violent practitioners, the city's public safety commissioner, Eugene "Bull" Connor. Into the early 2000s, even after I had taken my newspaper's NFL beat writer position, I would visit Shuttlesworth in his sparsely furnished home in Cincinnati's Roselawn neighborhood. He told me stories about his role in the civil rights movement. He encouraged me to keep writing — in his words, "the truth" – and to place my journalism in the context of my faith. He would be just one of my civil rights mentors.

Shuttlesworth told me of his personal struggles and triumphs. He was teacher, I the student. Two visits to the civil rights district in Birmingham took on greater meaning because of my relationship with him.

In April 2001, with Cincinnati poised on the edge of a racial explosion, the depth of the relationship I'd developed with Shuttlesworth revealed itself. A white Cincinnati police officer had fatally shot an unarmed black man, Timothy Thomas, 19, in an alley in the Over-the-Rhine neighborhood. (He left behind a 3-month-old son, Tywon, whom I would find and profile in December 2016.)

As the city teetered during that long, hot April of 2001, Shuttlesworth invited Martin Luther King III to his church. Editors had pulled me from the football beat for a month to help with news coverage of the riots and the declaration of martial law. King III was then president of the Southern Christian Leadership Conference, the civil rights organization founded by his father, Shuttlesworth, and other civil rights leaders 44 years earlier.

Before a Saturday afternoon speech by King at Greater New Light Baptist, Shuttlesworth gave me an exclusive interview with his guest. "This is a courageous reporter," Shuttlesworth said as King and I shook hands. "I can't believe he hasn't been thrown in jail for writing the truth around here about black people."

Never have I felt more unworthy of a compliment, especially when given to me by a man whose life's work and commitment defined courage and defied death.

These types of experiences – interacting with Shuttlesworth, King III, and many other African-Americans and their white allies – motivated me further, convincing me that the choice I'd made to focus my newspaper career there was indeed correct.

"How do I do more?" I more than once have asked another of my mentors, Nathaniel Jones. "Keep on keeping on" is how the retired federal judge and former NAACP general counsel answers me. Judge Jones, whom I profiled after his wife's death and interviewed many times, graciously agreed to write this book's foreword. I am honored, humbled, and inspired by his words.

I spent a day with Rosa Parks in suburban Detroit in 1998, ahead of her receipt of the first International Freedom Conductor Award from Cincinnati's National Underground Railroad

Freedom Center. Frail and 85, she said, "I will do what I can to further education, economic opportunity, and prosperity for all people. I will do as much as I can for as long as I can."

Fred Shuttlesworth, Nathaniel Jones, and Rosa Parks were some of the nationally known civil rights icons I would profile.

I would also get to know over the years many local heroes who comprise the backbone of Cincinnati's black community, the likes of day-care owner Margaret "Nanny" Andrews; business owner Cynthia Booth and her husband, Paul; pioneering ophthalmologist Chester Pryor; three men named Damon Lynch – Jr., III, and IV; and Pat McCollum, who adopted four of the more than 70 children she cared for as a foster mother.

* * *

Besides expanding my reading list – I go back frequently, among other titles, to Ta-Nehisi Coates's *Between the World and Me* and King's *Where Do We Go from Here?* – my work led me to protest songs and spirituals and speeches from the civil rights era. I listen to these almost as an antidote to the increasing number of angry phone calls and emails I receive from some white readers.

They complain I am not neutral and had swung to the "side" of African-Americans. A few use the N-word freely. I respond that I simply write the truth and let them know they may call my supervisor or write a letter to the editor. I won't argue with them. I have, however, asked a few of them if indeed African-Americans now have the advantage socially and legally over whites, "Would you trade places with a black man or black woman or want your child to be black in America?"

Even at the turn of the century, I'd seen much of America's racist bloodline. I envision racism and racial prejudice like a mist, circulating on the wind, there as an invisible pollutant or poison that can fall randomly at any time into the life of any African-American. Despite my concern, I know I can blend back into the privileged white crowd as another anonymous white face. I can hide in my race and tune out from the struggle, like switching off a television or light. I can take a day off. African-Americans do not have that luxury.

Increasingly attuned, though, I saw race and racial prejudice almost every day, almost everywhere, even when I took the job in July 2000 covering the National Football League.

In my third year on the beat, as the Cincinnati Bengals stumbled toward a franchise-worst single-season record of 2–14, it became clear that Dick LeBeau would not be retained as head coach. At the same time, I'd been contacted by civil rights attorneys Cyrus Mehri and Johnnie Cochran. They'd backed off a threat to sue the NFL about the lack of minorities hired as general managers, head coaches, and offensive and defensive coordinators. I interviewed Cincinnati Bengals President Mike Brown, who said the organization had not in its 34-year history interviewed a candidate of color for the top three coaching positions. Brown could have easily lied to me. He did not. Two months later, after the Bengals had hired an African-American head coach, Marvin Lewis, Mehri told me at the Super Bowl in San Diego that my story went all the way to the commissioner's office. He said it was used in the formation of the Rooney Rule, named for the late Pittsburgh Steelers owner Dan Rooney, which requires NFL teams to interview minority candidates for head coaching and senior football operation jobs.

The backlash to my initial story was strong. I received more than 90 emails, most saying I had forced race into a place it didn't belong and was attempting to paint Brown as a racist. "Stick to sports," multiple readers wrote. Another reader told me that he would no longer allow his son to read my Bengals coverage because I was a racist against white people. (Since returning to the *Enquirer* in 2016, I have received some handwritten letters from readers who don't like my race or immigration stories and suggest I go back to writing sports.)

On sports-writing road trips, I visited civil rights sites. In Atlanta to cover a Sunday night Bengals game, I went to service at Ebenezer Baptist Church and ended up sitting two pews behind Coretta Scott King. I walked through the historic sanctuary and the King Center for Nonviolent Social Change and sat quietly for several minutes beside the memorial pool that held Martin Luther King Jr.'s tomb.

In Birmingham, Alabama, during the NFL offseason to cover college basketball, I spent part of a day touring the city's Civil Rights District. Kelly Ingram Park, where police dogs and firehoses confronted students and child demonstrators in May 1963. The Civil Rights Institute, where a statue of Shuttlesworth greets visitors. And 16th Street Baptist Church, where dynamite planted by Ku Klux Klansmen killed four African-American girls on a Sunday morning in September 1963. I wrote a story for our Travel section that turned out flat and unemotional compared to what I experienced in the church. White guilt and privilege overwhelmed me, and I asked God to forgive me and my race.

I requested a transfer from the NFL beat in September 2008, effective at the end of that year. Nine seasons were more than enough. I felt like I was helping to make rich men even richer. I wanted to return to the local news section and write again about the issues that forced vulnerable people to society's margins. I wanted to tell their stories. By the time that I returned to the newsroom in January 2009, I'd made the two primary visits to Haiti to collect material for my first book. I went back to Haiti in February 2010 to cover the catastrophic earthquake of January 12 that struck near Port-au-Prince and killed tens of thousands of people.

Vanderbilt University Press published *A Promise in Haiti: A Reporter's Notes on Families and Daily Lives* in 2011.

I see my experiences in Haiti as complementary to those in Greater Cincinnati's communities of color. The systematic and historical oppression of people of African descent knows neither borders nor an end, it appears.

Back in the *Enquirer* newsroom, I agitated for a column and the latitude to write opinion pieces. Economic conditions caused by the recession prevented us from having a columnist on staff at a time of frequent and deep personnel layoffs. Local News editor Julie Engebrecht, who had hired me as NFL writer in 2000 when she was *Enquirer* Sports editor, challenged me to develop a stronger voice as a beat reporter covering social issues and race. "You can do that," she said, "by the subjects you choose to write about and how you write them. Take risks. I won't let you go too far."

I took Julie's advice to heart. Her endorsement, coupled with my having written a book, allowed me to move forward with greater confidence in myself and my mission.

I developed a series called "Saving Avondale," which detailed through 2012 and 2013 the attempts to revitalize Cincinnati's largest predominantly African-American neighborhood. Among dozens of others, stories looked at the need for improved housing, disparities in health outcomes for African-Americans compared to whites, development of a progressive youth council that helped young people earn money for college, and the creation of an urban food ministry.

In December 2012, the effort to rebuild Avondale as a mixed-income community, led by nonprofit developer The Community Builders Inc., would receive a major boost. It was named one of the four recipients nationally of a $29.5 million Choice Neighborhoods grant from the U.S. Department of Housing and Urban Development. After I broke and published the story of federal investment in Avondale, a reader who identified himself as a "white taxpayer" sent me an email that read, "I don't want my money wasted like this."

Some of my early series work, dating to stories published in March, was included in the HUD application. Attorney Ozie Davis III, executive director of the Avondale Comprehensive Development Corp. during those years, was my primary source.

"That deep of an investment you made in the community uncovered good things and some bad things," Davis told me. "Sometimes, we didn't want you to shine the light on some of the bad things. But you always did it with a certain amount of honesty. It was really honest. It was a real unbiased approach, and it always seemed you were working to find the solutions that could be created for whatever you were seeing."

Despite my affection for the people and their community, I did write about the bad things, including the scourge of urban violence. I profiled an African-American youth baseball coach, Vince Ward, who'd attended the funerals for 18 of his former Avondale Indians players from across the city in a 10-year period.

"The problem is they get older, leave you and fall under the influence of other people," Ward said.

Every now and then, my major coverage areas – race and the human side of U.S. policies governing immigration and refugee resettlement – intersected to make for the most fulfilling story.

I spent time with groups of African immigrants who were the region's newest black citizens. About 1,200 Fulani people, most recipients of political asylum from the West African nations of Senegal, Mauritania, and Guinea, had created a Muslim community in the predominantly black suburb of Lockland. They occupied all 68 units of Mulberry Court Apartments, designating one apartment for a language and culture school for youths and another on the third floor as a prayer room.

I later profiled Clarence Howell, a 78-year-old black man who had survived the Jim Crow South and hired a Syrian refugee and Muslim, Bassam Osman, 36, to work in his shoe repair shop in the Pleasant Ridge neighborhood.

"I had to cross the same kind of line he had to cross," said Howell, who explained how Jewish people had helped him, a Christian, when he migrated 57 years earlier to Cincinnati from rural Georgia. "When I met Bassam, he reminded me of myself."

\* \* \*

My newspaper work took me back twice to the Catholic church on California Avenue in Bond Hill.

In 2011, 18 years after I'd first gone to St. Agnes to talk about the intersection of race and religion, I made my first visit to the new Church of the Resurrection for a one-year anniversary on the merged faith community. It had formed the previous year when the archdiocese closed three predominantly African-American churches – St. Andrew in Avondale, St. Mark in Evanston, and St. Martin de Porres in suburban Lincoln Heights – and consolidated them at the former St. Agnes. Membership had declined in those parishes. The buildings were old and too expensive to maintain. Leaders of the four parishes had met two years before the merger and decided they couldn't afford to continue separately.

The St. Agnes building was large enough to accommodate the combined membership, and its building was newer and solid physically. Parishioners voted on the new name, Resurrection. Together, they said, they would rise and form anew.

Still, some people had hard feelings. Parishioner Wendell Washington, 62 at the time, was a St. Mark member for 40 years. The closure and merger, he said, "felt like being stabbed in the heart." The community persevered. Furniture – the St. Mark pulpit, altar chairs from St. Andrew, and the St. Martin baptismal font – was moved in.

Three weeks later, Washington changed his mind and went to Mass. "I had to pout and realize I had to listen to God," he said.

For African-Americans, including Catholics, the church has historically been a safe zone, away from the often-unjust society of the pre-civil rights movement era, an institution for blacks run by blacks with a collective wealth.

"It's the one place African-Americans' personal dignity is respected, even though in the larger Catholic Church they were not treated well," said Resurrection's founding pastor, the Rev. Dennis Chriszt, said. He is white and previously served a black Catholic parish on Chicago's South Side and as a missionary in the African nation of Tanzania.

In 2012, I was back at Resurrection for another story assignment. Students from Avondale's St. Andrew School, which had closed in 1965, held a reunion with the white nun – Sister Marilyn Rose Dietz – who had taught them in first grade. About 25 people, graying and in their 50s and 60s, met for Mass at 11 on Sunday morning, April 29. They had lunch and talked about when Avondale was a vibrant community, a city unto itself before the riots of 1967 and '68 gutted its business district and accelerated its decline.

I met Denise Price, 57, who grew up across Reading Road from St. Andrew. She sat next to Sister Dietz in a group photo and clutched her hand. They sang several songs, including "Hail Holy Queen." Every May, students at St. Andrew – in keeping with Catholic tradition – ceremonially crowned an image or likeness of the Blessed Virgin Mary to signify her as the queen of heaven and the mother of God.

"I loved that," said Price, who lived in suburban Silverton. "That was my favorite thing. May was so beautiful at St. Andrew."

I allowed myself to get lost briefly in our shared history, recalling my childhood parish in Dixon, Illinois, where for five years I attended St. Mary's elementary school. We, too, celebrated and revered her, our patron saint.

The present was not as sweet as the past. I dreaded what the next few days might bring in my personal life. I had waited 48 years to find Diana. We married November 11, 2011, the second marriage for both of us. Just six months after our wedding, Diana faced major surgery. A biopsy revealed abnormal cells in her uterus, less than two years after she'd received a similar diagnosis and underwent cancer surgery.

I didn't mention a word of her pending surgery to my hosts that Sunday at Resurrection.

Yet, the hopeful nature of the service and the warmth of the people – the sign of peace sometimes lasts 10 minutes, no exaggeration – comforted me and helped me remain optimistic about Diana's outcome. During the St. Andrew reunion in the gym after Mass, a couple of the former students insisted I eat. When I purposefully avoided getting in line and started interviewing other people, one of the women brought me a plate of food.

Mercifully, Diana's surgery revealed no additional irregular or cancerous cells. Eighteen months later, though, I would be diagnosed with colorectal cancer when doctors found a four-centimeter tumor during a colonoscopy.

Bruised and battered but alive, I made my way back in spring 2015 to Resurrection. Palm Sunday was my first Mass. I went not as a reporter or observer, not the ethnographer writing about a culture other than his own, but as a person in pain in the wake of life-threatening trauma.

My recovery benefitted from my relationships with both individual Resurrection members and the larger community. The resiliency of the people and their understanding of their own human brokenness – a struggle for all people – have played a big part in my emotional healing. More riches poured forth from that treasure chest I found across the color line.

I'd come to understand that I somewhat resembled this church community. It had been broken by the archdiocese's decision to close four churches and put them back together as one, like me, as a new body. The surgical scars that run horizontally and vertically across my abdomen have faded but are still plainly visible. My African-American friends and fellow Resurrection members bear scars of a different kind.

I hear them express variations on a single theme:

"God has gotten us through."

"God didn't bring me this far to let go of me now."

"God kept you because you still have work to do."

I say those words to myself now.

Though I shouldn't lose focus on the Mass and its message, my mind sometimes drifts. I get lost in the music, or I remember being 31 and new to town and the *Enquirer* and walking into the church for the first time in 1993. I can't believe 25 years have passed. Who gets to do this kind of work for that long in one place? My thoughts wander to some of the people I've interviewed and written about. Maybe I'm not off topic, because I most often end up thanking God for that gift. I experience even more gratitude during the Lord's Prayer, when as a parish we clasp hands with the people next to us. As the prayer comes to an end, we gently squeeze each other's hands – an affirmation – before letting go.

About a year after that fateful Mass when I broke down in tears, I had the opportunity to comfort in the way I had been comforted.

The choir had filled the church with beautiful hymns of praise and hope. The message in the homily reminded us that even when we fall off track or are in a storm that God is still with us.

"Can the church say 'amen'?'" Deacon Royce Winters Sr. asked as he preached.

"Amen!" A few hands raised with palms upward.

My emotions had leveled off thanks to hard and consistent PTSD therapy. That day at Mass – we were approaching the two-hour mark – I sat back in my pew after receiving communion.

As I propped the kneeler back into place, I heard a soft sniffle and looked to my right to see tears streaming down the face of my friend Shahidah. I moved over to her.

"My daughter has just been diagnosed with breast cancer," she said. A woman sitting in the pew in front of her handed her a small package of tissues. A woman sitting behind her placed her hand on Shahidah's back.

I wrapped my right arm around her. Shahidah dropped her head on my shoulder and wept. I held her and whispered that I would be there for her and her daughter. No other words were spoken or needed.

Then, the choir started to sing, so beautifully and with verve, another hymn, "I'll Say Yes to My Lord."

*Brought me out of darkness, into the marvelous light.*

# 1993: A POLITE SILENCE

*I had no idea when given the assignment for a week-long race series how the experience would change the direction of my career – and my life. I remain indebted to the executive editor who gave me the opportunity, the late Larry Beaupre, and to my series editor, Michael Roberts. I learned a great deal through the summer and fall of 1993 about Cincinnati, about its black community, about newspaper journalism, and about myself and what I wanted to be.*

## Divided by race

When it comes to race relations, Cincinnati has a tough time talking about its problems

*November 14, 1993*

Racial attitudes in Cincinnati come wrapped in a polite silence, a silence that each day contributes to a costly, widening gap between whites and blacks.

The *Enquirer* has spent four months examining race relations today in Cincinnati and the attitudes that shape them. Through interviews with hundreds of blacks and whites from all walks of life, a portrait emerges of two separate communities that know little about each other.

Discrimination, prejudice, and injustice persist in our community. But a stable economy, long-standing neighborhood identities, and an unspoken rule that rocking the boat won't do anyone any good, many people say, mute serious discussion of race relations.

"There is a denial in Cincinnati that we have a race problem," said Robert C. Harrod, executive director of the local chapter of the National Conference of Christians and Jews.

Harrod, who is white, has led cultural diversity training for employees of two dozen Greater Cincinnati businesses. Harrod said race relations in Cincinnati are tense. He described racial attitudes – the feelings and opinions that shape our behavior toward one another across racial lines – as stiff, slow to change and built mostly on indifference.

Many blacks say there is still an uneven playing field in most areas where whites and blacks co-exist. Black Cincinnatians feel they are required to be "superblacks" just to be accepted into mainstream white society, a requirement they say is every bit as divisive as the old rules of segregation.

Many whites, on the other hand, believe the scales of equality have tipped too far toward blacks. Equality, this group argues, should be colorblind when it comes to housing or employment, with no favoritism either way.

The average white Cincinnatian, Harrod said, considers race a non-issue today, a problem solved through civil rights battles 25 years ago. The average white person, Harrod said, concludes that if he does not wear a sheet, burn a cross, or use "the n-word," he does not have to worry about his own racial attitudes.

What is really happening, Harrod said, is that whites "employ a very limited definition of racism to distance ourselves from it," which allows race problems to grow worse.

"Cities that have made racial progress have made a lot of noise doing it. My hometown of Birmingham, Alabama, is one," said Daphne Sloan, executive director of the Walnut Hills Redevelopment Corporation, 48 and black. "Cincinnati has a denial and a behavioral fronting about it that suggests all is well. I think Cincinnati has been lying to itself for so long that it actually believes there is no race problem here whatsoever."

When the majority's racial attitude is denial, sociologists say, open discussion becomes a necessary first step to clearly understanding and solving problems. This week's six-part series will examine how racial attitudes shape our lives and how Cincinnati's peculiar silence might be broken in pursuit of positive change.

* * *

Race relations in the eight-county Greater Cincinnati area means black-white relations.

The city of Cincinnati is 60 percent white, 38 percent black. Hamilton County, including Cincinnati, is 77 percent white, 21 percent black. The combined eight-county area – Hamilton, Clermont, Butler and Warren, Northern Kentucky's Boone, Campbell and Kenton, and Indiana's Dearborn County – is 87 percent white and 12 percent black.

And events of the last year suggest Cincinnati is not a healthy community when it comes to race relations.

Incidents such as the controversy over Marge Schott's racist comments, the erection of a Ku Klux Klan cross on Fountain Square, or the black-white barroom fight that polarized Lower Price Hill, show how quickly racial attitudes here can escalate into racial flashpoints. In terms of racial attitudes, sociologists say, these incidents are symptoms of an unhealthy community.

Sociologists and urban experts describe an ideal, healthy community as one where all people feel they belong and can contribute, where diversity and constructive conflict are valued. For a community to move toward that ideal, experts say, people must know and trust each other enough to work together on difficult problems.

In Cincinnati, however, "blacks and whites just don't know each other," said Joe Jones, 73, a retired foundry worker from Springfield Township who was displaced from the West End by the construction of Interstate 75 in the 1960s. "I think people want them (race relations) to be better.

"They're just not willing to do what it takes to make them better, and that goes for both sides," said Jones, who is black.

Across the divide that separates black and white attitudes in Cincinnati, the sides seem to view each other with a mixture of fear and ignorance.

Michael Maloney, who teaches urban affairs at the University of Cincinnati and at Chatfield College in Brown County, said he thinks race relations in Cincinnati are "getting worse in every respect. Attitudes have hardened. Whites see the black world as twofold," said Maloney, who is white. "The perception of acceptable blacks continues to improve. And the attitude toward unacceptable blacks has hardened. These are the poor and working-class blacks. There's a lot of anger."

Much of the black anger, said Dr. Emmett Cooper, a psychiatrist and medical director at Emerson North Hospital, comes from small, day-to-day encounters, moments when an insensitive remark or action by a white person injects race as a stamp of inferiority.

"When you have no contact, you fill in the blank with whatever you've been taught by your family, institutions, and the media," said Cooper, who is black. "Many whites are taught that blacks are second-class citizens, and that is how they treat them."

In his new book, *The Rage of a Privileged Class* (HarperCollins), *Newsweek* contributing editor Ellis Cose writes that such everyday incidents for black professionals "are not so much isolated incidents as insistent and galling reminders that whatever they may accomplish in life, race remains their most salient feature as far as much of America is concerned."

The lack of open discussion or vigorous debate on race issues in Cincinnati, local observers say, is part of the city's character.

"Cincinnati is a pragmatic, nonconfrontational town that is more interested in results than in symbolic gestures," said the Rev. Duane Holm, director of the Metropolitan Area Religious Coalition of Cincinnati, an organization formed in the wake of the 1968 race riots to allow various denominations to work together on social concerns.

Said Sheila Adams, president of the Urban League of Greater Cincinnati, "You can tell Cincinnati is on the Mason-Dixon Line. We are behind the times. The city has a conservative tradition and has not spoken out honestly on race relations."

Dwight Tillery, 45, the native Cincinnatian who became the city's first popularly elected black mayor in 1991, but this month finished second to mayor-elect Roxanne Qualls, said, "I think that there is such a level of discomfort [that] people just want to get away from it as not existing. And if you want to talk about it [race relations], you're creating problems, making an issue."

Some people take issue with the view that Cincinnati suffers racist attitudes in silence.

Alfred Tuchfarber, director of the Institute of Public Policy Research at the University of Cincinnati, said, "I disagree with almost all of those points. . . . We have made race one of the central issues of our age, much to our great disadvantage. We must have equal civil rights for everybody. That's essential. But by emphasizing group benefits, we emphasize differences. We've moved beyond equal award of civil rights to a point where we're rewarding results on basis of group membership. I have done many studies that show people here are, in affirmative action issues, more liberal than the rest of the country."

Compared with some American cities, others say, Cincinnati's race relations are enviable. They point to the Los Angeles riots or the racially tinged New York City mayoral race. In contrast, the recent election here put three black members on a nine-member city council. Two of the four new Cincinnati school board members are also black.

"After all is said and done, Cincinnati is a fine place to be. Race relations are better here than most places," said Michael Rapp, executive director, Jewish Community Relations Council. "Sure, prejudice, bigotry, and scapegoating exist, and to deny their existence is erroneous and dangerous. There are those who want to underestimate the problem. There are those who say it's omnipresent. I would say it's someplace in between."

\* \* \*

But beneath the debate over Cincinnati's racial climate, statistics and anecdotal evidence show a community growing more racially separate and unequal.

The phenomenon of white flight is real: some whites, acting on the attitude that crime, drugs, and falling property values are caused by blacks, continue to move away from the city to predominantly white suburbs.

According to the 1990 Census, almost 50,000 whites moved to Clermont, Brown, Warren, and Boone counties between 1980 and 1990. For the same period, only about 1,100 blacks made the same move.

In that period, the city of Cincinnati's white population decreased by 31,000, while its black population increased by 8,000.

Employment: The disparity in Cincinnati's black and white unemployment rates – 15.8 percent for blacks and 4.7 percent for whites – was ninth highest of the 45 urban areas analyzed by the U.S. Department of Labor's Bureau of Labor Statistics in its *Geographic Profile of Employment and Unemployment, 1992.*

Education is another area in which unequal treatment by race is an issue. Plaintiffs in the 19-year-old school desegregation case *Bronson vs. Board of Education* settled on a plan last month to improve black students' achievement in the Cincinnati Public Schools. Concerns remain on the disparity in discipline rates of black and white students and the test scores of students enrolled in eight predominantly black, low-achieving schools.

Opportunity is also seen as unfairly distributed. Blacks who have negotiated the currents of corporate Cincinnati say their progress has been slowed, if not altogether stalled, by a glass ceiling. The pools of real power and big money remain the exclusive domain of white males.

"There's an attitude in Cincinnati business that the aggressive white male can push his way to the top," said Ed Rigaud, 50, vice president in food and beverage products at Procter & Gamble and one of only two black vice presidents in the company. "The same approach by a black male will be seen as too aggressive and downright militant."

On the other hand, says Paul L. Schneider, 32, an assistant manager at the FreeStore's FoodBank division and a Price Hill resident, there is considerable backlash against equal opportunity efforts.

"By their actions and words, blacks have established an us-vs.-them mentality," he said. "All I know is there are a lot of white middle-class guys sitting in bars with racist images in their heads who otherwise wouldn't have them because they didn't get a job because they were the wrong color."

Crime and punishment is also a site of differential treatment. Blacks in Cincinnati are four times as likely to be arrested on drug charges than whites, even though law enforcement officials say blacks and whites use drugs at nearly the same rate.

Police say drug traffic is easier to spot in black neighborhoods because it occurs out in the open. In suburban, predominantly white neighborhoods, dealers tend to sell only to people they know.

\* \* \*

Unchecked, many residents and urban experts say, the disparity in treatment of whites and blacks and widening gaps between the predominant white haves and black have-nots will further isolate Cincinnati's inner city and turn Cincinnati into a two-society city.

"One of the problems with racism is the great loss of community that accompanies it. Racism inspires a dog-eat-dog mentality among individuals," said former Ohio Gov. John Gilligan, guest lecturer at the University of Cincinnati College of Law and organizer of a spring 1993 civic forum seminar that discussed local attitudes about race.

That loss of community reaches well beyond an area's urban center. A study by the Federal Reserve Bank of Philadelphia suggests that the ghettoization and economic entrapment of much of Cincinnati's black population will catch up to its white suburbs.

Richard Voith, a senior economist and research adviser at the Federal Reserve Bank of Philadelphia, studied 28 metropolitan areas – including Cincinnati. His major finding: suburban growth has become increasingly dependent on the economic viability and growth of a downtown.

"Declining cities will eventually undermine suburban growth," Voith wrote in his 1992 report. "If city decline results in a concentration of the population with very little education and in a deteriorating physical infrastructure eventually the decline is likely to impose additional costs manifested by high crime, poor health, and unproductive workers."

# Schott, Klan opened a hard year in Cincinnati race relations

*November 14, 1993*

Questions about Cincinnati's racial attitudes have been a steady undercurrent in events of the past year.

It began a year ago, yesterday, November 13, 1992, the day former Cincinnati Reds controller Tim Sabo filed a wrongful-firing suit against Reds President and CEO Marge Schott in

Hamilton County Common Pleas Court. Sabo claimed Schott called former Reds outfielders Eric Davis and Dave Parker her "million-dollar niggers."

Schott apologized publicly December 9 for making "insensitive remarks," including when she allegedly said, "I'd rather have a trained monkey working for me than a nigger." Some in the community condemned Schott's insensitivity; others defended her.

The next day, December 10, the city of Cincinnati approved an application from the Ku Klux Klan to erect a cross on Fountain Square from December 21 through December 30. The Klan had argued it had the same First Amendment rights of free speech that allowed Christians and Jews to erect a menorah and a crèche on the square.

The Klan cross and Cincinnati became a running news story Christmas week as angry individuals – white and black – tried to tear the cross down while police and Klan supporters tried to protect it.

The year ended with late-night comedians making Cincinnati the butt of their jokes. A series of reports by national media, from NBC's Today show to the *Los Angeles Times*, painted Cincinnati as a racially intolerant city.

The Feb. 3 suspension of Schott by Major League Baseball did little to still the criticism.

Baseball suspended Schott for one year, fined her $25,000, and directed her to complete a course in cultural diversity training. After meeting those requirements, she was reinstated November 1.

Negative national portrayals kept coming.

In June, *GQ* magazine portrayed Cincinnati as a "Town Without Pity." Peter Richmond wrote that the city is "clean and safe and quiet and repressive, and resolved to keep itself that way" and is the "most enlightened 19th-century city in America."

With the Schott and Klan incidents as a backdrop, racial attitudes continued to play a role in a series of unrelated events:

- During the first week in January, vandals struck repeatedly in Northern Kentucky, defacing buildings of black historical significance with racial graffiti.

- On February 4, Dr. Stanley Broadnax resigned after 13 years as commissioner of the Cincinnati Health Department. *Enquirer* stories revealed he had abused city sick-leave policies to moonlight at the Southern Ohio Correctional Facility in Lucasville. Some black leaders charged the *Enquirer* and other Cincinnati media would not allow black leaders to succeed.

- In March, plaintiffs in the 19-year desegregation case against the Cincinnati Public Schools asked a federal judge to extend and expand court supervision of the district. In late October, all parties agreed on a plan to improve the achievement of black students without court supervision.

- On May 7, William Seitz said he would not run for re-election to the Cincinnati Board of Education. The previous June, Seitz criticized the number of jubilant outbursts by black families at a graduation ceremony, implying they reflected the cause of higher discipline rates for black students. The comments sparked calls for his resignation. Seitz ran instead for Green Township trustee. "After having fought a long, valiant, and often lonely battle for common-sense conservative values in the city," he said at the time, "I am ready to come home to serve the nearly 60,000 township residents who share my values of limited, efficient government and personal responsibility for one's home, one's family, and one's neighborhood." Seitz won the post.

- On May 24, popular Reds manager Tony Perez was fired by general manager Jim Bowden after the team's 20–24 start. Fans and others – black and white – charged that Perez, a Cuban, hired in October as baseball's fifth minority manager, was brought in to deflect attention from Schott's anti-black and anti-Jewish remarks and then let go without being given a fair opportunity. Bowden replaced Perez with Davey Johnson and said the move was made to salvage the 1993 season. The Reds finished in fifth place with a dismal 73–89 record. Johnson's record (53–65) was worse than Perez's.

- A July 18 Knothole baseball tournament game in Clermont County was halted by umpires when an all-black team of 10-year-olds from Evanston was greeted with racial taunts. Evanston manager Anthony Brown said players, coaches, and fans with the all-white team from Mount Orab called his players "niggers" and "coons."

- A fight between two drinking buddies, one white and one black, in Lower Price Hill erupted into a neighborhood confrontation on July 19. Dennis Bryant, 20, who is white, was arrested and charged with attempted aggravated burglary after police said they found him pounding on the door of Mark Whitson's apartment. Many of the neighborhood's 1,500 white residents are upset that Bryant was arrested and Whitson was not. Racially fueled incidents of rock throwing and window breaking followed the incident.

# Reporter postscript

The lesson that stays with me

*November 21, 1993*

I'm usually 5 to 10 minutes late.

Seems I'm always trying to squeeze in another phone call or wring out a few more paragraphs before I leave the office for an appointment. Writer's block lifts at only the moments I am scheduled to be someplace other than at my desk.

So, when I get where I'm going, I do apologize but expect to begin business without giving my tardiness a second thought.

A lot of people, I have learned, don't enjoy the luxury I take for granted.

Of the more than 350 interviews I did this summer for the *Enquirer*'s series, "A Polite Silence: Race Relations in Cincinnati," the lesson of one conversation in particular stays with me.

The source of my brush with empathy was a professional black man, in his late 20s, college educated. The first name was one of many things we had in common.

But some of the stories he told, well, I couldn't begin to understand them.

He talked about the horror and embarrassment of being pulled over behind the wheel of his late-model car by police in a predominantly white neighborhood; the stereotypical profile, he said, is drug dealer. He told me about stepping onto an elevator and seeing a group of white women secure their purses and slide to an opposite corner. He was wearing a business suit. He doesn't dare go anywhere without wearing a tie.

Then he made the connection: "And I can't be late," he said. "Never."

If he is late, he's often branded a "lazy, quota-filling nigger."

I explained my habit of trying to do too much and its consequences. He just shook his head, as if to say, "Must be nice."

This conversation, by the way, took place at the beginning of a stretch of interviews that took me into many corners of Cincinnati's black community, where I often was the only white person.

I met with organizations of black professionals, with civil rights leaders, and in private homes with groups of black people in order to form a framework for the series.

I was the minority. Race relations were not an easy subject to discuss, and I felt the weight of representing my race and being obligated to try to speak for it. I felt like my answers and conduct reflected on all white people.

I began to understand what it was like for my race to arrive ahead of me. Even if my black sources and hosts were not prejudging me – and I know most weren't – I couldn't escape the feeling that I was seen first as a white male who had enjoyed the path of least resistance.

And I was now the one whose values, education, contributions, personality, life experiences – my humanity – were afterthoughts.

I began to get preoccupied with surface features: Do I dare go without a tie? Do I use slang, or speak proper English and risk coming across as uptight? I woke up in the morning thinking about my race and how it would affect the rest of my day.

Dozens of blacks, including Mark, have told me that they learn how not to concentrate on prejudice. How to minimize its pull.

But, at the same time, they always keep up a guard. Always brace for the worst while hoping for the best. I can't begin to imagine the energy, creativity, and time it must use up.

All I know is that I'm going to give Mark a call and ask him to lunch. And I'm going to tell him to lose the tie and take his time.

# NEIGHBORHOODS

*African-Americans in Cincinnati identify strongly with their birth neighborhood, like the lifelong allegiance maintained by graduates of the region's Catholic high schools. Don't dare misidentify a native-born son of Avondale as being from Mount Airy. I will walk or drive through the industrial neighborhood of Queensgate and try to imagine the Kenyon-Barr community that vanished as the victim of the country's largest single "slum clearance" project. It displaced nearly 5,000 families. Such great loss.*

## Working hard at integration

Kennedy Heights was a neighborhood built on positive race relations
*November 14, 1993*

Thirty years ago, the blacks and whites who lived in Kennedy Heights were fighting a related war on two separate fronts.

Black owners of single-family homes in this northeast Cincinnati neighborhood wanted to stop a proposed zoning change that would allow apartment houses to be built along Coleridge Avenue and Plainfield Road.

White homeowners were concerned about the possibility of widespread "block busting" and panic selling. They didn't want real estate agents persuading whites to sell their homes to move away from blacks who were buying into the neighborhood.

While the issues were different, the goal was the same: To preserve the neighborhood.

Kennedy Heights has been a real-life example of the kind of discussion and action that can improve racial attitudes and race relations at the grassroots level.

On a July night in 1963, leaders from both camps met at the Kennedy Heights Presbyterian Church and realized their separate battles had a common goal, a desire to maintain the quality of life they both enjoyed. Together they formed the Kennedy Heights Community Council.

"The lesson of Kennedy Heights is that integration is an intellectual concept that doesn't just happen. It takes energy and a conscious effort to achieve and maintain," said Jim Cebula, a University of Cincinnati history professor and past president of the council who has lived in the neighborhood since 1971.

That energy and effort has led to:

- A council program called "Living Room Dialogues," which brings newcomers and longtime residents together to discuss neighborhood goals and traditions.

- An essay contest for high school graduates on what it means to grow up in an integrated neighborhood.

- Social events sponsored by various block clubs.

- Safe, affordable, integrated day care at the Kennedy Heights Parents' Cooperative Nursery.

- A neighborhood beautification committee, which undertakes a project each spring.

All the while, property values continue to appreciate. They're up 3.5 percent since 1990, according to the 1993 Hamilton County residential reappraisal.

The neighborhood attracts professionals, both black and white. The median price of a home is $59,400, although houses priced up to $250,000 are available.

"The downside is that we have to continually educate people as to what this and neighborhoods like it are all about. This concept is still foreign to many people," Cebula said. "The upside is that two generations of kids have grown up in this environment and gone out into the world with this mindset."

That's why John Burlew moved with his wife and two daughters to Kennedy Heights.

We could live just about anywhere," said Burlew, past president of the Cincinnati Bar Association and the only black elected to that position. "The world is not homogeneous. This is the real world. If you build a wall around kids, they will never learn how to get along with anybody but their own kind. Living here better prepares them for what they'll experience once they leave home."

Ahmad Qayoumi, assistant city engineer in Montgomery, and his wife, Jonna Papajohn, bought a 70-year-old, two-story house on Valley View Avenue last January because of the rising property values and the neighborhood's racial mix.

"There are several parts of town that are intolerant of racial differences," added Papajohn, 27. "We didn't want to live there."

---

# Bond Hill on verge of urban rebound

Redevelopment of a historic mall is vital to more change

*October 15, 2012*

Gardenia Roper has a new husband and a new career.

And as a new business owner and the newly elected president of the Bond Hill Business Association, the 31-year Bond Hill resident is confident that her neighborhood is on the verge of its own new beginning.

"I love Cincinnati, I love Bond Hill, and I am going to do everything I can to bring it back," said Roper, 67, a Procter & Gamble retiree.

In 2009, she opened Roper's Southern Style Cooking Restaurant & Catering on California Avenue with husband and chef Jesse Roper.

Plenty of evidence suggests Bond Hill is already coming back. At one time the geographic center of Cincinnati and its suburbs, the area since the 1960s had seen an increase in crime and decreases in home ownership and business activity. Its revival – which is attracting industry and jobs – promises to strengthen the Hamilton County tax base and the region's economy, in addition to improving the lives of residents and reducing demand for social services.

Outside developers note an uncommon single-purpose cooperation inside the neighborhood, where churches that have historically owned and developed property are working on new projects.

Even an apparent loss – an August decision by the Port of Greater Cincinnati Development Authority to cease negotiations with Corinthian Baptist Church to develop the former Showcase Cinemas site at Reading Road and the Norwood Lateral – turned into a likely victory.

---

## History lesson

*February 18, 2018*

Bond Hill's history is tied to its location on Mill Creek and the railroad.

For at least the first decade after its 1871 founding, Bond Hill was a temperance community, where the sale of alcohol was prohibited. Incorporated as a village in 1886, Bond Hill had grown to about 1,000 people when Cincinnati annexed it in 1903.

In 1910, Maketewah Country Club was carved out of a 127-acre dairy farm in the heart of Bond Hill. Grocery magnate Barney Kroger was a founding father.

The pastoral nature of Bond Hill endured until the 1950s, but change came with construction of highways and Swifton Shopping Center.

A few blocks down Seymour Avenue from Swifton stands Cincinnati Gardens, opened in 1949 with a seating capacity of 11,000, making it the seventh-largest indoor arena in the United States at the time. The Gardens – modeled after Toronto's Maple Leaf Gardens – was home to the NBA's Cincinnati Royals (now the Sacramento Kings) from 1957 through 1972. Xavier University's basketball team moved out in 2000 for an on-campus arena, Cintas Center.

---

Last week, Corinthian Baptist – which plans to move from Avondale to Bond Hill – reached a deal with a national developer out of Columbus, Equity Inc., to jump-start the Showcase project.

And the Port Authority in September agreed with another church, Allen Temple, to buy another high-profile Bond Hill commercial site less than two miles north on Reading Road. The authority wants to develop the 27-acre Jordan Crossing site and decaying outdoor mall at Reading and Seymour avenues into a mixed-use project that includes retail, offices, housing, and a hotel.

"It's been a long, slow, steady disinvestment," said Laura Brunner, Port Authority president, of both Bond Hill and the site, once known as the Swifton Shopping Center.

It was the city's first mall, opened in 1956, and its 66 retailers included a two-level department store and two groceries.

Rehabilitation of Jordan Crossing would be the single project that would most move the neighborhood forward, said Everett Gregory, president of the Bond Hill Community Council.

## "All it needs is some shining up"

Bond Hill has connections in Columbus. Alicia Reece, a neighborhood resident since 1993, represents it and the rest of the 33rd Ohio House District.

"All you might hear about is a police run on Reading Road, but Bond Hill has been quietly coming back," said Reece, whose father, Steve Reece, has operated the Integrity Hall banquet facility on Seymour Avenue in Bond Hill since 1988. "It's a diamond in the rough. All it needs is some shining up."

The elbow grease is starting to pay off.

The TechSolve Business Park on the northern edge of Bond Hill, on the site of the former Longworth State Hospital, has grown to 13 businesses that employ an estimated 1,900 workers.

One of the latest additions, in 2010, was the Graeter's ice cream production plant on Paddock Road and the former 66th Street, which was renamed Regina Graeter Way.

Rough Brothers, a greenhouse design and manufacturing firm, is expected later this year to begin construction of a new plant on Regina Graeter Way that will bring another 120 jobs to the city.

Procter & Gamble earlier this month announced a $2 million donation to the Reds Urban Youth Academy to be built at Roselawn Park – which is in Bond Hill.

Four renovated baseball diamonds and a 33,000-square-foot building will provide an all-weather baseball and softball training venue for youths ages 6–18 from throughout the region.

The Cincinnati–Hamilton County Community Action Agency moved from Walnut Hills to Bond Hill in 2005. Two years later, the merged Bond Hill and Roselawn branches of the Public Library of Cincinnati and Hamilton County moved into the agency's building at Jordan Crossing.

Across Reading Road from Jordan Crossing, the new Woodward Career Technical High School building opened in 2006.

A $30,000 grant will be used to erect signs and gateways to the neighborhood, whose major north-south arteries are Paddock and Reading roads running north from Tennessee Avenue to Seymour Avenue.

Bond Hill Business Association leaders are awaiting word on another $300,000 grant that would be used to buy five adjacent buildings at California Avenue and Reading Road.

The plan is to demolish the buildings and create a fenced-in green space and community garden while working to attract a developer.

California Avenue is the primary east-west route, connecting Paddock and Reading roads, that gives Bond Hill's commercial area its H-shape.

The Villages of Daybreak, a 60-acre development that surrounds the intersection of Langdon Farm Road and Rhode Island Avenue, has brought 92 new homeowners into Bond Hill.

The development is on the site of the failed former Huntington Meadows apartment community and its forerunner, Swifton Village.

New York developer Fred Trump bought Swifton Village for $5.7 million in 1962 and turned the 1,200-unit complex from 66 percent to 100 percent occupancy within two years.

His whiz-kid business school son, Donald Trump, worked on the Swifton project. The Trump Organization sold it for $1.05 million profit in 1972.

Villages of Daybreak was the site of two Citirama home development projects, in 2005 and 2011. A project led by NorthPoint Land Co., in partnership with two Bond Hill churches, the Allen Temple Foundation and Tryed Stone Family and Community Development Center, eventually should consist of 300 home sites.

Villages contributed to positive change in Bond Hill from 2000 to 2010. Though the neighborhood lost 27 percent of its population, falling just below 7,000, the percentage of home ownership increased from 45 to 55 percent. Bond Hill experienced another positive change in that same time frame. Its crime rate fell from 121.40 crimes per 1,000 people to 109.60 per 1,000 in 2010 – compared with an increase in Cincinnati's overall crime rate.

Deborah Robb moved in 2005 from suburban Forest Park to a single-family home in Villages. Director of Inclusion and Community Relations for the Port Authority, Robb liked Bond Hill because of the new housing stock and central location.

"I work downtown, and I didn't want to keep spending hours driving," she said. "I'm no more than 15 minutes from anywhere I want to go."

Interstate 75 runs through Bond Hill's western edge. The Norwood Lateral cuts across the southern end of Bond Hill and provides direct access to Interstates 75 and 71.

## "It's not going to happen overnight"

Demographic change came after the highways. The first black family moved to Bond Hill in 1964, and, fueled by unethical but legal real estate practices of the times, the racial composition changed within a generation.

By 1978, the neighborhood was 70 percent African-American. By 2010, the neighborhood had just 322 white residents (4.6 percent). Cincinnati's second black ghetto hopped North Avondale / Paddock Hills and swept through Bond Hill and neighboring Roselawn to its immediate north.

James Brown, now 94 and a widowed father of four, moved his family from Avondale to tree-lined Berkley Avenue in 1970.

"We wanted to buy a home, and when we came down Berkley and saw this one, we bought it," said Brown, who would retire in 1988 as a firefighter/engineer from Longview State Hospital.

His family enjoyed living in Bond Hill, where they were treated well by blacks and whites alike.

"The whites were too busy moving out, though," he said.

One of the white families that remains is the Bruggermans, who moved onto Berkley Avenue five years before James Brown.

"We needed a house, and the [five] kids were able to walk to St. Agnes School," said Dee Bruggerman, 77, a former math teacher at the school. "We're only seven miles from downtown, yet we're removed from all the traffic."

Bruggerman and Brown are members of the Church of the Resurrection, the former St. Agnes Church, formed when the Archdiocese of Cincinnati in 2010 closed three other predominately black churches, including St. Andrew in Avondale and St. Mark in Evanston.

Resurrection is a landmark on California Avenue, near Bond Hill Academy, a successful Cincinnati Public elementary school. Farther west, just on the other side of Paddock Road, is Gardenia and Jesse Roper's restaurant and catering business. His sweet potato pies will be available before the end of the month at Kroger, adding it to a list of other grocers.

Gardenia Roper is among Bond Hill's most unapologetic cheerleaders.

"The mindset has changed for the better," she said. "I can now see we are on the right track to become a thriving, bustling, walkable community. It's not going to happen overnight, but it's going to happen."

---

# History makes West End residents wary of FC Cincinnati stadium plan

*February 18, 2018*

Ralph Moon Jr. raised his voice in front of his family home on Dayton Street as he explained why he is against the proposed FC Cincinnati soccer stadium in the West End.

Moon, 69, is angry, no doubt, but he also had to speak loudly to be heard above the drone of Interstate 75 traffic to the immediate west.

"Behind me is I-75, which is indicative of the displacement of people in the neighborhood under the pretense of progress," said Moon, 69. "This kind of thing's been going on for over 60-some-odd years. A lot of broken promises."

West End residents have mixed opinions about a soccer-specific stadium being built in their historically black neighborhood – a stadium that FC Cincinnati executives say is necessary for them to secure a Major League Soccer berth. They have been expressing themselves at a series of public meetings over the past few weeks and have several more opportunities in the coming week.

Opponents are worried that more residents will be priced out of the community and that Cincinnati Public Schools will be cheated of property tax money.

"Many of the residents here are tired and not trusting of some of these fly-by-night ideas that may come up," said Moon, a 1966 graduate of Taft High School and retired educator who finished his career as a Walnut Hills High School math teacher.

Other people are for the stadium proposal, including former two-term Cincinnati Mayor Mark Mallory, whose politically influential family has deep roots in the neighborhood. He said the FC Cincinnati project is an unprecedented opportunity for West End residents to benefit from the gentrification that is gathering speed in the neighborhood.

"This is a real opportunity for the West End – a $200 million project that could bring new assets," Mallory said. "It's up to the community to say what it wants."

## Neighborhood already gentrifying

An *Enquirer* analysis of U.S. Census data shows the neighborhood is already changing – particularly the part closest to downtown and Cincinnati City Hall. Median household income in the area south of Court Street, which now has a majority of white residents, has risen to $49,000 compared to the area north of West Liberty, which is predominately black and has a median household income of $11,000.

The poverty rate north of Liberty is 61 percent, compared to 30 percent across the city.

The population of the West End as a whole is on the rise, growing 20 percent, to 7,980, just from 2010 to the middle of this decade. At the same time, the proportion that's African-American dropped 9 percentage points.

West End residents say they need only to look to their east to see the change in Over-the-Rhine, which has gentrified dramatically in the past decade and now has a majority-white population in its southern half, below Liberty Street.

No matter where they stand on the possibility of a soccer stadium coming into their neighborhood, current and former West End residents share a firm belief that few outsiders have really cared about their neighborhood until somebody wants a piece of it or to profit from it.

This time, it's the land that Cincinnati Public Schools' Stargel Stadium sits on, behind Taft IT High School on Ezzard Charles Drive. FC Cincinnati President and General Manager Jeff Berding wants to put the soccer stadium there if he gets an MLS franchise. In exchange, he says, he would build a new Stargel nearby.

As he makes the rounds of community and school board meetings, Berding is pitching what he says are the benefits to the neighborhood: jobs, improved athletic facilities for public school students, and the development of up to five dozen affordable housing units along Laurel Park Drive south of Wade Walk.

"I feel powerless, and I don't think I will benefit," said Marq Casey, 25, a forklift driver for DHL at Cincinnati / Northern Kentucky International Airport who lives in an apartment complex west of Linn Street.

A native of the area – Findlay Street in Over-the-Rhine – Casey said the proposed FC Cincinnati stadium "feels like it's not valuing our history and the history of the West End. So much of it is already lost."

Berding also is fighting 60 years of history that has generated cynicism among many people in the West End, especially African-Americans, of anything that sounds too good to be true.

## Historic neighborhood torn apart many times

Older residents can remember a self-contained community before construction of I-75 carved a wide gulch through the neighborhood.

The West End was the first Cincinnati stop for most African-Americans migrating from the South. By 1950, before expressway construction and urban renewal destroyed black communities in dozens of U.S. cities, almost half of all African-Americans living in Cincinnati – 36,000 of 78,000 – were squeezed into the West End. It stretched to the Brighton area north of Bank Street, south below Sixth Street, and to the west through what its now Queensgate.

While they went about clearing land for the expressway, city officials decided to take out a residential section of the West End just to the west of downtown and replace it with an industrial park that would become Queensgate. The idea was to attract light manufacturing to help the city compete with the suburban job boom.

That area, known as Kenyon-Barr, covered an estimated 435 acres south of Ezzard Charles. It was a densely populated community of some 30,000 people, almost all of them African-American. Lost in the demolition were 2,800 buildings – churches and other houses of worship, every kind of business ranging from corner stores and pharmacies to barber shops and funeral homes, schools, parks – and more than 10,000 housing units.

From 1959 through 1970, the Kenyon-Barr "slum clearance" displaced more families – 4,953 – than any other individual project in the nation, according to the University of Richmond's Digital Scholarship Lab report "Renewing Inequality." Of those moved, 97 percent were African-American.

In addition, a 58-acre project south of Liberty Street and west of Linn displaced another 1,500 families between 1952 and 1963, of which 90 percent were black.

Cincinnati Metropolitan Housing Authority attempted to move thousands of black families into public housing in white areas of the city and Hamilton County but ran into strong resistance from white neighbors. As a result, city planners ended up moving 12,600 displaced black families into the private housing market from 1955 through 1959. Segregation ruled the day, so many went to Avondale, which already had black housing.

"We all got shuffled around pretty good," said Fulton Jefferson Jr., 60, the oldest of four children in a family that first was displaced by I-75 and then from a home in Avondale a few years later by construction of Interstate 71.

His father, Fulton Sr., lived above a dry cleaner in the 500 block of West Fifth, a stretch of the street that was cleared for a tangle of I-75 ramps to the west of the Duke Energy Convention Center. West Fifth picks up a few blocks to the west, at Gest Street, in Queensgate – in the former Kenyon-Barr neighborhood.

## Stadium opponents: Learn from the past

Kenyon-Barr's history came up at Monday night's Cincinnati school board meeting, where West End native and former Cincinnati Mayor Dwight Tillery handed out copies of a 2017 magazine article about it.

Tillery didn't speak, but almost 50 other people did, and many of them spoke passionately against the soccer stadium as a threat to one of the few remaining pieces of black history in the neighborhood. Willard R. Stargel Stadium is named for a beloved African-American teacher and coach.

Earnestine Hill, 59, grew up in the West End, left and moved back into a new unit in the City West Apartments on Linn Street.

"A lot of us don't understand everything they're trying to do," Hill said. "A lot of people are concerned we're going to lose our housing. It has happened before."

The neighborhood looks far different than it did a generation ago.

In 1999, the city's Office of Architecture and Urban Design conducted a blight study in the West End and found that conditions existed that "constitute a serious menace to public health, safety (and) economic and social stability."

The most egregious offenders, officials said, were a pair of sprawling post-war public housing projects, Lincoln Court and Laurel Homes, that each had about 1,000 affordable units.

CHMA won a pair of $30 million-plus U.S. Department of Housing and Urban Development grants to tear down Lincoln and Laurel and replace them with mixed-income communities that significantly reduced the number of public housing units for low-income renters. About 2,000 people were displaced. At public meetings on the soccer stadium, some speakers said only one in ten displaced people were able to return.

The housing authority disputes that claim.

"CMHA has no record of any resident that wanted to return being turned down," agency spokeswoman Lesley Wardlow told the *Enquirer*. She said CMHA met its goal of creating a mix of affordable and market-rate housing in the Hope VI project, a government label for the program that's still used by residents.

Some former Lincoln and Laurel residents moved to scattered sites in the West End or other neighborhoods. CMHA, Wardlow said, also developed new senior housing in the Baldwin Grove project in suburban Springdale.

Still, hard feelings exist. Hope VI "decimated the community," said Joe Mallory, a former West End resident and vice president of the Cincinnati branch of the NAACP. The NAACP hasn't taken a position, but he is skeptical of putting the FC Cincinnati stadium in the West End, unlike brother Mark Mallory.

Mark Mallory supports the soccer stadium if the neighborhood can get tangible benefits from it. The 55-year-old former mayor gave two *Enquirer* journalists a driving tour of the West End on Tuesday.

He talked about how he and his brothers would peer through a barbershop window on Linn Street to see soul singer James Brown get his hair pressed. Across Linn Street, Mallory pointed out the former location of a Kroger grocery that moved out in 1973. Today it is one of the buildings housing the Cincinnati College Preparatory Academy.

"We had everything, but the community changed, like a lot of urban communities changed around the country," he said as he steered his black Ford north through the intersection of Linn and Liberty. "Now, if you look at the financial backers of FC Cincinnati, they are influential people. They have the ability to make things happen.

"I understand the concerns of the some in the community. They're afraid we'll lose the remaining fabric of the neighborhood. But I argue it's a chance to reinvest in the community and reassess the gentrification that's already taking place."

Ralph Moon, who grew up on the same street as the Mallory brothers, isn't buying. He stood in front of the home that has been in his family since 1945 and recalled walking a couple of blocks west to Crosley Field to see the Cincinnati Reds play. He talked about walking one block in the other direction to attend Heberle School, which a private owner is trying to redevelop into 59 apartments.

Moon referred several times to "broken promises," and took aim at the makeover of Lincoln Court and Laurel Homes as "a fiasco." The proposed soccer stadium, he finally said, "is another intentional effort to hijack the neighborhood."

At that, he let out a sharp sigh, adjusted his black fedora and glanced back at I-75.

*The* Enquirer's *Mark Wert contributed.*

# AVONDALE

*My favorite part of Cincinnati, Avondale is raw and real, unpretentious and unapologetic about its collective strengths and weaknesses. I reported several dozen stories out of this neighborhood from 2012 through 2014 for a series called "Saving Avondale," which documented its attempt at revitalization without displacing its long-time residents. Then I went to work there as an Urban League vice president in 2015 before going back to the Enquirer.*

# Saving Avondale

It's been scarred by riots, unemployment, and a festering malaise. But this neighborhood is filled with hope

*March 18, 2012*

Reading Road never recovered after it burned – once in 1967, then again in 1968.

Rioting along Avondale's main street accelerated the decline that had taken root a decade earlier.

Rush-hour traffic speeds south on Reading every morning and north at night as an alternative route to Interstate 71, but the in-between hours are eerily silent. A car dealer used to sell Buicks from behind now-boarded display windows shattered during the riots. Shin-high brown grass stands rigid, not bending to the wind, in the front yards of foreclosed four-family apartment houses sealed with plywood. The big stone Gothic-style Catholic church closed its doors two summers ago. A payday lender and a Burger King are among the most active businesses on the strip.

The jobless rate in Avondale is 40 percent. There's not a single grocery store or pharmacy in this community of 12,466. One-third of its kindergartners are overweight or obese. A quarter of its housing units are vacant.

Crime is up 16.1 percent from 2000, even after a decline in each of the past two years. Gunfire is frequent in parts of the neighborhood. Some residents on those blocks say their dogs reflexively stopped howling. Other residents have grown accustomed to the situation, and fearful of reporting criminal activity for fear of reprisal.

"There's nothing here," said Donna Jones Baker, president and chief executive of the Urban League of Greater Cincinnati, located a few doors south of Avondale's major crossroads, Reading and Rockdale. "There's an absence of vibrancy that makes a community strong."

Still, there is hope.

This time, hope is backed with money. Hope that Avondale won't continue on a path toward more unemployment and daytime drug-dealing but will be restored to its place among Cincinnati's most desirable neighborhoods, one with a mix of incomes and races and safe streets, where new businesses provide not just goods and services but jobs to the people who live here.

Harnessing the hope and addressing what ails Avondale is the job of Ozie Davis, named executive director in October of a neighborhood development organization unlike anything Avondale has seen. The Avondale Comprehensive Development Corp. has a professional staff and the mandate from a group of funders to pull together divergent neighborhood interests. With about $430,000 a year coming in from this group of generous yet demanding organizations – including the United Way of Greater Cincinnati – the nonprofit Davis leads has the resources to help turn around one of Cincinnati's most strategic neighborhoods.

The blueprint goals of this holistic approach – known as Place Matters – are to attract new businesses, investment, and housing to Avondale.

"Never before have we had the partners. Never before have we had the cooperation," Davis said. "We have a lot of work to do, but we will bring a renaissance to Avondale by 2019."

Davis, 46, is an Avondale leader and an Avondale resident, living with his family on the same street – Eden Avenue – on which he grew up.

"We understand now it's urgent," he said. And holy: "Our job is very much like the work of Nehemiah to rebuild Jerusalem."

Some stones of hope are in place:

- Hope in improved infant and new mother health, thanks to the Every Child Succeeds program in the basement of Carmel Presbyterian Church.

- Hope in Carmel and the 51 other Avondale churches that are socially vigorous and draw as many as two-thirds of their members from outside of the neighborhood.

- Hope in the popularity of the farmer's market and demand for urban gardens at the new Gabriel's Place community center.

- Hope in the gleaming new *Cincinnati Herald* building on Burnet Avenue on the other side of the neighborhood.

- Hope in the high three-year job-retention rate of workers who went through an Urban League landscape apprenticeship program.

- Hope that 39 units of abandoned housing on Glenwood Avenue and another 50 in the castle-like Ambassador on Gholson Avenue will be renovated within the next two years and rented with little or no subsidy.

- Hope that enough change can be shown in Avondale to persuade suburbanites who work within a mile or two at Cincinnati Children's or University hospitals that their time and money would be better spent rehabbing an empty Victorian than on long commutes.

"It's important that the people working in the city come to view our close-in neighborhoods as viable places to live," said Cincinnati Vice Mayor Roxanne Qualls. "We have the chance to make Avondale great again."

If people with a choice can't be brought back to Avondale, the city's population will continue a decline that has seen it shrink almost 25 percent, from 385,457 in 1980 to 296,943 in 2010. During that time, Avondale's population fell 37 percent, from 19,845 to 12,466.

The population isn't there now, but the jobs are, 50,000 of them – the second highest concentration in the region – at the hospitals and the University of Cincinnati and throughout an area of the city known as Uptown that includes Avondale. The reality check is that most of those jobs are out of the skill reach of the people who live there.

Davis, his team, and increasing numbers of residents, he said, envision a vibrant urban community, one that's safe to walk and even more diverse than pre-war Avondale.

That's when car dealers, groceries, and pharmacies lined Reading Road to the east and Burnet Avenue to the west. Almost a dozen synagogues dotted a neighborhood that was the heart of the city's Jewish community and home to 24,000 people in 1940. Black professional and middle-class homeowners moved there by choice from overcrowded conditions in the West End.

Yet it was that presence of African-Americans in Avondale that convinced city planners to force thousands of low-income black families there, when all-white city neighborhoods and first-generation suburbs rejected attempts to build new, scattered-site public housing for displaced blacks. The southern part of Avondale turned black and poor and officially "blighted" in 1956 by the city.

White families, and the black families that could, got out. Jewish families and mobile blacks moved to the other side of Clinton Springs Avenue, into what became known as North Avondale, or farther north to Paddock Hills. Many Jewish and other white families went out even farther, north on Reading Road to Roselawn, then filling up new suburbs such as Sharonville, Springdale, and Amberley Village – which became the center of Jewish life and culture.

For the people who couldn't leave Avondale then or can't get out today, they'd like to see their quality of life improve, though they are resigned that it won't – even as they agitate for amenities most communities take for granted, such as a grocery.

What remained of Avondale's once-thriving retail strips burned during the urban violence of June 1967 and April 1968. Growing frustration about the lack of fair employment and housing opportunities for African-Americans ignited the first outbreak, the assassination of the Rev. Martin Luther King the second.

Today, about 89 percent of Avondale's residents are black, making it Cincinnati's third-highest concentration of black population, behind Bond Hill and South Cumminsville–Millvale.

Yet Avondale is bigger and more populated. Its 2.2 square miles border Xavier University to the east, and the hospitals, zoo, and University of Cincinnati to the west. Location is its major asset.

"My belief is that, in a large number of minds, that so goes Avondale, so goes much of the city," said city council member Wendell Young, an Avondale native who worked as a police officer in the area from 1967 through 1992.

Revival of urban neighborhoods like Avondale would benefit the region in the global economy, said William Julius Wilson, a noted Harvard University sociologist.

"If you are looking to relocate to Greater Cincinnati or expand your business, you want to see a well-educated, strong workforce," said Wilson, who spoke at the National Underground Railroad Freedom Center in February. "The stronger the urban core, the stronger the suburbs."

Another national urban expert, New York City–based criminologist David Kennedy, who has worked on anti-crime initiatives in Cincinnati since 2007, is consulting with Avondale leaders on their latest effort to reduce violence in the community. Avondale and Over-the-Rhine led the city with 11 murders each in 2011.

"Avondale has become one of the places [where] we are trying to create a national break-through," said Kennedy, who is in contact with what he calls "troubled" communities across the country. "We will learn from Avondale. They're figuring out how to do things."

Reducing violence would go a long way toward helping turn Avondale back into a neighborhood where people choose to reside.

"Imagine [Avondale] with 7,000 to 8,000 more people and what that would do to the schools and businesses," said Liz Blume, executive director at Xavier University's Community Building Institute, a group of professional development consultants affiliated with the local United Way. "Avondale has everything an urban neighborhood needs to be successful: It's dense, you can walk it, it has deep church institutions, major employers as anchors and beautiful architecture. If we can't get it right here, where are we going to get it right?"

Getting Avondale right is a challenge Davis embraces.

Spending two days with him touring Avondale gives one the impression that he knows everybody. Davis has put together a board that gives everyone in the neighborhood a voice – churches, the Urban League, residents, banks, and perhaps its two best-known institutions, Cincinnati Children's Hospital Medical Center and the Cincinnati Zoo, which draw millions of people to the city each year and, for many, are the face of Cincinnati.

The zoo played a part in beginning the cleanup of the Mitchell Avenue-to-Vine Street entrance to Avondale from I-75. Zoo officials spent $30,000 in 2011 on a project to clear one acre and dilapidated housing at Vine Street and Forest Avenue. A new gateway sign built from stone welcomes visitors to Avondale and the zoo. New curbs, sidewalks, and landscaping were put in.

"It's a perceptible change, but we want to clean up the access to the zoo," said Bill Witten, an Avondale resident and former Procter & Gamble Co. executive who works as a paid consultant to the Avondale Community Council and the comprehensive development corporation. "We want to sell Avondale."

It's a tough sell for many suburbanites, who consider the two-mile drive from the Mitchell Avenue exit through Avondale a dangerous gauntlet.

The zoo, which covers 70 acres of Avondale, supports the youth council and neighborhood community gardens and is an educational partner with nearby Rockdale Academy elementary. Cincinnati Public has a 50-student magnet school at the zoo.

On the route to the zoo, on Vine Street near Glen Este Place, Davis and Witten pointed out three vacant apartment buildings they plan to develop.

## Avondale wants building projects

Place Matters funding has been used on several projects in Avondale since 2007. Yet Avondale built for the past five years – unlike the other two Place Matters communities, the Cincinnati neighborhood of Price Hill and the city of Covington, Kentucky – without a professional development staff. Now that expertise and paid staff are in place in Avondale.

Place Matters invested directly in social-improvement projects, such as mother-and-child health and job creation, through the volunteer Avondale Community Council. Avondale Comprehensive Development Corp. replaces the council as the neighborhood's lead Place Matters agency.

"It's going to be our bricks and mortar," said Fulton Jefferson, community council vice president and another key figure in developing programs funded the past six years by Place Matters.

With 25 percent of its 7,600 housing units vacant, Avondale is a hole in the city's tax pool but ripe as a place of redevelopment for workforce housing. The five founding members of the Uptown Consortium – the University of Cincinnati, Cincinnati Children's Hospital, TriHealth, UC Health, and the Cincinnati Zoo – employ nearly 50,000 people with a collective payroll of $1.4 billion.

The consortium heads development efforts in Uptown, which comprises Avondale and six other neighborhoods: Clifton, Clifton Heights, Corryville, Fairview, Mount Auburn, and University Heights.

The consortium led efforts to put up the Cincinnati Herald Building in 2009 and Forest Square senior housing in 2010 along Burnet Avenue. A Subway sandwich shop opened in October on the ground floor of the Herald Building.

"Ozie's group brings resources, energy, and an additional partner to help with development in areas we're not in now," said Beth Robinson, the consortium's president and chief executive.

The consortium supports a planned I-71 interchange at Martin Luther King Jr. Drive, scheduled for 2015 completion if state and federal money is made available. It would improve access to the hospital jobs and spur commercial development in the southern edge of Avondale.

It's just one of Davis's many wish-list projects. On the modest end, he is pursuing a deal in which a restaurant and reception hall would buy the former St. Andrew Catholic Church building on Reading Road, closed by the Archdiocese of Cincinnati in 2010 because of dwindling membership.

On a larger scale, Davis traveled to Chicago this month to meet with the Community Builders, a national nonprofit that is applying for a major federal grant on behalf of Avondale Comprehensive Development Corp.

The Choice Neighborhoods Implementation grant from the U.S. Department of Housing and Urban Development (HUD) would bring as much as $30 million over five years to

Avondale. In August 2011, HUD awarded its first grants, worth $122 million, to stimulate neighborhood revitalization in Boston, Chicago, New Orleans, San Francisco and Seattle.

Another four or five HUD Choice designations will be made in December. The focus is to improve housing and property management and to link those upgrades with improvements in transportation and education, including early childhood programs.

HUD money could connect to the Avondale Every Child Succeeds Home Visitation Program, which has received Place Matters funding since 2007. Another local program to build on is Gabriel's Place, a multi-disciplinary, food-based ministry in the former St. Michael and All Angels Episcopal Church. Dedicated in September and preparing for its first growing season, Gabriel's Place is a limited source of fresh fruit, vegetables, and fish while Avondale leaders continue to lure a grocery store. The last one, an Aldi, moved out of the Avondale Town Center in November 2008. Urban-apparel retailer Citi Trends has since leased the space.

Without a grocery, Avondale is considered a "food desert" because healthful food is not available to residents at a full-service grocery. Four- by six-foot garden plots are available for $20 annually at Gabriel's Place. Fruits and vegetables – lettuce, potatoes, onions, apples, oranges, and bananas – are brought to Gabriel's Place and are available at a farmer's market on the first and third Thursday each month.

## Doctor's family chooses Avondale

If the Avondale Comprehensive Development Corp. succeeds, more people like Geno Griffith and Johnie and Kenneth Davis will call the neighborhood home.

Mr. and Mrs. Davis, no relation to Ozie, brought up three daughters in the home they've owned on Forest Park Drive since 1984. Their cul-de-sac of two dozen houses has had little turnover. The street is freshly paved with new curbs. Lawns are neat. The housing stock is a mix of ranches and two-story Tudors.

"We are really happy here. We have great neighbors," said Mrs. Davis, an active volunteer at her church, Carmel Presbyterian. Her husband is a trauma surgeon at nearby University Hospital.

"Unfortunately," she said, "when bad things happen in Avondale, everything good here gets painted negatively."

Griffith, 18, lives in an apartment on Wilson Avenue with his mother, Gina, and younger brother, William, 17. He can walk the 15 minutes to Xavier University in neighboring Evanston, where he is on full academic scholarship. A graduate of Withrow International High School, Geno is a biology major and plans to become an anesthesiologist.

"There is a stigma to coming from Avondale that you don't have with Indian Hill or Blue Ash," said Geno, who attended Rockdale Academy in his elementary school days. He would like some day to live in a healthier Avondale.

The family had moved to Mount Auburn for a short time after they were evicted when a bank foreclosed on their landlord's property on Alaska Avenue. They returned a year ago. Gina Griffith, 53, has worked in environmental services at nearby Cincinnati Children's for 15 years. She has introduced her sons to doctors and other professionals there.

"We could live elsewhere, but why?" she said. "Avondale is home."

# Once decline started, it snowballed

By 1970, the Avondale of 1950 was gone

*March 19, 2012*

AVONDALE – Few Cincinnati neighborhoods experience the degree of change that left its mark on Avondale.

The transformation took place quickly in a single generation after World War II.

In 1950, Avondale still beat as the heart of the city's Jewish life and culture, 86 percent white, with a dozen concrete-and-stone synagogues standing like citadels and Jewish bakeries and delicatessens and kosher butcher shops lining Reading Road.

By 1970, Avondale had burned and been looted – twice – and with 91 percent of its population African-American, conjoined with Evanston and Walnut Hills to form Cincinnati's second black ghetto.

"What stands out about Avondale is how rapidly it became the center of the city's black community, when it had seemingly just been the center of the Jewish community," said Fritz Casey-Leininger, adjunct assistant professor of history at the University of Cincinnati, who has researched and written extensively about the neighborhood's history.

Fulton Jefferson Sr. lived it. His family's path to Avondale was typical for African-Americans.

"It was the center of pretty much everything," said Jefferson, 76, a widower who still lives in Avondale. "We were happy there."

He moved from Arkansas in 1954, toward the end of the migration of African-Americans to Northern cities. And like thousands before him who had moved to Cincinnati, he found housing in the West End, then the city's primary and segregated residence for African-Americans. Almost half of all blacks living in the city in 1950 – 36,000 of 78,000 – were squeezed into the West End.

Jefferson took a room on the third floor of a dry cleaner at 544 W. Fifth St. Gussie Bell, who would be part of the first Taft High School graduating class in 1954, lived on the second floor with her family.

A couple of years later, Fulton and Gussie would marry and move. They had to. The building they lived in was demolished to make room for Interstate 75.

The first idea was to clear the West End by building new public housing in other parts of Hamilton County. From 1945 to 1955, Cincinnati Metropolitan Housing Authority (CMHA) had little trouble filling the new English Woods and Winton Terrace developments with whites. Yet the agency ran into strong resistance in its efforts to relocate African-Americans in public housing in white neighborhoods, according to Casey-Leininger.

CMHA's failure caused city planners to decide that as many as 12,600 displaced black families would have to be absorbed into the private housing market between 1955 and 1959. And one of the only places African-Americans could go was Avondale because Avondale already had black housing.

"We all got shuffled around pretty good," said Fulton Jefferson Jr., 54, the oldest of his parents' four children and an Avondale resident, business owner and vice president of the neighborhood community council.

## Blacks move in, whites move out

Three enclaves of middle-class black families in Avondale – comprising about 10 percent of the neighborhood's population – had grown up just north of the Cincinnati Zoo, and to the east along Rockdale Avenue and farther south where present-day Martin Luther King Drive crosses what is now known as the Interstate 71 valley into Walnut Hills.

That valley, near the corner of Fredonia and Werhman avenues, is where Jefferson Sr. first rented a house that would eventually be demolished to make room for Interstate 71. The family was among the 16,000 African-Americans who moved to Avondale in the 1950s, when the neighborhood's black population increased from 14 percent to almost 70 percent.

"Whole streets flipped from white to black, almost overnight," Casey-Leininger said. "Real estate practices of the day were largely unscrupulous."

One method was known as "blockbusting," when an agent or lender would start a rumor that a black family was moving onto a street, that whites were moving out and homeowners should sell to avoid plummeting property values. Real estate listings in the *Enquirer* in 1954 advertised homes for sale in Avondale as "Colored Man's Dream" and "Unrestricted."

Panic selling by white homeowners played a major part in Avondale's swift racial composition change, Casey-Leininger said, as did the growing supply of new suburban housing. Cincinnati's white population decreased by 32,466 during the 1950s.

Lured by the new housing and attractive mortgage rates in the suburbs, whites left Avondale for areas to the north – Roselawn, Sharonville, Springdale, and Amberley

The corner of Reading Road and Rockdale Avenue in the Cincinnati neighborhood of Avondale burns during rioting on April 8, 1968. File photograph courtesy of the Cincinnati Enquirer. (Photo published April 9, 1968.)

## From high-end suburb to urban blight

*March 19, 2012*

- 1846: The first subdivision in Avondale is designated on records as "Plat of house lots at Clinton, three miles from Cincinnati." The community is called Clintonville.

- 1853: Ironworks owner Stephen Burton is one of the prominent Cincinnati business owners to make his family home in the neighborhood. His wife sees a resemblance between a stream near their home (today the site of 6-acre Martin Luther King Jr. Park) and the Avon River in England, and she begins calling the area Avondale.

- 1864: The Village of Avondale incorporates, primarily to try to curb lawlessness that spawns an outbreak of burglary, vagrancy, public drunkenness and public fighting. Burton is the first mayor.

- 1892: Robert Mitchell, owner of the Mitchell Furniture Co., builds a mile-long road to the brow of the hill overlooking the Mill Creek

Village. Jewish congregations eventually followed their members, vacating grand temples in Avondale that were eventually sold to black congregations or demolished.

"Avondale was such a lively community," said Michael Meyer, 74, who teaches Jewish history at Hebrew Union College-Jewish Institute of Religion and lived in South Avondale in the early 1960s. "It was sad to see the decline. [Housing] prices fell."

Founded in the mid-1800s as an exclusive suburb for Cincinnati's business and industrial elite who built testimonial mansions to their wealth, Avondale evolved in the early 1900s from a largely Protestant neighborhood to one in which Jews made up 60 percent of the population through the end of World War II.

The Jewish community wasn't the only one to leave Avondale. The Episcopal Diocese of Southern Ohio closed its last Avondale church, St. Michael and All Angels, in 2008, and the Archdiocese of Cincinnati shuttered St. Andrew Church in 2010 on Reading Road because membership – 1,800 in 1974 – dwindled to fewer than 100.

Congregation Ohav Shalom moved first to Roselawn and then Blue Ash, leaving its synagogue at 425 Forest Ave. Greater St. John AME Zion Church, displaced from the West End by I-75, bought the building and took occupancy in 1957. It was the Jefferson family's church.

## North Avondale rises, Reading Road burns

White residential migration continued out of Avondale, despite the failed efforts of two interracial resident organizations to maintain stable, mixed communities.

A third organization, the North Avondale Neighborhood Association, founded in 1960, succeeded. Black and white

(near the current Interstate 75 and Mitchell Avenue and through much of what is now North Avondale). Businessmen Andrew Erkenbrecher, Samuel Pogue, Frank Herschede and Barney Kroger build homes on these streets.

- 1896: Cincinnati annexes the village, and the city's fire and police services reduce crime and improve overall safety.

- 1903: New streetcar lines into Avondale open the community to less-affluent Greek Americans and Eastern European Jewish families who had settled originally in the West End. Haddon Hall Apartments is built as attractive housing for new residents.

- 1926: Forty-one businesses operate in the two-block area of Reading Road between Windham and Hutchins avenues. Among them: three groceries, two fruit markets, a hardware store, dry cleaner and bank. Three-fourths of Cincinnati's Jewish population lives in Avondale, and several synagogues are built during the early part of the 20th century. Among them is Louis Feinberg Synagogue, home of the Adath Israel congregation, which left the building in 1964 and dedicated its new synagogue in Amberley Village in 1967. Its old building is home to 3,000-member Southern Baptist Church.

- 1930: Avondale is the center of Jewish life in Cincinnati. The West End is the center of African-American life.

- 1955: "Slum clearance" project begins to move West End residents to make way for construction of Interstate 75. Clusters of black population near Cincinnati Zoo, on Rockdale Avenue and what would become known as the Interstate 71 valley (where Martin Luther King Drive crosses the highway), grow rapidly. The migration threatens

homeowners, well-connected at city hall, protected the newer and largely smaller homes from real estate speculators.

"A lot of good things were happening at the time, the [racial] integration of police and fire," said Meyer, who returned from teaching at Hebrew Union's Los Angeles campus to teach on its Clifton campus. He bought a house on Avondale Avenue in North Avondale in 1968 that he still owns.

Residents of North Avondale, the area north of Clinton Springs and Dana avenues toward Xavier University, had seen what happened in South Avondale. Large old houses were subdivided, often illegally, into low-rent apartments for the new residents. Property values fell far and fast in South Avondale but stayed high in North Avondale and Paddock Hills.

"The ghetto leap-frogs over North Avondale and Paddock Hills," historian Casey-Leininger said, "and starts again in Bond Hill."

The goal of financial and racial stability in North Avondale was achieved. Of its 6,326 residents in 2010, 48 percent are white, 47 percent black and 2 percent Hispanic. Avondale is 89 percent African-American.

Living conditions in Avondale worsened through the 1960s. City promises to improve housing were not honored. Increasing numbers of young African-American men were shut out of union jobs that white high school dropouts could get. The civil rights movement raised awareness nationally among African-Americans of economic and social inequalities. "There's a lot of anger," said Casey-Leininger. "It didn't take much to make it explode."

On June 11, 1967, Cincinnati police arrested a single African-American demonstrator, Peter Frakes, for blocking the sidewalk

to reach middle- and upper-class Clifton and North Avondale.

- 1956: City of Cincinnati officially declares Avondale "blighted" and needing rehabilitation.

- 1960: Twenty-nine businesses remain active in the immediate intersection of Reading and Rockdale.

- 1961: North Avondale Neighborhood Association holds its first meeting. A citizen group of residents living primarily north of Clinton Springs Avenue is founded to protect the community from falling home values and "unscrupulous" real estate practices of the era that had affected South Avondale. The organization will succeed in helping to maintain North Avondale and Paddock Hills (Census Tract 65), a stable neighborhood that is racially and economically integrated.

- 1967: On June 12, riots start in Avondale. Cincinnati's riot is one of 159 incidents in U.S. cities over the summer. Before tempers cool on June 15, one person is dead, 63 are injured, 404 are arrested, and the city sustains $2 million in property damage.

- 1968: On April 4, the assassination of the Rev. Martin Luther King Jr. ignites simmering racial tensions across the country. In Avondale, 1,500 African-Americans attend a peaceful outdoor memorial for King on April 8. A rumor that a white man had shot and killed a black woman in a nearby apartment building explodes into violence. Seventy fires are set, many of them major. Before rioting ends the next morning, two people are dead, and the city experiences $3 million in property damage.

- 1983: Avondale Town Center built. Retired basketball star Oscar Robertson develops the 40,000-square-foot center and lands an IGA grocery as the anchor tenant.

near the Lincoln statue at Reading and Rockdale in Avondale. Frakes carried a sign in support of his cousin, Posteal Laskey Jr., who became known as the Cincinnati Strangler and had been convicted in May for the murder of a white woman, according to *Enquirer* files.

A protest over Frakes's treatment the next evening at the same corner turned violent – kindled by frustration over lack of jobs, poor housing, and what black leaders said was the constant harassment of African-Americans by police.

- 2001: On April 11, four days after the police shooting of an unarmed black man, Timothy Thomas, in Over-the-Rhine, rioting and violence spread to Avondale. A bonfire burns at the intersection of Reading Road and Blair Avenue.

- 2008: Aldi grocery store closes in Avondale Town Center, leaving the community without a grocery store.

A thousand rioters smashed windows to loot businesses on Reading Road and Burnet Avenue. Gov. James Rhodes ordered 700 Ohio National Guard troops to Cincinnati. Before conditions cooled on June 15, one person was dead, 63 injured, 404 arrested, and the city sustained $2 million in property damage.

Less than a year later, on April 4, 1968, the assassination of the Rev. Martin Luther King Jr. in Memphis again ignited racial tensions across the country.

In Avondale, 1,500 African-Americans attended a peaceful outdoor memorial service for King the following Monday, April 8, at Avon Recreation Center. A rumor that a white man had shot a black woman at a nearby apartment building exploded into violence. Within an hour, dozens of buildings along Reading Road near Rockdale, most of them owned by whites, were burning out of control. The *Enquirer* reported that 55 firebombings occurred that night.

The National Guard deployed around 10 p.m. By the next morning, the worst was over, but a terrible toll had been exacted: two deaths, 220 arrests, and $3 million in property damage.

"Avondale couldn't come back from that; it just got worse for a long time," said Fulton Jefferson Jr., who graduated from Withrow High School in 1976 before enlisting in the Marine Corps. He spent 20 years in the military, most as a drill sergeant, before returning to Avondale in 1998.

"Things are better now than 10 years ago," he said. "We've got some good things happening now."

# Opinion

## A meditation on white privilege

*The Cincinnati Enquirer: August 5, 2015*

*Mark Curnutte is Vice President of Marketing, Communications & Key Initiatives at the Urban League of Greater Southwestern Ohio. He is a 30-year newspaper reporter, the final 21 at The Enquirer.*

The makeshift memorial, understandably, took form overnight Thursday and into Friday morning in the 700 block of Ridgeway Avenue.

Shaped by teddy bears, candles, a Christian cross, balloon, black-skinned baby doll, and two flowers — one wilted, the other fresh — it marked where 4-year-old Martaisha Thomas was shot in the face in a drive-by shooting at about 8:15 Thursday night. Police have arrested a suspect, who they say was aiming for someone else in a group of people at an outdoor party that included Martaisha. She remains hospitalized in critical condition.

I read about the shooting Thursday night, managed to get to sleep, but woke up for good around 2 a.m. The week already had emotionally drained many of us who live and work in Cincinnati. Former University of Cincinnati Police Officer Ray Tensing had been indicted on charges of murder and voluntary manslaughter for the July 19 shooting death of unarmed black motorist Samuel DuBose during a traffic stop in Mt. Auburn.

I had to work on a grant proposal Friday morning with a colleague at the Greater Cincinnati Urban League. It was for $40,000 and would go toward promoting and expanding our job-readiness programs that place 80 percent of graduates in jobs and help them stay there.

Most of the morning went to the grant work. A little before noon, I took off walking south of our office in the 3400 block of Reading Road. I had awakened overnight thinking about the last time a 4-year-old had been shot in Cincinnati. Khyren Landrum was hit in the hip on March 20, 2012, on Blair Avenue, as he walked home from a park with his mom and two older sisters.

Traffic sped by in the northbound lanes. I walked past the new housing unit going up on the corner of Reading and Maple Avenue, part of The Community Builders' $29.5 million federal Choice Neighborhoods grant. I moved past Somerset Manor, the imposing subsidized apartment building where Khyren and his family had lived.

Within sight of Ridgeway, I first noticed a local television reporter doing a stand-up near the apartment building. I turned the corner and caught sight of the memorial atop a low stone wall. Two officers in a Cincinnati Police cruiser, lights flashing in the noon-day sun, sat watching the scene.

I stood in front of the teddy bears and candles for a few minutes. A Cincinnati *Enquirer* reporter drove up. So did a reporter and videographer from another Cincinnati TV station.

I moved out of the way. Some neighbors walked over and discussed what they needed to add to the memorial. The shooting happened at a sharp bend in the road. I looked farther down Ridgeway, considered one of the most dangerous streets in Cincinnati, away from the gathering at the scene. A second police car drove up. I dislike crowds and media events. Martaisha's little shrine had become an attraction, one that media — and I am counting myself — treat as newsworthy, despite their frequency. They are the act of frustrated, angry, grieving people, most of them confined to lives of desperation and poverty in America's inner cities, who don't know what else to do to express that anger and frustration. It's the same with the rallies that, understandably, follow. Small children and adults alike sing a hymn and hold candles and handwritten cardboard signs at the scene of a shooting, imploring a peace that won't come.

## Denying "full citizenship"

Counting each of my steps from Martaisha's memorial, I walked down Ridgeway. On the night Khyren had been shot in 2012, I attended a meeting of the Community Police Partnering Center at Hirsch Community Center in Avondale. I had prewritten my story. Community leaders, including my now-colleague here at the Urban League, Dorothy Smoot, announced a new anti-violence initiative focused solely on Ridgeway Avenue. Called Moral Voice, the program had a relatively simple thesis: We know who's causing the trouble. It's a small group. We are sending people you know, intermediaries — a former teacher, coach, minister — to tell you the police know who you are. We are going to offer you help in terms of social services, child support adjustment, a reinstated driver's license, if you try to turn your life around. Otherwise, we'll be coming after you.

Back to Friday, the last day of July 2015. Notebook in hand, I walked. The night before, when I could not sleep, I reread part of what I consider one of the seminal books on race in the United States: *Two Nations: Black and White, Separate, Hostile, Unequal.* I'd scribbled some passages from the book, written by Andrew Hacker, professor emeritus in the Department of Political Science at Queens College, New York. Questions of race and race relations occupy my mind, by choice. They are the lenses through which I view the world around me.

At 100 steps, I stopped in front of a vacant lot, at which, in the center, stood an excavator. Near the street, in a row, several oversized concrete sewer pipes rested on their ends. "Dellway Sewer Replacement, 2/2/16 completion date," read the sign nailed to a tree.

I wrote down those details on a sheet near this line from Hacker's book: "From slavery through the present, the nation has never opened its doors sufficiently to give black Americans a chance to become full citizens."

Hacker believes, as I do, that white privilege is real. My life experiences have proven it so. I believe I benefit from it in ways that I — even as one who sees and knows it — don't realize. I do know I can be 10 minutes late for an appointment without being judged. I can grow my hair long and dress down as a professional. I can use slang and forego the King's English without someone questioning my intelligence. I can drive without being pulled over for no other reason than the color of my skin. I can be presumed innocent until proven guilty.

My sins are not the collective sins of all white people, as is often the perception of African-Americans. As a white man, I can work in a predominantly black neighborhood for a civil rights organization, but I can leave and blend in as another privileged white face in a privileged white crowd.

## Flags, garbage, hamburgers

I walked on. I had a destination. The only question was how many steps it would take me to get there.

At 175 steps, I stopped in front of a two-story house. An upstairs window was open to a screen. The window beside it held a fan. Stuck into the neatly mowed-and-trimmed yard were six sticks on which were stapled small U.S. flags.

At 195 steps, I saw — dumped in a small wooded area — a pile of garbage: A wood-framed rocking chair and 64-ounce white bottle that once contained Havoline motor oil.

At 380 steps, I paused across the street from a three-story apartment building. Music blared from an open window. I tried to recognize the rap but couldn't. A woman, talking on a phone, stood in the dirt yard. A man looked across the street at me — dressed in sport coat, open shirt, and jeans — and ducked back inside. Litter, several cardboard cigar boxes and clear plastic wrappers, choked the storm drain near my feet.

I walked on, and at 450 steps reached the corner of Ridgeway and Perkins avenues. A group of people, all African-American, sat in the shade of a porch. I waved. They waved back. I looked around. I was the only white person in sight. I jotted down more notes. I turned back to the page with excerpts from Hacker's race book.

"Few whites feel obligated to ponder how membership in the majority race gives them powers and privileges." Being white is the greatest benefit any American can have; "no matter how degraded their lives, they can never become black."

I thought of conversations I'd had with colleagues at the Urban League, where three of the 52 full-time employees are white. Some of my African-American co-workers said they've been depressed since the church shooting that left nine people dead in Charleston, South Carolina. That pall, one person said, had started to lift and then – literally, bang – Samuel DuBose is shot in the head for the "crime" of driving while black.

On the Avondale street corner, someone called my name. Startled, I looked across Perkins and saw three black men in Cincinnati Works T-shirts. One was a former *Enquirer* source, Mitch Morris, who had started a job-readiness course for returning citizens at the nonprofit, shortly after he'd been laid off from his job as a street outreach worker for the Cincinnati Human Relations Commission. Morris and his colleagues were blanketing the area with pamphlets promoting his program. Another television reporter and camera operator met him at the corner for an interview.

I walked on. At 595 steps, I had descended a small hill and reached the corner of Perkins and Blair. To my left, back up Blair, I could see the looming Somerset building and former St. Andrew Catholic Church, closed by the Cincinnati Archdiocese in 2010. I smelled hamburgers on a charcoal grill.

Nearing my destination, I started to walk across Blair but stopped when yet another police car — its blue and red lights twirling — drove slowly past.

Hacker touches on the phenomenon of urban violence in *Two Nations.* He calls it "self-inflicted genocide" but does not completely absolve white America of responsibility. Young black men suffer, he writes, "a despair that suffuses much of their race. These are young men who don't know whether they will live another year, and many have given up caring."

People kill within their race. Nationally, from 1974 through 2004, white assailants committed 86 percent of white murders, and 94 percent of black victims were killed by another black, according to the U.S. Department of Justice.

Individuals and families within the black community have personal responsibility for their choices and conduct. So, too, does the larger society have the responsibility to invest economically and socially in intentionally deprived communities.

## Blood stains sidewalk

I crossed Blair and turned right, toward the park and away from Reading Road. At 650 steps, I reached my destination: the place where Khyren was shot in the hip on the warm evening of March 20, 2012. His blood had stained the sidewalk in front of 842 Blair for a couple of months.

I had stayed in contact with Khyren's mother over the years. I had called her before taking off on my walk. She said a female police officer had helped her relocate to another neighborhood. Aiesha Landrum, now 33, said she and her children missed friends in Avondale but were now living in a more peaceful part of the city. I arranged to meet her that afternoon at 3 at a public library branch. She'd done temporary work for a warehouse distributor and was going to the library to fill out online applications.

Back on that warm March evening in 2012, at the spot where I now stood, a bullet tore through Khyren's hip and out his buttocks. I'd driven by Blair on Reading toward downtown and the *Enquirer* newsroom just before the shooting. The paper's night reporter met me at my desk and said a 4-year-old had been shot in Avondale. Did I know anything? I had gone back to insert a couple of paragraphs into my story. I added the details about the boy's shooting and sped back to Avondale.

Later, police said, two cars, one in pursuit of the other, had turned off Reading Road onto Blair. Where Perkins dead-ends into Blair, the driver of the chase car sped past the lead car and slammed on his brakes. The passenger from the first car got out and shot at the second. One bullet struck Khyren's left hip. He got up, tried to walk a couple of steps, stumbled and fell.

He would spend about a week in Cincinnati Children's and then have to undergo physical therapy to learn how to walk again. Aiesha Landrum pushed her son across the neighborhood in a wheelchair.

Two days after Khyren's shooting, Avondale and black community leaders gathered for a rally near the scene.

Khyren was big news for a while. Then he wasn't. The story of 4-year-old Martaisha will follow the same path before disappearing from the collective media and social consciousness.

Yet what has changed? Social service agencies blanketed Avondale after Khyren was shot and then went away. The same will happen this time. Police increased patrols then but went away. Politicians made forceful speeches filled with promises and then forgot them. What will change?

## "I will pray for her"

Someone new to Cincinnati asked me recently which city neighborhood is my favorite.

Without hesitation, "Avondale," I said. "I used to like Over-the-Rhine a lot. Not so much anymore."

I know too many good, hard-working, honest people in Avondale to think otherwise. They are without pretense and manipulation. Where some people see dysfunction in Avondale, I see order. Where some people see hopelessness, I see resilience; there are no people more resilient than Khyren, his mother, and sisters.

I drove to meet Aiesha and Khyren at the branch library. He had headphones on and was playing tic-tac-toe on a computer. He'd grown taller but was still thin. He'd lost his two front teeth. He gave me a fist bump. "Hi, Mr. Mark."

"He is doing better," Aiesha said. "He just started playing football."

They had TV news on Thursday night at home. "Khyren never watches but was watching for some reason," his mother said.

They heard about the 4-year-old girl who had been shot in Avondale.

"Like me?" Khyren said to his mother. "Is she dead?"

"No, she is still alive."

"I will pray for her."

Aiesha said she had babysat the girl's mother, who was now 28. "It crushed my heart," Aiesha said. "It brought back so many memories. I know how the mother is feeling, and Khyren was not as bad."

I drove back to Avondale to continue working on the $40,000 grant application. Grant writing and asking for money, I have learned, is a way of life at a nonprofit.

The Urban League provides most of its services for free, especially those for the most disadvantaged and marginalized — the chronically unemployed, returning citizens, at-risk youths at Woodward Career Technical High School. Graduates of the League's Solid Opportunities for Advancement and Retention (SOAR) program earn an average of almost $22,000 in their first year on the job. Graduates of its Accelerated Customer Service Education (ACE) program earned a starting hourly wage of $11.02. At Woodward, 146 of 175 tutored students earned grade promotion.

No matter how strong the economy, unemployment among black Americans is twice that of white America, and it's not because African-Americans don't want to work. Median black household income in Greater Cincinnati is $24,000, compared to $57,500 for whites. Hard to make a living when African-Americans make up 12.5 percent of the state's population yet account for 45 percent of the state's inmates.

Hacker notes: "Most white Americans believe that for the last [two generations] blacks have been given more than a fair chance and at least equal opportunity, if not outright advantages. [So few whites] feel obligated to ponder how membership in the majority race gives them power and privileges."

I finished work around 8 Friday night with my colleague B. Cato Mayberry, Urban League Vice President of Development. I drove home and picked at a small dinner before falling asleep on the couch with the Reds game on television. It was Avondale night at Great American Ball Park. Aiesha, Khyren and the two girls had gone. Aiesha sent me a text of Khyren wearing his new Reds T-shirt – his first.

Fridays are fireworks night at the ballpark. Khyren, who at 4 was shot in a hail of gunfire, has had an understandable problem with sudden loud noises and sirens. They frighten him badly.

Another friend from Avondale sent me a text that I would see overnight.

"Sitting here watching Khyren hold his ears as he TRIES to enjoy this fireworks show is tearing me apart."

---

# Devastated in '68, Avondale fought back, decade by decade, year by year

*April 8, 2018*

Fifty years ago this week, after the April 4 assassination of the Rev. Martin Luther King Jr., parts of Cincinnati seethed with anger, teetering on the brink of violence for four days.

Some cities – Detroit, New York, Washington – convulsed immediately but it was not until April 8, the Monday after Palm Sunday, that local events would lead to a full-scale eruption.

About 1,500 people were attending an outdoor memorial service in King's honor in the Avondale neighborhood. A speaker with the civil rights group the Congress of Racial Equality blamed white America for King's death and urged African-Americans to retaliate.

As the crowd filed into the streets after the memorial, a rumor spread that a white police officer had shot the wife of an African-American jewelry store owner in the neighborhood.

The rumor wasn't true. Jewelry store owner James Smith had struggled with robbers, who were also black, when his gun misfired, striking and killing his wife.

It didn't matter. Some African-Americans in Avondale and other parts of the city loosed their rage. In Mount Auburn, a group of eight black men pulled Noel Wright, a white student, from his car and stabbed him to death. They beat Wright's wife.

Seventy fires, many of them major, lit the night sky in the Avondale business corridors of Reading Road and Burnet Avenue.

By the night of April 9, some 1,500 National Guard troops had been brought in and a curfew imposed. Before order was restored, two people had died and the city had sustained $3 million in property damage, the equivalent of almost $22 million today.

Coming on the heels of rioting the previous June – in which 63 people had been arrested and $2 million in damages incurred – the vibrant, self-contained Avondale, previously filled with stores and restaurants, was in disarray, edging close to what many supposed was whole-sale abandonment.

Many white and black families with the financial means fled, following the Jewish migration of a generation earlier, north to Roselawn and new and established suburbs.

The Avondale they all left behind, it seemed, was a plywood-encased shell of its former self.

Today, Avondale is in the midst of what its boosters call a renaissance. Several hundred units of housing have been built or rehabbed in the past few years. The outdated Avondale Town Center is being rebuilt, and a medical clinic is rising to its immediate north on Reading Road. The academic scores of students at the neighborhood's two elementary schools – Rockdale Academy and South Avondale – are improving. So is child health.

It wasn't magic.

# Chapter 1: 1968–77

Aside from the racial unrest, the public looting and the self-immolation, the initial problem was that many people who could afford to leave Avondale started to move out.

Dr. Luther Lemon stayed. He kept his family home on Rockdale Avenue and his medical practice three blocks away on Hearne Avenue. He'd already been displaced once, almost two decades earlier, from the West End by the construction of Interstate 75. He wasn't moving again.

He understood that all of the professionals couldn't leave. If they did, he knew the neighborhood would absolutely fall apart.

"We never thought of leaving," said his daughter, Jan-Michele Lemon Kearney, publisher and editor of the African-American weekly newspaper the *Cincinnati Herald*.

Avondale lost almost 14 percent of its population from 1970 to 1980. The white population fell 24.4 percent. The black population decreased 12.5 percent. By 1980, a neighborhood that in 1950 had been home to more than 30,000 people — 60 percent white — was down to fewer than 20,000, 92 percent of them African-American.

Lemon knew the numbers as well as anyone. Yet Avondale was where he and his family belonged.

"It was wonderful growing up in Avondale," said Lemon Kearney. She and her older sister, Norma, rode their bicycles down Rockdale to Burnet, where they'd get hamburgers. The girls walked with their father down the street to the Cincinnati Zoo & Botanical Garden.

Lemon practiced family medicine. He made house calls. He delivered babies and cared for the elderly. He built a swing set in the backyard of his office. He paid for YMCA summer memberships for neighborhood children so they could take swim lessons.

He sent his children to the public school across the street from the house. If Rockdale Academy was good enough for neighborhood children, it was good enough for his daughters.

Lemon backed up his belief in his neighbors with his wallet. He made the first donation to the medical clinic run by Cincinnati Children's Hospital staff at Rockdale. (A plaque in the lobby today memorializes his sizable contribution.)

He kept fighting for the children and families of Avondale after his retirement from medicine in 1993. He joined the Avondale Community Council. At 80, though he was a major zoo patron, he joined a picket line to protest the zoo's effort to turn a neighborhood park on Dury Avenue into a parking lot.

Lemon stayed in Avondale until his death at 88 in 2003.

## Chapter 2: 1978–87

The next immediate problem was that no one from the outside wanted to move to or invest in Avondale. For several years after the riots, Reading Road and Burnet Avenue were still lined with abandoned and burnt building shells. While the community had some solidly middle-class and professional streets – Forest Park Drive, for example – safe and sanitary housing was in short supply.

In 1978, the Avondale Redevelopment Corp. was founded, growing out of the neighborhood's community council. Jim King, former council president, was hired as executive director.

King had lived with his mother in Avondale from 1963 to 1966. Then he went into the Air Force. He served at Okinawa until 1970. He didn't recognize the Avondale he came home to.

"It was devastating to see nothing that was here before," said King, now 72. "The Kroger on Forest Avenue, everything was gone."

Between 1970 and 1990, 800 buildings in Avondale had become vacant. The council organized a petition drive. More than 300 Avondale residents signed it, asking the city to demolish dozens of abandoned buildings.

King and his board went to work. Their formula was to use public money to leverage private investment.

In 1981, the redevelopment corporation finished its first building at the corner of Reading and Windham and moved its headquarters there. With its distinctive cornice, the building was one of the few in the immediate area to survive the riots and their aftermath.

In 1983, the 40,000-square-foot, 11-store Avondale Town Center opened at the corner of Reading and Rockdale. Despite its spotty history, marked by tenant turnover and the comings and goings of grocery anchors, the new construction symbolized the return of commercial activity.

And, in 1987, work began on the 28-unit Reading Green Condominiums complex between Prospect Place and Maple Avenue. The tax-abated 1,900-square-foot units sold for $85,000. The selling plan targeted households earning between $18,000 and $35,000. Down payment assistance was available.

They sold out in seven months.

"That first decade we were in business, we were able to stabilize the neighborhood," King said. "Our plan was to build housing on all that vacant land. We were naive. We thought we could get it all done in five years."

Reading Green was a major victory. Yet losses came with the wins. A proposed Reading Green II complex to the north of Prospect – today a parking lot for the Greater Cincinnati Urban League – was never built.

## Chapter 3: 1988–97

The problem now was that progress was slow and people needed caring for.

The Rev. Clarence Wallace was 29 when he came to Cincinnati in 1978 to become pastor of Carmel Presbyterian Church in the center of Avondale. He came from South Carolina, where he worked as an addiction counselor. That sensitivity would show up soon in his Carmel ministry with a long-standing and robust Alcoholics Anonymous meeting.

There was a need for an AA group, Wallace said, and it was the church's responsibility to provide it.

In 1983, the same year the Town Center opened on the other side of the Carmel parking lot, the church's 200 members voted to stay and remodel the sanctuary instead of leaving for suburban Forest Park.

Wallace created a summer program in which Avondale youths interacted on service and leadership projects with teens from Indian Hill Episcopal-Presbyterian Church.

Wallace created a soup kitchen, pantry and men's clothing ministry in the church.

"He was never one to tell you what to do," Carmel member JoEllen Grady said. "He'd ask you, 'We have this problem. What do you think we should do?'"

The community's need for food assistance grew into Sunday morning breakfasts and a fellowship lunch after the 11 o'clock service. Carmel sponsored summer academic enrichment programs for youths.

"You stay involved," Wallace told the *Enquirer* about his philosophy of social action.

Another need Wallace saw was to boost the sagging Avondale Town Center. It had fallen into disrepair and was without an owner after the original developer, the Oscar Robertson Co., which held the lease and mortgage, dissolved in 1987.

In November 1996, Wallace was one of four neighborhood ministers in the Avondale Coalition of Churches who bought the center. Wallace, who did not seek the spotlight, nevertheless agreed to take on the coalition presidency. (Its first president, Southern Baptist Church pastor the Rev. James Milton, had died the day before the coalition closed on the Town Center loan.)

The coalition was able to land a grocery store, Aldi, to fill the vacant anchor tenant space.

# Chapter 4: 1998–2007

The problems in Avondale were always bigger than buildings. Many children were not thriving, and too many were dying before their first birthday. Yet, at the turn of the century, an old problem screamed back into the forefront: violent crime.

A landlord was gunned down while renovating his property. Armed robbers pistol-whipped their victims. Another victim had his gold-capped teeth snatched from his mouth. Elderly residents were afraid to step outside of their apartment, even into hallways, where, they feared, criminals waited.

And all the while, babies were dying in Avondale and other urban neighborhoods at a Third World rate. The number of babies who died there before their first birthday in Avondale was 21 per 1,000 live births, roughly the same as the rate found in Guatemala and Mongolia.

Indeed, across the country, as the new century dawned, African-American babies were twice as likely as white infants to be premature, to have a low birth weight, and to die at birth.

In 2006, Dominique Love lost her first child. The daughter she named Domika Heavenly was stillborn. She had hydrocephalus, an excessive accumulation of cerebrospinal fluid in the brain. The baby, delivered at 25 weeks, also had a buildup of fluid in the chest.

Enough was enough. Wallace and his Carmel Presbyterian Church formed a partnership with Cincinnati Children's Hospital to house a program for at-risk first-time mothers, Every Child Succeeds. The program had existed across the region but had no physical home. It did now, opening in November 2006 in Carmel's basement.

Yet housing this program wasn't enough. Wallace saw the need these low-income mothers had for basic baby supplies. So in 2007 Carmel established the Avondale Caring Network Pantry, which provided free formula and diapers.

In other neighborhoods, Every Child Succeeds' home visitation program reached 25 percent of eligible mothers. In Avondale, within the first two years, 85 percent of eligible mothers were receiving services and home visitation.

Love found her way there in 2011 when she became pregnant again. She received home visits. She attended classes at Carmel on child development, parenting, and nutrition. She was part of a moms' group. (Carmel also was the site of a dads' group.)

Love delivered a healthy baby boy, Kelijah, in May 2012. He was one week overdue and was born at 7 pounds, 6 ounces.

"I met all the right people and developed a huge support system and network," she said. "I learned so much and was more confident."

During that decade, because of Every Child Succeeds and other prenatal and home visitation programs in Avondale, the infant mortality rate there dropped to 8 deaths for every 1,000 live births. Other indicators of infant health, including full-term births at 37 weeks, also have increased dramatically.

# Chapter 5: 2008–17

The problem was the lure of the streets. Growing up in Avondale was tough for many teenagers. Too much poverty. Too many shootings and drug deals. Too much idle time. Too little supervision and structure.

In 2006, the Avondale Youth Council was created to provide neighborhood children structure and incentive and keep them busy. Founded by two Avondale men – one was a military veteran, another was an Indiana University law graduate – the council bloomed by 2008. It was a place where kids belonged, where grown men meted out love and discipline, where mothers believed that change could happen. And because, at first at least, the kids were paid to show up.

Twice-monthly meetings were the foundation for field trips, personal development classes, and mandatory community service. Members, between the ages of 12 and 18, had to wear a uniform of a golf shirt or youth council hoody and a baseball cap.

If members maintained a C average in school, they were paid $5 an hour for community service work, $2 of which went into an account they would receive at graduation. Some members received as much as $1,000 a year toward college. The council's $30,000 annual budget came from a variety of sources, public and private, including Chase Bank, the Model Group, and the Uptown Consortium.

About a half dozen of those first youth council members have come back home to live. Daniel Watkins, 25, a Northern Kentucky University graduate in organizational leadership and sports management, inherited a house from a family member on Harvey Avenue. "When you're out there picking up trash and working to make things better, you develop a lot of pride in where you're from," he said.

Rasalyn Williams, 26, is planning to come back to Avondale. She lives downtown. She has worked for six years as a health unit coordinator in the Emergency Department at University of Cincinnati Medical Center.

Turns out Luther Lemon and other professional families had the right idea 50 years ago in those shaky years after the 1968 riots. If he stayed in Avondale, it would be worth coming back to.

## Epilogue

The problem is that for decades the perception was that nothing good could come out of Avondale.

Now one of the best ideas Avondale ever had – its youth council – is being exported to a handful of Cincinnati's other predominantly African-American neighborhoods. The woman doing a lot of that work is an Avondale Youth Council alumna.

Jasmine Humphries explains that "the last thing I was going to do was come back." Humphries, a 2008 Withrow High School graduate and original youth council member in 2006, is now a community engagement specialist at the partnering center, which is part of the Greater Cincinnati Urban League.

Humphries, who has an economics degree from the University of Cincinnati and studied in China, is helping to replicate the Avondale Youth Council model in the West End, Walnut Hills, Winton Hills, and Bond Hill.

According to some, this is the time for Avondale's rebirth. Town Center's progress is proof of that. The best and brightest young people are coming home.

Pieces are in place. People, too.

Dr. Lemon's house, for the record, is still there.

# BLACK HISTORY MONTH

*For years we were expected to commemorate Black History Month, even as increasing numbers of our African-Americans readers told us they didn't like the idea of their history being confined to the shortest month. Black history, they'd say, is American history. I agree. Yet, during February, I worked to take advantage of the opportunity to do stories that I'd have a harder time getting into the paper during, say, July. Only one of the stories in this chapter published outside of February.*

# Beacon for better education

Jennie Davis Porter stirred thousands of students to "lift as we climb"
*February 7, 1997*

In 1928, when she became the first black woman to earn a Ph.D. from the University of Cincinnati – and only the fourth black woman Ph.D. nationally – the late Jennie Davis Porter wrote that segregated black schools were better for students than integrated ones.

She cited psychological and achievement tests of students at the three all-black Cincinnati schools she ran – Stowe, Jackson, and Sherman – and often held up future Cincinnati mayor Theodore Berry as the shining manifestation of her philosophy.

Segregated black schools provided a positive environment for development of students' self-esteem, Dr. Porter wrote, and were a source of good jobs for black teachers.

The issue divided blacks. Supporters said quality and equal education for black children was more important than racial integration. Others said any form of segregation invited racial discrimination.

Today, almost 70 years after she wrote her dissertation and 60 years after her death, Dr. Porter's argument for segregated schools has returned to the center of a growing debate among educators. In fact, her dissertation – "The Problem of Negro Education in Northern and Border Cities" – is still requested at least a half-dozen times a year from UC archives by black educators nationally who advocate a return to segregated, neighborhood schools.

Dr. Porter influenced two generations of black educators and was responsible for the education of thousands of Cincinnati's black children. Without her iron will to provide all children a quality education, hundreds of young African-Americans would not have attended school.

Mr. Berry, chosen by city council as Cincinnati's first black mayor in 1973, believes Dr. Porter's philosophy was rooted in her concern for the children of black families migrating from the South a century ago. "Instead of nine months of schooling, they only received six months because of their work in the cotton fields," says Mr. Berry, now 91 and living in Hartwell. "She sold the school board on a special school that would help bridge that gap."

## Must help others

Dr. Porter's father, William, was a former slave who became Cincinnati's first black undertaker. She was born in Cincinnati on Oct. 9, 1876, to Ethlinda Porter, a teacher.

Her family's wealth didn't blind her to the plight of less fortunate blacks. She developed one of her favorite slogans – "We must lift as we climb" – at an early age. After earning her bachelor's degree in education at UC, with specialties in art and music, Dr. Porter taught from 1897 to 1914 at Douglass School, Walnut Hills. One of her first-grade students was William DeHart Hubbard, who, competing in the long jump at the 1924 Paris Olympics, became the first black athlete to win a gold medal in an individual event.

Dr. Porter's teaching philosophy was patterned after Booker T. Washington's self-help edict. (Mr. Washington, of the Tuskegee, Alabama, Industrial School, later came to Cincinnati several times to confer with Dr. Porter. She was also a trusted confidant of Hull House founder Jane Addams, who sought Dr. Porter's advice on social problems affecting blacks.)

In 1911, Dr. Porter established a private kindergarten for West End blacks. By the end of the first year, enrollment had jumped from 72 to 125. White philanthropist Annie Laws funded the school.

In 1913, when Dr. Porter and other influential blacks discovered that 147 black children ages 9 to 14 were not attending school, she organized a summer school at the old Hughes High School, West End. Again, Ms. Laws provided funding.

In 1914, Dr. Porter persuaded Cincinnati Public Schools Superintendent John Withrow to establish Cincinnati's first all-black school at the former Hughes site and rename the building Harriet Beecher Stowe School. Ms. Stowe, author of *Uncle Tom's Cabin*, had taught in a girl's school near Hughes in the 1830s. Dr. Porter was named Stowe's principal, a first for a black woman in Cincinnati.

Enrollment increased from 350 to 650 in the first year, and she successfully lobbied the board of education to erect a new building. But World War I delayed construction.

Mr. Berry was a member of Stowe's Class of 1920. "Miss Porter sponsored a series of public events to promote the school," he says. "I made my first public speech on the occasion of one of her festivals."

Mary E. Rozier, 79, of Hyde Park, attended Stowe from kindergarten through ninth grade and was a member of its Class of 1933. "She had a gruff voice," Ms. Rozier, who worked for many years as a legal secretary, says of Dr. Porter. "When she'd speak, we'd jump out of our skin. She insisted that kids be neat, and if the family didn't have the means, she spent her own money on you" for school clothes and other supplies. Dr. Porter also insisted that black children learn about black history.

"The teachers made sure we had pride in our racial background," Ms. Rozier says. "The standards were very high. We had to be very quiet in the hallways, especially when we were on the same floor as Dr. Porter's office."

## Community leader

Dr. Porter's influence among black Cincinnatians had grown several-fold by the early 1920s.

The school board put her in charge of the "Colored Farm," a site in College Hill where black students received agricultural training. She also oversaw 15 black clubs, a cultural center and a social service bureau.

"Power begets power," Mr. Berry says. "Miss Porter knew this."

On Thanksgiving Day 1923, the new Stowe School was dedicated at 635 W. Seventh St., in what is now the Queensgate building that houses, among other businesses, the offices of WXIX-TV Channel 19.

The school's 2,000-student enrollment quickly grew to 3,080. Stowe was Cincinnati's largest school. The building included two open-air classrooms, vocational and home-economics facilities, a swimming pool, gymnasium, doctor's office, prenatal clinic, and an auditorium that featured a pipe organ. The school had a national reputation for excellence and drew notable visitors such as Marian Anderson and George Washington Carver.

Even one of her critics, Wendell Dabney, publisher and editor of Cincinnati's black *Union* newspaper who opposed her segregationist viewpoint, admired her and the school. "She has found time to take deep interest in the betterment of thousands of school children who have been under her jurisdiction," Mr. Dabney wrote in 1926. "Stowe School is the only school in the city organized on a psychological basis to prove statistically that the Negro is not mentally inferior." Dr. Porter's 1925 master's thesis at UC was written on the reorganization of Stowe School.

Jackson School, built in 1883 at Fifth and Mound streets, the West End, was closed during the 1950s and demolished to make way for Interstate 75 construction. Sherman, at Eighth and John, was built in 1879. Centennial Plaza now sits on that site.

## A gentle side

In spite of Stowe's extra features, Dr. Porter believed in basic education that stressed reading, writing and math. Porter Middle School, built in 1953 in the West End, is named in her honor. Her portrait hangs in the lobby. The school's creed was her motto: "Take what you have and make what you want."

"She was determined to find students who had been left behind and get them on the road to success," says Vera Edwards, 81, of Avondale, a UC professor emerita.

Ms. Edwards, who came to UC from her native Texas to earn her master's degree in educational psychology in 1931, considers Dr. Porter a role model for black women who went into the field at that time. "She had great influence and was well-known," Ms. Edwards says. "She was a taskmaster but had a gentle side."

That gentle side was expressed often in her art. Two of her paintings have been displayed in exhibits at the Cincinnati Museum Center.

She was a member of Union Baptist Church and died at her Walnut Hills home on July 3, 1936. She was still principal of Stowe School, which would close in 1962 and be turned into a vocational school. Dr. Porter never married. She was inducted in the Ohio Women's Hall of Fame in 1989. Upon her death, she left her $50,000 estate to create a trust fund for the education of black youths.

Two of her brothers, abolitionists, challenged the document in court. Mr. Berry, who received his law degree from UC in 1931, defended his former principal's will and won the case.

# Eye on life lessons

Ophthalmologist has spent 40 years prescribing medical and personal advice

*February 10, 1998*

''Howard, this is Dr. Pryor,'' Howard Melvin Sr. said to his son.

Howard Jr., a 10-year-old fourth-grader, reached out and limply shook the eye doctor's hand while he stared at the floor.

Before Dr. Chester Pryor would examine Howard Jr.'s eyes, he examined the boy's behavior.

''Young man,'' Dr. Pryor said, ''that is not the way you shake a man's hand. You shake his hand firmly and look him in the eye.''

''And then he made me practice shaking hands,'' Dr. Howard ''Daryl'' Melvin said today, 37 years later.

In almost four decades of ophthalmology practice, Chester Pryor has dispensed eye care and life lessons in equal doses. He's as likely to diagnose a character flaw as he does glaucoma or macular degeneration.

Dr. Pryor's philosophy is based on his family upbringing and the teaching of segregated black schools: "Don't worry what the other guy is doing, even if he's trying to keep you down. Worry about what you can do to excel."

So when he encourages black youths growing up in the 1990s not to use racism as a crutch, he's not telling them anything he didn't practice beginning in the 1930s.

''Disease and illness are very ubiquitous terms,'' said Dr. Pryor, 68, of North Avondale. ''If people can't take care of themselves, they're going to be more susceptible to the things (poverty, substance abuse) that will make them sick.''

Or as Dr. Melvin, now 47 and an ophthalmologist, said of Dr. Pryor: ''He talks the talk because he walks the walk. Whether he's telling you to straighten your tie, lose a few pounds, curb your lavish spending, stop cutting church or do better in school, he has lived his life exactly to those high standards.''

Adhering to strict self-discipline is how Dr. Pryor managed to succeed as a black man in a largely unwelcoming white world.

"Black teachers were very insistent that [black] students be excellent with the knowledge they would be competing with people who had the advantage of being white," said Donald Spencer, 83, who taught young Chester social studies at Walnut Hills' segregated Douglass Jr. High. "We told them, 'We don't want you to come back here complaining about racial problems.'"

Staying true to those words is how Dr. Pryor overcame prejudice to compile a long list of "black firsts." He was the first black ophthalmologist in Cincinnati (1962) after becoming the first African-American to intern at a private Cincinnati hospital, Jewish, in 1954 and 1955.

He was also the first black ophthalmologist certified in Ohio (1960), the first black treasurer of the Academy of Medicine in Cincinnati (1969), and the first black president of the Cincinnati Eye Society (1976).

Many white doctors at Jewish, unhappy that a black doctor was interning there, ignored him in protest, Dr. Pryor says. He was rejected by many white patients who didn't want a black doctor to examine them. His first attempt to join the Cincinnati Ophthalmology Society was refused before a compromise allowed him to attend lectures and conferences but not the dinners that always followed.

Finally, a ranking white doctor in the society worked without Dr. Pryor's knowledge to gain him full membership.

## Strength from faith

While enduring these and other racial slights, Dr. Pryor never lost his composure, said his wife of 44 years, the former Audrey Jean Keels of Bidwell, Ohio. "I never knew many of these stories," said Mrs. Pryor, who is her husband's office manager. "He never came home and got upset in private. He was very consistent."

Back then, as they still do, his days started with prayer and Bible reading. "He'd always get up 15 minutes, a half-hour early to have quiet time," Mrs. Pryor said. "His faith is his strength. I'm the sleepy head who goes to bed early. He never sleeps more than five or six hours a night."

But he isn't slowing down. Dr. Pryor still sees as many as 75 patients a week in his clinic. He's in surgery Friday morning. Part of Tuesday is spent working with University Hospital residents in the eye clinic.

Dr. Pryor is guided by the words of one of his mentors. In the 1940s, the late Dr. Raymond E. Clarke was the first black doctor to perform surgery in a white hospital in Cincinnati. His portrait hangs in the lobby of Dr. Pryor's Highland Eye Medical Center in Mount Auburn.

"Dr. Clarke said to me, 'Even if they're wrong, always do right,'" Dr. Pryor said while looking at the portrait. "'First, always do your work. Always be respectful. Always be honest and never plot revenge.'"

Chester Pryor did seek revenge once, but only once, as one of only a handful of black students at Withrow High School in the mid-1940s.

It was against a white math teacher who didn't like black students. "He was a racist," Dr. Pryor said. "He made fun of my clothes in class. My mother made my sweaters, and he asked me, 'Did you get that at a pawn shop?' The last thing he wanted to do was give me a good grade. [But] I aimed for and achieved the highest grade in the class."

## Likely to succeed

Mr. Spencer, Dr. Pryor's middle school teacher, isn't surprised by his former student's success.

"He was always carrying all of his books," Mr. Spencer said. "He was strictly business. Even when the other kids were cutting up, he was about his lessons. He always won a prize for knowing the most black history at the end of Negro History Month."

Dr. Pryor's boyhood friends aren't surprised, either, by his personal and professional success.

"He was always the one pointing out wrong and right and the way to improve the situation," said lifelong friend Carl Tuggle, 73, of Paddock Hills and retired Aiken High School assistant principal. "The biggest force in his life was his mother. She instilled that in him."

Francis Pryor was born in Alabama and moved with her family to Cincinnati, where she met and later married Percy Pryor. Chester, born in Walnut Hills, was their only child.

Percy Pryor worked for more than 40 years at Provident Bank, where he was in charge of the supply room and retired as assistant secretary treasurer – the first black officer in the company. Francis Pryor attended Central State College (now University) in Wilberforce at the same time as her son.

She earned an education degree there and later taught business classes at Cincinnati's Bloom School (now Bloom Middle School in the West End). She was the district's first black business teacher but was not allowed to teach in high schools.  "My parents taught me honesty, respect, obedience, hard work, to stay within your means, to work in the church and in the school," Dr. Pryor said. "We were never party people."

The values have lasted a lifetime. Friends say Dr. Pryor's non-work activities are serious ones. He's involved in his boyhood church, Allen Temple AME Church in Bond Hill, and formerly held the highest Masonic office in the state.

As a member of the Mason's True American Lodge No. 2 in Avondale, Dr. Pryor is most concerned with raising money for college and vocational school scholarships.

## Concern for the young

Dr. Pryor has always had a heart for young people and continues to offer advice, even if many black youths today consider him outdated and meddlesome, said Dr. Melvin, his former patient and clinic mate.

"He's the reason I became an ophthalmologist," said Dr. Melvin, who rented office space from Dr. Pryor for four years before opening his own clinic around the corner from his mentor's. "I had to do a report on the eye when I was 13, and my parents suggested I see him. I remember him being very busy but taking an hour for me. He loaned me several books that were over my head, but I did my best and got an A. After that report, I knew what I would be."

Dr. Melvin has patterned his practice after Dr. Pryor's. "I take welfare referrals from hospitals, just like he does," he said. "I'd say half of his patients, black or white, don't pay him. But he doesn't turn them away. He always makes time for people. He cares about people."

He showed that concern for Dr. Melvin's two young sons on a recent Sunday morning at Allen Temple. Dr. Melvin introduced the boys to Dr. Pryor. But they shook his hand without

looking him in the eye. "I had to chuckle when Dr. Pryor sat them down to talk and make them practice shaking hands."

# A Legacy in Action

Soon-to-be retired L. V. Booth steered ministry into
banking and housing

*February 20, 1998*

In 1952, when the Rev. Lavaughn Venchael (L.V.) Booth came to town, Cincinnati's black churches pretty much kept to the business of saving souls. But the Rev. Booth's arrival ushered in an array of church-based economic development and social outreach programs that have forever changed the role of local black religious organizations.

He used the financial strength of his first Tristate congregation, Zion Baptist Church, to secure credit to build hundreds of low-income housing units and a church-run nursing home. He later established the region's first black-owned bank.

He often explained his actions by saying, "We should have concern for the physical as well as the spiritual well-being of people." The Rev. Booth is widely regarded as a visionary with the perseverance to get tough jobs done.

He latched on to the national black-empowerment trend coming out of Philadelphia's black churches and brought it to Cincinnati.

"He is truly a pioneer," says the Rev. Calvin Harper, 57, pastor of Morning Star Baptist Church, Walnut Hills, who worked with the Rev. Booth to open the Hamilton County State Bank in 1980. "Our problem was we didn't pick up soon enough on what Rev. Booth was doing. He was a man ahead of his time."

The Rev. Booth, now 79 and in his 15th year as pastor of Silverton's Olivet Baptist Church, will retire soon, May at the latest. He plans to move to Daleville, Ind., where his wife, the former Yvette Livers, 38, will be executive director of a Girl Scout council. The Rev. Booth's first wife, Georgia Booth, died from cancer in 1993.

"I've made my journey," he says. "I married [Yvette] to empower her. I am leaving to support her." They met at Olivet, which she attended upon the recommendation of her former pastor in Louisville.

"She was in a character-building organization, and I was amazed when she agreed to marry me," he says. The marriage "didn't sit well with my children or the people in the church, but she's good company. She's understanding." Yvette Livers Booth thinks her husband will keep busy in Indiana. "I know him," she says. "He will move on and find new challenges."

## A storied figure

Still regarded as a "storied figure in Baptist circles," the Rev. Booth in January came to the defense of the beleaguered Rev. Henry Lyons, president of the National Baptist Convention

U.S.A. (The Rev. Lyons is accused of misusing church funds but has promised to enact reforms within the 8.5 million-member organization.)

Speaking at its winter board meeting in Los Angeles, the Rev. Booth suggested the convention cover some of the Rev. Lyons's legal expenses, an idea that was not formally considered. The Rev. Booth's appeal was for unity: "You have a great convention. You have a great president. You don't have to kill a man to save a convention."

In 1961, it was the Rev. Booth and the Rev. Martin Luther King Jr. who founded the Progressive National Baptist Convention. It split from the National Baptist Convention and formed a denomination that would play a more active role in the civil rights movement by linking with groups such as the Southern Christian Leadership Conference and providing the Rev. King a national platform. The Rev. Booth was its president from 1971 to 1974.

Progressives today have 2.5 million members in 1,800 churches. The Rev. Booth's focus, however, was his local ministry, which he viewed as communitywide. His economic-development work won him many admirers, though he never sought the spotlight. "To God be the glory," is his standard response to acclaim.

One admirer was then-Ohio Gov. James Rhodes, who in 1968 appointed the Rev. Booth as the first African-American on the University of Cincinnati Board of Trustees (1968), where he served until 1989.

Another admirer is financier Carl Lindner, whose investments and donations helped the Rev. Booth establish the Hamilton County State Bank and Olivet Baptist Church and publish, in 1997, a book of poetry, *Through It All ... Keep on Praying* (Inspiring Word Publications).

"I sensed early on that he had great leadership ability, was smart and hard working," Mr. Lindner says in a written statement. "I was delighted to help him when he started the Hamilton County State Bank. His goal has always been to help others help themselves."

Rev. Donald Jordan Sr. is pastor of Allen Temple AME Church in Bond Hill and a successful Tristate businessman: the chief operating officer of Thompson, Hall, and Jordan Funeral Homes. "Rev. Booth believed racial progress was made by economic development," the Rev. Jordan says. "When you judge him by his works, he stands among the elite ministers."

## The Golden Rule

The Rev. Booth's work while Zion Baptist pastor stands as his most lasting and influential. Before he arrived, the church operated a handful of low-income housing units next to the church on West Ninth Street, but they didn't pass his "Golden Rule" test. "Church people should not be housing other people in housing they would not live in," he said at the time.

So he had the building leveled and replaced by a parking lot. In 1958, the church built two low-income housing developments in Westwood on Western Northern Boulevard: Shelton Gardens and Reid's Valley View Manor. He was the first African-American to borrow $1 million from the First National Bank (now Star Bank). He cultivated trusting relationships with First National bankers and officials at Western-Southern Life Insurance Co., whom he still refers to as "friends."

The construction of Interstate 75 forced Zion Baptist to move from the West End. The congregation purchased land and built a church and neighboring nursing home in Avondale

– another Cincinnati first. The 50-bed Zion Nursing Home (now Zion Care Center) sits on the corner of Glenwood and Washington avenues.

In 1995, the center was expanded, adding a rehabilitation building, chapel, boardroom and dining room. J. William Poole, a 40-year Zion Baptist member and chairman of its board of deacons, is vice president and CEO of Zion Care Center, Inc. It is Medicare- and Medicaid-approved. "Rev. Booth believed that other elderly facilities were not up to par," Mr. Poole says. "He had great vision and stamina to make this a reality."

Three more multi-unit apartment buildings were developed by the church under the Rev. Booth's direction, bringing to 339 the number of units under church control. Four of the five facilities are for elderly residents, and each is operated in conjunction with the U.S. Department of Housing and Urban Development (HUD). He also had a hand in the development of Avondale Town Center.

Zion Baptist was also the base from which he worked to establish the black-controlled bank. Mr. Lindner contributed almost $1 million to help the Rev. Booth found the Hamilton County State Bank in 1980. It closed in 1987, and its $14 million in assets were purchased by Provident Bank, of which Mr. Linder is the majority shareholder.

## Church turmoil

It was the Rev. Booth's activity outside the church that led to problems inside. "Some younger people in the church were concerned with its financial might and political power," he says. "There was much discontent in the church. Some people thought I was giving too much to community service and neglecting the church. Membership had dropped from 1,000 to 700."

Looking back, he admits he wasn't good at delegating responsibility and that some members didn't feel they could have a significant role in the church. The Rev. Booth resigned in 1984, and 88 Zion members followed him to his current church, Olivet Baptist. Mr. Lindner again provided financial assistance, and the Rev. Booth says he will leave the church with only a $129,000 mortgage balance and manageable monthly payments.

A high point in Olivet's history was allowing the fledgling Marva Collins Preparatory School to operate rent-free in the church basement for three years. It opened at Olivet in 1990 with 43 students and two teachers and moved to a Roselawn building in 1993. Named for Chicago educator Marva Collins, the local school educates children considered to be unteachable. Today, it has 201 students and 13 teachers.

When school organizers needed a home, "it was kind of automatic to go to Rev. Booth," says Cleaster V. Mims, Collins school CEO and board president, who taught English at Western Hills High School for 27 years. "Some of the ministers are very reactionary, but Rev. Booth was always proactive. If you wanted to get something started, you could go to him."

Letting the Collins School establish itself was consistent with the Rev. Booth's ministerial style, said Paul Booth, 43, the youngest of L.V. and Georgia Booth's five children. "He saw all of this as a way the church could serve the community," says Mr. Booth, a local property manager, board president of the Citizens' Committee on Youth and former Cincinnati Council member. His siblings include a Baptist minister, pediatrician, attorney and another professional property manager.

**Family is important to L.V. Booth.**

When he was honored by Zion Baptist in 1977 for 25 years of service, he said: "I think one of my greatest achievements is in bringing up our own children and getting them to make the most of their talents to serve the community. If we had not been able to do this, all other things would have been lacking."

Through the years, the Rev. Booth maintained a low profile and said little about himself. "He was not the marcher," his son says. "He worked behind the scenes to get things done."

The Rev. Booth will continue to work. He plans to write the histories of Zion Baptist families who were involved when the church was a stop on the Underground Railroad. He has no complaints as his service to Cincinnati comes to an end. "My ministry has been a giving ministry, but in giving I have received a great deal," he says. "There's a little bit of hurt and loneliness sometimes because I will not be with familiar people and things. But my adventurous spirit tells me there is more ahead. You don't know what is out there. I've worked by faith through the years and will continue to work by faith."

# The children came first

For more than 30 years, Margaret "Nanny" Andrews has kept an eye on the community's youngest

*February 26, 1998*

Before it was a tired political slogan, the African proverb "It takes a village to raise a child" was the code by which Margaret "Nanny" Andrews lived.

She never met a child she couldn't love, and her concern for children has grown into a child-care business that is one of the black community's most trusted institutions.

Mrs. Andrews, 85, known widely as Nanny, didn't plan to watch more than 1,000 Tristate kids over all the years. It was her desire to help out a young neighbor that gave rise to what today is Nanny's Multilevel Learning Center on Reading Road in Avondale.

The time was the mid-1960s. "The gal across the street got a good job at the courthouse, too good to pass up, except she didn't have anyone to watch her baby," Nanny says. "I knew I could help her out." She remembers her first kid's name – Steven.

Nanny sits in the parlor of her Avondale home, surrounded by dozens of family pictures and hundreds of dolls and stuffed animals that have become the traditional parting gift of appreciative parents and kindergarten-age children.

"I have a whole bag of teddy bears in the closet," she says. Arthritis and a 1991 heart attack forced her to "retire," though she daily finds herself in the company of children who find their way into her home.

It was that way from the beginning.

"I didn't have to go out and get a job," she says. "The jobs came to me."

A week after she took in her first child, she had a second. The following week she was caring for four preschoolers. Word of her devotion to children spread from mother to mother.

One of Nanny's first families was that of a classmate in adult night school at Stowe School in the West End. Nanny earned her GED in 1963, more than 30 years after she left high school in her native Johnstown, Pennsylvania, to marry and have a child.

The friend told her sister about Nanny. A single mother, Margo Lattimore took her daughter, Alicia, to Nanny when the girl was 3. She stayed for two years, and even after she entered school, Alicia wanted to visit Nanny on weekends.

"It was always more than a day-care center at Nanny's," says Ms. Lattimore, now 46, of Kennedy Heights and a retired Cincinnati Bell technician. "She treated kids like they were part of her family." Many mothers turned to Nanny for advice.

"You could talk to her about anything," Ms. Lattimore says. "She never made you feel rushed, and she always gave you a thoughtful answer. She never steered me wrong."

Ms. Lattimore never missed a payment, but some families did. Nanny put children's well-being ahead of her own, say the Tristate parents who have known her for three decades. Single parents pulling weekend military hitches and those parents with drug or alcohol problems left their children at Nanny's home for days – even weeks – at a time.

"I always said, 'Just pay me when you can,'" Nanny says.

## Then came trouble

By the mid-1970s, Nanny and a small staff were caring for 40 children in a child-care center she had established in her remodeled basement. She charged no late pick-up penalties. Some people did take advantage of her, she says, and Nanny's generosity and inability to turn anyone away got her into trouble.

In March 1982, after receiving complaints about the traffic congestion Nanny's business was causing her neighbors, the Cincinnati Health Department's Child Day Care Licensing Office investigated in conjunction with building and fire officials. They found Nanny's day care in violation because there was only one basement exit and too many children.

"It was not in the best interest to close her down and push 40 children into 'underground' day care," says Bonnie Cipollone, the health department official who investigated. "We worked with her." She helped Nanny find a new location in the basement of a Walnut Hills church and get a license for 56 children. But in a year, the health department took Nanny to court for violating her license. At one point, she was watching 95 children.

"Ms. Andrews always wanted to do the right thing," Ms. Cipollone says. "She wanted to comply with the regulations, but I wasn't there every day watching. She had to choose between what she saw as two 'right things.' Complying or watching children."

After her court appearance, in which Nanny was fined $50 and court costs, she found a larger facility in another church. Nanny's daughter, LaVerne Briggs, who had been teaching in the center, gradually took control of the business; she also completed child development courses at the University of Cincinnati. In 1988, Nanny's moved to its current location on Reading Road.

Today, Nanny's serves 50 children, with 13 on a waiting list. In a time of upheaval about child-care staff turnover, Nanny's five employees have been there an average of almost 10 years.

## A second mother

While locations changed, customer satisfaction has not. Evelyne Butts, 41, of Madisonville took her two sons to Nanny's. "To me, she was like a second mother," Joey Butts, 16, a sophomore at Hughes Center high school, says of Nanny. He and his brother, Everett, 13, were under Mrs. Andrews' care.

Mrs. Butts remembers how hard Nanny worked. Beyond the traditional nap, lunch, and arts-and-crafts fare, she took children on field trips to pumpkin patches, museums, and around the city to see the lights.

"She really brought with her the knowledge and wisdom of a lifetime and shared it with the children and families," says Mrs. Butts, a systems analyst with Jewish Hospital.

Nanny, known as June Bug to her father, grew up in an environment that cultivated a caring heart. The late Hobert B. Hawkins nurtured that natural empathy. At age 9, young Margaret noticed that the girl who lived across the street – Queenie, who was 7 – wore a threadbare winter coat.

"I said to her, 'Queenie, my dad will buy you a coat,'" Nanny says. "She said, 'My brother needs shoes.' I went to Daddy. He said, 'Now what is it June Bug?' I said, 'Queenie needs a coat.' He said, 'Not tonight. Tomorrow.' The next day, Queenie had her coat and her brother had his shoes."

Her heart stayed soft despite years of hard work and disappointment. In 1932, she owned and operated Margaret's Snack Shack and a rooming house in Johnstown. A lease misunderstanding forced her to close in a year. She thought she had signed for five years.

Later, during the Depression, she made a living from a private nightclub she opened in Florence, S.C. During World War II, she was called to Cincinnati to collect an inheritance that didn't materialize. She had planned to use the money to build a hotel in Florence.

She stayed in the area. She moved to Springfield, Ohio, and went to work for the railroad, in a farm tractor factory, as a theater ticket taker. She had been a seafood cook in the South.

## "A living saint"

She moved to Cincinnati in 1962 and was hired as an in-home nurse for a Clifton man. Four years later, when they parted ways, the man's wife gave Nanny a music box she had received as a wedding present. It hangs on a wall in Nanny's parlor.

She volunteered as a reading instructor and babysitter at Avondale's Burton Elementary, near her home. All the while, she let people – adults, families, children – stay with her in her home.

"She is a Christian soldier, a living saint," says Sharon Rogers, 42, of Bond Hill. Nanny watched her son, who's now 14.

"One little girl stands out," says Mrs. Rogers, who works in the University of Cincinnati's public relations department. The child, age 2, was being neglected. Nanny made arrangements with the family to keep the girl and tried to adopt her, which didn't work out. Nanny cared for her, off and on, until the girl was in kindergarten and reunited with family, an aunt.

Nanny paid for the girl's upbringing like she was her own and not once, friends say, did she take public assistance money to defray her costs. She got out of the business in 1991 when she suffered the heart attack.

Mrs. Briggs, now 68, runs a tighter ship than her mother did. "It's a business," she says. "You have to be this way. Times have changed."

What endures is her mother's legacy of selfless love for children.

"She always believed God would provide for her if she did his work," Mrs. Briggs says. "She's true to God and to her culture as an African-American. Part of our heritage is to stay together and look out for each other. We had to."

# The heart of a lion

Founder in 1985 of the Women of Color Quilters Network, Carolyn Mazloomi is honored for her quilts and her many achievements

*February 1, 2014*

Carolyn Mazloomi searched through piles of quilts in her sprawling basement studio.

She finally came upon the one she was looking for, "one that will get me in trouble around here," she said. She pinned the black-and-white quilt, titled "Certain Restrictions Do Apply," to a fabric wall. At its center is the Statue of Liberty holding a stop sign and surrounded by small boats carrying people of color.

"It was inspired by the Haitian people who lost their lives trying to get to Miami," she said of the 2013 piece. "I don't advocate people coming illegally, but everyone should be treated fairly when trying to emigrate."

For African-Americans quilting is a way to keep history alive, and Mazloomi's work is filled with historical themes that often connect to a shared African experience. During this Black History Month, she will be one of four people honored Friday as Glorifying the Lions award winners by the Urban League of Greater Southwestern Ohio at its 65th annual meeting.

The name of the award, presented to people 65 or older, originates in the African proverb that says, "Until the lions have their own historian, tales of hunting will always glorify the hunter."

Mazloomi works in narrative quilts. Subject matter includes the African-American experience during the civil rights movement and music, especially jazz and blues, an interest inspired by an aunt who owned a Louisiana juke joint. Her own experiences add to the richness of her work.

Born in Baton Rouge, Louisiana, in a family of amateur painters and artists, Mazloomi ended up in California. She graduated from Northrop University in Inglewood, and worked in Los Angeles as an aerospace engineer. She earned a Ph.D. in aerospace engineering from the University of Southern California in 1984 and continued her career as a crash site investigator for the Federal Aviation Administration. She has a pilot's license.

She describes her life as "family, art, and airplanes."

Family led her to Ohio. Some 20 years ago, she and her husband, Rezvan Mazloomi, an engineer originally from Iran, wanted a better place to bring up their three sons.

"L.A. is not where I wanted to raise them," she said. "My children got very good educations here and were safe."

Two of her sons – they're all in their 30s – live and work locally.

It's here that her career as an artist, historian, author, and exhibit curator took off.

An exhibition of her work just returned from a two-year tour of museums in China. Sponsored by the U.S. Department of State, the exhibit opened in Shanghai and closed at the Beijing Museum of Women. Her quilts have been included in five exhibitions at the Smithsonian's Renwick Gallery. Her artwork can be found in many museums and corporate collections, such as the Wadsworth Museum, the Smithsonian American Art Museum, American Museum of Design, Bell Telephone, the Cleveland Clinic, and Exxon.

Founder of the Women of Color Quilters Network, she is one of six artists commissioned to create artwork for the National Underground Railroad Freedom Center. She is curator of an exhibit opening in July in Johannesburg that pays tribute to the late South African President Nelson Mandela. In 2003, Mazloomi was awarded the first Ohio Heritage Fellowship Award, recognizing her as one of the state's living cultural treasures.

For all of her personal acclaim and standing, Mazloomi didn't forget the women who depended on quilting for a livelihood. It was in 1985 that she founded the Quilters Network, a nonprofit designed to preserve and foster the art of quiltmaking among women of color. Work of the 1,700 network members has been displayed nationally and internationally.

Kathy Wade, a longtime friend and jazz vocalist and educator, said Mazloomi "is a genius, a quiet genius, she has all that aeronautics and math and geometry plus the understanding of the need to present our history."

Women are an important subject to Mazloomi. "It's our charge to raise decent human beings," she said. "In my work, it doesn't matter their color. I try to remind women that they are the caretakers of the world."

Her quilt "Grandmother's Love" shows an elderly woman in her garden surrounding by grandchildren. "No Greater Love" illustrates a woman holding a child.

Promoting an art form and preserving African-American history are her goals, even if writing and curating have taken time away from her own art.

"Here as African-Americans we always learned about other folks' history," Mazloomi said.

"Most white folks don't know our history. Art in any medium is the greatest educator. Art brings humankind together."

# Sole mates

A Syrian refugee bonds with a survivor of the Jim Crow South
in a shoe repair shop

*July 26, 2017*

The storefront smells of fresh leather, glue, and rubber, circulated into a mixture by the small industrial fan above the door.

An older man, a life-long Christian who worked with his parents in the cotton fields of the Jim Crow South, takes an unblemished pair of men's soles and heels from a shelf.

He hands them to a younger man, smaller and bearded, who speaks no English beyond basic greetings, he says through an Arabic interpreter. He is a Muslim from Syria, a refugee displaced by his country's civil war.

The men wear identical blue golf shirts and full-length aprons. The older man holds out a well-worn pair of dress shoes. With a thick, almost muscular right index finger the color of dark chocolate, he taps the heel and the sole, twice each. The Syrian man nods. From beneath the bills of their matching baseball caps, they make eye contact, smile, and head toward opposite ends of Clarence Howell Shoe Repair in Pleasant Ridge.

The relationship of Clarence Howell, 78, and Bassam Osman, 36, is built on shared expertise in shoemaking and repair and shared experiences as outsiders looking for a safe place.

"When I met him, he reminded me of myself," Howell said in a deep voice still dripping with rural Georgia after 57 years in Cincinnati.

Osman, the married father of (now) five children – the latest a U.S.-citizen son born earlier this month – came from the city of Aleppo, where war has claimed 31,000 lives and destroyed 33,000 buildings. He worked in a shoe factory before it was bombed.

Osman fled first in December 2011 to Turkey with a seriously ill daughter, before uniting his family in a United Nations camp there. After two years of intense vetting involving five interviews and document searches, the family arrived in July in Cincinnati.

Osman and his family members are among the 86 Syrian refugees resettled here since July 1, 2016, by Catholic Charities Southwestern Ohio. The agency celebrated World Refugee Day locally June 17.

## Men find refuge in Cincinnati, five decades apart

The Osman family arrived six months before the Trump administration announced a ban that seeks to prevent most travel from Syria and six other predominantly Muslim countries.

The ban, almost all parts of which have been blocked by federal courts, also seeks to suspend the U.S. refugee program for 120 days. It was spelled out in an executive order called "Protecting the Nation from Foreign Terrorist Entry into the United States" that President Trump signed January 27.

Despite some strong opposition to Syrian refugees entering the country, Osman said he has experienced a positive reception here. "It is a very kind nation. In Turkey, my kids were called scavengers and dirty," he said.

Howell can relate to name-calling and second-class citizenship. He grew up with it.

"If you met a white lady, you had to turn your head and look away, or they would hang you," he said of his years in Georgia. "We had to sit upstairs in theaters. I remember being 11 or 12 when my mother was working in the fields. She said we couldn't be playing when Mr. Charlie – he was the white man in the truck – drove past."

So when a Catholic Charities volunteer introduced Osman and Howell in November, the shop owner decided to give him the same chance he received when he came to Cincinnati in 1960 and landed a factory job.

"I had to cross the same kind of line he had to cross," Howell said. "I try to help people who gone through what I gone through. I know when you're shuckin' and jivin' me. Bassam ain't doing that. Some Jewish people helped me when I got here and didn't hold nothing against me."

Three hours a day in the shop turned to four and quickly to full-time work for Osman. Howell switched a former full-time worker to part-time to make room for him.

Osman's salary rose from $9 an hour to $10 to $10.50 and finally to its current $11.

"He's a hard worker. He's very grateful. He gets the job done, he's not lazy," Howell said. "At 6 o'clock, the American workers stop, sometimes at 10 minutes of 6. Bassam is working at 6:20 to finish a job. He works fast. I have to tell him he doesn't have to work so fast."

"I have nephews and grandkids who don't work like that."

Sometimes, Howell will fix one shoe and have Osman repair the other. "Never need to show him twice," Howell said. "He can do everything I can do if I show him."

Howell worked the front desk on a slow summer morning. Osman was in the back of the shop at a machine called a master finisher that resembles a standing, encased power sander. He inked and polished a new pair of men's heels. He put the shoes on a shelf in front of a box fan to dry.

## Job central to long-term independence

Osman's job complements the web of supports he has received since resettling here.

The U.S. Conference of Catholic Bishops provides $1,075 for each refugee to use upon their arrival. Catholic Charities administers that money to help families set up a household.

The local Syrian American Foundation provided the Osman family with furniture for its Roselawn apartment. They attend services at the Islamic Center of Greater Cincinnati in West Chester Township.

He said his children's teachers at Roselawn Condon School have helped them learn English and adapt to American culture. A Catholic Charities volunteer tutors them.

Osman saved enough to buy a used car. By the eighth month here, he had to start to repay the U.S. State Department for the airfare and travel loan.

For all of the assistance, most of Osman's affection is directed toward Howell, whom he calls "Uncle" in English.

"He is a great man. I can tell he cares about me and my family," Osman said.

Osman's children decorated eggs during their first Easter season in the United States. They gave some to Howell.

"They love him, too. They run up to him and hug his legs," said Osman, who smiled at the memory as he rubbed his thin, dark beard with his right hand. "My kids know I am happy when I come home from work."

For all of his good fortune, Osman faces challenges. Two of his children, a son and his oldest child, a daughter, Zulekha, have Wilson's disease. It is a rare inherited disorder that causes copper to accumulate to dangerous levels in the liver. They are treated with medication by doctors at Cincinnati Children's Hospital Medical Center. Zulekha was twice misdiagnosed in Turkish hospitals with liver cancer and given chemotherapy. Another Turkish doctor said she needed a transplant.

Howell, a grandfather and the married father of three adult daughters, understands Osman's need to be with his children at the hospital. Sometimes, visits can take four hours. The children will require lifetime treatment for the disease, which can worsen and have serious side effects.

No such complications exist at the shoe repair shop.

"The way he treats me, he makes me want to give 100 percent to him all the time," Osman said. "We do not speak the same language. We know we love each other."

Said Howell, matter-of-factly, "I feel like he's a family member. I love him like he's one of my brothers."

# CHAPTER 5

# COMING OF AGE

*Some of my most challenging but most rewarding stories have focused on young black Cincin-
natians and their attempts to grow up in a society that often fears them or views them suspi-
ciously or as second-class citizens. I won't take for granted how these young people trusted me
enough to open parts of their lives to me to such a vulnerable degree. I consider that access a
privilege, not some sort of journalistic right.*

# The last right thing

Michael McCoy, who died saving a baby from a drive-by shooting,
made something of his life

*December 22, 1995*

For most of his young life, it seemed, Michael McCoy tried to do the right thing. That's
why he was known as Spike – after filmmaker Spike Lee. At times, doing the right thing
meant scolding his older sister, Nikki, for shoplifting. It meant fighting at school to defend his
mother and sisters. Shaming friends and going home when they went to steal cigars from a
drugstore. Trying to resolve conflicting stepfamily loyalties.

And on the afternoon of Monday, April 10, doing the right thing meant shielding a baby
girl from gunfire.

On that warm afternoon, Spike, 13, stood holding 15-month-old Paris Gunterman on an
Evanston sidewalk. Gunshots were fired from a passing car, and when Spike heard them, he
bent over to cover the baby. A bullet struck Spike on the top of the head. He would lose consciousness a few minutes later.

He died at 10:24 the next morning.

\* \* \*

Michael Vincent McCoy Jr. was born October 17, 1981, in Zanesville, Ohio.

His mother, Sharon McCoy, had two daughters before she was married. Nikki and Sarah
Cooper were 3 and 1 when Michael was born. His father, Michael Sr., a Tennessee native who
grew up in Akron, Ohio, worked at a Zanesville wire factory. He and his wife were 22.

Spike was brought up in the Church of God and Saints of Christ. He could recite the Lord's Prayer and knew the alphabet before he was 2. At 7 months, he could walk.

The weekend before he died, Spike – independent by nature – had been abnormally clingy to his mother. He had gone with her and her live-in boyfriend, Al Johnson, to watch them shoot pool.

Johnson is a generation older than Spike's father, who is now 36, remarried and living in Columbus, Ohio, with a 2-year-old son, Evan.

Johnson was not always patient with Spike, but they had made peace. The man had begun attending Spike's baseball games. Spike would get angry with his father on the phone and say Johnson was now his dad. Spike was jealous of the attention his father paid to his new son.

On Sunday night, Sharon, Al, and Spike had gone to see the movie *Bad Boys* at Western Hills Plaza. When they returned home that night, Spike finished the leftovers from dinner – fried chicken, stuffing, and greens – before going to bed.

\* \* \*

April 10 dawned clear, hinting of mid-60-degree temperatures to come. Though it was the first day of spring vacation for Cincinnati Public School students, Spike didn't sleep in. The Peoples Middle School seventh-grader, who lived at Westwood's Aspen Village apartments with his two sisters, mother, and Johnson, had a morning routine to keep: eat two bowls of Cap'n Crunch cereal while watching the Dennis the Menace cartoon and Mighty Morphin Power Rangers in his silk boxer shorts, purple with green polka dots.

After watching the two shows, Spike had a habit of turning off the television and goading his sisters into role-playing Power Rangers.

But Spike was alone that morning. His sisters had spent the night at a friend's house in Walnut Hills, not far from the 3600 block of Clarion Avenue in Evanston, where the family had lived for most of 1994.

"Every night you'd hear gunshots going off," says Sharon McCoy, who moved her family to Westwood last December. "I didn't want to stay there." Still, her three children spent a lot of time in Evanston. Most of their friends lived in that area.

Spike was acutely aware of his size. It kept him humble. At 6, he looked 4, yet he insisted on playing peewee football in Zanesville. His helmet and shoulder pads had to be ordered. At 13, he was still small, 10 pounds lighter and 4 inches shorter than average.

At noon that day, Nikki phoned Spike. They made plans to take pictures at Owl's Nest Park on Madison Road in O'Bryonville that afternoon. Spike took a bus to Five Points in Evanston, where Gilbert Avenue turns into Montgomery Road and intersects with Woodburn and Hewitt avenues. He walked to the St. Leger Apartments, to the home of a family friend whose children he had often watched. Spike was a prized baby-sitter. He once scolded another baby's mother for not giving the child medicine at the right time.

"He just loved little children," his mother says. "They were always around him. They would find each other. He understood what it was like to be small."

Spike had that soft spot for children and a cool side he'd show to the streets. He'd often dangle a toothpick from his mouth and speak in a slow, slurred voice. He prided himself on being just as comfortable with babies as he was with his many older friends, some of whom were in street gangs.

* * *

Sharon McCoy was laid off from her construction job the Friday before her son was shot. She is still unemployed but tends some bar on weekends.

In 1991, Sharon moved her daughters and son to Cincinnati from Zanesville to find work. The family settled in Westwood. The apartment on Westwood-Northern Boulevard would be their first of four Cincinnati addresses in less than four years.

His parents had discussed sending Spike to live with Michael Sr., who had moved to Columbus and taken a job in an auto parts factory.

"Spike said he had to stay with his sisters," his father says. "He didn't want to split the family up even more."

* * *

After visiting the family friend and her children at St. Leger Apartments that afternoon, Spike walked to the Kentucky Fried Chicken restaurant at Five Points. His sisters were late getting to Evanston for the photos. At KFC, Spike saw Joan "Summer" Taylor, one of his sisters' friends from Walnut Hills and the mother of 15-month-old Paris.

Spike and Summer ordered a two-piece chicken dinner – Spike's favorite food – with strawberry shortcake for dessert.

He and Summer talked about the future. "Spike said how much he wanted to be a daddy," says Summer, 17. "He was saying how he'd take his child everywhere and how, if he got his girlfriend pregnant, he wouldn't make her go to court for child support, how he'd just pay it. He told me he wanted to be Paris's godfather."

* * *

Spike spent most of the summers of 1992, 1993, and 1994 at the home of Sharon's sister, Vanessa Booker, and her husband, Jim. They live in rural Pataskala, Ohio, just east of Columbus. Spike rose early each morning to fish.

The Bookers had spoken with Sharon about having Spike move in with them and attend school in Pataskala. Sharon says none of her three children had adjusted well to life in Cincinnati. But Spike stayed because he felt he had to take care of his mom and sisters.

Spike's moodiness was the result of the fractured relationship with his father, Sharon says. Michael McCoy Sr. attributes them to "being caught in the ego battles" of a divorced couple.

* * *

It was after 6 p.m. when Spike and Summer decided to finish their meal at the apartment of her cousin, who lived at 1555 St. Leger Place.

One of Spike's older friends, D. Gaines, 18, of Evanston, tried to get Spike to join him for some basketball at the Evanston Recreation Center, just south of Five Points on Woodburn

Avenue. Spike declined Gaines's offer. Summer had too much to carry. He told him he might join up with him later.

Spike carried the coats and the food. Summer pushed Paris down the block in a stroller. It was an unseasonably warm afternoon. The streets were filled with people.

\* \* \*

Each time the family moved, Spike changed schools. His sixth-grade year at Rothenberg Elementary, Over-the-Rhine, was his best in Cincinnati. He played football and baseball with other boys who went to school there. He joined the school's Boy Scout troupe. He sang a solo at sixth-grade graduation.

Spike was first assigned to special education teacher Donda Lukas. This boy was too smart to be in a learning disabilities (LD) class, Lukas thought, only to learn later that he had been put there because he had been disruptive in regular classrooms.

"I mainstreamed him out. He excelled in science and loved music. He had a beautiful singing voice," says Lukas, 34, who has transferred to Winton Montessori.

Spike was most interested in electronics. He tinkered with broken VCRs and cassette tape players. His own tape player had broken not too long before his death, and "Spike worked on it until he fixed it," his mother says.

The boy placed the well-being of his mother and sisters ahead of all else. He saw himself as the man of the family. "He felt very responsible for them and tried to protect them," Lukas says.

In seventh grade at Peoples Middle School, Spike was suspended for fighting with another boy who had insulted his mother. He picked fights, he once confided in his uncle, Jim Booker, to keep from having other people pick fights with him. The aggressor, at least, had some sense of control.

"My son is no angel, but he wasn't out there stealing or selling drugs," Sharon McCoy says. Adds Nikki: "The kind of things he did was chasing after girls. He'd knock on somebody's door and run. He don't approve of stealing."

\* \* \*

Late that afternoon, when Spike and Summer got to the door at 1555 St. Leger Place, he handed her the coats – including his own black Carolina Panthers jacket by Starter and matching stocking cap – and picked up Paris.

Summer walked up the concrete stairs first. Spike stayed outside with the baby. The heavy security door slammed behind her – three times on the rock that was used to prop it open.

By the time Summer left the apartment, she heard screaming and saw people running. Shots had been fired. The first person she saw was Lamont Brown, 18, of Bond Hill, who had been standing next to Spike. Brown had been hit in the buttock with a .22-caliber bullet but managed to get inside the building.

Police say Brown was the intended target and had ties to the Bloods street gang. He had been involved in a weekend fight in which the shooter, Deatrick Beard, 17, of Jackson, Tennessee, had been stabbed in the back.

Beard and his cousin, Mark Williams, 18, of the West End, were members of the rival Folk Nation gang, who wear signature blue-and-black clothing. A witness told police that Beard and Williams had been cruising St. Leger in a stolen car all day.

Summer found Spike sitting on the sidewalk, his back against some landscape timbers. Paris was sitting on his lap. He was stroking the baby's hair. Summer could see the bullet lodged in the top of his head. Blood was streaming down the side of his face and neck. Spike, despite the serious wound, was calm.

"He handed Paris up to me and said, 'I'm all right, baby girl. Now get Paris in the house,'" Summer says. "He didn't panic because he didn't want to upset Paris. She was still playing with his hands."

Other people panicked. They moved Spike into an apartment. He slipped into a coma. Summer remembers his last words. "People kept telling him to hang on, and he said, 'I'm trying, I'm trying, but I can't. I can't. I'm too tired.'"

\* \* \*

Beard pleaded guilty to murder and to firing the fatal shot. He is serving an 18 years-to-life sentence. A jury convicted Williams, a passenger in the stolen 1985 Chevrolet Cavalier, of murder and three counts of felonious assault. He is serving 34 years to life.

Sarah Cooper, 15, is having the hardest time with her brother's death. "She's not dealing with it," Sharon says. "She's doing stupid stuff. She walks out that door and I don't know if I'll ever see her again. Then she'll come home, sit down and start crying."

Nikki, 17, is doing better and plans to return to school to get her GED. She and her mom often talk about Spike.

Sharon McCoy says her ex-husband didn't come back into their son's life until September 1994, seven months before Spike's death.

Michael McCoy Sr., who says he regrets not spending more time with his son, was profoundly affected by the boy's bravery.

"He made something out of his life. Even in the brevity of his life, it is a large life," Michael Sr. says. "He summarized his life in that single moment. In all the chaos of that neighborhood, he provided some sanity. He was trying to take charge of his life, and he certainly took charge of his death. He wasn't a victim. He saw a situation and made a decision to protect someone who couldn't protect herself. His greatness shames me. I'm humbled by it, to call him my son. I could have been a better father. I've learned so much from him. I'm trying to do that with his little brother" (McCoy's son Evan).

Summer, who is now four months pregnant with her second child, keeps one of Spike's memorial cards on her dresser at home. "Paris would have got hit, too, if it wasn't for Spike," she says. "He's a true hero. I know he could have dropped her and run."

A photo of a smiling Paris rested in the open lid of Spike's casket during visitation.

Sometimes, Summer brings Paris over to see Sharon. She plays with the baby. She bought the child a Christmas present. She says she can see Spike in the baby's eyes. Sharon, Nikki and Sarah tell Paris that Spike "is her boy."

Spike was eulogized as a hero.

"He had an energy and a desire to please people," said Elder Gregory McNeil of the Church of God and Saints in Christ Tabernacle, Cumminsville, and the boy's minister. "I always thought of Michael as a rose growing in a field of debris. He was a beautiful flower that had sprouted up among decay and deterioration. He exemplified unselfishness, performing an act of supreme unselfishness."

"Greater love hath no man than this, that a man lay down his life for his friends." – John 15:13.

Sharon McCoy clings to that passage. It comforts her. But, she says, her life is "in a rut. ... Some days, I can't even get out of bed or get dressed. Some days, I just don't care. But I'm trying to get out of this. I have two other children. I have lost control of them at one time or another since he died. I have to take care of them."

Sharon donated Spike's organs. The thought of part of him living on, too, gives some comfort. But she still has funeral expenses to pay. She can't afford a headstone for her son's grave in Zanesville.

At times, she wonders about what Spike would have been had he lived. She thinks about the ghetto. "It still hurts. It was cruel the way they did it. But maybe Michael's life – maybe I wouldn't have been so happy with his life."

Sharon slept in her son's bed the night he died. It was the first time she had what has become a reoccurring dream. "When I have dreams about him, he's always in a swing, smiling, with his teeth showing. And the swing is always coming to me, and he's smiling, saying 'whee.' It's a kids' swing at a park. And he looks so happy. I believe Michael is in heaven. God is pleased with him. He is a hero. He saved that little girl's life. His good work followed him to his judgment day."

---

# For some black students, failing is safer

Many who strive to do well often face peers who call them "'too white"
*May 28, 1998*

For as long as she can remember, Carrie Lucas has kept her guard up around white people. The 17-year-old Taft High School junior says it's no secret that a lot of whites don't want African-Americans to succeed.

But at 14, she was shocked to learn that a lot of blacks didn't want her to succeed either.

Since she began achieving high grades as a freshman three years ago, the Mount Auburn teen has endured a stream of verbal harassment from some of her African-American peers.

"It was always, 'Why are you trying to be white? Are you trying to be better than us?'" Carrie says.

It's the time of year when schools recognize academic accomplishments at honors assemblies and graduation ceremonies. While ambitious students of all ethnic and racial backgrounds have always been teased by their peers, black students often face a more pointed taunt from an unexpected source – other black youths.

The putdown equates academic achievement with "selling out" and "trying to be white."

The anti-achievement ethos is often an insidious pull on African-American students' performance, so much so that it recently attracted the attention of several national black advocacy organizations.

In April, in partnership with the National Congress of Black Churches and other groups, the national Urban League introduced an initiative to promote black student success. The Campaign for African American Achievement will try to counter negative peer pressure and lack of parental involvement.

The program has already started in 20 of the Urban League's 115 chapters. The Urban League of Greater Cincinnati plans to establish a national honors club, the Thurgood Marshall National Achievers Society, by next spring. It will provide clothing and scholarship incentives to students for keeping a B-average and performing community service.

The Urban League effort is similar to an Ohio State University extension program in Cincinnati Public Schools since 1988.

OSU's Young Scholars initiative identifies urban, low-income, minority youths in the sixth grade in nine Ohio districts and attempts to provide them with support to overcome peer pressure and other educational obstacles. The promise is college financial aid if they graduate high school with a B-average or better.

"The black kids who are academically sound still want to be friends with the kids on the block, but they need support not to be drug down by their desire to fit in," says Clarence Frazier, Cincinnati Young Scholars coordinator and former assistant principal at Withrow High School.

Statewide, a survey of Young Scholars determined that negative peer pressure is the No. 1 obstacle for academic achievement. The key to success, the survey showed, is reducing time spent with negative peers without cutting ties to them.

Peer pressure isn't the only factor inhibiting black student performance. Other factors include poverty, limited access to role models and positive images and low societal expectations.

Black peer-group pressure to underachieve, while difficult to quantify, is omnipresent. Some educators and sociologists say it contributes to blacks' statistically poorer academic performance. In 1997, ninth-grade Ohio proficiency test results show that lower percentages of African-Americans in Cincinnati Public Schools passed than whites in each of four subjects, including a 62-27 percent difference in math.

"It's real," Ellie Johnson, principal at Woodward High School, says.

Says Bill Soloman, a Taft High math teacher who is African-American, "To be 'in' is not to be a good student."

And the racial dig is especially painful.

"I didn't expect this from black people. We're supposed to help lift each other up because we've all been oppressed," says Carrie, who has a 3.3 grade-point average and plans to attend Northeastern University in Boston or Washington University in St. Louis to study pre-law and law. "A lot of (black people) are rude. They're judgmental. They criticize you for wanting to do something else with your life."

Many black students would rather underachieve and fit in among their peers than excel and risk being ostracized, says Signithia Fordham, an assistant professor of education at the University of Maryland-Baltimore County and author of *Blacked Out: Dilemmas of Race, Identity and Success at Capital High* (University of Chicago Press, 1996).

These students, she says, will stop doing their best in school, skip classes and even drop out.

## In different worlds

Joseph Day lives in different worlds but says he belongs in neither.

He lives with his grandmother, who's on a fixed-income, in Pleasant Ridge. He hangs out with friends he has known since their years at Roselawn Condon elementary. Some of them are high school dropouts. A couple are gang members. A few of them work.

His buddies want Joseph to skip school and party with them during the day, which he sometimes does. This is what Joseph calls his "black world."

Joseph's other world is Walnut Hills High School, a demanding college-prep institution that his black friends refer to as a "white school," even though 40 percent of its students are African-American. It's there that Joseph, 18 and a senior, studies physics, Spanish, and statistics.

"It's been real, real hard," Joseph says.

Many of Walnut Hills' students are from middle- and upper-class white families. They have computers at home and the money for field trips, the latest clothes and extracurricular activities.

Joseph does not.

His neighborhood friends don't understand why he sometimes stays in to study before coming out late at night.

"There are so many distractions here," Joseph says while sitting on a couch in his grandmother's living room. "But I've got to stay on good terms with these guys. We've got to stay tight. They have to know they're important to me. You can't make it through life if you don't fit in."

At the same time, Joseph won't let his neighborhood friends tell him what to do. "My dreams are so much bigger than theirs," he says. "I don't want to be rich; I just want a safe place to have a family."

Joseph is considering enlisting in the armed services as a way to escape. "UC [the University of Cincinnati] is a good school, but not for me," he says. "I've got to get out of Cincinnati."

He'd like to be an engineer. Math and science are his strongest subjects. He has a 2.5 GPA at Walnut Hills, and scored 1,100 on his SAT.

"I'm a lot smarter than I let on," Joseph says. "If I would have tried harder and not been pulled down, I could have done so much better. I messed up so bad. Sometimes I wonder what it's like to be white and not have to deal with all this stuff. Being white has to be so much easier than being black."

## Blackness vs. whiteness

Academic achievement isn't the only activity that some black youths say is "white." Involvement in mainstream culture, such as theater, having white friends, and speaking standard

English also make black students vulnerable to the taunt that they are selling out. These are activities that much of general society – and many African-Americans – do not associate with "being black."

Blackness, according to this reasoning, is defined by a preoccupation with basketball, an affinity with rap music and the ability to fistfight, author and education consultant Jawanza Kunjufu writes in *To Be Popular or Smart: The Black Peer Group* (African-American Images, 1989).

"It has increased," says Mr. Kunjufu, an African-American, in an interview from his Chicago office. "It is increasingly difficult to go against the peer group."

## Even a black student's college choice can be criticized.

Why choose Miami?

Kitalena Mason, valedictorian of Withrow High School's Class of 1998, will attend Miami University in Oxford this fall. She was surprised when her college choice drew odd responses from black peers: "Why you want to go to that white school? You think you better than us? Why ain't you going to Fisk?"

Fisk University in Nashville, Tenn., is one of the nation's historically black colleges. Miami is 93 percent white.

"I have a friend who is black who is at Miami, and he's told me everything is OK," says Kitalena, 18, a Mount Healthy resident who plans to study communications and Spanish. "It's so petty to racially stereotype people. I want to ask these people, 'How far has that gotten you?'" The taunt was an irritant, she says, but nothing that could detour her from her goals. She has too much support at home to fall prey to this. Kitalena's the daughter of a Thai mother and an African-American father who insisted on excellence. "If [youths who taunted her] really thought about what they were saying, they'd realize they were insulting themselves," she says.

## Fear of abandonment

African-American youths who hurl "selling out" insults often do so out of fear of abandonment. As the black middle class continues to expand, many African-Americans see themselves hopelessly left behind, says Dr. Alvin Poussaint, clinical professor of psychiatry at Harvard University Medical School and co-author of *Raising Black Children* (Plume, 1992).

"Sometimes it's family members who reject a smart kid because they feel the smart child will desert them for the white community," says Dr. Poussaint, who is African-American.

Forty years ago, at the dawn of the modern civil rights movement, 60 percent of African-Americans lived in poverty. Today that number is 29 percent, according to the Census Bureau. (The federal poverty level for a family of three is $20,004.) At the same time, the black middle class has grown to 40 percent.

But poor-performing black students try to hold up their grades as the norm, Dr. Poussaint says. The success of academically successful black students makes them feel even more like failures.

Gifted black students are often hazed as "traitors" to their race for getting good grades, he says. That's because academic failure is often regarded as a kind of camaraderie among African-American students.

Both groups of black students are responding to the same societal stigma that African-Americans are inferior, says Ms. Fordham, the Maryland teacher and author. "Some students resist the claim that African-Americans can't achieve by being on time every day, doing their homework, getting vested in a school," she says. "Other students avoid school success because they feel school will not make a difference in their lives."

As a result, studies of integrated schools show that African-Americans, primarily males, dominate remedial and special education classrooms and are missing from gifted programs.

Going against this low standard – attending private school, for example – draws negative peer pressure.

## Hanging on to talent

Earlier this semester, Bobby Payne had been scoring in the 90s in his religion class at Purcell-Marian High School.

Then the freshman's scores dropped into the 70s. When his teacher, the Rev. William Cross, inquired, the answer was negative comments from some of his black friends. He wasn't studying as much as he had been. He had stopped trying his best.

Bobby, 15, a freshman from Kennedy Heights, says he is teased by his cousins and some neighbors who attend public schools that he is a "little rich white boy" because he goes to a Catholic school.

"They think it's a white school," says Bobby, who attended a predominantly black Catholic elementary school, St. Francis de Sales, which is around the corner from Purcell-Marian in Walnut Hills. About a third of Purcell-Marian's 730 students are African-American.

High school brought on social changes for Bobby, his mother says. "His group of friends is older and larger," Oymma Barker, 40, says. "His cousins now have older friends from public schools, and Bobby is listening to some of them. He's the only one not in public school."

Talks with his mother and Father Cross have helped him get back on track, says Bobby, who wants to attend Georgia Tech or Morehouse or Clark colleges to study chemical or electrical engineering. He's again scoring in the 90s.

He also had a dream. "God told me to do my best," Bobby says. "God gives us certain talents, but if we don't use them, he takes them away. I don't want to lose the talents I've been given."

## Tracing the beginnings

Sociologists and other scholars date the rise of the black anti-achievement attitude to the 1960s. That's when two fundamental changes occurred in society:

Much of the black middle class left for the suburbs, taking with it several role models whose success reinforced the importance of education in predominantly black neighborhoods.

Public school desegregation brought with it forced busing that moved black children out of their neighborhood schools and into predominantly white schools.

Integration cultivated an idea that blacks should accept white values of success, many sociologists say. The message was that African-Americans had to copy whites. Resistance to such ideas is at the heart of black life in the United States. Black children, as the behavior is modeled for them, resist efforts that they perceive as attempts to make them white, says Ms. Fordham of the University of Maryland.

The black peer group pressure often hits in middle school. "In K–6, a student can do well on tests and get good grades and be on the honor roll and still have an excuse," Mr. Kunjufu says. "The excuse is, 'Well, I didn't study. I didn't try to get a good grade.'"

From sixth grade on, when schoolwork becomes more challenging and peer opinion matters more, he says, scores often begin to decline.

Says Mr. Frazier, director of Cincinnati Young Scholars program: After sixth grade "parents tend to become a little more hands-off. The schools are bigger. All of a sudden it's not so cool to be carrying those books around."

## "Way to go, white boy"

Steven Kennedy did his math homework religiously for weeks. He studied for the test the night before. It was long division with decimals. As his sixth-grade teacher at predominantly black Douglass Elementary in Walnut Hills returned the exams, Steven was confident he had done well.

"'Steven got the highest grade,' "he remembers the teacher telling the class. "'He got the only A.'"

As a smile spread across his face, Steven heard some black students sitting around him say, "Way to go, white boy."

"You ain't black."

"Hey, Oreo."

"I'm not a white boy," Steven shot back. He still wasn't sure why he'd been teased. It was the first time he'd experienced the insult.

Steven, now 16 and a sophomore at Hughes Center in Clifton, asked his mother, Sharon Pope, why he had been called white. She explained that some African-American students don't want others to succeed in school.

A few months later, Mrs. Pope gave her son a biography of Harriet Tubman, the escaped slave who returned to the South many times to help guide other escapees North on the Underground Railroad.

"[The story] touched him," says Mrs. Pope, 42, and the mother of three sons. Steven, her middle son, wants to attend the University of Texas to study aerospace engineering. "Steven came back to me and said, 'Mom, we have to take advantage of the opportunities people like her set for us. It wouldn't be right to waste my chance.' "

Says Steven: "Yes, there is racism. But each person has the power to get out of the situation they're in – through education."

## Black history matters

Too many students don't know enough black history. If these black youths knew the story of African-Americans, they would know it's the story of achievement in the face of oppression.

Education, hard work, family values and community are the foundations of black identity in the United States.

For centuries, slaves in this country risked punishment, or death, to learn to read and write. While enslaved, they resisted the larger society's image of a good slave as an illiterate slave.

Just four years after the 1863 Emancipation Proclamation, African-Americans founded Morehouse College in Atlanta and co-founded Howard University in Washington, D.C.

The literacy rate among African-Americans in the South increased from 20 percent to 70 percent between the end of the Civil War and 1910.

But only recently has society begun to realize the scope of black history and the contributions of African-Americans. Still, the celebration of black history remains segregated in a single month, February. "Our achievements have been 'blacked out' of the public imagination," says Ms. Fordham, the cultural anthropologist.

## "Be who you are"

Leah Derkson has three heroes from contemporary black history. Their lives provide the Holmes High School senior with models of excellence.

But as a student who ranks in the top 10 percent of her class, she received a different message during her first few years at Holmes. "Black kids said I was 'selling out, that I was a 'Tom,'" says Leah, 18, of Covington, who will attend Northern Kentucky University on a full academic scholarship.

Walking through school corridors earlier this month with a white *Enquirer* photographer drew the same type of response: "Look at Leah, trying to be a white girl again."

Leah discovered her first hero while researching the life of the Rev. Fred Shuttlesworth, the black Baptist minister now living in North Avondale who led the fight against segregated Birmingham, Alabama, during the 1950s and 1960s. Along with the Revs. Martin Luther King Jr. and Ralph Abernathy, he is widely considered one of the "big three" of the civil rights movement.

Leah also explored the accomplishments of Theodore Berry, a lawyer and civil rights activist who became Cincinnati's first black mayor.

Then she started reading the poetry of Maya Angelou.

*You may shoot me with your words,*
*You may cut me with your eyes,*
*You may kill me with your hatefulness,*
*But still, like air, I'll rise.*

"You have to be who you are," says Leah, who plans on returning to Holmes to teach history after she completes college. "I've learned you can't let anyone take away the things that you believe."

## Possible solutions

Beyond black youths learning more black history, there are other changes that could reduce negative black peer pressure.

On a large scale, race relations experts say, society must continue to chip away at institutional racism that marginalizes African-American lives. Civil rights activists and some educators and politicians say predominantly black urban schools must receive fair funding.

Mr. Kunjufu suggests that requirements for advanced placement and honors courses be altered to allow in more African-American students. The result, he says, would be a larger group of black students who could support each other and reduce feelings of racial isolation.

Schools could expand black history courses, create black history clubs, hold more assemblies to honor an increasing number and wider variety of academic achievements among black students.

Away from school, parents should find playmates for their children from families who value education. That way, say educators and ministers, children can begin to develop social support that helps them withstand the anti-achievement pressure they'll face.

"I have always tried to get my children around other positive influences – kids, parents," says Nina Teasley, 39, of Clifton, the mother of Mikkia Lawrence, 18, a Walnut Hills senior. "No boy sits outside in his car and honks his horn for my daughter. She has been taught not to answer to 'ho' and 'bitch.'"

Mikkia, who attended Winton Woods High School, Forest Park, for 10th and 11th grades, has always been around positive black peers. "If everybody around you is negative," she says, "you'll become negative."

If black youths find themselves encountering negative peer pressure without support, they should turn to their neighborhood church, says the Rev. Damon Lynch Jr.

"No church or minister espouses dumbing-down," says the Rev. Lynch, pastor of New Jerusalem Baptist Church, Carthage, which recognizes student members with at least B-averages during one Sunday service a month.

New Jerusalem is also among the many black Tristate churches that offer a rites-of-passage program for young African-American males. "Simba" introduces young people to positive adult role models and teaches them how to function in larger society without feeling as if they're sacrificing their heritage.

## A success story

Then there are black youths like Carrie Lucas, whose personal determination and will are enough to see them through.

She had more reason than most black youths to give up. She could have yielded to the stereotype of a black female who was being put upon by her family.

Before she was 15, Carrie had lived with her mother, grandmother, and an aunt.

Her teen years arrived with this edict from her aunt, who was caring for Carrie and her three siblings: You stay home. You cook. You clean. You watch the little ones.

Carrie went to court to become a ward of the state. She wanted a foster parent. She wanted to be left alone to go to school. She won and, while in court, discovered that she wanted to be a lawyer.

She has been in foster care in a Mount Auburn home for two years.

"I thought, 'I am a child. I am not a mother or a maid. I'm getting out,'" Carrie says. "The only way to a better life is education – no matter what color you are. Being smart doesn't belong to any one race."

# Sam DuBose's children moving forward

## A year ago, Cincinnati man was shot to death during a traffic stop

*July 19, 2016*

Four of Sam DuBose's children tumbled into DaShonda Reid's car on a recent summer evening. They were hurrying to boxing lessons.

As she climbed into the driver's seat, a few inches from a dashboard placard bearing his picture and the words, "Justice for Samuel DuBose," Reid looked back over her left shoulder and said, "This tragedy is not going to stop his children from being successful. If anything, it's fuel that will help make them successful."

They are following her example. They will thrive, not merely survive. They will be strong mentally and physically.

One year ago today, Reid lost the man she'd been with off and on for 16 years and who, just two days before his death, had proposed and given her an engagement ring. She is the mother of three of his children and stepmother, DuBose had said, to three more of his children. She also took in another of DuBose's children whose mother had died of cancer in 2014.

A total of 13 children lost their father, a man they say was loving and attentive, a firm and effective disciplinarian, yet blessed with a sense of humor that could defuse the most stressed situation.

In a time of heightened national racial tensions and inflamed police-community relations, Samuel DuBose has taken a place in the litany of names of unarmed African-Americans who have died at the hands of police. Eric Garner. John Crawford III. Michael Brown Jr. Tamir Rice. Walter Scott. Freddie Gray. Philando Castile. These are just some of the better-known names. The list consists of hundreds more.

Reid and the children know about those cases. They know all the details of their father's death. He was pulled over for a missing front license plate on a Mount Auburn street on a Sunday evening. The stop escalated to the point where a white University of Cincinnati police officer, Ray Tensing, shot him point blank. After viewing the officer's body camera footage, Hamilton County Prosecutor Joe Deters said Tensing would face a murder charge. The trial for Tensing, who was fired by UC, will begin Oct. 24.

"They know about the killer," Reid said on a recent afternoon from her living room of the four-bedroom house on a quiet suburban street. "They know when the trial is. They know everything that happened. We don't and won't sugarcoat it."

They know how this man they all loved and mourn had his character attacked posthumously. His lengthy rap sheet was reported. He'd been charged almost 100 times since the late 1980s for minor offenses, almost all of them traffic-related. He used to sell and still used marijuana; a small amount was found in his car at the time of his death. His driver's license had been revoked.

Yet they don't dwell on the negative or their loss. Those things are out of their control. Paralysis is not an option. They look forward and keep moving. Besides boxing, the children swim and are involved in activities at school, including student government. She is teaching her children to be proud of their black American culture and said, "We are not ashamed of the melanin in our skin, even if some people are frightened by it."

DuBose comes to Reid in her dreams, she said, and gives her nonverbal messages. His spirit fills the house, the way his music and scent still do. It is that of his cologne, a brand called Thallium, mixed with marijuana.

Just 43, DuBose was there one moment and dead the next. He did not fade away from a long disease.

The night of his death, Reid slept on his side of the bed. She'd taken laundry that he'd worn from a basket and surrounded herself in bed with his white T-shirts.

"Surreal, a lot of crying, a lot of family support," Reid said when asked to recount the first few days and weeks. "Flesh is just that. Your spirit still lives. His spirit is within us and everywhere in this house. His soul is everywhere. It did not go into his grave."

They did not sit still. Reid took the children to Kings Island less than a week after his death. She said she had to get the children out of the house and away from the TV. "His murder just kept popping up all the time everywhere," Reid said.

She works for a company in new business development. She has an associate's degree in paralegal studies.

On Martin Luther King Jr. Day in January, UC announced it had reached a financial settlement with the family. In May, a judge decided how the $4.8 million settlement would be split among family members. Each of DuBose's children will receive $218,000.

Teaila Williamston, 17, is DuBose's daughter by another woman, who died in 2014. Teaila played one of his songs at the Black Lives Matter Cincinnati rally July 10. In "Global Warming," a song about the "genocide of black men in American society," the girl said, her father eerily predicts his death in a police stop gone bad.

Teaila and her sister, Chyna DuBose-Reid, 15, have recorded music together. Teaila raps. Chyna can rap but is gifted with a singing voice. They wrote and recorded a song together called "Sparks," a love song that includes the lyric, "We got a future, I ain't worried."

Before he died, DuBose told Chyna that she had received the talent for music and how he wanted her to dream big.

The girls have written and recorded several songs in honor of their father. Reid's favorite is "Write Your Name in the Sky."

Samuel Vincent DuBose Jr., 10, always waited eagerly for his father to come home.

"We were all just happy," he said. "The night he died, I kept waiting for him to come home. Now I just want to keep my mom happy. I feel bad because he only had Vincent for four years, and Vincent only had him for four years."

Vincent Samuel DuBose, 5, used to sleep between his parents in their bed. He'd end up with his feet on his dad's back. The little boy will still make his way to his mother's bed.

"I want to be close to her," he said. "I want it to be like it was back then."

Reid and her children know their lives will never be the same, of course.

At times, they look back in gratitude. Other days are hard. Determined, they choose to look to the future.

# Spoken word poets

Another voice for black Cincinnati

*July 29, 2016*

Standing at a microphone, stretching her long arms and fingers forward as if to snatch an image from air and memory, her clear brown eyes fixed on a distant point, Siri Imani stared down the long lager tunnel that a century ago housed fermenting beer and described the contemporary reality of a 21-year-old black woman.

*So I love society*
*For pretty much condemning everything I feel inside of me*
*Until I express myself*
*And they'll probably call it rioting*

Her satirical spoken word piece is called "I Love You," one of dozens of poems in Imani's repertoire and one of the two she performed Thursday night during the Speak event at the Mockbee in the Brighton area of Over-the-Rhine.

Built in the 19th century into a Central Parkway hillside, the former Bellevue Brewing Co. serves as a historically apropos venue for these series of performances by the newest generation of local spoken word artists. They are part of the lineage of African-American oral tradition that traces back to slavery and encompasses the black church and spirituals, jazz and blues, the Harlem Renaissance and hip-hop and spoken word poetry.

The oral tradition isn't just about documenting history. They protest and triumph. They celebrate and mourn.

Today, these sensitive, observant poets and their pieces provide insight into the 21st-century black American experience.

For Imani, a former Withrow High School basketball star who played under her given name, Siri Huey, present-day spoken word shows the diversity of experiences and interests of young African-Americans. It also has value to the listener who comes from outside of the black community.

"If they were to listen, maybe the next time they see us on the street they might not be afraid," she said. "Maybe they'd realize we are intellectual. We're angry, yes, but we're scared."

The intellect, the anger, fear and hope are all on display on the third Tuesday of every month in the Speak events. White and red rose petals lead from the Central Parkway sidewalk into the rounded spaces of the Mockbee. Strings of white party lights frame the doorway and railing. Admission is $10, $8 with a can of food to be donated to a food bank.

Speak is produced by another young black woman, Alexis Cox, 22, a University of Cincinnati student from Westwood. The title of the Thursday event was, "The Evolution of Man's Rhymes."

"In the African-American community, all we have is our ancestors," said the organizational leadership major. "Spoken word allows us to say what's on our minds. It's important to have a space to uplift each other."

Besides Imani, five other spoken word artists – all under 25 – performed this past Thursday. The pieces included the erotic – a story from a young man who attracted the attention of one of his father's former girlfriends – and addressed love, both romantic and self-love. They were spiritual. Most of all, they identified the places young black Americans inhabit in a larger society that is not altogether the most welcoming at all times.

## True art must reflect the times

The Thursday show, attended by about 60 people, featured local artist Laurent Che. He is a 2011 St. Xavier High School graduate who grew up in Northside and the son of a Cameroon immigrant father. A graduate of Kent State University, Che, 24, is leaving soon to work towards a master's degree in marketing and advertising.

His formal education served as the backdrop to his first piece, a new composition he debuted titled "Fear." Not surprising, in the age of the Black Lives Matter movement both nationally and locally, "Fear" is about the treatment African-Americans experience at the hands of police. Che references the police shooting earlier this month of Alton Sterling in Baton Rouge, Louisiana. He died in a convenience store parking lot, where he had been selling compact discs.

*Lord, we are trying our best*
*But what can we do*
*When they kill us over CDs?*

"I don't know who said it, but you can't be a true artist without reflecting the times," Che said before the show. "I try to speak from the heart. I stopped trying to be too cool for school. You can't be honest if you're more concerned about being cool."

In "Fear," he anticipates his own parenthood – and that the current crisis won't improve.

*So what am I supposed to tell my future son*
*When he passes his driver's test?*

"I know some of us, black men, thought if we carried ourselves a certain way and were educated that we would be immune to police brutality," he said. "That's not the case."

## No room for negativity; just love, expression

Words are at the center of all of the art performed by Aziza Love.

She is a 2013 Walnut Hills High School graduate and senior at Miami University, Oxford, where she is studying civil and regional development with a minor in educational psychology. Aziza – aka Alexis Thompson, 20, of Clifton – is a singer-songwriter and multi-instrumentalist who regularly performs at Prime 47, Downtown, and throughout southern and central Ohio.

With her hair wrapped in a scarf, she paced the sidewalk outside of the Mockbee before her first of two pieces, "Love Is." It is new. She needed to rehearse in her mind.

Without a hiccup, she spoke and sang behind the microphone:

*Love is diversified classic art*
*Love is Joss Stone*
*Love is Kendrick Lamar and Mozart*

*Love is from the heart*
*Love is every part*

"I wrote it yesterday. I pull from the sky and the world around me," she said during intermission. She had an upcoming performance in Dayton, Ohio, to prepare for. She also is a yoga practitioner and event coordinator.

"Everything I do, my performances and events, is for people to express themselves," Aziza said.

She wants people to listen in order to learn and not just to formulate a response.

"We don't need more negativity. We don't have any more room for that," she said. "We don't know people's first, middle, and last names. We don't know each others' stories. That's the value of what we're doing here tonight."

In the face of ongoing racism and other obstacles, these young spoken word artists do remain optimistic. They say their words and the opportunity to express them are vital to their perseverance, just as they were for their forebears.

## Giving a voice to her generation

On July 10, as a crowd swelled in front of Cincinnati police headquarters in the West End for the Black Lives Matter rally and march, Siri Imani read one of her pieces, "Lost Generation."

She'd been invited by organizers to speak, in part, for the young people involved in the movement.

*Which brings me to a series of unfortunate questions*
*With equally unfortunate answers*
*Mr. Officer, I wonder, if you saw Grandma's face at the family reunion*
*When she counts seven instead of eight grandsons*
*Then would you show remorse for the life of the one? ...*
*See, I got so many questions*
*But I fear if I ask*
*I'll be answered by Smith and Wesson.*

She ends the piece with an anguished expression of hopelessness, brought on by the deaths of many contemporaries.

Yet, in poem and conversation, Imani said, "we're not without hope."

# Being Timothy Thomas's son

Tywon Thomas was 3 months old in April 2001, when his father's death led to changes in Cincinnati Police procedures

*December 22, 2016*

Tywon Thomas knows what he likes and what he does not, in a typical, uncomplicated teen-aged boy sort of way. He does not like *Romeo and Juliet*, the book he is reading in freshman English class, saying, "All I know is he's a boy who's in love with a girl."

He does not always like having to help look after his youngest siblings. He turns the TV to cartoons. He reheats food in the microwave. He checks homework and makes sure they get a shower. He said he understands that his mother works and is taking college classes.

Tywon obsesses about football and gym shoes. He watches New England Patriots and Ohio State football games on TV. He imagines himself playing professionally and making one-handed catches like his favorite player, New York Giants wide receiver Odell Beckham Jr. Tywon does not like Beckham's blond dye job.

Having turned 16 Tuesday, Tywon stands 5-feet-8, weighs 126 pounds and has a waist up to his neck and man-sized hands, suggesting that he will grow into his father's 6-foot-3 frame.

Tywon already looks like his dad. He has the same slow smile, dark complexion, high cheekbones and upturned almond-shaped eyes that shine from a photo of his father that most of the country saw 15 years ago.

It's his father who makes Tywon different from other teen-aged boys.

Tywon was 3 months old when Timothy Thomas was shot and killed by a Cincinnati police officer in an Over-the-Rhine alley. His death in the early morning hours of April 7, 2001, touched off days of social unrest and violence and led to an agreement that changed how the Cincinnati Police Department does its job.

Tywon knows how his father died but not how it altered the course of the city.

"It's like my dad is famous," Tywon said during lunch in an Over-the-Rhine that is gentrified and far different than the one in which his parents and extended family members lived.

He paused.

"I wish he was famous for something different," he finally said. With his mother's permission, Tywon agreed to talk about growing up fatherless, a private pain that nonetheless is playing out in public because of the nature of his father's death.

At 16, Tywon said he does not yet want to be part of the cause that Timothy Thomas still embodies – police reform and community relations. Tywon said he does not want to appear at rallies or make short speeches until he is comfortable. He plans to read more about his father's death and its aftereffects once he turns 18. "I might be ready then," he said.

For now he just wants to be a kid, finish high school, go to college and stay out of the kind of legal trouble that already has found him twice as a juvenile.

## Son inherits his father's enduring legacy

Just as the anniversary of Timothy Thomas's death begins to fade from memory, the police shooting death of another unarmed black man somewhere in the country brings it back. Thomas was the 15th black man killed by Cincinnati police officers in the five years previous to 2001, a span in which police did not shoot and kill a white man. Thomas's death was the tipping point. Over-the-Rhine erupted in violence.

The City of Cincinnati, Fraternal Order of Police, and Black United Front were among groups in 2002 that signed the Collaborative Agreement, which brought sweeping reforms to the police department. It would change how it tracked and recorded its use of force, modify foot-pursuit policies and add computers to cruisers. The emphasis would now be community-oriented policing.

In August 2014, members of the Black United Front handed out copies of the Collaborative Agreement in Ferguson, Missouri. The shooting death there of unarmed black man

Michael Brown by a white officer touched off rioting and elevated the Black Lives Matter movement to the national stage.

Cincinnati again was in that unwanted spotlight in July 2015. A white University of Cincinnati police officer, Ray Tensing, shot and killed an unarmed black man, Sam DuBose, during a traffic stop in Mount Auburn. In the days following DuBose's death, city officials hailed the Collaborative Agreement for helping keep the fragile peace. They invoked the name of Timothy Thomas, as if martyred.

Tensing's murder trial ended in November in a hung jury. He will be tried again in May in Hamilton County.

Like many teenagers, Tywon Thomas detaches from news coverage. He said he knew little about the shooting. When he learned that DuBose had children his age, Tywon said the case reminded him of the situation of a friend at Hamilton High School. A classmate there recently lost his father to street violence in Cincinnati.

Tywon is the oldest of Monique Crutchfield's six children. She works as a home health aide and is taking classes to become certified as a medical assistant, which would increase her hourly wage.

This fall, she moved from an apartment in Hamilton and doubled-up with Timothy's sister in her split-level house in Colerain Township. The arrangement is an economic necessity. Crutchfield wants to move her family back, where her children attend school. Tywon is a freshman at Hamilton High.

He has younger sisters who are 14 and, 4 and brothers who are 10, 8 and, 3. Crutchfield is married but said that her husband is serving jail time. Tywon said his stepfather was involved in a shooting but that he still talks to him occasionally and likes him.

Crutchfield, 36, is tall and thin and speaks in a candid, unadorned manner. Tywon takes after her, too.

"I just try to help keep him on the straight and narrow, do the right thing," she said of her oldest son.

Tywon started to ask about his father when he was 3.

In a 2006 interview with the *Enquirer*, Timothy's mother, Angela Leisure, said her grandson would ask where he was.

Leisure said she made a copy of her 2000 wedding video so Tywon could see his father on a happy day.

She said she would frequently find Tywon in front of a TV, watching the video.

After Thomas was killed, Leisure gave reporters a copy of a photograph of her son in a tuxedo from her wedding. A framed copy sits on a table in the house in Colerain Township. Another is in a thick album of family photos.

His mother told Tywon what has become his favorite story about his father. Monique and Timothy argued. He told her that she could have anything else if they split up but that he was keeping Tywon.

"That's what made him get a little bit serious about life," Tywon said of his father. "They both got serious about life when I was born."

Thomas had finished his GED. Just a few days before he died, he'd gotten a job through temporary service. He was to start two days after his death. He aspired to a career in electronics.

## Minor scrapes with the law, just like his father

Tywon knows that at the time of his death, his father had 14 misdemeanor charges against him, all related to traffic.

Shortly after midnight on Saturday morning, April 7, 2001, Timothy Thomas left his infant son and his mother in their apartment at 1319 Republic St. He said he was walking to a nearby convenience store to buy cigarettes.

Off-duty officers working security details recognized Thomas and knew about the traffic charges. Five were for driving without a license and three for driving with an expired one.

Officer Stephen Roach, a white, four-year Cincinnati Police veteran, joined in the 10-minute chase. Half a block from Thomas's apartment, Roach surprised him in a dark alley at 13th and Republic streets. Roach said Thomas appeared to be reaching into the waistband of his pants for a weapon. Roach fired once. He hit Thomas in the chest. The unarmed Thomas died within the hour at University Hospital.

Tywon and his mother talk about the decision his father made that night to run. She tells him to comply with police. They also talk about police and the two legal scrapes that Tywon has already had as a juvenile.

When he was 12, Tywon went with a friend to a big box store and tried to steal pellet guns. Guards stopped them before they got out of the store. Police were called. The boys had to pay fines.

In 2015, Tywon and his mother said Tywon and some other boys were outside of their house in Hamilton when they were accused of throwing rocks at a passing motorcyclist.

Tywon insisted he did not throw the rocks but was found guilty by Butler County juvenile officials and sentenced to pick up litter as a way to pay restitution.

## At 13th and Republic, for the first time

All that remains of the large memorial to Timothy Thomas are the faded letters RIP, spray-painted on the old bricks above the alley where he was shot. A back room, site of the shrine – candles, flowers, stuffed animals, empty bottles of liquor – is gone.

In the past month, Tywon has visited the site with Terry Thomas, Timothy's younger brother. Terry, who lives in Pleasant Ridge with his wife and children, is 32.

Terry took Tywon to the Republic Street address where he lived with his parents. Then they stood at the foot of the faded RIP graffiti.

On 13th Street, closer to Vine Street than Republic, someone fashioned a weatherproof image of Timothy Thomas from a sign and strapped it to a tree with bike chain. The two-sided image was adapted from the tuxedo photo that Thomas's mother had given to the media after his death.

"It's weird," Tywon said while looking at the painting of his father. "It looks like me, like a mirror."

Seeing the painting is another reminder of how much Tywon misses his father.

"I always say he's in heaven," he said. "I wish I knew my dad. If wishes were real, that would be my first wish."

In May 2003, just two years after Timothy Thomas was killed, the City of Cincinnati agreed to pay $4.5 million to 16 plaintiffs in what was the largest legal settlement to date in the city's history. The settlement ended the wrongful death case of Timothy Thomas and other complaints of excessive use of force and police misconduct. The city and police officers named admitted no wrongdoing.

Crutchfield said that Timothy's mother, Angela Leisure, handled the case. Crutchfield said she knows little about the settlement, other than Tywon receives a small monthly payment and will get a larger lump sum when he turns 18 or 21, she's not sure which. Terms of the agreements are confidential.

His mother said Tywon talks of wanting to do for other family members to lift them out of poverty.

Still, he said of the money, "I would trade it to have my dad, for real, all of it."

# CHAPTER 6

# MILITARY

*Stories about African-American veterans or active military always interested me. They ask piercing questions about service, sacrifice, and racial equality. I'd forgotten the story about Mary Moore and her Vietnam MIA son, Greg Moore, and was thankful to rediscover it. I have two older brothers who were in high school at the same time as Greg. My brothers had college deferments. I couldn't help but see how having an MIA son would have emotionally torn up our mother, too.*

# America's forgotten heroes

Tuskegee Airmen, black veterans still fighting for recognition

*November 11, 1994*

First Lt. John Leahr flew more than 100 bombing missions over Italy during World War II and was once chased across Austria by the Luftwaffe, but his most frightening war story comes from a Memphis street corner in 1946.

That's the night a good ole country boy told a white police officer that he had "killed me a lot of niggers in my life but never killed no nigger officers, so I guess I will now."

Leahr and three other black military officers, all of them distinguished war veterans, huddled on the sidewalk, trying to shield themselves against boots, fists and clubs, as a crowd of whites gathered around to watch.

The cop drove off. If not for a white sailor who just happened by and helped get the black men safely on a bus, "I, a decorated military pilot who risked my life to protect my country, would have died at the hands of these idiots," said Leahr, 74, of Kennedy Heights.

They had helped win the Big War. Thousands died, including 66 of Leahr's Tuskegee Airmen compatriots, yet almost 900,000 black veterans came home to a nation that refused to even acknowledge they had served.

This Veterans Day finds these veterans still fighting, some 50 years later, for recognition and to clear the name of segregated black units whose contributions, they say, are either ignored or misrepresented in U.S. military history.

There is a sense of urgency to this campaign, which many of them consider their final battle, a last push for overdue attention.

"When we go, and a lot of us are already gone, these stories go with us," said retired Lt. Col. William Jones, 80, of Paddock Hills, who served with the Army in the Pacific Theater in World War II and later in Korea and Vietnam.

An informal local organization – retired soldiers like Jones and Leahr – would like to see a black veterans' memorial in Cincinnati. But even more, they want the military accomplishments of African-Americans taught in elementary and high schools. They are willing to speak to students and civic groups. They'd like to see teachers pressure textbook publishers to include them.

"People do not know we were there, that we fought and bled," said Rollon Thompson, 73, of Silverton, a retired Army major. "We are invisible in the history books. We weren't invisible when it came to dying."

The local veterans were moved to action by the omission of African-Americans from 50th anniversary celebrations of D-Day earlier this year.

More than 1,700 black troops landed on Normandy, according to U.S. Army data. One of them, James Madaris, 72, of Silverton, is a retired Army warrant officer.

They were not allowed to fight in com-

David McPheeters, a member of the Tuskegee Airmen from Cincinnati, attends a program to honor his unit. McPheeters, who had a distinguished 43-year military career, died in 2015 at age 93. Photograph by Joseph Fuqua II, courtesy of the Cincinnati Enquirer. (Photo published Sept. 27, 2009.)

## Blacks in the U.S. military
*November 11, 1994*

African-Americans were serving in the U.S. military long before Tuskegee Airmen took to the air in World War II:

More than 5,000 black troops participated in the Revolutionary War at places such as Valley Forge, Yorktown, and Bunker Hill.

Crispus Attucks, a runaway slave, was one of five African-Americans to die in the Boston Massacre in 1770.

Peter Salem, a former slave, was a hero at Bunker Hill for shooting the British officer who led the assault on the minutemen at Lexington.

Nearly 200,000 African-Americans fought in the Union Army during the Civil War. One of them, Robert Blake, won the Navy Medal of Honor for distinguished service aboard the USS *Marblehead*. There were 161 black regiments in the Union Army.

bat units, but African-Americans served as radio dispatchers and medics, in transportation units and in kitchens, performing all sorts of menial labor. Still other black soldiers manned helium-filled balloons as shields against enemy air attacks.

"The bullets," Madaris said, "didn't make no distinction about skin color."

The armed services were officially integrated in 1948 by an executive order of President Harry Truman. Some units remained segregated through Korea. But by the Vietnam War, all units were fully integrated, and several thousand blacks were among the 58,000 Americans who died in that war. The military recently revised its casualty figures, reporting that fewer than 7,000 African-Americans died in Vietnam, down from initial estimates of 13,000.

Black troops, known as Buffalo Soldiers, formed some of the most highly decorated regiments on the frontier, historians say. Still, white generals considered them inferior fighting men.

During World War I, the first two American troops decorated by France, Henry Johnson and Needham Roberts, were African-Americans.

In 1940, a veteran of the Spanish-American War, B. O. Davis Sr., became the first black general. His son, B. O. Davis Jr., commanded the Tuskegee Airmen.

It's another example, some black veterans say, of the military's attempt to diminish their contributions.

## Tuskegee Airmen: Inferior planes, "hidden history"

Even though the military was the first U.S. institution to integrate, it held fast to an Army study done in the 1920s that purported to claim that African-Americans were physically and mentally unqualified for combat. It allowed generals to restrict black GIs to menial jobs.

But in the late 1930s, as it grew increasingly clear that Americans were going to have to fight German and Japanese aggression, black newspapers such as the *Pittsburgh Courier* demanded that African-Americans be included in the rearmament effort.

So, as part of its Civilian Training Pilot Program, Franklin Roosevelt's administration made flight instruction available at selected black colleges. Tuskegee Institute in Alabama, founded by Booker T. Washington, was one of the schools selected.

Thanks to Eleanor Roosevelt, a prominent challenger of the military's racial attitudes, black pilots finally were being commissioned. They, however, still were a segregated unit, the 332nd Fighter Group. By war's end, it graduated 926 pilots, including John Leahr of Cincinnati.

He, like the rest of the unit, served in North Africa and Europe.

Flying propeller-driven planes, Tuskegee pilots escorted American bombers over Nazi-occupied Europe and never lost a bomber to enemy fire in 15,000 sorties, Leahr said.

Tuskegee pilots also shot down 409 Nazi planes in the process. On strafing missions, they took out almost 1,000 trucks and railroad cars and even sank a German destroyer, though their planes were equipped with nothing more than machine guns.

Still, to keep white and black pilots from fraternizing, the Army once bulldozed two runways out of the desert sand in North Africa. The strips were about 5 miles apart: One was for whites; the other for blacks.

"They hid our history," Leahr said of the U.S. Army.

The black pilots decided if the Army wouldn't tell the truth, they would. The Tuskegee Airmen organized nationally in 1972.

"The main objective was to inspire young blacks to consider the military," Leahr said.

The Army Air Corps, which split off from the U.S. Army in 1947 and became the U.S. Air Force, was the first branch of the service to integrate its ranks because of the success of the Tuskegee fliers.

In addition to word getting out in textbooks, Tuskegee veterans are hoping filmmaker George Lucas – creator of *Star Wars* – gets a feature film project about the Tuskegee Airmen off the ground before they die.

Lucas has tried unsuccessfully with five writers in four years to come up with a script to tell their story. The working title is Red Tails, in reference to the unit's nickname. Tuskegee pilots splashed red paint on the back ends of their planes.

## A hollow day

Despite some recognition and official historical redress, many black fighting men say Veterans Day still rings sadly hollow.

"We're not heroes, but we are patriots who love our country. We're not asking for anything more than white veterans have received," said retired Lt. Commander David McPheeters, 72, of Bethel.

He'll be in uniform today, in New Richmond, for the dedication of a Merchant Marine statue. McPheeters was a Merchant Marine late in his career, after serving in the Army in World War II and the Air Force in Korea.

The memories are hard.

It was white MPs telling black officers they "won't salute a nigger."

It was inferior equipment and out-of-the-way barracks and mess halls.

It was riding in open-air trucks through harsh weather while whites rode in covered trucks.

It was being expected to fight as team players when even recreational softball teams were segregated.

It was donating blood while knowing many white soldiers would still rather bleed to death than use it.

It was being treated with more dignity and acceptance in Germany and other foreign nations than in their own country.

"The hardest part of it all was not being allowed to live up to your full potential," said retired Lt. Col. Maurice Adams, 67, of Paddock Hills, who served in Korea and Vietnam. "They held you back when you were willing to give the ultimate sacrifice. That was the worst."

Until they came home – to Jim Crow.

Leahr recalled driving with three other black officers through Atlanta en route to a military function. The war had ended. He was a flight instructor at Tuskegee.

They were pulled over by a white police officer.

"The cop said, 'Where you niggers going all dressed up?'" Leahr said. "I said, 'We're United States military officers on official business.'"

The cop's face turned red. He started shaking, pulled out his pistol, cocked it and held it to Leahr's head.

"He said, 'OK, you nigger son-of-a-bitch, don't say a word about this to anyone, or you're dead,'" Leahr said. "He put the gun away and drove off. You have to remember, we were helpless because there were no federal anti-lynching laws yet."

He resigned his commission soon after and entered private business. No private airline, of course, would hire black pilots – even a Tuskegee Airman with a distinguished flying record.

"We really thought it would change when we came back," Leahr said. "We thought we would come back to a different country. We thought this [World War II] was the big fix. We were over there, willing to die. We thought people would finally get over the race issue. We were wrong. We're still wrong."

Black soldiers were fighting for a country they hoped their country would be, but still has not become.

# United in duty, separated by race

WWII comrades finally embrace

*March 7, 1998*

Because John Leahr is black and Herbert Heilbrun white, they didn't meet until last year.

Yet the paths of these two Cincinnati men crossed many times – most dramatically in the skies over Europe during World War II.

After graduating, respectively, from Withrow and Hughes high schools in 1938, they both worked at Wright Aeronautical in Evendale, but never met each other.

From there, the men took different routes into combat.

Mr. Leahr was relegated to a segregated unit, the 332nd Fighter Group, also known as the Tuskegee Airmen, which distinguished itself by flying escort for heavy bombers. He came home to a country that – because of his race – didn't recognize his military service and prevented him from flying for a commercial airline.

Mr. Heilbrun piloted a B-17 Flying Fortress, the workhorse of the Allied bombing campaign against Germany, and was a test pilot after the war at Wright Field (now Wright-Patterson Air Force Base) in Dayton, Ohio.

Friday morning, at an assembly at Sellman Middle School in Madeira, the men made their first public appearance together.

This time, Mr. Heilbrun was the escort on a friend's mission. Mr. Leahr, 77, of Kennedy Heights has worked tirelessly since 1975 to publicize his compatriots' accomplishments.

Piloting P-51 fighter planes, Tuskegee fliers flew 1,578 missions over Europe, shooting down or destroying hundreds of Nazi planes without losing a U.S. bomber in their escort. Mr. Leahr, a first lieutenant, was part of 72 combat missions.

"I'm not in a nameless grave in Germany or at the bottom of the Adriatic Sea because of this man and his fellow airmen," said Mr. Heilbrun, also 77, of Sycamore Township. "They flew hand-me-down planes but were excellent fliers. I thank God for them."

Mr. Leahr has made hundreds of appearances, primarily in schools and churches, on behalf of his unit. The Sellman School program was the first time a white pilot joined him.

"It's nice to have him say for himself what I've been saying all these years," Mr. Leahr said.

Sellman students saw a short film about the Tuskegee Airmen before Mr. Leahr and Mr. Heilbrun spoke, answered questions and displayed models of the planes they flew.

Steve Hurst, 12, a sixth-grader, learned this lesson: "Don't ever think someone is better than you," he said afterward.

The pilots met for the first time last summer at another Tuskegee program, where Mr. Heilbrun sought out Mr. Leahr and hugged him.

"I said, 'I've waited 52 years to put my arms around you and thank you for everything you did,'" said Mr. Heilbrun, a commercial real estate salesman.

The respect and admiration are mutual.

"Those guys had it rough," Mr. Leahr said of bomber pilots. "They dropped down (as low as 18,000 feet) over targets. A lot of those boys didn't make it."

The men recently compared mission logs and discovered that Mr. Leahr accompanied Mr. Heilbrun and crew at least twice. The first was December 16, 1944, for a raid on an oil refinery in Czechoslovakia. The next day, Mr. Leahr was among Tuskegee fliers escorting Mr. Heilbrun's and other B-17s to an oil refinery strike in Germany.

"You felt a lot better with the Tuskegee Airmen up there with you," said Mr. Heilbrun, a first lieutenant who flew 35 bombing missions.

Comrades in the sky, WWII pilots were segregated on the ground.

White fliers landed their planes on one airstrip. Tuskegee Airmen touched down on another runway, often several miles away.

Therein lies their lament. Segregation delayed a friendship more than five decades.

Since meeting, Mr. Leahr, a widower, has had dinner with Mr. Heilbrun and his wife. Mr. Heilbrun has attended meetings with Mr. Leahr and other local black military veterans fighting to get their contributions recorded as American history.

Retired Tuskegee Airmen mobilized nationally in 1972 to publicize their service and, as a result, the military service of other African-American troops. The group also included the late Coleman Young, former mayor of Detroit, which was home of the nationwide effort.

Mr. Leahr attended the national meeting and organized public speaking engagements for local black military veterans. He retired from CG&E and also worked as a stockbroker, at GE Aircraft Engines and in the catalog supply department at Wright-Patterson.

All he ever wanted to do was fly, but no airline would hire him, even though he was more qualified than many white pilots who landed jobs.

"It's a terrible thing that has happened to them," Mr. Heilbrun said of the Tuskegee Airmen. "I love John Leahr, and that's not a word I pass around lightly. I'm amazed that we can still have racism, bigotry and racial hatred in this country. I just know I wouldn't be here if not for their ability and dedication to duty. That's the statement I want to make."

# Over there

A Tristate veteran offers an oral history of the "war to end all wars"
*May 27, 1996*

On this Memorial Day, a holiday set aside to honor Americans who gave their lives for their country in military service, the *Enquirer* recorded the oral histories of the Tristate's few remaining World War I veterans.

There is a shortage of oral histories from Americans who fought these battles, historians say. Generals and admirals have been interviewed, but few GIs have had the opportunity to commit their memories and accomplishments for record.

After three months of research, the *Enquirer* found six veterans in the eight-county Tristate: Clayton Batchelor, 98, of Lawrenceburg, Ind.; Joseph Fussner, 100, of Mount Washington; Albert Harnist Sr., 96, of Fort Thomas; Lawrence Scaletta, 99, of Lawrenceburg; and James Everett Warren Sr., 101, of College Hill, are white. A sixth local WWI veteran, Morrison Blackwell of Fort Thomas, was interviewed February 8 but died March 12, a week before his 105th birthday.

Nationally, of the more than 4.7 million Americans in uniform for World War I, fewer than 12,000 are alive today. There were 74,800 WWI veterans alive in 1991. The average age of living WWI veterans is 97, and they range from 89 to 112.

## Morrison Blackwell, 104, Fort Thomas

Morrison Blackwell was born March 19, 1891 in Chatham, Va. He moved with his four sisters, two brothers, and parents, Stephen Peter and Lucy Blackwell, to Westwood in 1900.

Morrison Blackwell went into the fifth grade before leaving school to begin carrying a hod at a Westwood brickyard.

He enlisted August 4, 1918, in the U.S. Army and was a member of the 813th Pioneer Infantry, a segregated African-American unit. It was a detail assigned to the Army Corps of Engineers.

The U.S. military was not officially integrated until 1948, by an executive order of President Harry Truman. Some units remained segregated through Korea. But by the Vietnam war, all units were fully integrated.

Most of Private Blackwell's service was spent in France, where he dug graves in the American cemetery for the 18,000 American troops who died during the Meuse-Argonne offensive of September–November 1918. Almost 1 million Americans took part in the campaign.

Working conditions were miserable for African-American soldiers. Their work was considered "disciplinary action" for white troops who ran afoul in their units. Still, Mr. Blackwell never complained about his experiences nor never wavered in his sense of patriotism, his family says.

"Never, never, never did he say a bad word about it," his oldest son, Stephen P. Blackwell Sr., of Springdale, says. "He always said he had a job to do and did it.

"He was out there with shells exploding all around him and no protection for his ears. It cost him his hearing in one ear, but he never would file for extra benefits and would say, 'The good Lord blessed me with one good ear.'"

Private Blackwell was discharged July 21, 1919, and returned home.

He married the former Ada Lear in 1923. She died in 1990. The couple lived in the West End, Avondale, Walnut Hills, and Roselawn. He worked for General Motors from 1933 until his retirement in 1969.

Mr. Blackwell spent decades without receiving the medals he was due. He finally received the World War I Victory Medal with Battle Clasp and Bronze Victory Button in 1988.

Of their 10 children, eight are still living. He had 26 grandchildren, 30 great-grandchildren, and five great-great grandchildren. On February 8, he sat for an interview with the *Enquirer* at the Veteran Affairs Nursing Home in Fort Thomas, where he had moved in 1990. Even with the help of his daughter, Pearl Lewis, of Forest Park, Mr. Blackwell was able to answer only one question:

What did he remember about his time in the service?

"Our boys was getting hit from all sides," he said. "For 75 miles, they were hitting us. I was on guard duty out in the woods, and there would be trains coming through with wounded soldiers. I got down in there and dug graves for the boys."

He also spoke of his voyage to Europe, when his troop ship was struck by a torpedo fired from a German submarine.

"We were lucky that it hit above the water line, or else we wouldn't have made it," he said.

Shortly after this interview, he became ill with pneumonia and could not recover. Mr. Blackwell died March 12, a week before his 105th birthday.

❖──◆──❖

# "We had to be perfect"

## WWII service provided no racial sanctuary for Cincinnati women, but the experience paid off

*May 26, 1997*

Mary Williams was looking for a way out of the slum.

Mary Rozier was looking for something to do while her husband served in the U.S. Navy.

The former West End women weren't looking to make history or a civil rights statement, but they did. During World War II, they were part of the first and only group of 855 African-American women to serve overseas.

The 6888th Central Postal Directory Battalion of the Women's Army Corps (WAC) functioned as the post office for the U.S. Army and Army Air Corps in Europe.

Battalion members served in Birmingham, England, and Paris and Rouen, France, from February through November 1945. That was three years before an executive order by President Truman desegregated the armed forces.

Of the half-dozen Tristate women who served in the 6888th, Mrs. Williams and Mrs. Rozier are the only ones still living in the area, they say. (Two others are longtime residents of Anchorage, Alaska, and New York.)

They were aware of their unique position but didn't see themselves as pioneers. Simply doing a good job in harm's way, they hoped, would be enough to close some of the distance between the races back home.

Mrs. Rozier, 79, of Hyde Park is proud of her military service.

"Sorting the mail seemed like a small thing, but it was needed," she says. "But I wonder more now than before, 'How much good did it really do?' You thought you would come home and finally be a first-class citizen. But the longer you live, the more you realize things are not much different."

In the early years of World War II, servicewomen were part of a separate organization – the Women's Auxiliary Army Corps (WAAC) – which was established in May 1942, six months after the United States entered the war.

A year after it was founded, the WAAC became part of the Army of the United States, and its name was shortened to WAC.

During WWII, more than 17,000 WACs served overseas. The members of the 6888th were the only African-American WACs to leave the country.

Plans originally called for black WAC units to be shipped to Europe as early as 1942, but War Department officials decided they would not be sent to Europe or the Pacific until they were a "necessity."

With civil rights organizations and black newspapers applying pressure, the War Department decided a black WAC unit was needed in Europe to run the post office – but not before declaring that "Negro" women were not filling any existing military jobs.

In December 1944, black WACs were asked if they wanted to serve overseas. Surprisingly, many declined, says Mrs. Rozier, who was working in medical records at Fort Atterbury in Indianapolis.

"I wanted to go over," she says. "I wanted the adventure. But, mainly, I wanted to serve my country."

She went to Fort Oglethorpe, Ga., for overseas training. It was there Mrs. Rozier met Mary Daniels (Williams), another Cincinnatian and volunteer who had been stationed as a cook at Fort Leonard Wood, Missouri.

"I didn't want to be a cook, so as soon as I could, I got out of that," says Mrs. Williams, 76, of Kennedy Heights.

## Shouldering a burden

Training was difficult at Fort Oglethorpe.

"We were given gas masks. We had to go through the gas chamber," Mrs. Rozier says. "We had to crawl under barbed wire. We had to climb the cargo netting."

African-American WACs were put up in segregated living quarters. They didn't know whether conditions were better or worse than they were for white women, because the black women never saw the other side of the camp.

After three weeks of training, the 6888th was sent to New York. From there, the black WACs would be sent to Europe. They arrived in Scotland by ship in early February 1945.

Two years later, Jackie Robinson would break the color barrier in Major League Baseball. For the first few years, he would carry the weight of his race and couldn't fight back.

The 6888th shouldered the same burden.

"If any of us made the tiniest mistake, it would go against the whole 6888th and all black women and black people," Mrs. Williams says. "We had to be perfect. There could be no fighting. No one ever fell down drunk. Our [black] officers never raised their voices with us."

The African-American women received proper and warm greetings from Europeans. Mrs. Rozier recalls a crowd greeting them in Birmingham, where they would set up the post office.

"We were a curiosity," she says. "We were invited to teas and dinners by the English, and when we got to France, it was the same thing. Our officers encouraged us to do this. We would be in uniform and representing the 6888th. People were very kind to us and interested in what life was like for us, as Negroes, back home. They knew about the racism."

But foreign soil provided no sanctuary from racial taunts.

"I was walking down a street in France when I came upon an American serviceman walking with a French woman," Mrs. Rozier says. "He said to this woman, 'Now say hello to the blackie,' which she did. I could not say anything. I just walked on quietly."

But for every taunt, there were dozens of appreciative comments from Europeans.

"I was waiting with some other girls to cross a street in Belgium, and a Belgian man said to us, 'You look like a bouquet of beautiful flowers. Look at all of those beautiful colors,'" Mrs. Rozier says.

## Distinguished service

Operated previously by enlisted men and civilians, the postal directory in Birmingham was in chaos. There was a warehouse filled with 3 million backlogged parcels.

One room was filled with birthday and Christmas packages of spoiled cakes and cookies. Running around were rats as large as cats. Wearing water-repellent clothing and boots, the women opened the packages, discarded the rotten food and repackaged and redirected whatever was salvageable.

The 6888th worked two shifts, of eight hours, each day. In sixteen hours, they processed an average of 130,000 pieces of mail.

"In three months, we got the place cleaned out," Mrs. Williams says. "A lot of the mail came back from the front stamped 'Killed in Action.' You could see whenever one of us saw that . . . you couldn't help but get a little choked up. Sometimes, we'd write little notes on the back of envelopes, like 'Keep up the great work. We're proud of you.' You see, we were all in this together."

The 6888th broke previous U.S. Army records for redirecting mail, said high-ranking officials in the European Theater of Operations: "No particular difficulties were reported in discipline and administration. The unit was congratulated by the theater on its 'exceptionally fine' special services program. Its observance of military courtesies was pronounced exemplary, as were grooming and appearance by members and the maintenance of quarters."

That review of the 6888th's performance is part of a 1996 book about the battalion, *To Serve My Country, To Serve My Race*, by Brenda L. Moore (New York University Press). Still, there was no official Army citation.

The battalion also worked in Rouen and Paris before shipping home in November 1945.

In Rouen, they saw where, in 1431, Joan of Arc was burned at the stake. They marched in a Joan of Arc day parade and visited the sites of Paris.

"I really wanted to go over," Mrs. Rozier says, "and I really wanted to come home."

## Racism at home

Mrs. Rozier thought she would return to a different country – a country that could, at last, see past skin color. She had worked with the Cincinnati chapter of the National Association for the Advancement of Colored People (NAACP) throughout the 1930s.

Shortly after she was reunited with her husband, who had served in the Navy in the Pacific, Mrs. Rozier was denied admission to a Cincinnati business college because of her race.

"I was very disgusted," she says, "but I didn't let it stop me."

She used her Army training in medical records to land a job as a medical secretary at the former General Hospital (now University Hospital). She and another woman opened a secretarial service and ran it from 1948 through 1959. Then she went to work for the local office of the National Labor Relations Board before retiring in 1976.

## A way out

Mrs. Williams also used her military service to her advantage. The GI Bill paid for her education at the University of Cincinnati, where she earned an undergraduate degree in sociology and a master's degree in social work.

She first went to work in the mailroom of the Hamilton County Department of Human Services and gained the support of her supervisors to pursue her education.

"I was different," says Mrs. Williams, widowed in 1996 after 41 years of marriage. "I had to get out of the West End. I knew I would go no place there. I used the Army as a step out. I fought my way out. G.E.D. Night school. Whatever it took. I brought my brothers and sisters with me. I was tough. I told them they had to get an education. A lot of people were content to stay there. I wasn't."

Mrs. Williams also lifted others. After earning her master's degree, she was promoted to social caseworker. That was her position when she retired in 1986. Many of her clients through the years were members of West End families.

"They would tell me, 'I can't do this. I can't get out,' " Mrs. Williams says. "I said, 'Yes you can. I did. I used to live right over there on Wade Street. The slums didn't get any deeper than that in the Depression."

Military service was but a chapter in her life, and not the central chapter at that. But, Mrs. Williams says, military service made her stronger than she already was.

"I learned a great deal about self-discipline and commitment," she says. "I could never accept that there wasn't a way out. The Army gave me a way out."

# Last of a storied cavalry fights for recognition

All-black unit of Buffalo Soldiers served in WWII after a long history

*February 9, 2000*

In 1943, Lorenzo Denson was one of about two dozen men from Cincinnati drafted to serve in an all-black cavalry unit on the Mexican border.

"The only horse I'd ever seen was the milkman's horse on Seventh Street," he said.

Shortages of men in segregated black infantry units took Mr. Denson and other Cincinnatians overseas – without their horses – to North Africa, Iran and Italy. They worked as everything from paratroopers to combat engineers. Mr. Denson was a firefighter at an airfield.

"We did our job," he said. "We did what we were told."

These Tristate men also found their way into history as the last of the Buffalo Soldiers, members of the renowned all-black cavalry units formed during the Indian wars. The U.S. Army disbanded all horseback cavalry units in 1944.

This month – Black History Month – finds Cincinnati's Buffalo Soldiers on a final ride. Like the Tuskegee Airmen and other groups of black veterans before them, the Buffalo Soldiers are trying to win recognition for contributions that they say have been overlooked for more than fifty years.

Mr. Denson, now 79, retired and living in Columbia Township, will be among a group of nine living World War II-era Buffalo Soldiers scheduled to make its first Tristate appearance Thursday at the public library in Corryville.

"We helped to win World War II," said Linwood Greene Jr., 79, of Silverton, another Buffalo Soldier.

At least 14 of Cincinnati's World War II Buffalo Soldiers are dead – none was killed in action – and chances are this piece of Tristate history would have faded away if not for George Hicks III. A retired Army veteran who's a fan of the all-black cavalry units, Mr. Hicks moved from Washington, D.C., to the Tristate a couple of years ago and immediately organized the Cincinnati-based Heartland Chapter of the Ninth and Tenth Horse Cavalry Association.

"These men are American heroes," said Mr. Hicks, 50.

There are 20 domestic chapters of the Ninth and Tenth Association and one in Germany. About 650 black cavalry veterans from World War II are still living.

"We owe a lot to George," said Mr. Denson, who appeared at the Buffalo Soldiers booth at the Indiana Black Expo in July in Indianapolis. Public reaction there added urgency to the black troopers' mission.

People, black and white alike, didn't know who they were. "They thought we were actors," Mr. Denson said.

The men sported black hats with crossed cavalry swords and the No. 10 affixed to the front. With blue shirts, they wore the cavalry's standard yellow neckerchief.

"Once people found out who we were and what we did, they wanted to have their pictures taken with us," Mr. Denson said.

William Snow, 77, of New Burlington will appear at the library with Mr. Denson and at least three other men.

"Overseas, we did everything we were instructed to do," said Mr. Snow, a Walnut Hills native and retired postal worker. "I was proud to be in the cavalry. I am proud to be part of the history."

The black cavalry dates to post–Civil War North America. Its first recruits in 1866 were former slaves who patrolled the frontier from Texas to Montana. They guarded settlers and protected wagon trains.

Buffalo Soldiers earned respect, and their nickname, from the Cheyenne, Arapahoe, Kiowa, Comanche, and Apache Indians they sometimes fought, a story captured in the song "Buffalo Soldier" by the late reggae icon Bob Marley. Indians said black soldiers' hair resembled buffalo fur.

Four all-black regiments, stationed throughout the western territories, were known as some of the fiercest fighters of the Indian wars.

They were among Theodore Roosevelt's Rough Riders in Cuba during the Spanish-American War and crossed into Mexico in 1916 under Gen. John J. Pershing.

During World War II, fearing a Japanese land invasion through Mexico's Baja Peninsula, the government placed cavalry units, first white, then black, along the rugged border terrain. Armed units on horseback protected dams, power stations, and rail lines important to San Diego's war industries.

Black troopers from Cincinnati were sworn in at Fort Thomas and sent to train at Camp Lockett near San Diego.

"We were trained in infantry and how to be infantry on horseback," Mr. Denson said. "When you were assigned a horse, you were instructed to treat this animal like it was your best friend."

African-Americans could not rise beyond the rank of sergeant, so all commanding officers were white.

"They treated black troopers very well," Mr. Denson said.

Patrolling the border is how Buffalo Soldiers figured they would close out the war. But within a year of arriving in California, the cavalry troopers were put on alert to go overseas. They were put aboard a segregated train for a two-day ride to Newport News, Virginia.

A stop in Houston showed the men that many of their white countrymen wouldn't accept them, even though the troopers would put their lives on the line for them.

"We were in cramped quarters on the train, and the colonel got us out and had us marching up and down the platform to stretch our legs," said Mr. Greene, the Madisonville native who lives in Silverton.

"The mayor of Houston heard we were there, and he came out and said, 'Get them niggers back on the train.' And that's exactly what he said. So the colonel has us go back to a train car and assemble our .50-caliber machine guns. We went back out and marched until it was time to switch trains."

Many historians consider Buffalo Soldiers unsung heroes, troopers who did jobs a lot of white soldiers didn't want to.

"Blacks were second-class citizens in the military, and blacks were second-class citizens in society," said Pat O'Brien, a history professor and twentieth-century America expert at Emporia State University in Emporia, Kansas.

Emporia is near Junction City, Kansas, home of the Ninth and Tenth Cavalry Association, which is raising money to build a Buffalo Soldiers memorial there.

"In many ways, World War II – and the performance of the black soldiers – provided the context for the civil rights movement," Mr. O'Brien said. "It readily exposed the paradox – how could you fight against one thing overseas and promote it at home."

Mr. Greene, who joined the combat engineers and worked as a welder, landed at Normandy on D-Day. He was wounded six days later when the Jeep in which he was riding ran over a mine.

He took shrapnel in the head, hand, and stomach. The next fourteen days were a blur. He received the Purple Heart and an honorable discharge at a Cleveland hospital on August 4, 1945.

Mr. Greene came home to Cincinnati and went to work as a railway mail clerk. He experienced more racism at home than he did abroad.

"I was in the same boxcars sorting the same mail, and they wouldn't let me join the union," he said.

Paul Greene, his son, was a U.S. Marine killed in Vietnam in 1966. Paul Greene was 19.

"I'm proud of my son's service to his country," Linwood Greene Jr. said slowly. "I'm proud of my service to my country."

Mr. Snow, who also received an honorable discharge, didn't think he would live to see the United States again.

"I had as much fun as I could because I thought I would be gone at any minute," he said. "God was with me. That's how I didn't get hurt."

Mr. Denson is most proud of his honorable discharge, dated November 6, 1945. He also received the American Theater Ribbon, Good Conduct Medal, and Victory Medal.

"A lot of things happen in the service, and they had a lot of ways of busting you down," said Mr. Denson, who retired in 1981 from Cincinnati Public Schools as a plant operator.

Not far behind are his feelings for his unit.

"I liked the outfit. I liked the horses. I learned a lot," he said. "We didn't come in until the tail end, but we did a good job. No, we weren't actors. We were the real thing."

# Clinging to a glimmer of hope

After 30 years, a Vietnam MIA's mother struggles with loss and doubt

*Editor's note: This month marks the 25th anniversary of the fall of Saigon and the end of the war in Vietnam. More than 58,000 U.S. troops died in the war, and more than 2,000 remain missing in action.*

*April 2, 2000*

Mary Moore's son has been missing in action in Vietnam since 1969. She asks herself the same question nearly every day: Would I rather know if Greg were dead?

She began asking the question shortly after two men came to her Clifton apartment that October.

They told her that Sgt. Raymond Gregory Moore's helicopter had sunk in a river in South Vietnam. He was 20.

The men told Ms. Moore that two soldiers survived the crash. The remains of another were recovered. Five men, including Sgt. Moore, were unaccounted for.

"It's a feeling I can hardly describe," Ms. Moore said last week, more than thirty years after that visit. She last saw her son when he was 19, before he shipped out.

Casualties of war aren't found only on the battlefield. For every one of the 2,029 servicemen still missing in Southeast Asia – twelve from Greater Cincinnati – there are mothers and fathers and siblings and wives and children who focus on slivers of light in the darkness. They face countless questions but don't find many answers.

They realize they probably won't see their loved ones again but can't fully grieve. Uncertainty is enemy and friend.

Once outgoing, Ms. Moore has closed up emotionally. She suffers anxiety-related health problems. In March, she was hospitalized for gallstones.

Many nights are sleepless. Other nights, she wakes up at 4 in the morning, rolls over, sees a portrait of Greg and says hello to him.

"I always wake up thinking about him," she said.

Her two surviving sons lost direction in their lives because of what happened to their brother, Ms. Moore said. They live out of town. Her daughter has a house in Avondale.

Ms. Moore is wounded every time her hopes rise and fall, as they did last month. Defense Secretary William Cohen visited Vietnam to call attention to a joint U.S.–Vietnamese effort to recover and bring home remains of American servicemen.

What if they find Greg?

Today is Greg Moore's fifty-first birthday.

Ms. Moore doesn't celebrate, other than sometimes lying awake in bed for a few extra minutes to think about him.

She pictures him as middle-school aged – not middle-aged – and the family lives on Elmore Street in Northside. Greg has chickens and ducks in the yard. He runs through the forest, shooting targets (never animals) with a pellet gun. He would be a sharpshooter in the Army. He loved the military. He volunteered shortly after his 1968 graduation from Courter Tech High School. He figured he'd be drafted.

He goes to school. Mrs. Moore opens the pantry door and hears a hissing sound coming from a shoebox. There's a snake inside. Greg put it there. He comes home after school.

"Don't worry, Ma," he says. "It won't hurt you."

Greg has an aquarium in his room. There's one in the front room, too. Mother and son together take care of the fish.

Weeks after learning her son is missing, Ms. Moore can't face the aquariums alone and gets rid of them.

It seems that every day she allows herself to answer a question: What would he be like if he had come home?

"I wonder how he'd have matured," she said. "I wonder how he would be as a father. He's a very compassionate person. He would be career military or be working with animals."

Ms. Moore didn't have the luxury to mourn. She had three other children.

She had been separated from her husband when Greg was 4 and brought up four children as a single parent. (Raymond Moore, her former husband, died in 1990.)

All three siblings were affected when their brother was declared missing. Greg had been the glue.

"He was the man of the house," Ms. Moore said. "Greg was protective of me. He would go to the bank with me. I could send him to pay the telephone and gas and electric bill."

Her other children, especially the boys, "got real moody," Ms. Moore said.

"One boy tried to be macho for my benefit, but he was hurting," Ms. Moore said. "He'd say, 'Mom, remember when Greg did this.' He just stopped caring about everything when Greg didn't come back. Greg could keep the other boys in line. They all went into their shell."

Ms. Moore would occasionally retreat to her room.

If the door was cracked, one of the children would call, "Ma, are you OK?"

"It was very hard on all of us," she said. "I know they had their moments, but they didn't want me to see."

Some images were too horrific to think about, but they would come nonetheless. What if he survived the crash and was captured? What if he's being tortured?

During the day, Ms. Moore worked at local hospitals as a nurse's aide. Then she worked at night sewing shirts in a factory. Work kept her mind occupied.

Then she hurt her back and had to retire.

Helen Wanda Moore, who's 48, keeps an eye on her mother. So, too, does Ms. Moore's daughter, Cessalea, 12.

"I think the government gave my mother a lot of false hope," Wanda Moore said.

The Army told her mother that someone survived the helicopter crash and walked away. Army investigators said they found footprints, size 9, the size Greg wore, in the mud.

"It does something to your life," Wanda Moore said.

Mary Moore baby-sat Cessalea before she started school.

She still helps out her daughter by keeping track of the girl after school these days.

"She and Wanda pull me out," Ms. Moore said.

Almost a year to the day her son came up missing, Ms. Moore received a telegram from the Army.

Sgt. Raymond Gregory Moore of Cincinnati is declared "killed, body not recovered," it read.

A casualty officer from the Army recruiting station in Bond Hill paid her a visit.

"They have to finalize it," Ms. Moore said of the Army.

A mother can't.

She held a memorial service – not a funeral; Greg Moore has never had a funeral – at First Baptist Church in Cumminsville. People sang and prayed for Greg's safety and return home.

"I've never fully accepted that he is dead."

Still, Ms. Moore went to court in 1972 to challenge the $10,000 death benefit she had been paid by the government.

Between the time of her son's 1969 disappearance and the declaration of death in 1970, the Department of Veterans Affairs increased the benefit to $15,000. Ms. Moore said she was due the higher amount because her son, according to the military, died in October 1970.

She won, and her case set a legal precedent that won the additional $5,000 for another dozen families in the same situation.

There are constant reminders that Greg is missing and presumed dead.

Every year since 1970, Ms. Moore has received a Christmas greeting from the White House.

That's six presidents. Nixon, Ford, Carter, Reagan, Bush, and Clinton. The signature is stamped. The condolence is the same.

"Concerning your loss, we sympathize with you. You are in our prayers."

In March, the Army sent her what's called a "family member update" saying that her son's status had not changed. They're sent to MIA families from the Cold War, Korea, and Vietnam.

The updates used to come every few months. Now they come every year or so.

"They said he was still dead and they hadn't found him," Ms. Moore said.

Then there are news events.

On March 24, the remains of Marine Pfc. John Morris Smith, a World War II MIA, were returned to his family in Lincoln Heights.

Pfc. Smith disappeared July 14, 1945, as Americans fought Japanese on Okinawa during World War II. The remains of Pfc. Smith and two other Marines were found in a cave near the city of Nago in 1998.

"In some ways, I find myself being a little jealous," Ms. Moore said. "But if the Army can't tell me anything positive about my son, then I'm not jealous. I'm happy for that family. She can have some closure and peace."

But then comes the question and images of rifle shots and an honor guard, of a lone bugler playing taps, of pressed khaki uniforms and precise salutes, of a bright red-white-and-blue flag adorning a casket.

Would I like to have Greg back to bury him?

Ms. Moore leans on God. She doesn't blame him.

She is a member of New Jerusalem Baptist Church, Carthage, and is part of a women's prayer group led by Barbara Lynch, wife of pastor the Rev. Damon Lynch Jr.

Prayer soothes Ms. Moore's soul and mind.

"You can see the pain she's in. It has been kind of a nightmare, having hope and then doubt," Mrs. Lynch said.

"We pray for her. We pray for her son."

Marva Coffey is another church member and close friend of Ms. Moore's.

"We try to talk just about every day," said Ms. Coffey, 59, of Forest Park.

And she prays the same prayer for her friend.

"I'm praying for the day she can put it behind her and know where he is, that he's in God's hand."

Ms. Moore is not angry at God, even though she has lived with one dreadful question for 30 years.

Is Greg dead?

"I believe your life expectancy is set out before you," she said. "I ask God to watch over him. I know he will. If Greg's in heaven, he's with God. I know that.

"I'm still grateful for the other kids I have."

On October 9, 1969, Sgt. Moore was part of a rescue team aboard an extraction helicopter above a minefield in eastern Long Khanh Province, South Vietnam.

One of the rotor blades struck a tree, causing the helicopter to lose altitude. The pilot headed west down a river valley in an attempt to regain lift. The aircraft struck 15 to 20 feet of water and sank in the Song Dong Nai River in less than 10 seconds.

That night, some 8,700 miles away, Ms. Moore had a vision. It was different from dreams she had had when she was holding Greg's hand and he was wearing a little white sunsuit.

"I was sleeping that night, and I woke up when I heard him call my name, 'Mama,'" she said.

"He was standing in the doorway to my room and he was wearing muddy fatigues. He called my name, 'Mama.' I sat up in bed and moved closer to him. But the closer I got to him, the more he faded out until he was gone."

What remains today are questions, one in particular: Would I rather know if Greg were dead?

"A mother never gives up hope," she said. "I wish and hope and pray that, if he is dead, that it was quick and he didn't lay there suffering. But I can't accept that he is dead. People tell me to let it go. I don't express that much around certain people.

"I can't give up hope. If I accepted that he was dead, that would help me find closure, but it would knock out the glimmer of hope that he's still alive. You wish you had closure. But you still want the hope, the opening, the glimmer that you'll see your son alive again."

## "Pardon my tears:" Letter to a lost son

The *Enquirer* asked Mary Moore, 71, to write a letter to her son, Sgt. Raymond "Greg" Moore, who has been missing in action in Vietnam since Oct. 9, 1969. Today is his fifty-first birthday.

> April 2, 2000
> My Dearest Greg,
> I'm writing you this letter to let you know how much I love and miss you. The part of my heart that belongs to you is very sad and lonely. I know you wouldn't want me to feel this way, but I'm your mother and I have the right to do so.
> No one or no thing can fill this empty void in my life but you, so it will be there forever. Pardon my tears, but my heart is so full at this very moment that I can't stop the tears from running down my cheeks, falling off my chin. When I look at your handsome picture, so young and only 19 years of age, never to see you again. It's been 31 years. Yes, I have good memories and I thank God for you. I pray for your safe keeping in heaven with him.
> I know you are with me in spirit and love.
> I'll always love you, my son.
>
> Love,
> Forever yours,
> Mom.

Wendell P. Dabney published black newspapers *Ohio Enterprise* (1902–1907) and *The Union* (1907–1952), and in 1926 released the book *Cincinnati's Colored Citizens*, an ambitious project that provided portraits of the city's influential African-Americans and thumbnail sketches of black institutions. Photograph from the *Cincinnati Enquirer* archives. (Introduction, "Into the Marvelous Light.")

Elaine Nelson of Bond Hill and John Bruggeman of Pleasant Ridge greet during the sign of peace at St. Agnes Catholic Church in Bond Hill in 1993. Photograph by Kevin Miyazaki, courtesy of the *Cincinnati Enquirer*. (Introduction, "Into the Marvelous Light.")

Margaret "Nanny" Andrews, 85 in this 1998 photograph, sits in the parlor of her Avondale home with granddaughters Prashia Andrews, 7, left, and Tarma Franklin, 16, top, and a neighbor whom Nanny Andrews has watched for three years, Taylor Larkin, 8. She holds one of her favorite dolls, whom she named Rebecca. Photograph by Dick Swaim, courtesy of the *Cincinnati Enquirer*. (Chapter 4, "The children came first," published Feb. 26, 1998.)

Dr. Chester Pryor stands as Ohio's first certified black ophthalmologist (1960) and Cincinnati's first (1962). He had a practice in Mount Auburn and was named a Great Living Cincinnatian in 2017. Photograph by Craig Ruttle, courtesy of the *Cincinnati Enquirer*. (Chapter 4, "Eye on life lessons," published Feb. 10, 1998.)

Jennie Davis Porter, who died in 1936, is remembered as a pioneering black educator in Cincinnati. Photograph courtesy of *The Cincinnati Enquirer*. (Chapter 4, "Beacon for better education," published Feb. 7, 1997.)

The name Damon Lynch is synonymous with civil rights and the black church for the past 50 years in Cincinnati. Three men share the name: Damon IV (left), the Rev. Damon Jr., and the Rev. Damon III. Photograph by Cara Owsley, courtesy of *The Cincinnati Enquirer*. (Chapter 9, "What's in a name?" published Feb. 20, 2016.)

Carrie Lucas says she started to endure racial taunts at age 14 from fellow black students who equated her academic success with a desire to be "white." Photograph by Steven M. Herppich, courtesy of the *Cincinnati Enquirer*. (Chapter 5, "For some black students, failing is safer," published May 28, 1998.)

Kitalena Mason is a graduate of Miami University in Oxford, Ohio, a predominantly white school. Her Withrow High School classmates often asked their class valedictorian why she wanted to attend "a white college." Photograph by Steven M. Herppich, courtesy of the *Cincinnati Enquirer*. (Chapter 5, "For some black students, failing is safer," published May 28, 1998.)

Siri Imani is a former high school basketball star who has made a name for her searing, evocative spoken word poetry. Photograph by Sam Greene, courtesy of the *Cincinnati Enquirer*. (Chapter 5, "Spoken word poets," published July 29, 2016.)

Tywon Thomas was 3 months old in April 2001, when the police shooting death of his unarmed father, Timothy Thomas, brought about reforms in Cincinnati Police Department procedures. Photograph by Carrie Cochran, courtesy of the *Cincinnati Enquirer*. (Chapter 5, "Being Timothy Thomas's son," published Dec. 22, 2016.)

Mary Rozier recalls her service in Europe during World War II as part of an all-black, all-female postal battalion. Photograph by Tony Jones, courtesy of the *Cincinnati Enquirer*. (Chapter 6, "'We had to be perfect,'" published May 26, 1997.)

Mary Moore holds a portrait of her son, Sgt. Gregory Moore, which includes a newspaper clipping from 1969 about how he had been declared missing in action in Vietnam. Photograph by Glenn Hartong, courtesy of the *Cincinnati Enquirer*. (Chapter 6, "Clinging to a glimmer of hope," published April 2, 2000.)

Morrison Blackwell enlisted in the U.S. Army in 1918 and served in an all-black unit that dug graves for white servicemen in U.S. cemeteries in Europe. Photography courtesy of the Blackwell family. (Chapter 6, "Over there," published May 27, 1996.)

Tuskegee Airman John Leahr and bomber pilot Herbert Heilbrun make an appearance at an elementary school and discuss how they served in World War II but were kept apart by racial segregation. Photograph by Tony Jones, courtesy of the *Cincinnati Enquirer*. (Chapter 6, "United in duty, separated by race," published March 7, 1998.)

Jerome Goodwin, far left, cuts the hair of Al Lamb of Fairfield at Goodwin's II in Woodlawn. Fellow barbers Leon Williams and Jewell Jett take care of their customers. Photography by Craig Ruttle, courtesy of the *Cincinnati Enquirer*. (Chapter 7, "The barbershop: A haven for black men," published Jan. 11, 1999.)

Milton Hinton, a retired University of Cincinnati vice provost for minority affairs, was elected to his first of two terms as Cincinnati NAACP branch president in 1994. Photograph by Ernest Coleman, courtesy of the *Cincinnati Enquirer*. (Chapter 8, "Hinton invigorates NAACP" published May 23, 1995.)

Cincinnati NAACP executive committee member Nicole Taylor and her son, Jordan Stephens, 9. "He is going to be a young black man and looked at as a threat." Photograph by Sam Greene, courtesy of the *Cincinnati Enquirer*. (Chapter 8, "'These are no ordinary times,'" published July 10, 2016.)

DJ McCollum, burned over 85 percent of his body as an infant, is among the four of more than 70 foster children that Pat McCollum has adopted. Photograph by Cara Owsley, courtesy of the *Cincinnati Enquirer*. (Chapter 9, "Then she saw the love in DJ's eyes," published June 8, 2012.)

Sonny Webb: the $210 he spent to attend the Million Man March was the best money he ever spent. Photograph from the *Cincinnati Enquirer* archives by Jym Wilson, Gannett News Service. (Chapter 10, "Local men add their voices to today's 'Million' in Washington, D.C.," published Oct. 16, 1995.)

The Rev. Fred Shuttlesworth, who won the civil rights battle of Birmingham, Alabama, stands outside of his Cincinnati church, Greater New Light Baptist. Photograph by Glenn Hartong, courtesy of the *Cincinnati Enquirer*. (Chapter 11, "In the name of civil rights," published Jan. 20, 1997.)

Retired federal judge Nathaniel Jones perseveres through the death of his wife, Lillian, in November 2011 to complete his autobiography. Photograph by Liz Dufour, courtesy of the Cincinnati Enquirer. (Chapter 11, "Book helps Judge Jones cope with wife's death," published Jan. 7, 2012.

After the death of her NFL-player son, Chris Henry, Carolyn Henry Glaspy became the voice of organ donation nationwide. Photograph by Michael Keating, courtesy of the *Cincinnati Enquirer*. (Chapter 12, "She lost a son but found a cause," published Sept. 25, 2011.)

Former Cincinnati Reds player Eddie Milner went through rehab multiple times to treat a cocaine addiction. Photograph by Saed Hindash, courtesy of the *Cincinnati Enquirer*. (Chapter 13, "Faith helps former Reds outfielder Eddie Milner fight his addiction," published Sept. 10, 1998.)

Vince Ward spoke at funerals for 18 of his former Avondale Indians youth baseball players in a 10-year period. Photograph by Amanda Rossmann, courtesy of the *Cincinnati Enquirer*. (Chapter 13, "His ongoing quest? Teach them how to live," published May 5, 2013.)

Dominic Duren helps former prisoners adjust to life in society after he was incarcerated for 12 years. Photograph by Patrick Reddy, courtesy of the *Cincinnati Enquirer*. (Chapter 16, "Returning citizen 'perfect for job,'" published Feb. 21, 2015.)

Iris Roley of the Cincinnati Black United Front has worked to improve police-community relations for 20 years. Photograph by Carrie Cochran, courtesy of the *Cincinnati Enquirer*. (Chapter 17, "Black community holds fast to the Collaborative Agreement," published Nov. 17, 2017.)

The Rev. Clarence Wallace was a church pastor for 34 years and a humble community leader in one of Cincinnati's most impoverished neighborhoods. Photograph by Gary Landers, courtesy of the *Cincinnati Enquirer*. (Chapter 18, "Rev. Clarence Wallace, 63, led Avondale's Carmel Presbyterian," published Dec. 19, 2012.)

# CHAPTER 7

# INSTITUTIONS

*I figured out quickly that if I wanted to work the urban affairs beat that I'd better get to know black pastors and be in the black church. And once in the church, it was a short distance to the black barbershop, newspaper, and radio station. That time in the black church made me realize how the larger Christian church – and many white Christians, especially today – failed to make good on common ground to close our racial gap. Racism seems to be stronger than a shared faith in Jesus.*

# The *Cincinnati Herald* at 40

An African-American paper chronicles different world

*September 9, 1995*

A steady rain matted the garbage littering the street in front of the *Cincinnati Herald* offices Friday.

Publisher William Spillers called the Cincinnati Sanitation Department a couple of times during the day. But by 4:30 p.m., no one had come to Walnut Hills to clean up the mess that had dropped from a garbage truck earlier that morning.

"Do you think they'd leave it go if it was in front of the *Enquirer*?" Spillers asked. "No way. It's just different worlds. We live it every day. You can't understand unless you live it. That's why we're here."

The *Herald* has been documenting life in Cincinnati's black communities for 40 years. A banquet will celebrate that anniversary tonight at the Albert B. Sabin Convention Center.

"Our niche is to try to help the black community understand what's happening here and how all these changes [in public policy] affect us," said Spillers, who is running for a seat on the Cincinnati Board of Education at the request of the teachers' union.

The *Herald*, one of six black newspapers in Ohio and 184 nationally, has a paid weekly circulation of 25,000. It has been the primary black newspaper in Cincinnati since 1955, when it was founded by Gerald Porter, a newspaper publisher from Dayton, Ohio.

In its early years, the *Herald* played an important role in building support for the state's first equal employment opportunity legislation, said former Cincinnati Mayor Theodore Berry Sr.

"At the time the *Herald* started, we had two national Negro newspapers, the *Chicago Defender* and the *Pittsburgh Courier*, that gave us perspective on national issues and events in other urban communities," Berry said Friday. "The *Herald* gave us the African-American perspective on local issues. It filled a need and continues to perform a great service."

When Porter died in a car accident in 1963, his widow, Marjorie Parham, took over the financially strapped newspaper, turned it into a profit-maker and ran it until retiring a few years ago.

Spillers, Parham's son, has run the paper since his mother's retirement.

The paper's 30th anniversary in 1985 was almost its last – not because of financial pressures but because the publishers thought it might have outlived its usefulness.

Black and white Cincinnatians were looking as if they finally had figured out how to get along, at least had agreed to disagree, Spillers said.

But progress slowed. It stalled. And then it slipped into reverse. As the economy grew more uncertain, people looked for someone to blame. By the 1990s, there was a resurgence of white supremacist groups.

"It was like everything we had fought for was for naught," Spillers said.

Betty Winfield, a professor of journalism at the University of Missouri School of Journalism, Columbia, and a mass media historian, said that the black press is as vital today as it was when the first paper was founded in 1827.

"The black press gives people a sense of community and shared goals, and that's good," Winfield said Friday. "These publications are necessary. The first paper, *Freedom's Journal*, had the motto: 'We wish to plead our cause. Too long have others spoken for us.' That's as true today as ever, unfortunately."

She points to studies that say that while only 30 percent of those living in poverty in the United States are African-American, 62 percent of depictions in the mainstream print media and 65 percent of network portrayals of poverty have a black face.

"And you ask if a black press is necessary," Winfield said.

On specific issues, she said, the black press is often the only source of the African-American point of view.

Spillers said the *Herald*'s high point came in the mid-1960s, when it warned of racial tensions that then exploded in the Avondale riots of 1967 and 1968.

"We told them it would happen, and the politicians kept saying, 'Detroit, Chicago, yes. But Cincinnati? No. Not here,'" he said. "We then did all we could to appeal for calm and reflection and mediation of differences. We'd like to think we made a difference."

The *Herald* made news itself in March 1994, when it was hit by a firebomb. A second-floor newsroom was destroyed. Equipment melted in the fire's heat, and stacks of papers and files were burned. No one was injured.

Spillers said a man had telephoned the newsroom receptionist several times before the blast, threatening retaliation against the newspaper over a guest column published on the commentary page. The column, titled "Blacks and Islam," by a writer named Michael R. Burks, questioned why blacks identify with Islam, an Arabic religion, when blacks "are not Arabs or descendants of Arabia."

"Nobody was going to shut us down," Spillers said.

The newspaper has failed to publish only once in 40 years, when pages were lost en route to the printer and not found until after the publication date.

Spillers is planning. The paper has outgrown its Walnut Hills offices. He's thinking of expanding to Columbus, once Amos Lynch, publisher of the *Columbus Call and Post*, retires.

He aims to improve the quality of the *Herald* by reducing the number of typographical errors, and increasing the sophistication of the writing and coverage.

"They have really grown as a product," said Edna Howell, news director at Bond Hill's WIZF radio (100.9 FM), another major voice in the black community and one of the city's top-rated radio stations. "I think African-Americans who may not have viewed black media as legitimate are coming to respect us [black-targeted media]."

Spillers's foremost goal for the paper mirrors his hope for the black community.

"This is our community," he said. "We know what we need to do. We've got to right our own wrongs."

# Faith in action

The city's black churches preach economic development
and civic involvement

*December 10, 1995*

Sunday morning, 9:15. Senior Pastor Michael Dantley is preaching Isaiah 60 and economic development at Christ Emmanuel Christian Fellowship in Walnut Hills.

"The government couldn't do it. The system couldn't do it. The kingdom of God has the answers to our problems."

Shouts of "amen" rise from the pews.

"If you need housing, it's God," he says. "If you are tired of poverty, it's God. It's not welfare, it's God."

Dantley wipes his brow with a handkerchief. His coat is off; his white shirt is soaking wet. With an organ's music rising and a drum urging them on, the faithful are on their feet.

The preacher stalks around the pulpit and pounds the lectern with his fist: "God – [*bam*] –will not fail us."

Dantley's is but one voice in a chorus speaking to black congregations across the country – in rousing Pentecostal churches like his, in more sober settings such as the AME churches, in black Baptist churches that run the emotional gamut. The refrain: community and economic development are necessary expressions of faith.

At a time when the federal government is scaling back a half century of social welfare programs, African-American churches are trying to meet the growing needs of their communities and sounding a call for black self-reliance.

Witness the Million Man March in October: 837,000 black men from around the country gathered in Washington, D.C., to hear a message of responsibility and self-respect preached, mainly, by ministers.

Witness the document released November 17 by the National Congress of Black Churches Inc., which represents 68,000 black congregations nationwide. Its 10-point plan of action includes calls for churches to stimulate economic recovery and adopt a neighborhood school.

---

## Strength in numbers
### *December 10, 1995*

Cincinnati's black churches are represented by two major organizations:

The Baptist Ministers Conference includes almost 100 churches and 150 ministers whose total membership exceeds 75,000. Its president is the Rev. Damon Lynch Jr.

The Interdenominational Ministerial Alliance is 50 congregations – mainly African Methodist Episcopal (A.M.E.), A.M.E.-Zion, Christian Methodist Episcopal (C.M.E.), Seventh Day Adventist, and United Methodist – with about 10,000 congregants. Its president is the Rev. Taylor Thompson.

---

And witness what's happening in Greater Cincinnati's black churches:

- Economic development: The churches are applying for and pooling resources to buy property, renovate housing, improve access to mortgage loans, create jobs, and form a church-run credit union in the Avondale Town Center – which a group of four neighborhood ministers are trying to buy from the City of Cincinnati.

- Public policy: Black pastors in Cincinnati, who say they can deliver thousands of votes, are courted by police administrators to help keep the peace during times of strained race relations and by public school officials to support levies. At the urging of ministers, many black voters turned out in unusually high numbers to support two successful school levies last month.

- Social outreach: Both as individual congregations and coalitions, the church is weaving an ever-expanding safety net of programs. Among them are learning centers for students expelled from Cincinnati Public Schools, free health screenings, child care, and Head Start programs.

"The white church is not dealing with the poverty levels we are," said the Rev. John Wyatt, pastor of Avondale's St. John AME Zion Church. "Black denominations serve congregations in the urban centers where the need is greatest."

Even many non-church-going African-Americans and those who do not belong to the traditional black churches look to black preachers for leadership. One is Gerald Glaspie, a marketing consultant from Roselawn, who attends his wife's Catholic church.

"They are very much in touch with what the community feels and don't lose sight of that, even when it's not what they are preaching," said Glaspie, 40.

And black churches have the money and the ability to secure major credit. Nationally, they collected $2 billion in offerings last year, which represented three of every four charitable dollars given by African-Americans. The church also receives one of every three hours African-Americans volunteer. And most of those hours come from women, who make up a majority of church membership.

Emily Spicer, 69, a retired school administrator, contributes her time and money to her church, Carmel Presbyterian in Avondale. "The needs are so great, and if the church doesn't do it, who will?" said Spicer, a former Taft High School principal from Forest Park. "The church is the place to be if you want to be a part of the solution."

## Economic development: From home loans to credit unions

Black churches, which have historically tried to address the economic problems of black communities, are employing new methods in their efforts to rebuild neighborhoods.

The economic gap between whites and blacks has widened to a gulf: Median black household income was 64 percent the household income of whites in 1980. By 1990, it had dropped to 51 percent.

One method: increase home ownership. A church-sponsored program is helping more African-Americans get mortgage loans.

Steve and Dawn Causey, of North College Hill, were denied a mortgage the first time they applied. They then completed a church-sponsored course for prospective African-American buyers, and now own a home.

"African-Americans feel something is more trustworthy if it comes through the church," said Steve Causey, 28, a member of Bethel No. 2 Apostolic Church in South Fairmount.

Their trust was supplied by Tryed Stone Baptist Church, a 3,000-member congregation in Bond Hill that is one of two dozen black churches in Cincinnati that are part of Huntington Bank's Community Centered Banking program. The ministers endorse the bank and its products and provide a meeting place for bank officials and churchgoers. The bank provides credit counseling for applicants like the Causeys, and guarantees approval once counseling is completed.

In 1992, the year before striking the relationship with ministers, Huntington Bank's mortgage division collected 34 mortgage applications from black residents, compared with 700 from white applicants. In less than three years, more than 400 African-Americans have applied.

"We tried all kinds of advertising and worked with various community groups, but we couldn't get anything done in the black community. Until we worked with the churches," said Jim Shumate, Huntington's Community Reinvestment Act (CRA) officer. "They helped us overcome the fact that minority communities do not trust banks."

The Baptist Ministers Conference is taking another approach. It plans to open a federally insured credit union, modeled after one run by Cleveland churches, in the Avondale Town Center on May 1. The conference has signed a lease for the former Hamilton County State Bank building.

The ministers are working with Star Bank and Bank One, and several local financial institutions have pledged to make $100,000 in benevolent deposits.

The ministers' credit union will provide savings and checking accounts, and make loans to people who live, work, or worship in Avondale before expanding to allow in all church members, said the Rev. K. Z. Smith, pastor of Avondale's Corinthian Baptist Church and the conference's credit union organizer.

In addition to a credit union, Avondale might soon have a grocery store, if the Rev. James Milton and three other Avondale-based ministers have their way. Milton, the Rev. Clarence Wallace of Carmel Presbyterian, the Rev. Donald Jones of Greater New Hope Baptist, and Smith have formed a nonprofit corporation and are trying to buy Avondale Town Center. The program is based on successful black church-led developments in Detroit and Atlanta.

"This community does not have a viable grocery store," said Milton, pastor of 3,000-member Southern Baptist. "If we owned it, we could encourage parishioners to support it and create new jobs in the community."

Creating jobs for African-Americans is also the goal of a larger Baptist Ministers Conference project in Over-the-Rhine.

The conference purchased a 43,000-square-foot building at 37 Back St. The minister's building will be called Lighthouse Industries and will, at first, be a place for people to work repackaging damaged goods for local companies, including Procter & Gamble Co., said the Rev. Damon Lynch Jr., president of the Baptist Ministers Conference and pastor of 1,000-member New Jerusalem Baptist Church, Carthage.

The ministers are also talking by phone with businesses in Asia, hoping to bring unassembled shirts and shoes to the building, Lynch said. Employees would put them together, giving them a tag that reads, "Made in America."

Andi Udris, director of the Department of Economic Development for the city of Cincinnati, applauds the economic development efforts of the black churches.

"The only way to get enough equity together is through church-based development," he said. "The churches know the neighborhoods and care about the communities. They are vested."

Christ Emmanuel Christian Fellowship, Senior Pastor Michael Dantley's Walnut Hills church, now counts an Ohio License Bureau office among its holdings.

The Jireh (Hebrew for "provider") License Branch was awarded to the church's Jireh Corp. and opened in July on North Bend Road in Finneytown. The branch was moved from College Hill.

Dantley, pastor of the 5,100-member church, the city's largest black congregation, said, "The church has to be in the marketplace, physically and spiritually."

Some of the branch's six employees are Christ Emmanuel members.

"This is about a way of treating people in a service industry that leaves no doubt that the spirit is there," he said.

## Public policy: Ministers step into political arena

In October 1994, the shooting of a black teen by a white police officer in Lexington, Kentucky, sparked groups of African-Americans to twice march on downtown. Rocks and bottles were thrown, injuring six people and leading to four arrests.

Pastor Ennis F. Tait leads prayer at the site of a homicide in the Cincinnati neighborhood of Millvale. Tait's anti-violence and anti-poverty work continues a tradition of social action in the black church. Photograph by Cara Owsley, courtesy of the Cincinnati Enquirer. (Photo published Jan. 17, 2012.)

## Churches' history rooted in activism

*December 10, 1995*

Community and economic development are nothing new in the black church. In fact, says retired Duke University sociologist C. Eric Lincoln, they are the foundation on which the black church in America was built.

"It was the only organization concerned with the social welfare of black people," said Lincoln, author of *The Black Church in the African-American Experience*.

In the 19th century, black churches created institutions for African-Americans that provided economic opportunity and stability: banks, building and loan associations, funeral homes, and stores, and provided jobs, training, food, counseling, and housing.

"We've come back to the roots," Lincoln said.

Driving the return to church activity is a change in the nation's political attitude.

"The government is withdrawing from Job Corps and housing programs, and as the

In July, after Indianapolis police reportedly brutalized a black suspect during a drug-related arrest, a pharmacy was looted by black teens. Car windows were shattered. A dozen people were injured and 39 arrested.

In April, Cincinnati similarly was poised on the edge of racial unrest. The April 25 arrest of black Northside teen Pharon Crosby at Sixth and Vine streets, caught on videotape by WLWT (Channel 5) and aired repeatedly, sparked feelings of institutionalized racism and police brutality.

But in Cincinnati, the ministers of some African-American churches stepped forward to appeal for calm and helped focus community attention on police reform.

Some ministers organized short-lived pickets of local businesses. The Baptist Ministers and Interdenominational Alliance joined an NAACP-led coalition of groups demanding changes in the Police Division training methods.

The city, however tense and racially polarized, remained peaceful.

"Two other cities . . . had race riots. We didn't," Safety Division Director William Gustavson said. "The ministers kept the community from overreacting and resorting to violence. We had a lot of disagreements: the ministers supported strong measures against the officers. Our position was, it was important to complete the investigation. The overriding issue we agreed on was keeping the community calm."

Cincinnati's black churches exert this kind of political influence in the community and its institutions for two reasons, said Gene Beaupre, who teaches political science at Xavier University.

First, the traditional sources of power in the black community – namely civil-rights organizations – have "atrophied." Second, loyalty and discipline within the traditional political parties are fading, attributes that remain strong in the churches.

"Ministers can motivate and educate and mobilize their congregants," Beaupre said.

In many ways, ministers in the black community serve like elected officials.

"African-Americans have access to their pastors, and [they have] influence in the corridors of city hall, in the banks and other institutions," said Arzell Nelson, executive director of the Cincinnati Human Relations Commission.

Other local political observers say the Cincinnati Businesses Community (CBC) underestimated the influence and ability of the black church to defeat the CBC-led "strong-mayor" plan – Issue 1, on the August ballot.

The Baptist Ministers held press conferences and rallies to voice its opposition to Issue 1. The Interdenominational Ministerial Alliance distributed leaflets against the initiative, saying it would lessen black representation on the city council.

"We urged our people to vote their conscience," said Ministerial Alliance President Taylor Thompson, pastor of Allen Temple AME Church, Roselawn.

The groups also pay close attention to the business of the Cincinnati Public Schools.

"The support of the black churches is critical," Superintendent J. Michael Brandt said. "We need them to support levies."

In 1993, the Baptist Ministers led the defeat of a levy that would have financed building repairs because, its leaders said,

city, county, and state governments tighten their belts, black people are feeling the pinch because we still are at the tail end of the economic scale," he said.

Two Cincinnati pastors – L. V. Booth and the late Wilbur Page – were among the first to pursue economic development opportunities. Page's Union Baptist Church stayed downtown after its first building was demolished during urban renewal and built a new church and the 14-story Page Tower apartments. Booth, pastor of Silverton's Olivet Baptist Church, opened the Hamilton County State Bank in the Avondale Town Center in 1980. It closed seven years later.

Few local black pastors followed their leads, and larger-scale attempts at economic and community development did not occur, said the Rev. Damon Lynch III, pastor of Over-the-Rhine's New Prospect Baptist Church.

"We got into building churches, which only serve the one purpose," he said. "My vision is to build communities, not church buildings."

That vision is now the prevailing one in Cincinnati and in many other U.S. cities among black church leaders.

A sampling of other activity:

In Detroit, Hartford Memorial Baptist Church bought eight blocks of land in rundown northwest Detroit. Today the area is home to an 800,000-square-foot, church-owned shopping center and a housing development.

In Atlanta, the Wheat Street Baptist Church holds $33 million in real estate, including a pair of shopping centers and dozens of single-family homes.

In Meridian, Mississippi, a church's grocery store has grown into a business that includes a funeral home, hog farms, and an auto-repair shop - and 49 percent of a Jackson bank.

the district should first spend to improve academic performance. This year, the ministers endorsed both a renewal levy worth $19 million and a second, $26 million increase that would replace some programs slashed during the past year. Both levies passed.

## Social outreach: Programs reach out to young and elderly

Black churches do more than take stands on issues, say Brandt and other city leaders. The churches take action, trying to force positive change through hands-on outreach programs.

There are a wide variety of church-based rite-of-passage and summer camp programs for youths, literacy programs for adults and soup kitchens and food pantries for families. The programs are both big and small.

Small like the weekly open house for seniors living in the neighborhood of Avondale's St. John AME – Zion Church. That's where Yvonne Gray and a half-dozen other church women entertain as many as 20 people – many of them non-church members – for four hours each Thursday.

Said Gray, 57, of Mount Healthy, "It's important to reach out as a Christian in any way you can."

That's the spirit of the learning centers, a big program run by the Baptist Ministers Conference.

The centers, located in five Baptist churches, are places where suspended Cincinnati Public Schools students can go for daily academic lessons and counseling. Staffed by pastors and church volunteers, the centers have guided more than 300 students back into school since 1992.

One center is at Consolation Baptist Church in Mount Auburn. Consolation and the other four host churches – Avondale's Corinthian and Greater New Hope Missionary, New Jerusalem in Carthage, and St. Elizabeth in North Fairmount – absorb most of the program costs.

Two of the center's students are 15-year-old boys – friends – recently suspended from high school for 80 days for assaulting another student. One of the boys' fathers is a 54-year-old West End man who is not a churchgoer.

"It was the church or the juvenile detention center, and he's a lot better off here," he said after a parent-student meeting.

Another big program is being formed by the Baptist Ministers Conference: health insurance coverage for its members.

Lynch, the conference president, was a member of the Ohio Health Association, a Columbus-based organization brought together when President Clinton was promoting his national health-care policies in 1993.

The unprecedented unity of local black church leaders, Lynch said, and their increased sophistication will allow churches to acquire federal Community Block Grants.

Lynch's church, New Jerusalem, for example, recently acquired a $2.5 million HUD grant to construct a 43-unit home for the elderly and disabled in Oakley.

Sunday morning, 11:30. Lynch is preaching James 2 and economic development at New Jerusalem.

"We got three things in abundance in the black community," says Lynch, a towering 6-foot-4 figure dressed in a white robe. "We got liquor stores. We got check-cashing joints.

And we got churches. If you put your money in our credit union, you'll help us drive the check-cashing joints out of the community."

A sermon that started quietly is building to a fevered finish. A woman faints in the front pew; the preacher doesn't miss a beat.

"I don't care what [House Speaker Newt] Gingrich and the boys are doing in Washington. I don't believe God brought me this far to leave me here," Lynch says.

"But we can't let God do it by himself. It's not enough to have faith. It's not enough to do good works. You do good works because you're so thankful to be saved. You can't have one without the other."

Lynch lurches his lanky frame forward. He's all elbows and knees.

"I want you to turn to your neighbor and say, 'I ain't gonna let God do it by himself.'"

The faithful repeat the words in the same rhythm. It sounds as sweet as a song.

"I ain't gonna let God do it by himself."

They're on their feet for the final call-and-response.

"I got a faith that functions."

# Strong radio voice

"Lincoln's entertaining, he's informed, and he reflects
the black urban audience"

*October 29, 1998*

Lincoln Ware's WCIN talk show is required listening in the African-American community. Minutes before 11 on a recent Wednesday morning, an ad aired on WCIN-AM featuring the Rev. Damon Lynch Jr. and other members of the Baptist Ministers Conference. They were endorsing Janet Howard for the Ohio State Senate.

Minutes after 11, Caleb Brown Jr., a downtown lawyer and regular caller to Talk 1480 with Lincoln Ware, dialed in: "Why aren't these ministers doing a spot for [domestic relations court judge] Deborah Gaines?"

"Good question," Mr. Ware said.

During the next commercial break, a station secretary delivered the answer to Mr. Ware in the studio: "Rev. Lynch called," she said. "He said he supports Judge Gaines and would be happy to come in and tape a commercial for her if she asked. She hasn't asked."

Don't be fooled by WCIN's weak signal and low Arbitron ratings. (It usually places about 20th out of 30 Tristate radio stations.) Even if they're not listening in big numbers, people do pay attention to Lincoln Ware from 10 a.m. to 2 p.m. weekdays. Local movers and shakers – preachers, politicians, police, pundits – want to know what black folks are thinking.

"It is probably the broadest forum for African-Americans to speak and be heard, and from that point of view, that is very positive," Councilman Dwight Tillery said of Talk 1480.

"From time to time, I listen. We have to keep it on. My staff or other people in the community, they let me know if I should be aware of something."

Moderating the discussion is Mr. Ware, 48, a native Cincinnatian and host of 1480 Talk for five years. About a month ago, when the show's length was doubled from two hours, Mr. Ware became the first African-American to have a regular four-hour talk slot on Cincinnati radio.

What he has done is update and build on the original mission of WCIN: to inform and entertain African-Americans.

"When I was growing up, people listened to this station to find out what was going on in the community. You're not going to hear it on WLW," said Mr. Ware, who grew up in Silverton and graduated from Woodward High School in 1968. "They still depend on WCIN as the source of information about the protest or rally."

As WCIN celebrates its past this weekend with a 45th anniversary ball, station management is banking much of its future on Mr. Ware's ability to cultivate and grow his audience.

---

## WCIN anniversary
*October 29, 1998*

WCIN was Cincinnati's first radio station to play "black" music 100 percent of the time and is widely known as the nation's third-oldest R&B station.

It went on the air in 1953 from a studio on Beekman Street. WCIN and its early disc jockeys – Ed Castleberry, Jack Gibson, and Charles "Buggs" Scruggs – introduced listeners to Sam Cooke and Aretha Franklin. Motown Records founder Berry Gordy Jr. is said to have had WCIN on his list of the nation's most important black radio stations and tried to get his records played by its DJs.

WCIN's call-in contests were so popular that the local telephone company created the 749-contest line that most stations now use. WCIN's programming today is a mix of classic R&B, talk radio, and religious shows. A new tower should be ready by year's end and will increase the station's signal from 1,000 watts to 5,000 watts.

---

If this late October day is any indication, there is no shortage of callers. Or subjects.

This show began – like many – with a discussion of the police. Police–community relations is the hottest topic on the Talk 1480 hit parade.

Mr. Ware opened by updating listeners about the case of a Cincinnati police officer punished for seizing and later circulating sexually explicit photographs of a black Walnut Hills woman during an unrelated search of her home. City officials now question whether a written reprimand is enough punishment for Spec. John Horn, who is white.

"My callers are always complaining about stuff like this going on," Mr. Ware said during a commercial.

The first caller, Edward, said, "there are a lot of renegade cops out there."

"There are a few renegade cops," Mr. Ware said. "I'd say 80–90 percent of them are decent human beings. We need the police."

A few minutes later, though, Mr. Ware tweaked his defense of the police into this race-hinged question: "If a black cop stole photos of a white woman, would he be out on his tush?"

That device is a standard Lincoln Ware move, said Keith Fangman, Fraternal Order of Police president and a nine-time 1480 guest.

"Many times, his positions are drawn along racial lines, depending on the color of the officer or the citizen," he said.

At the same time, Mr. Fangman added, "Lincoln is one of the few black leaders who has the courage to speak about the epidemic of black-on-black violence."

## Views aren't automatic

New listeners are often surprised to learn that, even as moderator of this black-oriented forum, Mr. Ware doesn't automatically take the traditional black point of view on issues. His critics who are African-American are quick to use the c-word: conservative.

"I am conservative, compared to my callers," Mr. Ware said before going on the air.

One such opinion led to the "bald" look he has sported since 1995. Convinced of O. J. Simpson's guilt, Mr. Ware bet a caller that he would shave his head if the former football star were acquitted of murder charges. He's now a Montel Williams look-alike.

Mr. Ware started this day by scanning the *Enquirer, Cincinnati Post,* and *USA Today*, while sipping coffee. He keeps a razor blade on the console of his bare-bones studio to clip articles of interest to African-Americans.

Some people – especially African-Americans who've come here from other cities – say Mr. Ware typifies black Cincinnati's unusual conservatism. "He tries to be liberal," the Alabama-born Mr. Brown said, "but Lincoln is a closet conservative."

Others say Mr. Ware is typical of talk-show hosts, black or white, focused only on ratings and willing to let callers make the most outrageous comments on the air to stir controversy.

"He's gotten pretty adept at playing devil's advocate," Mr. Tillery said.

Ernie Waits Jr., the retired dean of local African-American radio personalities, admires Mr. Ware's independent streak. "You can't put Lincoln in a box," he said. "He's his own man."

Bill Cunningham, WLW's operations manager, is also a fan. "Lincoln's entertaining, he's informed, and he reflects the black urban audience in a way, I believe, that has not been done before."

## 25 years on radio

Now in his 25th year on Tristate radio, 22 of them at WCIN, Mr. Ware fields between 50 and 60 calls per show. He's most proud of the caliber of studio guests the show attracts – the likes of Steve Forbes, Johnnie Cochran, and Rep. Maxine Waters (D-Calif.).

But Mr. Ware is not a workaholic. He works to maintain balance in his life. He and his wife of 20 years, Sharon, 42, have two daughters. And it's from his perspective as a father that Mr. Ware most often reveals his strongest beliefs on the air.

When a Wednesday caller brought up the case of a 19-year-old Westwood man charged with raping his girlfriend's 7-month-old son, Mr. Ware pulled no punches.

"People need to be more careful about who they leave their children with," he said. "I'd like to take an electric cattle prod, put it up his rear end, and charge it a few times."

Mr. Ware is also disturbed by the sight of young African-Americans loitering outside his studio window on Reading Road at the Avondale Town Center. He has notified police about truants he sees on the street.

"The guys hanging out on the corner, instead of standing out there on the corner, they should serve the country in some branch of the service," said Mr. Ware, a former U.S. Marine. "There should be mandatory military service for two years at age 18."

On this program, the discussion bounced from topic to topic:

Schools that aren't meeting the needs of African-American students.

Comments made by Louis Farrakhan on a recent TV talk show.

Two-way or one-way Vine Street in Over-the-Rhine.

The military.

Religion.

Police. Always police.

Mr. Ware has doubled as WCIN's program director since 1992, but he is not an activist. He's neither comfortable with nor willing to organize or lead community protests and rallies. He is sometimes criticized for not being more involved, but that's nothing new. He recalled a lesson he learned 30 years ago as a Woodward senior and track star.

Spring 1968 was a time of unrest. The Rev. Dr. Martin Luther King Jr. had been assassinated. At Woodward, administrators ruled that if athletes had unexcused absences, they couldn't compete. Lincoln, a district champion in the 440-yard run, chose to go to class instead of participating in a protest.

"They said, 'You turned your back for track,'" he said 30 years later with a hearty laugh. "I wanted to run in the meet after school."

The lesson is especially helpful in his line of work.

"You learn," Mr. Ware said, "that you can't make everybody happy. You've got to say what you think is right."

# The barbershop: A haven for black men

True feelings flow at Jerome Goodwin's Place in Woodlawn

*January 11, 1999*

Sometimes, when Jim Graves walks into Goodwin's II barbershop in Woodlawn, he wants to sit down while he waits for a haircut and watch whatever's on the big-screen TV (often boxing or *The Young and the Restless*).

Sometimes, Mr. Graves, 36, simply listens to the conversation.

And sometimes, the Woodlawn resident and cinema manager is right in the middle of the discussion. Especially if the subject is what he says is the "witch hunt" against President Clinton.

Mr. Graves is free to voice his opinions in the barbershop without fear of repercussion. "It's a sanctuary," he said.

The black barbershop is not just a barbershop; it's a singular institution in this country. And it's unlike other bedrock black institutions.

The barbershop has none of the religious constraints of the black church. There aren't the academic requirements of the black college. Everyone's welcome in the barbershop, and everyone's welcome to speak out.

Melvin Murphy thinks even more of the barbershop. In his self-published book, *Barbershop Talk: The Other Side of Black Men* ($24.95), the Virginia-based author suggests the barbershop is where black men – free of negative stereotypes that often shadow them in larger society – can be themselves. Relaxed. Unaffected.

"It's one of the few places where African-American men gather and do not feel threatened as black men," Mr. Murphy writes. "The barbershop has provided an emotional safe-haven for men who have endured exploitation for more than 200 years."

There's no exploitation at Goodwin's II, just plenty of exposition and exaggeration.

"Hey, Rome," Goodwin's II owner, Jerome Goodwin, calls to customer and former Hughes High School classmate Rome Adkins. "You'd better not look at this. You're gonna have a flashback."

"What do you mean?" asks Mr. Adkins, a truck driver from Madisonville.

"You're going to remember when I hit you that hard in school," Mr. Goodwin says as a smile spreads across his bearded face.

The dozen men in the shop burst out laughing. They're watching a tape of the first Evander Holyfield – Mike Tyson heavyweight title fight from November 1996.

"Holyfield's gonna hit him so hard the dust on the TV's going to jump," says Mr. Goodwin, drawing another round of hoots and hollers.

Mr. Goodwin, 53, has cut hair since 1965. He opened Goodwin's II on Martin Luther King Day in 1995 in a converted garage. He holds court from the first chair, next to the front window and door. His clients include Bengals Carl Pickens and James Francis and several former players.

But Mr. Goodwin is more than a barber. He's part preacher, just like his father, the late Rev. A. L. Goodwin, founding pastor in 1926 of Jerriel Baptist Church in the West End.

"We talk to the kids who come in," Jerome Goodwin says. "We let them know it only takes three seconds to get into trouble but a lifetime to get out of it."

He hasn't met a customer he couldn't draw into a conversation. "Just ask them what they think about Clinton or the Bengals," Mr. Goodwin says.

The television remote, like the business phone, is within arm's reach. "Sometimes, we shut the TV off," says Mr. Goodwin, a big fan of *The Young and the Restless*.

"Then there are times we turn it up to shut somebody down."

Mr. Goodwin puts in a tape of the Holyfield – Tyson rematch from June 1997, the fight in which Tyson bit off the tip of Holyfield's ear.

"There's only two reasons Mike did it," Mr. Goodwin says in his big voice toward Mr. Adkins. "He was either hungry or wanted to get disqualified because Holyfield was whupping him."

The TV sits diagonally in the corner that opens toward the four barber chairs and 17 seats where customers wait their turn. The seats are arranged in five uneven rows facing the television.

Alexander Okafor, 48, of Finneytown, and his three children fill the second row. He has brought in his sons, 10-year-old Chibuzo and Ameche, 6, for haircuts. Daughter Ijeoma, 8, is here for the culture.

The end of Spike Lee's *Malcolm X* is playing when they arrive.

"I have gone to mixed [race] shops, but I feel more at home here," says Mr. Okafor, a native Nigerian and senior chemist with SunChemical who moved here from Long Island, N.Y. "We have the same cultural background, the same experiences."

The second chair at Goodwin's belongs to 77-year-old Leon Williams. He has cut hair in local barbershops since 1948.

"I love it," he says. "You meet so many people in here. All ages, babies up to 96-year-olds. And everybody's got a different opinion about everything." The only concessions he has made to time are the padded mat circling his chair – "Helps the feet," he says – and cutting down to four days a week.

"I'll quit when I can't stand up any more," Mr. Williams says.

Today he's cutting the hair of Walter Mitchell, 82, a retired social worker from Wyoming. Mr. Williams has cut his hair, Mr. Mitchell says, "since I was old enough to pay myself. I can't remember anyone else cutting my hair."

Mr. Williams started at the Dupree Barber Shop in Lockland. He worked at Drake Hospital for 14 years and merged his business with Mr. Goodwin's seven years ago.

The most exciting time to be a barber was the 1960s, at the peak of the civil rights movement. "We had the TV on all the time, and the discussions we'd get in, oh my," says Mr. Williams, running his clippers across the back of a customer's neck.

"That [Martin Luther] King was a heck of a man. I went to his funeral, but I didn't get in. Too many celebrities."

Goodwin's is not for black men only. Women bring their young sons in for haircuts, and some women come by to have Mr. Goodwin trim their eyebrows.

Thomasina Forte is in from Forest Park with her daughter, Ebony, 18, a University of Cincinnati freshman.

"I love just sitting here and listening to the guys talk," Thomasina Forte says. "I like how they bicker with each other. Who tells the most lies. The nicknames they throw at each other. I like watching them when a nice-looking lady comes in. It gets quiet. Their facial expressions change."

When women are in the shop, the topics are tamer. There's no cussing or smoking allowed at any time.

Goodwin's also has some white customers.

"Hair is hair," Jerome Goodwin says.

Rewind to Tyson–Holyfield I. The tape is running. So are the mouths.

"Tyson's confused," Mr. Adkins says. "He hit Holyfield with his best shot, and Holyfield's still standing."

Mr. Goodwin shouts down from the first chair to the third chair, where Lamont Sanders, 24, is cutting hair: "Lamont, bet you 50 bucks Holyfield knocks him out."

"Bet you he don't," Mr. Sanders says.

Mr. Goodwin: "I'll do better than that. Bet you they stop the fight in the 11th round."

"Mike's fighting for his life," Mr. Adkins shouts.

End of Round 6.

"Mike ain't nothing but a chump," Mr. Goodwin says.

The hours pass. Men come and go. Mr. Goodwin changes tapes in the VCR. Tyson–Holyfield yields to reruns of *Sanford and Son* starring Redd Foxx. Next is NFL Films' *100 Greatest Tackles.*

Jimmie Brown, 58, of Glendale waits for his haircut. He's a retired mechanical engineer from Procter & Gamble, a deacon at Lincoln Heights Missionary Baptist Church and a fan of *The Young and the Restless.*

He climbs into Mr. Goodwin's chair and fills him in on the latest from the soap: "Victoria's moving in with him today," Mr. Brown says.

"Him who?" Mr. Goodwin asks.

"Neil."

"You don't say."

After his haircut, Mr. Brown explains what the barbershop means to him.

"There is a camaraderie that's relaxing," he says. "The discussions can be especially heated around election time, and especially when a politician is not performing up to his or her duties."

Issues of race are brought up, too.

"But I don't think you'd find them one-sided," Mr. Brown says. "You'll find blacks who say their experience has shown them that changing your behavior will change your situation. Sometimes we make ourselves victims through our thought processes."

A scream shoots from the big-screen TV.

Mr. Goodwin has put in a tape of Jurassic Park. Some more children have come in with their father.

# Event honors those trained to serve

## Pullman porters helped pave the way for civil rights

*May 4, 2009*

In the heyday of train travel, in the early decades of the 20th century, Pullman porters numbered more than 20,000.

Today their ranks have dwindled to fewer than 100, and a precious four of them, including a Bond Hill man, are headed this weekend to Philadelphia to take part in National Train Day ceremonies. The gathering surely will be the last reunion of a proud group of African-American men who worked hard, made a good living, and helped usher in the modern civil rights movement.

Amtrak will cover the expense of putting the participating Pullman porters on flights Friday to Washington. Then they will be placed on an Amtrak train for a ride to Philadelphia. Once aboard, they will receive the same royal treatment they afforded passengers during much of the 20th century.

I. T. Hector, 93, of Bond Hill, will attend, health permitting. He was a Pullman porter from 1943 to 1958 at Cincinnati's Union Terminal.

"I liked it a lot," said Hector, who primarily made beds in sleeping cars, cleaned the cars, and served riders in passenger cars. "I knew for a black man it was a pretty good job. It kept you from having [to work] cleaning toilets."

Some porters did. They gave dignity to sometimes undignified tasks.

The Pullman Palace Co. of Chicago built, owned and operated many passenger trains in the first half of the 20th century. It hired African-American men exclusively as porters.

Serving primarily wealthy whites, the porters worked tirelessly and with exquisite manners and professionalism to make the exchanges as positive as possible in the days of racial segregation.

"We were aware of opportunity to interact with all sorts of people," said another former Pullman porter, Robert Tate, 90, of Walnut Hills. He has been ill and said he will not be able to attend the weekend reunion.

"We knew we had the opportunity to become familiar with each other [blacks and whites], and we treated everyone with the highest level of respect," said Tate, a porter from 1942 to 1968. There is no official end to the Pullman porter era, but it is generally considered 1867 to 1969.

Tate regularly served Henry Ford Jr. and his family on train rides to Florida, where they would board their yacht at Pompano Beach.

African-American celebrities rode, too. Tate met Sammy Davis Jr. and Lena Horne.

Service, not servitude, was the unofficial motto of the all-black group. They organized in 1925 as the Brotherhood of Sleeping Car Porters.

Under the leadership of A. Philip Randolph, the porters were the first African-American labor union to sign a collective bargaining agreement with a major U.S. corporation. The Pullman Co. would not recognize the union until 1937. The union won $2 million in pay increases for employees, a shorter workweek and overtime pay.

Hector once made $20,000 a year, most of it in tips. Pullman porters had to work 400 hours a month or travel 11,000 miles, whichever came first, to earn full pay.

The Pullman Porter Museum in Chicago, located in the historic Pullman district, bears Randolph's name. It was founded in 1995 by a Cincinnati native, Lyn Hughes, who compiled and wrote *An Anthology of Respect: The Pullman Porters National Historic Registry of African-American Railroad Employees* (Hughes-Peterson Publishing, 2007).

"An unwritten fact is that Pullman porters were the foundation of the black middle class," said Hughes, who is the featured speaker at the reunion. "More often than not, they were well educated. They were not allowed to work in their chosen fields. But for a black man, the job of Pullman porter was a coveted position."

As porters, they took tickets, dusted jackets and fetched coffee and tea.

"It was a clean job," Hughes said. "And they did it with a self-imposed standard of excellence."

Hector, who had owned a restaurant in his hometown of Atlanta and still owns a printing shop on Lincoln Avenue in Walnut Hills, said there wasn't a whole lot of talking.

"'Yes, sir' and 'No, sir' were what we said," he said while sitting in the dining room of his home. "You did not talk back, no, sir."

Hector traveled to all 48 of the continental United States. He worked out of Cincinnati with some 100 other Pullman porters.

He loved Seattle because of the huge apples. He recalls the sad living conditions of American Indians when he rolled through New Mexico. In Atlanta, he met Mary McLeod Bethune, founder of a school in Daytona Beach, Florida, that became Bethune-Cookman University, and an adviser on African-American affairs to four presidents – including Franklin Roosevelt.

Hector served her on a trip to Washington to meet with the president and first lady Eleanor Roosevelt.

During and after World War II, the Pullman cars moved thousands of U.S. troops across the country. Hector would be gone for up to 30 days. It took four to five days and nights to get from Cincinnati to Los Angeles. Then there might be a layover.

The porters would play cards in their off hours. Hector said he did a lot of walking through cities and liked to window shop.

The Pullman porters played a major role in the civil rights movement. Union boss Randolph planned a March on Washington in 1941 to protest government hiring practices that excluded African-Americans. The threat of the protest moved Roosevelt in June of that year to sign Executive Order 8802, which prohibited government contractors – including the defense industry – from engaging in employment discrimination. Randolph also helped organize the 1963 March on Washington.

The porters did their part. They would secretly circulate and deliver copies of prominent black newspapers, including the *Chicago Defender*, to areas in the South that could not get news of progress for blacks in the North.

All the while, train travel ground nearly to a halt because of the expansion of air flight.

To the end, there was that Pullman porter standard.

"We," Hector said, "had dignity."

---

# Urban League convention

## Cincinnati is a tale of two cities that threatens the region's growth and appeal

*July 22, 2014*

The 8,000 participants in the National Urban League convention this week will see a Cincinnati brimming with downtown development, a bustling riverfront, and investment in the streetcar.

What they're unlikely to see, unless they venture outside of the central business district, is the other Cincinnati – neighborhoods such as Avondale and Evanston and suburbs such as Mount Healthy, where much of the region's African-American population lives cut off from the city's growing vitality and financial promise.

Cincinnati is not unlike many large American cities in which significant economic divides separate black from white. The gap is wider here, though, a new Urban League study shows, risking the safe futures of thousands of residents and undercutting a sound economic foundation needed for new jobs and regional growth.

The national disparity will be discussed at the convention, "One Nation Underemployed: Bridges to Jobs and Justice," running Wednesday through Saturday at the Duke Energy Convention Center.

Metropolitan Cincinnati, which includes Hamilton and Middletown among five counties in Southwest Ohio, seven counties in Northern Kentucky and three in Southeast Indiana, has nearly the worst median household-income gap between blacks and whites compared to other metropolitan areas. Of the 77 cities analyzed by the National Urban League in its report, "State of Black America," Greater Cincinnati ranks 73rd, with median black income at $24,272, compared to $57,481 for whites.

In unemployment, the region ranks 47th of the 77 metropolitan areas, with black unemployment standing at 17.1 percent compared to 7.1 percent for whites.

"My first reaction is that I wish we were further up the lists," said Mary Stagaman, executive director of Agenda 360, a long-range project of the Cincinnati USA Regional Chamber designed to lift low-income residents out of poverty in the region's 15 counties. "But I am not surprised. We've known for some time we've had disparities."

What's new is the growing belief that the solution to improved economic health is a regional issue – not one confined to the urban core cities of Cincinnati, Covington, and Newport.

"In the 21st century, those communities with broad divides are going to be less attractive for business expansion and business relocation," Marc Morial, president of the National Urban League and former New Orleans mayor, told the *Enquirer* in an interview.

The obvious consequences to an unchecked economic gap, Morial said, are worse overall economic health and business climate and "the negative impact on public safety and violence."

## Economic disparity has ties to health, education inequality

The National Urban League credits Cincinnati for making strides in police–community relations since the April 2001 shooting of an unarmed black man by a Cincinnati Police officer.

The shooting of Timothy Thomas in Over-the-Rhine led to a black-led boycott of downtown. Bill Cosby and other national entertainment acts refused to perform in Cincinnati, and the Urban League was one of several organizations to move its conventions from Cincinnati to other cities.

The Urban League planned to meet here in 2003, and city leaders, including then–Mayor Charlie Luken, lobbied the group hard to come here, citing reforms within the police department. But in July 2002, following the suspension of the police department's highest-ranking African-American officer, the Urban League decided to go elsewhere.

At the time, Assistant Chief Ronald Twitty was being investigated for allegedly lying about a car accident. Twitty later worked as police chief in suburban Lincoln Heights.

Morial recently praised Cincinnati for its downtown development and "sea change" in police–community relations since the 2001 race riots.

That civil unrest, though, underscored problems beyond police–community relations.

"The riots . . . were also about economic frustration," said Donna Jones Baker, president and chief executive since 2003 of the Urban League of Greater Southwestern Ohio. "These economic gaps continue. And while we have a vibrancy in the city because of wonderful things happening, we have a group of people who can't access them. We can't expect people to suffer in silence forever."

Baker said she is concerned because social goals to elevate the region as a whole often mask conditions in the urban core.

Additional economic, education, and health data show how wide that chasm is. Within the city of Cincinnati:

- Unemployment for African-Americans is 19 percent and 7.1 percent for whites.

- Two in five African-Americans in Cincinnati live below federal poverty lines, compared to fewer than one in five whites.

- 11.8 percent of African-Americans 25 years or older have a bachelor's degree, compared to 45.1 percent for whites.

- Economic and education indicators translate to racial health disparities. In 2011, the U.S. Centers for Disease Control and Prevention used data to show how poor people are at higher risk for serious disease and premature death. Poor residents also have reduced access to health care and receive inadequate quality care.

- African-Americans on average don't live as long as whites. They have less access to private health care and healthful foods, and they are significantly more likely to suffer from diseases and conditions ranging from cancer and diabetes to high blood pressure and obesity.

## Region trying to develop future, current workforces

The region's response so far, led by the United Way of Greater Cincinnati, is to focus on early childhood education and job training for adults.

Stagaman, of Agenda 360, applauded the work being done through the United Way's Success by 6 program, a national strategy in more than 350 U.S. cities. "We build the workforce of the future by making sure children are ready for kindergarten and are reading at grade level by third grade," she said.

Current workforce challenges – including shortages of skilled workers – are being addressed by agencies including Partners for a Competitive Workforce, Cincinnati Works, and the local Urban League.

The Urban League's signature job readiness program is SOAR, or Solid Opportunities for Advancement and Retention. In the past five years through its Avondale headquarters, the local Urban League has enrolled 300 students a year in SOAR – and most of them have criminal records.

Eighty-one percent graduate the intense, three-week employment boot camp. They now earn an average of $21,625 a year, injecting $4 million a year into the local economy and reducing the drain on social services.

Eusi Saddyk, 34, of Covedale graduated from SOAR in 2012 and went right into the Urban League's Construction Connections program.

Both programs were vital to the success he has enjoyed since. He earned $16 an hour doing concrete work from September 2012 through last month. He is now painting for a local company and is opening his own business – which he calls property protection – which involves roof and gutter work, drywalling, and painting.

"SOAR gave me the confidence I could get out in the field and make maximum wage," said Saddyk, who served almost a year in prison for selling cocaine in Illinois. The felony remains on his record.

"I learned so much in Construction Connections, how to operate all kinds of equipment and how to be safety conscious on a construction site," he said. "I knew I could go into a job interview and prove and show what I could do. I never stopped looking to advance."

# Freedom Center sheds its chains of doubt

Museum celebrates its 10th anniversary on a road to financial health and future growth

*August 3, 2014*

The National Underground Railroad Freedom Center marks the 10th anniversary of its opening Sunday, celebrating a decade in which it survived derision, doubts, and debt that nearly shut it down.

Today, an *Enquirer* review of the center's financial documents and interviews with key civic and business leaders finds an institution poised for growth in the next 10 years.

After early struggles with financing and disappointing attendance, the Freedom Center is enjoying a surge in its endowment, a balanced budget, beefed-up programming, and growing national renown.

"I see us becoming increasingly stronger financially and playing a major role here and abroad in promoting a particular type of freedom – inclusive freedom," center President Clarence G. Newsome said. "It is predicated on the equality of all people of all races and ethnicities. In history, a select group of people have experienced it, while many groups have not."

It was a hard 10 years.

The Freedom Center opened on August 3, 2004, seeking an elusive identity as both museum for Underground Railroad artifacts and living space for the discussion of modern-day slavery. Just three years after the 2001 riots, its reception was split – either welcomed or scorned – while growing red ink sapped taxpayer dollars and patience.

As recently as December 2011, the center's leaders told the *Enquirer* that the institution had only a year to live if a stubborn $1.5 million budget shortfall could not be closed. The exclusive *Enquirer* report generated both financial aid and in-kind service help.

The W. K. Kellogg Foundation offered a $1.8 million America Healing program grant. And more than a dozen professional firms, ranging from accountants to marketing specialists, provided free or deeply discounted services to help turn around the center.

Now, the center is looking forward to a series of commemorative events that includes a visit by former Polish President Lech Walesa, and it will honor former South African President Nelson Mandela.

As the Freedom Center enters its next decade, challenges remain.

## Maintaining, building stronger financial base

Late in 2011, center officials stared at a 2012 budget that had $4.5 million in expenses but just $3 million in revenues.

"We're scratching and clawing," Kim Robinson, then-Freedom Center president and chief executive, said at the time.

That was the bottom. But financial fortunes would soon turn around.

In July 2012, the Freedom Center merged with the Cincinnati Museum Center, and a projected $1.3 million in savings were realized.

The Freedom Center will earn revenue from a traveling exhibit. Famed quilter Carolyn Mazloomi was one of six artists commissioned to create artwork for the Freedom Center's "And Still We Rise" quilt exhibit that closes September 1. Co-created by the Freedom Center and the Museum Center, the exhibit is already booked to travel and show in an Orlando, Florida, museum beginning in January and in a museum in Austin, Texas, in June. Two other contracts for the exhibit that would have it on the road well into 2016 are under review.

The Freedom Center had a balanced budget of $5.4 million for fiscal year 2012–13.

Its endowment, which stood at $1.6 million at the end of June 2012, now is $4.8 million. A 1:1 endowment match up to $5 million, guaranteed by former Freedom Center board co-chairman John Pepper and his wife, Francie, was extended one year to the end of 2014. The Peppers, who have made contributions in excess of $15 million to the Freedom Center, want to see the endowment reach $10 million.

"We have a much stronger financial foundation," Pepper told the *Enquirer*. "But the [fund-raising] battle is never over. We are looking to create a sustainable financial structure."

Attendance reached 121,449 in 2013, the highest since 2008, and attendance revenue increased 35 percent, according to Freedom Center documents.

The center paid off its mortgage in 2011 and owns its building. The amount of taxpayer money received has dropped to less than 7 percent of the budget, and it comes almost exclusively from contracts and grants with the U.S. Department of State – for a foreign visitor program that teaches democracy – and the U.S. Department of Education.

Students in the Schooled on Freedom program accounted for about one-third of center visitors in 2013. The total cost per student, $12.50, which includes admission and busing to the Freedom Center, is paid by private donations.

## Upgrading, expanding collections, programming

Still, as a relatively young institution – just 10 years old – the Freedom Center is working to expand its internal exhibit and artifact offerings and continue to contribute to the worldwide movement linking 19th-century U.S. slavery to forms of contemporary slavery that ensnare an estimated 27 million people.

Two recent acquisitions have added to the center's collection. The first is a cast iron cooking pot believed to have belonged to Margaret Garner. Born in Boone County and enslaved, she escaped in 1856 with her husband and children across the Ohio River but was captured in Cincinnati. The story of how Garner killed her daughter rather than allow her return to slavery is the basis of the 1987 Toni Morrison novel *Beloved*.

The cooking pot is on loan to the Freedom Center after its excavation from the Gaines plantation in Northern Kentucky.

The other is the original headstone of Salmon P. Chase, who died in 1873 when he was presiding Chief Justice of the U.S. Supreme Court. Originally buried near Washington, D.C., Chase's remains were moved to Spring Grove Cemetery in 1886, and the original tombstone was deposited on the property.

Both artifacts are on display in the Slavery to Freedom exhibit.

The Freedom Center partnered with the State Department in 2012 to produce the documentary *Journey to Freedom*, which marries the story of Solomon Northup, a captured free man forced into slavery for 12 years during the 19th century, with several examples of contemporary slavery worldwide. The film showed at more than 50 U.S. embassies worldwide. The center recently acquired an original 1853 copy of Northup's book, titled *Twelve Years a Slave*. Each year, the State Department brings its international Trafficking in Persons heroes to the Freedom Center for a reception following their introduction in Washington, D.C.

The Freedom Center has the first museum-quality exhibit devoted to contemporary bondage, "Invisible: Slavery Today," which opened in 2010. Earlier this year, the Freedom Center earned accreditation from the American Alliance of Museums, given only to 3 percent of 35,000 specialized museums nationwide.

"We have a number of partnerships we have formed with many groups – the State Department, Historians Against Slavery, the Smithsonian Institution, International Justice Mission – that will help us grow and expand in the next 10 years," center chief executive Newsome said.

## Improving outreach, national recognition

The Freedom Center continues to improve its outreach and attachment to the local community. Its regional partnerships involve the University of Cincinnati, Xavier University, Northern Kentucky University, and several social service agencies, including those that bring young mothers and fathers and their children to the center for training and cultural development. STEM students (Science, Technology, Engineering, and Mathematics) come from local high schools.

One of the center's unique relationships is with General Electric, an original donor to its construction and development. GE's Global Operations Center building is rising just to the west of the Freedom Center, and the vibrancy of The Banks, including the Freedom Center, helped GE choose its location over Mason and Oakley. GE Aviation is also working as a financial partner with the Freedom Center to help it develop a business and convening center on its fourth and fifth floors, facing north into downtown.

"We're committed to helping the center develop and promote this conference center," said Pat Zerbe, community relations manager for GE Aviation. "Our expectation is this plan not only will increase revenues but also provide more options for the center's use."

GE and the Freedom Center worked together during the July National Urban League Convention in Cincinnati. The two organizations played host to 300 high school students in a leadership summit that ended with a Center tour.

The Freedom Center reached out to the National Urban League. Its president, Marc Morial, met privately with Newsome. And the National Urban League conference and Macy's Music Festival were responsible for doubling the Freedom Center's attendance for the weekend of July 26–27.

In fact, the Freedom Center is responsible for helping to attract up to $8 million in convention business each year, according to a University of Cincinnati study. "The nature and location of the Freedom Center has been hugely instrumental in bringing numerous conventions," said Dan Lincoln, president of the Cincinnati USA Convention & Visitors Bureau. "Cincinnati has gotten more repeat attention."

Cincinnati Reds chief operating officer Phil Castellini said the Freedom Center helped to win Major League Baseball's Civil Rights Games at Great American Ball Park in 2009 and 2010. "The Freedom Center's proximity to the ballpark and message were key factors . . . and ultimately led to securing the bid to host the 2015 Major League All-Star Game," he said.

Newsome sees the Freedom Center becoming a national household name in the next 10 years.

"I see us making Cincinnati very proud," he said, envisioning partnerships with arts, civil rights, and religious groups to spur cultural and economic development.

# THE NAACP

*Milton Hinton, a retired University of Cincinnati administrator, emerged in 1993 as my primary source for background and perspective. I'd go to his house in North Avondale and be shown to his upstairs reading room, where I'd ask a question and listen. He was a former New Jersey NAACP chapter president, and by the time he was elected Cincinnati branch president, we had a strong relationship. (I was at their home so frequently that, even years later, his wife referred to me in public as "my white son.")*

# Hinton invigorates NAACP

NAACP President moves the group back into the spotlight

*May 23, 1995*

Rewind to the early 1990s. The Ku Klux Klan cross on Fountain Square. Marge Schott's alleged racist remarks. The racially charged backlash against the *Enquirer* for its investigation of former Cincinnati Health Commissioner Dr. Stanley Broadnax. The ongoing Bronson school desegregation case against Cincinnati Public Schools. The debate over how to elect city council members to ensure minority representation.

The Cincinnati chapter of the NAACP speaks out each time but as just another voice in the chorus.

Fast forward to 1995. The NAACP is the featured soloist.

The difference? New chapter President Milton Hinton.

March: The local chapter, angry about the *Enquirer*'s depiction of black men in a series on the Ohio parole system, pickets the newspaper's office.

May: The NAACP organizes and leads a coalition of a dozen local civil-rights groups demanding the firing of three Cincinnati police officers involved in the April 25 arrest of a black teenager. The two official city investigations of the incident involving Pharon Crosby, 17, of Northside, are expected to be released Wednesday.

When he was elected in November, Hinton promised aggressive action from the NAACP, perhaps civil disobedience, to reinvigorate the local branch.

When it came time to respond to the Crosby arrest, which many people in the black community said was another case of excessive force by the Cincinnati Police Division against an African-American, Hinton was ready.

"I reached out and said, 'Here's a matter that concerns all our constituencies,'" Hinton said. "The issue of excessive force is one common to all of the folks. Others [coalitions] might not be this easy."

Hinton presided over several private coalition meetings and three public rallies, including the May 13 delivery of the coalition report on the arrest to City Manager John Shirey at City Hall.

The renewed public activity of the National Association for the Advancement of Colored People has sparked new interest in the organization, the nation's oldest civil-rights group, incorporated in New York in 1911.

"Dr. Hinton . . . is helping restore the vigor of the organization," Cincinnati City Councilman Tyrone Yates said.

What Yates calls vigor, critics of Hinton call opportunism.

"The NAACP and racism are an industry," said Cincinnati Police Sgt. Paul Hilmer, president of the Fraternal Order of Police. "Hinton has an easy job. He just has to find an issue to try to raise money. They've blown Sixth and Vine [site of the Crosby arrest] out of proportion. Hinton was just looking for a cause, real or imagined. He hasn't been the calming factor I've heard him portrayed to be, and has done nothing to advance communication between the black community and the city."

## "The publicity helps"

Hinton takes the criticism, like the praise, in stride. "The publicity," he said with a long pause, "helps the organization."

In the six months since he was elected chapter president by a 2-1 margin to succeed Frank Allison, who had retired in November, Hinton has managed to move a largely dormant organization into the spotlight by resurrecting two basic NAACP principles: inclusion and consensus building. Allison, who died in February, was president for five years.

The coalition he has put together in the Crosby response consists of the Baptist Ministers Conference, the Greater Cincinnati AME Ministerial Alliance, the Urban League of Greater Cincinnati, Housing Opportunities Made Equal of Greater Cincinnati, the Black Male Coalition, the local Nation of Islam community, and the Black Law Student Association of the University of Cincinnati.

Another organization came aboard last week – when a representative of the Interdenominational Ministers Association walked into Hinton's NAACP office, handed him a $500 check for a lifetime NAACP membership and said the group was joining the coalition.

Dorothy Coleman, who lost twice to Allison and again to Hinton for the chapter presidency, said under Allison, the chapter did not hold monthly membership meetings and had allowed some committees to go long periods without chairmen.

She also said the chapter had lost the respect of the African-American community because "it hasn't done anything." As the head of the membership committee, Coleman said an all-too-often refrain was, "Why should I join?"

The chapter is different – inside and out – under Hinton.

"Hinton has a different style about him," said Tim Burke, chairman of the Hamilton County Democratic Party, an NAACP ally against efforts to eliminate Cincinnati's city-manager form of government.

"He has a calming influence that allows people to listen to each other. He has also done an impressive job going back to his constituents and presenting a more unified front."

## East Coast roots

Two new committees – the Stand-By Committee, which performs secretarial chores on short notice; and the Demonstration/March Committee, which secures permits for public displays of unity and protest – are up and running, joining 13 other committees that are all now functioning.

Hinton deflects most of the credit and invitations to compare his administration to others.

"Leadership always takes responsibility for an organization's pluses or minuses," he said. "I have been able to pull in some new people, and they have been willing to pull in other people."

Hinton, 67, is a retired University of Cincinnati vice provost for minority affairs. He was president of the NAACP's Glassboro, N.J., branch during the late 1950s and 1960s, a period of heightened civil unrest. He and the young people he recruited into the organization drove around South Jersey picketing restaurants that wouldn't serve them.

He has a bare-bones office in the equally sparse NAACP suite at the Kemper Lane Apartments building, Walnut Hills.

The former chairman of UC's Early Childhood and Special Education Department, Hinton was promoted to vice provost, in part, to recruit and maintain minority staff members and graduate students.

"He was masterful in confronting issues, not personalities," said Marylyn J. Smith, associate dean of UC's University College. "What came through at all times was his profound respect for all human beings, including those with adversarial positions."

After his retirement from UC in 1991, Hinton founded the Committee of 51, a multiracial group of citizens from various walks of life who met to discuss issues in minority and integrated communities.

Comments made by Cincinnati school board member William Seitz attracted the bulk of the committee's attention. Seitz had drawn a parallel between disruptions at a high school graduation and the lack of discipline in African-American homes in 1992.

## Hinton sought out

The Committee of 51 called for Seitz's resignation and backed up the call with action, preparing a nationwide mailing to organizations planning to hold conventions in Cincinnati during the next three years. Seitz did not seek re-election and is now a Green Township trustee.

The Committee of 51 attracted the attention of the NAACP.

Hinton said people within the chapter approached him about running for president; they wanted Hinton to do on a larger scale what he had been doing with the committee.

"I wish it wouldn't have been necessary to do this," he said, "but there is a need, and it must be addressed. I am hoping that with some of the young persons in the organization, that mine will not be a long term. People see us involved, and it conveys to the public that the NAACP is doing something."

---

# "These are no ordinary times"

## The NAACP is returning to Cincinnati for its 107th annual convention
### *July 10, 2016*

Noah Sherman is a big, dark-complected young man. He knows what it means when he physically goes out into the world.

"I am perceived as scary," said the 19-year-old Westwood resident who stands 6-foot-7 and weighs 260 pounds. "I have to come into a room with a smile. I have to be jolly. Otherwise, I am seen as the menacing and angry black man."

A second-year criminal justice major at the University of Cincinnati, Sherman has long-range concerns like "getting a job, having a future. I worry about it. It's scary. We have a lot of this going in with society."

Fear is all around him. He is feared. He fears how some people might treat him or what they think of him. Others fear him.

The country is rocked with fear of "the other" – Mexican and Central American immigrants, Muslims, the federal government. Donald Trump supporters. Some whites fear blacks. Some blacks fear whites. Fear is our new national pastime.

Noah Sherman is one witness to where we are in America. In terms of race relations, he is not in a good place. By extension, as a nation, neither are we.

The NAACP comes to Cincinnati this week with an estimated 10,000 delegates for its 107th annual convention. Cornell William Brooks, its president and CEO, prefaced this meeting with the simple but clear declaration: "These are no ordinary times."

Are these times in which it is critical to ask where the fear and rage come from? Is it prompted, in part, by questions like: Isn't the civil rights movement over? Weren't those issues resolved 50 years ago?

And, if so, doesn't that make the NAACP obsolete and irrelevant?

The NAACP last brought its national convention to Cincinnati eight years ago – in 2008 – when one of the notable guest speakers was the then-junior Senator from Illinois, Barack Obama. "Eight years ago," Brooks said, "we were on the eve of a post-millennial civil rights movement."

If we are there, it has not turned out as some had hoped. Trayvon Martin. Eric Garvey. "I can't breathe." John Crawford III. The Emmanuel Nine in Charleston, South Carolina.

Poisoned water in Flint. Michael Brown Jr. Ferguson, Missouri. Baltimore. Freddie Gray. Tamir Rice. Black Lives Matter. Samuel DuBose. *Shelby v. Holder* and the Voting Rights Act.

We are here.

"We are on the eve of the first presidential election in 50 years without the full protection of the Voting Rights Act," Brooks said. "It's a very significant moment. We are about to elect a president in a radically different political landscape than Barack Obama walked upon in 2008."

In 2013, the U.S. Supreme Court ruled in *Shelby v. Holder* that two provisions of the Voting Rights Act of 1965 were unconstitutional. To date, 17 states – including Ohio, which has reduced the number of early-voting days and is purging inactive voters from its rolls – will have new voting restrictions in place for the first time in a presidential election. The new laws include strict photo ID requirements, early voting cutbacks, and registration restrictions.

"Jim Crow 2.0," Brooks said.

## Been here before

The NAACP had been to Cincinnati twice before 2008 for its national convention, in 1946 and 1970.

In 1946, the year before Jackie Robinson would break Major League Baseball's color barrier, the issues of great importance to Cincinnati's black community involved housing and education. Whites had been moved out of the West End to public housing to the north (English Woods and Winton Terrace) and the Laurel Homes project in the West End would be converted to all-black residency. The Cincinnati Board of Education would cooperate by building "new Negro" middle and high schools in the West End.

In 1970, two years after the assassination of the Rev. Martin Luther King Jr. and the second of two consecutive years of rioting in Avondale, race-related fights would close two Greater Cincinnati high schools (Withrow and North College Hill) for days at a time. NAACP lawyers would not file the *Bronson v. The Cincinnati Board of Education* lawsuit seeking complete desegregation of public schools for another four years. The practice of prohibiting the sale of homes to black buyers – it's called "redlining" – was common throughout Hamilton County.

Now a former federal judge, Nathaniel Jones attended the 1970 convention as the national NAACP's general counsel.

"We heard from the outside in 1970 that we were irrelevant," said Jones, who will be honored at the convention's closing-night banquet June 20 with the NAACP's Spingarn Medal. "What's happening this year makes this year's convention of tremendous importance."

## The divide gets wider

As dated as the concerns of the 1940s and 1970s might appear in retrospect, an ever-increasing number of signs point to a widening racial gap. The arc of the Obama presidency from 2008 to 2016 has brought about its own brand of racial backlash.

The number of hate groups spiked with Obama's 2008 election before trailing off. The number dropped to 784 in 2014 but increased again to 892 in 2015, according to the Southern Poverty Law Center of Montgomery, Alabama.

Tea Party rallies, designed to protest "big government" and "high taxes," have featured increasing numbers of anti-black and anti-Obama messages, including some suggesting the president should be lynched on the White House grounds.

In the new book *White Rage: The Unspoken Truth of Our Racial Divide*, author Carol Anderson tracks the efforts of white Americans over the centuries to limit or reverse black progress.

The Pew Research Center in late June released a report on the state of race relations in America. It shows that 88 percent of blacks say the United States needs to continue to make legal and social changes in order for African-Americans to have equal rights with whites. Just 53 percent of whites say the country needs to make those improvements for blacks to achieve equality.

The Pew report also reflects the nation's political polarization: "About six in 10 (59 percent) white Republicans say too much attention is paid to race and racial issues these days, while only 21 percent of white Democrats agree."

The NAACP will be in Cincinnati on July 19, the one-year anniversary of DuBose's death at the hands of white University of Cincinnati police officer Ray Tensing during a traffic stop for a missing front license plate in Mount Auburn. Tensing faces a murder charge when he goes to trial October 24.

The NAACP comes to a city enjoying a rebirth that, statistically, is benefitting white residents far more than its black population. Government-funded redevelopment of The Banks and Over-the-Rhine is generally out of reach of the city's African-Americans.

The 2016 National Urban League State of Black America report shows that median household income for the region's African-Americans is less than half of that for whites – $28,600 compared to $58,000. Meanwhile, the black unemployment rate is double that for whites.

The national Urban League report followed a 164-page local Urban League publication, "The State of Black Cincinnati 2015: Two Cities," that documented race-based disparities across the board in education, income, incarceration, health, and life expectancy.

"Until and unless we allow everyone the opportunity to realize their full potential, our region will never be as vibrant or as rich as it could be," said Donna Jones Baker, president and CEO of the Urban League of Southwestern Ohio, which covers the Cincinnati and Dayton, Ohio, areas.

The lack of white acceptance of such facts focuses frequently on a perceived lack of work ethic among African-Americans – if only they tried harder, like the Irish and Italian immigrants – and violent crime, particularly the phenomenon known as black-on-black crime. It asserts the supposition that African-Americans are largely responsible for their substandard conditions.

NAACP president and CEO Brooks said the organization promotes personal responsibility and supports churches, mosques, and other institutions in the black community that make the same call. Yet, he said, crime is a product of a toxic combination of poor schools, poor policing, and the lack of jobs.

"It is that way in any community that is inundated with guns and drugs with ineffective policing and insufficient economic hope – regardless of race," Brooks said.

Earlier in June, Georgetown University sociologist and author Michael Eric Dyson gave the keynote address at a community event called the "Black Agenda Cincinnati." It drew 1,500 people to a daylong workshop at Woodward Career Technical High School in Bond Hill.

He said white references to black-on-black crime are intended to distract and to divert attention from larger issues of economic inequality and police misconduct. According to the U.S. Department of Justice, 93 percent of black homicide victims are killed by another black person; 84 percent of white homicide victims are killed by another white.

"If you want integrated homicide rates, you've got to have integrated communities," Dyson said.

Cincinnati is the nation's fifth most residentially segregated metropolitan region. African-Americans have not shared in economic growth nationally and locally. As efforts at racial integration have fallen apart, blacks have been ghettoized in low-income, economically deprived, higher-crime neighborhoods that its residents say offer a small bridge out.

"The masses of black people do not do well," Dyson said. "They suffer in poor housing and poor schools. They are disproportionately put in prison. They are disproportionately expelled from kindergarten through high school. It's the best of times for some upper- and middle-class African-American people and the worst of times for the masses stuck at the bottom."

## One barrier down, many to go

These types of race-based economic, housing, police–community, health, and criminal-justice issues play out in the daily lives of African-Americans here and across the country.

Noah Sherman sees plenty of people stuck on the bottom of the city's economic ladder in his home neighborhood of Westwood. He also remembers what he, even as an 11-year-old boy, felt at the dawn of the Obama presidency.

"He broke down barriers, but I remember being afraid that he wasn't going to be able to get stuff done," Sherman said.

As he aged through the Obama years, issues of race became more pronounced in the young black man's life. As a student at DePaul Cristo Rey High School, Clifton, Sherman recalls a conversation with a white classmate in which she said race didn't play any role in society.

"I've learned from my life experiences that race plays a part in everything," he said. That's one of the reasons Sherman became involved in the NAACP at age 13 when he joined the local youth council. Today he is president of the NAACP's Ohio state Youth and College Division and a full voting member of the Cincinnati branch.

He is interested in law, even if he decides not to pursue it as a career. Knowledge is power, he said. He wants to know his legal rights. He wants to educate other African-Americans who either don't know their rights or don't make the effort to know them. He sees many people in his community who are "tormented" by job discrimination or by interactions with police in which their civil rights are violated, he said.

Fear of the police is omnipresent in the black experience here, even though, Sherman said, "I know some good police officers. Not all police offers are bad."

For the most part, Sherman avoided the trapdoors of growing up black and male in this society. He talked in 2014 at a town hall meeting in Evanston about a white police officer in a cruiser following him slowly for no reason as he walked home on foot.

"How can I feel safe from the police?" Sherman asked a panel that included former Cincinnati police chief Jeffrey Blackwell and councilman Chris Seelbach.

That fear motivates Nicole Taylor to invest a great deal of her time in the NAACP as its third vice president. The 36-year-old mother of three from Westwood also chairs the Cincinnati NAACP's criminal justice and public safety committee.

Her fear is more intense and more personal than her anger. Taylor has two daughters, 6 and 18, the oldest a 2016 Dater High School graduate who will attend Tuskegee University.

Her 9-year-old child is a son, Jordan Stephens.

"In a few years, he is going to be a young black man and looked at as a threat," Taylor said. "I couldn't imagine losing him in an open-carry state."

In Ohio, 570,000 people have received new concealed-carry handgun licenses or have renewed them, according to state documents. In 2015 alone, 97,000 new permits were issued, a 50 percent increase from 2012.

Taylor fears citizens who carry guns. She fears police. She knows details of cases in which black men and boys have died. John Crawford III, 22, was shot and killed by police in a suburban Dayton, Ohio, Walmart store while holding a toy BB gun. "Tamir, Trayvon, none of them deserved to die."

In March 2012, Taylor took her son, then 5, to a rally on Fountain Square that protested the death of Martin, the Florida teenager gunned down by self-appointed neighborhood watchman George Zimmerman. Taylor blinked back tears in a sharp early spring western sun that evening and said, "While I can't imagine that he will be looked at and feared, I know he will be."

In her role with the NAACP, Taylor helped to craft a resolution that will go to the entire national delegation for a vote. It calls for mandatory increases in police de-escalation training. If approved, the resolution would become part of the NAACP's national platform.

"It happens over and over and over, unarmed black men being killed by police. It hurts," said Taylor, who works for an international labor union. "It's so overwhelming that you feel helpless, but I reject that. We have the right to live in a society that is not racist."

⸻ ◆ ⸻

# NAACP's top legal eagle from Madisonville

"Some people run from where they're from. Not me"

*July 18, 2016*

Bradford Berry talked Saturday over the noon hour about the arc of his days. How did a black child growing up in Madisonville end up with one of the country's most important civil rights jobs as chief lawyer of the NAACP?

"I remember playing Knothole baseball in this big park on Stewart Avenue, right there at Chandler," said Berry, 53, back in his hometown as NAACP general counsel for the organization's 107th annual convention this week. "My parents were bound and determined to keep me and my brothers out of the streets. So piano lessons, baseball, all kinds of things to keep us occupied.

"Really, it's through God's grace. I feel like a lot of doors have been opened to me. I've been given a lot of opportunities. I tried to take advantage of those opportunities. But there's no way to explain it other than through God's grace."

At the end of a 45-minute interview, Berry posed for a portrait in the Duke Energy Convention Center and rushed off to an NAACP board meeting.

Unknown to him at the time was the breaking news that another child growing up in Madisonville — on Chandler Street, just a couple of blocks from where Berry spent the same kind of hot, sticky summer day on a ball diamond — would not have the same opportunities he had. A 5-year-old boy was shot and killed shortly after 12 p.m. Saturday. He was upstairs with his 11-year-old brother in their home in the 6200 block of Chandler.

On Wednesday night, as Berry and NAACP delegates started to arrive in Cincinnati, a 2-year-old and a man were left in critical condition following a shooting in Madisonville on Whetsel Avenue near Chandler.

The violence contrasted with the path Berry has forged in his life and career, a clear signal of the work that remains to be done at the NAACP and in society.

"That's my neighborhood," Berry said Sunday when told about the shootings. "I walked those streets daily. I am heartbroken, and chances are I know someone in those families."

## "I was offended by what I perceived to be discrimination"

Don't let the serene demeanor and verbal eloquence mislead, say family members and people who best know Berry. Inside burns a passion for racial justice. It is fueled by a strong intellect and almost three decades of far-reaching legal work — not to mention personal experiences as a black male profiled by white authorities both as a child in Cincinnati and as an adult professional driving to and from his suburban Washington, D.C., home.

"I remember having the impression that African-American kids, our interactions with the police were different," Berry said. "I remember coming Downtown to go shopping and getting followed around stores, and that offended me. I was offended by what I perceived to be discrimination."

Forty years later, he still is. Wearing dark-rimmed glasses and a dark suit, Berry recalls a conversation with his 19-year-old son.

"You have to know what you're doing. And you have to look like you know what you're doing," he said. "It is still the case where African-Americans have to score high in every category. Nothing gets overlooked. We continue to be denied opportunities that we should get because our flaws are magnified. We all have flaws, but ours are magnified."

His parents gave Berry and his three older brothers the same message in the family home in Madisonville. They were solidly middle-class. Woodvill Berry worked in Oakley on the floor at Cincinnati Milacron, an industrial technology company serving the plastics processing industry (and known today simply as Milacron). Their late mother, Addie, reviewed tax returns for the Internal Review Service in Covington. Both came from rural Kentucky and did not have access to higher education. They would make sure their sons went to college.

Bradford Berry graduated in 1981 from Walnut Hills High School, where he noticed that other black students lived in predominantly black neighborhoods and had gone to segregated schools.

He took careful note of the world around him and mindfully processed what he heard and saw.

"My brother always had a calmness to his approach to any situation," said Darrell Berry, 58, who still lives in Madisonville. "What he had as a child most people don't develop until later in life. Brad reacts rationally to matters most of us react irrationally or too quickly to."

He went to George Washington University for an economics degree and onto Yale Law School. Bradford Berry worked for a year as a law clerk for Judge Nathaniel Jones in the U.S. Court of Appeals for the Sixth Circuit in Cincinnati.

Jones had served as NAACP general counsel from 1969 through his 1979 appointment to the federal bench. Jones argued school desegregation cases and defenses of affirmative action before the U.S. Supreme Court.

"He's a very bright lawyer, measured and thoughtful," Jones said of Berry, who expressed to Jones his interest to one day serving the NAACP. "It is a civil rights organization. It is not a social work or a social organization. He has the expertise to guide it back in that direction. The issues are critical."

Berry has worked in Washington for both private law firms and in the federal government for the Federal Communications Commission and the Department of Justice.

## Part of NAACP president's "dream team"

Praising Berry's ability to community with people of various backgrounds, NAACP President and CEO Cornell William Brooks recruited him in June 2015 to be part of his "dream team." Berry runs the organization's legal department, which consists of just two other staff attorneys. Much of the work required of the department is to serve legal needs of 2,200 NAACP units around the country. Its other work consists of outside legal challenges — including those brought against some states for alleged illegal voting rights restrictions and a class action lawsuit filed in May against Michigan officials over the Flint water crisis.

It's those efforts that consume scarce resources and attract most of the attention. And they have historically, dating to Charles Hamilton Houston's attacks on separate-but-equal laws in the 1930s and 1940s and Thurgood Marshall's *Brown v. Board of Education* victory against segregated public education more than 60 years ago.

"Big shoes to fill," Berry said.

Behind the scenes, in the face of finite resources, he has worked to strengthen relationships with and secure work from outside law firms on behalf of the NAACP. Much of the legal work done by Berry's office and its partners focuses on three areas: voting rights, policing, and education:

*Voting rights:* In 2013, the U.S. Supreme Court voted 5-4 to overturn Section 5 of the Voting Rights Act that had required some states and local governments to obtain federal preclearance before implementing any changes to their voting laws.

"A lot of states could not wait to enact some of these voting restrictions," he said. Legal battles continue in North Carolina, Texas, and Georgia.

*Policing:* "We're talking about standards, screening, and training to standards," Berry said.

"The thing that is missing in much of the discussion is are they temperamentally fit to work in a predominantly African-American neighborhood?" he said of some police officers. "If you are afraid of African-Americans, African-American men, and big African-American men, then you have no business policing in a black neighborhood."

*Education:* "It is really priority one. Every year, we have kids dropping out of school or graduating without the skills to go to college or get a job. What are these people supposed to do? We have to find a strategy to improve the performance of the K-12 public education system for our kids."

Each of these issues alone stand tall as obstacles, Berry said; they are daunting when taken collectively.

Yet, Berry said Saturday as he walked to an NAACP board meeting at the convention, he wants to stay in the job as long as the organization will keep him.

"I feel," he said, "like I'm exactly where I'm supposed to be."

His journey started in Madisonville and still leads back. He planned to drive there Sunday night to visit his father.

"You know, some people run from where they're from. Not me," he said. "Me, I'm a Madisonville kid through and through."

# CHAPTER 9

# THE BLACK FAMILY

*Even years before I became the first (and only) of seven siblings in a Catholic family to divorce and later remarry, I didn't quite understand the narrow definition of "family" that some people insisted on using, and how they would direct it disparagingly at African-Americans. Here are four black families of different shapes and sizes that I've had the good fortune to know.*

# Then she saw the love in DJ's eyes

Experienced foster mother Pat McCollum didn't think
she could handle a severely disabled child

*June 8, 2012*

DJ McCollum leans his left ear – his only one – near his mother's mouth.

"I love you," Pat McCollum says in a loud, clear tone.

DJ squeals and grunts and waves his arms in happiness. Then he pinches a grape with his left thumb and index finger, pops it into his mouth and leans in again.

"I love you," Pat says.

The pattern stops only when DJ's plate is empty of grapes.

"They tell me he's deaf," Pat said later. "I don't believe them."

DJ and Pat have been proving experts wrong for a long time. DJ wasn't supposed to live past 2, a year after an older child in his Winton Place home dropped a match into DJ's crib, burning him over 85 percent of his body, leaving him disfigured without both feet and his right hand and ear or the ability to speak or hear or function intellectually beyond the level of an 18-month-old.

He's now 21. He came into Pat's life in 1998 at age 7 as a foster child, one of more than 70 she has had in her College Hill home in the past 21 years. She had adopted three. DJ became the fourth in 2002.

Their relationship has taught Pat about resilience, patience, and love. And when she thinks back 14 years to the day she met the boy, she remembers that she didn't initially want him. A former teen mother and high school dropout, Pat doubted that she could handle such a severely disabled child, even though she'd gained a reputation for caring for special needs foster children. And her friends reminded her that DJ would force her to rearrange her own life that she had worked hard to put right.

DJ did change everything, including Pat's perspective.

"I say he's normal," she said. "There is so much in there to draw out."

DJ McCollum's life entered a new phase this week.

He is spending three days in Fairfield at Sonny Spot Too, a day center that helps adults with developmental disabilities learn skills. In his first week there with 40 other adults, DJ strung beads and used scissors for the first time.

"I am so proud of my baby," Pat said.

DJ is going to Blue Ash the other two days of the week, to Jewish Vocational Service, where he is being assessed to determine what kind of work he can perform before joining a workforce of about 150. One possibility for DJ is labeling, assembling, and mailing dog leashes.

"Now he is on to the rest of his life," Pat said, "like any other young man his age."

## Milestones mark a young life

DJ graduated May 18 from Woodward Career Technical High School, with a full diploma. Wearing his prosthetic legs of different lengths beneath his gown, DJ pushed his walker across the stage at Xavier University's Cintas Center.

"DJ is a very strong young man with a very strong advocate in Miss Pat," said Woodward Principal Shauna Murphy. "He touched a lot of lives here in four years. The reaction of our students and staff was very heartfelt."

Pat had watched as students and parents erupted in cheers. "Eight steps," she said. "He made it up eight steps."

DJ completed his goals in Woodward's special program for teens with disabilities, learning how to walk with new artificial legs and developing such skills as folding a towel.

DJ had used a wheelchair for several years, even though most of his right leg had been saved from the fire. In 2009, his mother, doctors, and physical therapists decided to have the leg amputated above the knee because it would give him the chance to walk with artificial legs.

"There were no guarantees he would be able to walk," Pat said. "I felt it was unfair that he wouldn't have the chance, though."

Hard work and teamwork made it happen.

"He was so tall, a full 6 feet," Pat said. "They measured his femur (thigh bone). I thought he would be about 5-4."

## Mom understands hard road, too

The challenges are many and often messy. DJ likes to remove his diaper as often as possible. At times, other children have reacted to his disfigured face and body by crying. One day at the Winton Woods water park, three boys started beating DJ as he sat playing in the spray.

"I ran up, grabbed those boys and yelled, 'Where's your mother?'" Pat said.

She discovered how much DJ loves water when her pastor, the Rev. Damon Lynch, Jr., baptized DJ. He didn't want to get out of the font.

"I remember when she took him in," said Lynch, pastor of New Jerusalem Baptist Church, Carthage. "I didn't think she could do it. I'd seen these stories in the movies, but I'd never seem someone take on somebody so challenged in real life. There must have been something there in the plan of God."

Pat agrees. Yet she is no stranger to long odds.

Never married, she had her first child in high school and dropped out. She went to night school and summer school and graduated a year ahead of her classmates. She was the first African-American bunny in Cincinnati's Playboy Club. She went on to earn a bachelor's and a master's in social work from the University of Cincinnati and has worked there as an adjunct instructor. Pat has trained incoming foster parents.

She knows DJ will live with her the rest of his life.

"Either I die first, or he does. I will never separate from him," she said.

Yet she encourages people to take on children with special needs. Her message is simple and direct.

"It's OK to foster these kids," Pat said. "These children have the right to a family, to have love and to be pushed to their highest potential."

She first had to convince herself.

She started as a foster parent in 1991 for the county agency. She quickly adapted and specialized in children with special needs. But when a caseworker called Pat in a panic, described DJ and asked her to care for him, Pat said, "Hell, no."

Later that day, the caseworker called back and asked Pat to take him until another family returned from vacation.

She agreed, reluctantly.

## DJ finds a mother and a big family

Yet DJ won over Pat and the rest of the family, including birth daughter Detra McCollum, now 48 and a hair stylist.

Detra has twisted DJ's hair into dreadlocks. Pat wanted to grow out DJ's hair to prevent children from being afraid of him.

Besides styling DJ's hair, Detra is teaching DJ more American Sign Language. He knows the signs for *stop, bad, more, candy,* and *soda pop.* "What a sweet tooth," Detra said. DJ likes to slap hands and fist bump. He can often dress himself with minimal help.

"I mean, he's family," said Detra, an adoptive mother herself of seven former foster children. "He just fits in and can get the attention he needs. To me, that's just my little brother."

And Pat's son. They share a defiant resilience.

"He was sitting on my lap one day, and I was singing to him," during the first week she cared for him, she said. "I was supposed to give him back to the county."

He reached up to her face with his left hand and the stump of his right arm. He cupped his left hand on her cheek, guiding her face near his ear.

"Right then, he had me," she said. "I love his beautiful little self. I see in his eyes how much he loves me when I walk into his room. He is the love of my life."

---

# Father's Day for a nontraditional father

"Their last chance to see how a man is supposed to treat a woman"

*June 16, 2013*

Some 20 years ago, when Jackie and Robert Humphries decided to become foster parents, one prevailing goal drove them to open their home to teen girls – an especially difficult group to place because newborns and infants are most in demand.

"It was their last chance to see how a man is supposed to treat a woman," Jackie Humphries said.

Today, even as the most recent of their 25 foster children has found refuge and routine in the same Clifton house the newlyweds bought in 1984, they've accomplished their mission. Many of the girls they brought up as their own have finished college and delayed marriage and motherhood until they found men who – like Robert does Jackie – treat them like their queen.

And on this Father's Day, several of the Humphries' former foster daughters will visit or call the man they still refer to as "Uncle Robert" to thank him for helping change their lives for the better.

## Husband, wife complement each other as parents

Hundreds of children in Hamilton County alone need these kinds of homes. At any given time, an average of 850 children up to age 17 are in county custody because of abuse and neglect.

"I don't know my birth father. This is my father," said Theresa Warren, 28, of Silverton, who was in and out of foster homes before settling with the Humphries for seven years and graduating in 2004 from Withrow High School.

Jackie Humphries, now 55, didn't make it easy on the foster children. She kept them busy in extracurricular activities ranging from school-based sports teams and the Girl Scouts to the Avondale Youth Council.

Kennetha Harris-Godfrey, now 32 and the married mother of three daughters – 10, 4, and a newborn – described the household as "strict but loving."

"No nail polish, no makeup, no boyfriends, no phone calls with boys," said Harris-Godfrey, a track and volleyball star at Aiken High School who went on to run at Kentucky State University. She had been in three foster homes before coming to the Humphries in third grade. She left in seventh grade and came back in tenth, when she stayed through graduation.

"I was a virgin when I went to college because they told us how boys were only interested in one thing," said Harris-Godfrey, who lives in Columbus with her family but still frequently visits the Humphries. "I see now how they are my models as a wife and a mother. They made me feel like the man I was going to get was not going to be the running back. He was going to be the quarterback. And he was."

The dress code was strict, too. Jackie was the enforcer by design. Robert, now 62, was the good cop who'd come home from his job as a Hamilton County juvenile court bailiff and round sharp edges, taking a foster child for a drive and attending a sporting event.

Still, he had the look, a trimmed mustache and the clear, sharp eyes of law enforcement. Former foster children say they were intimidated if not sometimes scared. He and his wife complement each other as parents. He is measured and calm; Jackie, with big hair flying, is in constant motion.

"I told the girls all the time, 'You don't have to dress overly revealing to look attractive,'" Robert said.

After a while, the girls policed each other and themselves in the house, three stories with a tall central stairwell and filled with clean but well-worn furniture. One of the family's favorite stories, as Jackie tells it, is how one foster daughter was dressed "like a hoochie mama with a blue jeans skirt halfway up her butt," she said. "But when she saw Robert coming home, she ran upstairs and changed."

## Humphries' foster kids strive to emulate their relationship

The couple didn't intend to be foster parents. They have two of their own birth children. Ricardo, 28, is in the Army National Guard. Jasmine, 22, is majoring in chemistry at the University of Cincinnati and is now studying as an exchange student in China.

Their first two foster children were Jackie's sister's granddaughters, who were 7 and 8 when they came from a troubled home in California to live in Clifton.

"It was about kinship," Jackie said of a tradition in African-American families. "You take care of each other."

They really were Aunt Jackie and Uncle Robert to the first two, and when other foster children showed up, the names stuck. They took the leap into foster parenting, first working directly with Hamilton County and now through Lighthouse Youth Services.

Lighthouse foster care director Jami Clarke says the couple "holds the children accountable. They are naturals," she said.

Perhaps a reason is that both come from large families. Robert is the ninth of eleven children and grew up in Covington. Jackie was fourth of eight and grew up in Corryville and Avondale. Five of their foster daughters were teen mothers.

They formally adopted one child, a son, Terrell, now 27, who came to them as a foster child when he was 7 and never left. They adopted him right before he turned 18. He changed his last name to Humphries.

"Really, if not for Aunt Jackie and Uncle Robert, I'd be on the street or locked up, like my twin brother, who's been in jail for 11 years," said Terrell, who works as an ambulance driver for a private company.

He recalls being overwhelmed in school and far behind when he got to the Humphries.

"Aunt Jackie taught me mathematics," he said.

Uncle Robert taught him how to be a man.

"Walk away when you're angry, get up and go to work every day, stay healthy, don't drink or smoke, buy for a girl on a date, always hold the door for a woman" are some of the lessons he saw his adoptive father live each and every day.

Terrell is unmarried, has no children, and has remained unattached. His standards, he said, are high.

"I want to get married and have a family, but what I want in my wife is a woman like Aunt Jackie, and what I want to be as a husband is my Uncle Robert," Terrell said.

On this Father's Day, Aunt Jackie said her husband remains the answer to a prayer she had as a teenager.

"He has such high morals and compassion," Jackie said. "When I was 15 and 16, I prayed for a man like my daddy. My daddy loved my mother so much. He would do anything for her. My husband treats me that way. And that is what we try to pass on. These girls have to know their self-worth."

# What's in a name?

If it's Damon Lynch, a lot

*February 20, 2016*

Police snapped handcuffs on six people the night of July 31 at Fountain Square. The arrests came at the end of a rally protesting the police shooting death twelve days earlier of black motorist Samuel DuBose in Mount Auburn.

One of those six names printed August 1 on the Hamilton County Common Pleas Court docket stood out: Damon Lynch.

Damon Lynch IV, 31, son and grandson of two of the city's most prominent black church pastors and civil rights activists, would plead guilty in January to disorderly conduct and pay a fine. A judge dropped the charge of resisting arrest.

"I don't need a tragedy to protest," Lynch IV said. "I protest daily because I understand the system is flawed. I want to be there. I want to do better than they did."

"They" are his two forebears of the same name: his grandfather, the Rev. Damon Lynch Jr., 77, and father, the Rev. Damon Lynch III, 55. And bettering them will be a tall order, even for a man who gladly carries the weight of his name and who stands, fully bearded, 6 feet, 6 inches – two inches taller than his previous two namesakes. They share a famous local name and a passion for justice and civil rights. But make no mistake, they are their own men whose tactics reflect their differing times. To wit: The frustration the newest generation of African-Americans is experiencing in terms of race-based economic and criminal justice disparities.

"His generation inherits a deficiency, a deficit," Lynch III said of his son. "I don't want people to be afraid, especially black people, to say that right now it's worse than it was in the 1950s or the '40s."

He understands the anger behind his son's arrest. "You always need somebody, I don't care what the movement is, somebody's going to climb the flagpole," Lynch III said. "We applaud those people."

Since the late 1960s, a man named Damon Lynch has been central to civil rights agitation in Cincinnati, first as a participant but emerging as the leader in the 1990s when fellow preachers voted Lynch Jr. president of the Baptist Ministers Conference.

Lynch Jr.'s tenure brought the conference back to 1960s-style church-based development in the city's predominantly black neighborhoods and protests against police treatment of African-Americans. That post vaulted Lynch Jr. into a position of individual influence in the building of the National Underground Railroad Freedom Center and bringing the Rev. Billy Graham to Cincinnati for a 2002 revival at Paul Brown Stadium at which Graham, for the first time, proclaimed racism a sin.

In 2001, after eleven years as an Over-the-Rhine Baptist church pastor, another Damon Lynch emerged in newspaper headlines. Lynch III, as a leader of Cincinnati Black United Front, organized marches and the downtown boycott of restaurants and entertainment venues following the police shooting death of an unarmed black man, Timothy Thomas, by a white Cincinnati police officer just blocks from what then was the location of Lynch III's New Prospect Baptist Church. One of the signatures on Cincinnati's still-hailed 2002 Collaborative Agreement, which changed how the city's police department did its job, is that of Damon Lynch III.

## "Corporate, grassroots, underground"

Besides their height, the four men named Damon Lynch have much in common.

The original Damon Lynch, born in rural Georgia in 1897 and standing 6 foot 3, migrated north to Lincoln Heights and worked first in construction and then as a barber. He lived late in life with Damon Jr. and his wife, Barbara, before his death in 1976.

By that time, Lynch Jr. had entered his seventh year as pastor of New Jerusalem Baptist Church in Carthage, where he remains today.

The congregation of New Prospect called Lynch III as its pastor in 1990. The church moved to Roselawn in 2013. Lynch IV works for his father at the church in an urban agriculture project. His business card reads, "High Urban Media Specialist," with expertise in marketing and branding.

"They live through me, and that makes me feel real good to know I'll be walking around here for a long time," said Lynch Jr., honored in 2010 by the Cincinnati USA Regional Chamber as a Great Living Cincinnatian.

Barbara Lynch, 74, has been married 56 years to Lynch Jr. They met growing up in Lincoln Heights.

Of her husband, son, and their namesake grandson, she said, "They all three have a deep concern for the welfare and treatment of all people, especially for African-American people."

Eric Lynch, 26, brother of Damon IV, is an actor at the Goodman Theatre in Chicago.

"I see three men who are standing upright, uncompromising, principled," said Eric, who has appeared on *Chicago Fire* and *Chicago P.D.*

The three Damon Lynches recognize similarities – they are especially communicative and are independent thinkers. Lynch Jr. said, for example, he and his wife did not push their son into the ministry. Family members and friends note similarities but say their personalities reveal the differences in the times when their activism came of age.

Barbara Lynch said her husband is patient and "can talk at length to build a consensus. My son is not as patient and seeks to bring about change more rapidly. My grandson is very passionate about his generation and wants instant change."

The consensus is Lynch Jr. is "diplomatic," with the ability to talk with kings and paupers. Lynch III is described by a friend as a "tortured introvert" like his mother. Lynch III's sermons burn with intellectual intensity and social perspective – such as saying the gentrification of Over-the-Rhine did not solve poverty and homelessness, just moved it somewhere else – while his father's preaching style normally builds to a sweat-soaked, theatric finish. No wonder, say family members, Lynch Jr. wanted to be an actor, a talent grandson Eric clearly inherited.

"People ask me, 'When are you going to preach?,'" said Lynch IV, active on social media. "I am not a pastor, but I preach everywhere I go."

He supports Bernie Sanders for president and is concerned about food and water safety, especially given the lead crisis in Flint, Michigan. Earlier this month he spoke at a news conference about teen suicide in the black community at Church of the Living God in Avondale, where he promoted a movement called "I Shall Live and Not Die."

"My grandfather is corporate," Lynch IV said. "My father is grassroots. I'm, at this point, underground."

## A respectful "clash of ideologies"

Protests of the Samuel DuBose shooting might have pushed Damon Lynch IV into his public life. The police shooting of another unarmed black man, Timothy Thomas, in 2001, made Lynch III a leader rivaling his father's influence, though they differed on how to bring about change.

Lynch Jr. sought diplomacy and peace through efforts to build the $110 million Freedom Center on the riverfront and to bring Graham here.

Lynch III confronted the larger problem of police–community relations.

"We had a clash or two on ideology," Lynch Jr. said. "My son showed how tenacious he is to get his message across."

Lynch Jr. had arranged to bring entertainer and activist Harry Belafonte here in support of the Freedom Center. Lynch III "siphoned" off Belafonte and took him on a walk through Over-the-Rhine.

"When he saw what was going on there, [Belafonte] joined me," said Lynch III, who opposed the building of the Freedom Center and wanted that money invested in impoverished Cincinnati neighborhoods.

As part of leading a boycott of downtown, Lynch III picketed the Graham crusade but, ultimately, met the evangelist backstage.

National civil rights leaders who came through Cincinnati during the long, hot summer of 2001 – Belafonte, the Rev. Al Sharpton, Martin Luther King III, the Rev. Jesse Jackson Sr. – all ended up in Lynch Jr.'s North Avondale home for meetings. Lynch III participated.

Lynch IV, a Princeton High School junior, watched and listened and said the experience helped to shape his activism.

Despite the intra-family disagreements, the two prominent local preachers as father and son maintained a high level of discourse, Lynch Jr. said. "We kept our integrity."

They taped an interview for CNN with host Paula Zahn at the WCET-TV's studio in the West End.

"They wanted him to cuss me out," Lynch Jr. said of his son. "We did not. We debated but respected each other's views. It never aired. I guess 'if it doesn't bleed, it doesn't lead.'"

That behavior is typical of the Lynch family, said longtime friend Iris Roley, a Bond Hill business owner who has worked for two decades with Lynch Jr. on police reform.

"Everything they do," she said, "they do with elegance and grace."

Like Lynch Jr. and his son, Roley expects an even greater civil rights contribution will be made by Lynch IV, which is difficult to imagine given the transformational work done by his father and grandfather.

"The Fourth is very intentional about his steps and very aware of the name and its legacy," she said. "He is connected and capable as far as social justice work and his ability to bring people together."

So with Lynch IV's future apparently well focused, just one question remains.

Will there be a Damon Lynch V?

"Of course," Lynch IV said. "Lord willing."

# Marriage of faith, food, and music

"Celebrate our historic strengths that have kept us alive"

*August 19, 2016*

Paul and Cynthia Booth have donated their time and money to the Midwest Black Family Reunion since its beginning in 1989.

The Booths gave freely because of their belief in the core mission of the annual event: to promote the strengths, traditions, values, and coping skills of the black family and dispel negative contemporary myths and stereotypes of its demise.

The Cincinnati event is the nation's longest-running Black Family Reunion. The 28th annual celebration will be Friday through Sunday at Sawyer Point and other locations throughout Greater Cincinnati.

The Booths, of Amberley Village, will be honored as Midwest Black Family Reunion's Family of the Year.

The overall event features three days of activities and traditions central to the black family: faith, food, music – adding up to togetherness. It transforms Sawyer Point into a carnival midway, where fun and games balance the serious, such as a Sunday morning religious service and two days' worth of free screenings that address race-based health disparities.

Today, some outsiders allege the black family has deteriorated and thus created economic and social problems among African-Americans. Yet the Booths and others inside the black community say the black family remains resilient and vital.

"The state of the black family is not different than any other ethnicity, any other family," said Paul Booth, Sr., 62, a former two-time Cincinnati City Council member and Congressional aide to David Mann. "That being said, does the black family have some work to do? Yes.

"That's what the Black Family Reunion is all about: going back to our roots. The Black Family Reunion is no different than the Hispanic Festival or the Oktoberfest. It celebrates the legacy of the black family."

He and his wife, married for 36 years, said they held fast to their forebears' traditions, family meals and family prayer among them.

"I hope the black family never loses the ability to pray," said Cynthia Booth, owner of six regional McDonald's franchises that ring the Interstate 275 beltline and employs 400 people. "No matter the trials and tribulations they face, I hope they can still pray. It sustains us. The family becomes stronger through prayer.

"There is not a time that our children have not heard us pray, collectively, and for them. We are constantly praying for their wellbeing and their futures. Prayer has been a very strong force in the black family and needs to take even a greater role as we try to sustain ourselves."

## The "total of community"

The late Dorothy I. Height, president emerita of the National Council of Negro Women, created the Black Family Reunion. The first, held on the National Mall in 1986, was sponsored by Cincinnati-based Procter & Gamble. The second was held three years later in Cincinnati.

In a 2008 interview with the *Enquirer*, Height said she came up with the reunion concept after watching a Bill Moyers television documentary titled "The Vanishing Black Family."

She said the documentary focused only on teen pregnancy, not unique to the black community but endemic in society as a whole. Instead of protesting, she said, Height wanted to create something positive.

"We felt we needed to show the total of the black family, to celebrate our historic strengths and valued traditions that have kept us alive," she told the *Enquirer*.

Cincinnati is the only Black Family Reunion remaining of the original dozen-plus that were held across the country in major markets that included Philadelphia, Chicago, and Los Angeles. Outside of Cincinnati, the only other Black Family Reunion is held in a small city in north-central Illinois, Rockford, where its chapter of the National Council of Negro Women has since organized an annual event.

Thirty years after the Moyers 1986 documentary aired, the black family remains under assault from some corners of American society. Critics point to a 2013 report by the U.S. Centers for Disease Control and Prevention (CDC) showing that 72 percent of births to non-Hispanic black women occur outside of marriage.

Yet the same report shows that black fathers were statistically the most involved with their children on a daily basis than any other group of fathers – whether black fathers lived with their children or at another home – in a number of measurable areas: helping their children with homework, discussing events of children's days with them, taking them to and from activities outside the home, and frequency of eating meals with them.

The black family and black church are two institutions that have helped to sustain African-Americans in the face of economic, educational and health disparities, said the Rev. K. Z. Smith, pastor of Avondale's Corinthian Baptist Church, host church of the Midwest Black Family Reunion.

"The two are linked, the family and the church," he said. "As long as I can remember, it was rare to find black children who didn't go to church. Even if the parents didn't go, they made sure their children did."

Yet as the black middle class grew, Smith said, dependence on the church waned and some parents no longer require their children to go to services.

The Midwest Family Reunion, if nothing else, aims to cement that bond between the black family and the black church

Friday's lead-off event, the Heritage Breakfast, will be held at The Word of Deliverance Ministries for the World, Inc., in Forest Park and will feature a keynote address by national civil rights leader the Rev. Otis Moss Jr., one-time pastor of Mount Zion Baptist Church in Lockland.

Sunday morning starts at the reunion with an outdoor service at Sawyer Point. This year, it will feature Pastor Donnie McClurkin, of Perfecting Faith Ministries in Freeport, New York, and a prominent gospel music artist. Attendees can be baptized during the service.

For more black families than not, like the Booths, they said, the church remains an integral part of life.

## The next generation

Paul and Cynthia Booth are members of Greater New Hope Missionary Baptist Church, Avondale. It was there in 2007 that Paul Booth Jr. was ordained. The 34-year-old pastor and his wife, Asha, now have a new daughter, 4-month-old Laila. He also has a new church, start-up Legacy Pointe in Kenwood. Paul Jr. is a sixth-generation minister in the Booth family, a string that skipped only Paul Sr. and whose most notable member is Paul Sr.'s father, the late Lavaughn Venchael (L.V.) Booth, a national pioneer in black church-based economic and community development.

Paul Booth Jr. has inherited the even demeanor of a preacher beneath which burns intensity and conviction: calling out the media for focusing more on the shortcomings of the black family than its greater number of achievements, praising the historic and enduring work ethic of African-Americans, and the strong desire of his people to be educated and achieve.

He and his now 25-year-old brother Martin both attended Cincinnati Hills Christian Academy. Paul Jr. then earned a political science degree from DePauw University in Green Castle, Indiana, before moving to Atlanta and finishing a master's degree in divinity at Emory University.

"We're living in some challenging times for the family unit as we know it, both socially and politically," he said. "And the black family is not enduring any challenges other families are not. But what is covered is what is highlighted and resonates in peoples' minds. I believe that the foundation of the black family is very strong."

Martin Booth – named after the Rev. Dr. Martin Luther King Jr., an associate of his minister grandfather – earned an undergraduate business degree from Wake Forest University before moving to Atlanta, where he worked as an account manager at Coca-Cola Enterprises. He recently returned to Cincinnati to work in the family business, running McDonald's restaurants, but plans to pursue an MBA beginning next year at the University of Chicago or Northwestern University.

"We, as the black family, as you sit and listen to us, we don't want to be viewed as the exception, we want to be viewed as the norm," Martin Booth said. "I believe, going back to how we're viewed on television, that's what we're seen as. We have to educate people as to what you stand for. The black family is strong. We are intelligent. We are hardworking. We are constantly trying to break down barriers and advance ourselves.

"I don't think our values are an exception. I think it's based on the opportunities you are granted. I think what we have tried to do is try to live out the values we were taught at home."

# CHAPTER 10

# MILLION MAN MARCH

*I remain grateful to the then-leader of Cincinnati's Nation of Islam community, Minister James X Robinson, who rebuked a junior associate during a group interview who'd questioned whether I, a white reporter, should be trusted to write accurately about the event and its buildup. "He has proven himself to be qualified and fair," said Robinson, who cooperated with me for many years. During the march in Washington —and a prayer service on the National Mall — I was moved to the verge of tears by the challenge to be a better husband, father, and citizen. Fatigued from the long weekend of bus travel and work and knowing I still had to get to the USA Today office in suburban Virginia to write and file, I took a deep breath and let my notebook and pen drop to the grass. Black men I didn't know standing on either side of me each reached openly for my hands and invited me to pray with them. I did.*

## Black men's march inspires and divides

*October 11, 1995*

Saturday night, when he boards one of 75 to 100 buses leaving the Tristate bound for Washington, D.C., Reggie Brazzile said he will become a warrior for his people.

"My job as a young black man is to get knowledge," said Brazzile, 31, a University of Cincinnati graduate student and one of an estimated 7,800 local black men from Cincinnati expected to participate Monday in the Million Man March on Washington, D.C.

"This is about self-determination and independence, and I have to do my part," he said.

National organizers say the march is a show of unity by African-American men, and will emphasize that most black men stay in school, work hard, and care for their families.

The march is also described as a call for all black men to dedicate themselves to ending the urban cycles of crime, unemployment, drugs, and other conditions that feed negative media portrayals of black men.

A two-day program around the march will include speakers, musical performances, and a voter registration drive. The march begins at 11 a.m. at the Capitol building,

The man behind the march is Minister Louis Farrakhan, leader of the Nation of Islam.

"The black man is specifically under assault, and all of the legislation, for instance, that is coming on the heels of the new crime bill, is focused on filling new prisons with black men," Farrakhan wrote in a recent issue of *Emerge Magazine*. "We want to reverse the ugly look of black men around the world by giving the world a positive look at dedicated, sober, determined black men.

"Our men are ready if somebody will guide them. They are ready to shoulder their responsibility."

While the march has drawn support from many black organizations and leaders, the participation of Farrakhan – whose rhetoric some consider anti-Semitic – has alienated others.

The president of the National Baptist Convention USA Inc., the Rev. Henry Lyons of St. Petersburg, Fla., has urged its 33,000 affiliated churches and 8 million members to boycott the march.

In the Tristate, where more than 200 black Baptist churches are affiliated with the convention, two ministers declined to comment on the march directly, saying only that they supported Lyons's decision to boycott. Some other Baptist ministers are privately supporting congregants' participation.

There are other points of contention.

The Anti-Defamation League took out a large ad in the *New York Times*, saying the march will "unfortunately . . . be the most mainstream event led by an anti-Semite in recent American history. And that cannot be ignored."

Cincinnati Councilman Phil Heimlich repeated a similar message last week on the floor of the council when two local march organizers asked for Mayor Roxanne Qualls to proclaim October 16 "Million Man March" day in Cincinnati and for the council to approve a resolution supporting the march.

"Mr. Farrakhan has advocated racial division and has used the Jews consistently as a scapegoat," Heimlich said in an interview. "We are in a time when we need racial healing. I will vote against any such resolution."

Council is expected to address the matter again today.

Differences among major black organizations and religious groups can be overcome, said Farrakhan's local representative and the leader of the Nation of Islam community in the Tristate, Minister James X Robinson.

"It is clear the problems we face are much greater than the differences we might have," he said. Robinson said God has spoken through Farrakhan.

"This is a beginning to correct the ills immorality and the absence of God have caused. How can you love God when you hate your brother? The only thing that can save America is God."

A study by the Sentencing Project released last week shows that nearly one-third of black men in their 20s are in jail, prison, on probation or parole – a sharp increase over the one-in-four proportion of five years ago.

The organization, which is critical of stiffer sentencing policies and the "war on drugs," also found that black women in their 20s showed the greatest jump of all demographic groups under criminal justice supervision, up 78 percent from 1989 to 1994.

The march has been endorsed by many African-American organizations and leaders – such as the National NAACP; Dorothy Height, president of the National Council of Negro Women; Jessie Jackson; the National Black Police Association and the Black Social Workers.

Several local African-American groups also support the march, including the Cincinnati NAACP chapter, which gave its endorsement at a September 27 organizational meeting in Walnut Hills led by the Rev. Benjamin Chavis. Chavis, the former head of the NAACP, is the national director of the march.

Notable local participants will include Judge Leslie Isaiah Gaines of Hamilton County Municipal Court and former Cincinnati council member and former Cincinnati NAACP chapter president Paul Booth, who plans to attend with his son.

Robinson and other local march organizers criticized what they call white establishment organizations – including the mainstream media – which focus stories on the schisms, not on what they say promises to be a powerful show of unity.

The Rev. William Land, pastor of Freeman United Church of Christ in Walnut Hills and regional coordinator of the African-American Leadership Summit, said the march was bringing together African-Americans who are Christian and Muslim, Republican and Democrat, apolitical and atheist; 150,000 black men from Ohio, Kentucky, Indiana, and West Virginia are expected to march in Washington.

"This will be another example of the black man energizing all of American society. That is our history," Land said. "Even when we were enslaved, God used African men in America for that purpose. It is time again."

Reggie Brazzile knows it is time. "The day is significant," he said, "if after that day we begin to repair ourselves and our people."

◆

# Steps of hope, march of unity

Local men add their voices to today's "Million" in Washington, D.C.
*October 16, 1995*

WASHINGTON, D.C. – William L. "Sonny" Webb took the first steps on his path to the Million Man March almost fifty years ago.

His journey began as a child when he learned that his race made a difference. He was in fourth grade at Assumption Catholic School in colorblind Walnut Hills, where the children of first- and second-generation Italian immigrants played stickball with the grandchildren of freed slaves.

The public-school kids went to the zoo for their end-of-the-year field trip. The kids in parochial school went to Coney Island.

"I can remember the day like it was going to happen tomorrow," he said. "My mother put on my nicest white shirt, my neatest trousers, and me and my friends, we took the bus out to

Coney Island. All my friends got in, one by one, but when I got up to the entrance gate, the lady in the booth looked at me and said, 'I'm sorry, son.'

"Until then, race had been insignificant in my life. I was crushed. I could feel the pain just spread across my face."

Webb sits in a chartered bus heading east on Interstate 70, two miles outside Quaker City, Ohio. It is 5:35 Sunday morning. The dark bus cab is illuminated only by the glow of two overhead televisions, showing a film about segregated black sailors in World War II, *Proudly We Serve: The Men of the* U.S.S. Mason.

The caravan – three buses, a couple of vans, and some private cars – departed Swifton Commons Mall in Bond Hill and the Avondale Town Center shortly before 2 a.m. and stopped to pick up a handful of other marchers two hours later in Columbus.

## Beyond the hurt

Webb looks around the bus as he tells his Coney Island story. The hurt of a child appears on the man's face, but only for a moment. To him, this day is not about pain. It's about determination.

His face reflects that spirit.

"I'm coming here to gain insight into the solutions that are going to be discussed," said Webb, 59, a Kennedy Heights widower with three grown children. "Some of the problems have been inflicted on us. Some of them are self-inflicted."

Organizers promise to develop a new framework for renewing the nation's black communities.

Today's march, they say, is a first step. Between 500,000 and 1 million men are expected to attend the main program, 11 a.m. to 4 p.m. at the U.S. Capitol.

Webb, one of between 5,000 and 8,000 Tristate men participating, is focusing on the message of unity and positive change, not on the controversy surrounding the central figure, Minister Louis Farrakhan of the Nation of Islam.

"I'm a Catholic, and I don't agree with everything Farrakhan says," Webb said. "But the only way anything is going to happen is for us to come together and make it happen."

## Field of dreams

It is 7:48 a.m. The caravan pulls into a Smithton, Pennsylvania, truck stop. Daylight wakes napping riders. Groans greet *Forrest Gump* as the film begins to roll on the bus televisions.

Webb, a group leader at General Electric Aircraft Engines in Evendale and a former professional baseball player, has a specific solution to help black youth.

It's baseball. His voice rises with excitement when he talks about turning two dozen acres of inherited land near Blanchester into a summer sports retreat for urban children, black and white.

"Learning to play baseball can teach kids some responsibility," said Webb, who played part of the 1962 season for the Washington Senators farm club in Wilson, North Carolina. "You learn discipline. You learn that failure is part of life. You learn that the team is more important than the individual."

He remembers a time when ballfields were there – in the West End and Walnut Hills – for youngsters.

Webb and four friends, all former players, have formed a nonprofit corporation called SWAP, Seniors with a Purpose. They lead instructional clinics for young baseball players each summer. The Blanchester complex would allow them to reach more children. Webb's new nickname is "Field of Dreams."

Anticipation rises on the bus as the monuments come into view. Some men hold cameras up to windows to snap pictures.

For Webb, the march is another highlight of his African-American experience. He counts the march with Jesse Jackson's 1988 presidential bid; when his friend and former Reds outfielder Frank Robinson became the first black manager in major league baseball, 1975; and his hopes for Gen. Colin Powell in national politics.

"Some of these things were just inconceivable when I was a kid," Webb said.

The bus crosses the Theodore Roosevelt Bridge and swings past the Lincoln Memorial.

"It's also inconceivable to me that we have so many young black men standing on street corners, doing nothing and going nowhere. I'm here because we got to do something about it. I spent $210 to be here. It's the best $210 I've ever spent."

# Million Man March

Black men resolve to unite

*October 17, 1995*

WASHINGTON, D.C. – The Million Man March all but turned the nation's most political city into a church.

They came, hundreds of thousands of black men from across the country, and accepted a message of atonement and reconciliation with heartfelt reverence. They left resolved to go home to put the words into action.

More than two dozen speakers – most of them ministers – delivered just as many variations on one theme: Repent by shouldering the lead role in repairing the nation's black communities.

"We're not here to tear America down. America is tearing itself down. We're here to begin to rebuild it," said Minister Louis Farrakhan during a two-and-a-half-hour oration. The Nation of Islam leader, the keynote speaker and event organizer, has been criticized widely for statements many consider anti-Semitic, sexist, and divisive.

Farrakhan defended himself, saying that efforts to oppress African-Americans by setting them against each other no longer work.

"You came today through the call of God that was delivered through me," he said. "He wouldn't bring it through me if my heart were dark. And how could my heart be so dark if the light is so bright?"

Beneath a brilliant blue sky, the rally stretched from a stage on the Capitol Building's west facade to the base of the Washington Monument, 10 city blocks away. National Park Service officials estimated the crowd to be 400,000; organizers said as many as 2 million attended.

At times throughout the day, the men were chastised, as when they were told by a former Los Angeles gang member to "drop the crack, drop the guns, and pick up your lives."

At other times they were coddled, told by Dorothy Height, director of the National Council of Negro Women, that "your black women love you and salute you."

Throughout the six hours that made up the core program, the men were rapt. While food booths and vendors festively clustered on the edge of the Mall, within it the atmosphere was deeply serious. Very few men sat down. They stood, eyes fixed on the stage or on any of the three large video screens positioned every couple of blocks.

Hundreds of black women attended, as did a sprinkling of whites – many came out on their lunch breaks and after nearby government offices closed – but the day clearly belonged to black men.

And judging by the expressions on their faces, the message was one they were thirsting to hear. For many, the day was without question a religious experience.

"I personally was inspired . . . moved to tears by the poetry of Maya Angelou and the children," said Lovell Love, 46, of Roselawn, director of the Positive Peer Posse Inc. "I am inspired to go back to Cincinnati and try to do even more for children. I was looking for a blessing, and I received it."

Many others said the rally accomplished its central mission: to unify black men.

Brian McCrary, 21, a Xavier University senior from Junction City, Georgia, rode a bus to Washington. His experience has taught him that issues of class have fractured the black community.

"From now on, when I see a brother or sister on the street, I'm going to ask them how they're doing and what I can do for them," he said. "We've never had an opportunity like this to express our unity."

Some participants carried homemade signs. One supported Christopher Darden, the lawyer from the Los Angeles County prosecutor's office who tried O. J. Simpson, for president. Other marchers carried flags from African nations; one of the largest banners featured the image of Bob Marley.

The Rev. Jesse Jackson of the National Rainbow Coalition answered his own question. "Why are we here? We're here because there are 300,000 more black men in prison than in college," he said. "Why are we here? Because our children attend second-class schools" while American cities are building "first-class jails and ballparks."

Marchers vowed to take the messages of unity and self-reliance home – messages that shouldn't be dismissed because of the messenger, Farrakhan, said the Rev. Steve Brown, 41, associate pastor of St. Paul AME Church in Walnut Hills.

"The differences are obvious, but we have more similarities," said Brown, who wore a gray sweatshirt that read "A Million Blackmen Strong."

"This might signal to black politicians and other ministers, the traditional leaders in the black community, that they are not tapping into the concerns of black men."

# CHAPTER 11

# ICONS

*My profile of the Rev. Fred Shuttlesworth is displayed in the small museum dedicated to him in the church he founded in North Avondale, Greater New Light Baptist. I have stayed close to two of his daughters, Ruby Shuttlesworth Bester and Patricia Shuttlesworth Massengill, and they told me that this 1997 story was one of his favorites. Thank you, Reverend. I am pulling for author Andrew Manis and his efforts to get his fine biography, A Fire You Can't Put Out, turned into a biopic so more people will know about Fred Shuttlesworth.*

# In the name of civil rights

The Rev. Fred Shuttlesworth carries on a 40-year
fight as the  movement's "battlefield general"

*January 20, 1997*

December 26, 1956, would be a big day.

Buoyed by the U.S. Supreme Court decision that bus segregation in Montgomery, Alabama, was illegal, more than 200 blacks in Birmingham would ride in the white sections of city buses for the first time.

The night before, the Rev. Fred Shuttlesworth had gone to bed early. His wife and three of his four children were watching television in another room of the Bethel Baptist Church parsonage.

It was a few minutes after 9 o'clock, Christmas night, 1956.

Bang! In a violent flash, sixteen sticks of dynamite exploded outside his bedroom wall. Shards of glass and wood flew across the room and pierced his coat and hat, which hung on a hook. The walls shook. The floors buckled. The Rev. Shuttlesworth, on his mattress, tumbled into the basement.

The blast was the first of three times that the Rev. Shuttlesworth was almost killed in the name of civil rights. He was the undisputed leader of the long battle to integrate Birmingham, which carried the tag "Johannesburg of North America" for its brutally enforced segregation policy.

Although he moved in 1961 to pastor a Cincinnati church, he returned often to Birmingham. He invited the Rev. Dr. Martin Luther King Jr. and the Southern Christian Leadership Conference (SCLC) there in 1963. Those demonstrations led directly to the passage of the 1964 Civil Rights Act.

The Rev. Shuttlesworth, now 74 and in his thirty-second year as pastor of North Avondale's Greater New Light Baptist Church, remains one of the unsung heroes of the modern civil rights movement.

And today, Martin Luther King Jr. Day honors not only the movement's leader but the movement itself.

"Martin had tremendous respect for Fred," Coretta Scott King, Dr. King's widow, says in an interview from her Atlanta office. "He considered Fred a man of great courage, raw courage. Many people were committed to the movement but lacked courage to suffer the consequences of their beliefs. The Rev. Shuttlesworth was prepared to give his life."

Some historians consider the Rev. Shuttlesworth one of the civil rights movement's "big three," along with the Rev. King and the Rev. Ralph Abernathy, the Rev. King's successor at the helm of the SCLC. The Rev. Shuttlesworth was one of the group's founders.

For his part, the Rev. Shuttlesworth isn't worried about his place in history. He says he did what God called him to do – repeatedly stick his head in the mouth of the lion that was segregated Birmingham.

"I saw King as God's person to be the spokesman," the Rev. Shuttlesworth says today while sitting in his church office, lined with plaques, photographs, and other civil rights mementos. "A person who wasn't thinking about the movement, when they heard King, would start thinking about it. That was Martin's challenge. He wasn't to take the brutal work, although he paid with his life. The brutal work was my challenge. I was a battlefield general. I would never ask anyone to do anything that I wouldn't."

Immediately following the blast, Fred Shuttlesworth yelled to his family that he wasn't hurt, says one of his three daughters, Ruby F. "Ricky" Bester, now 52, of Forest Park.

"He was so calm. His calm settled us," says Ms. Bester, who was 11 the night of the blast.

Police discovered the Rev. Shuttlesworth and a deacon – who was visiting – beneath fallen lumber. In the rubble, the Rev. Shuttlesworth managed to find a coat and some pants to put over his undershorts. Another officer met him as he strode from the back of the house.

"He said: 'Reverend, oh reverend, I'm sorry. I'm really sorry. I didn't think they would go this far,'" he says. "I didn't say anything and walked around the side of the house toward the street.

"Then he said, 'Reverend, I tell you what I would do if I was you. I'd get out of town and never come back.'

"I said, 'Well, officer, you're not me. Now you go back and tell your [Ku Klux] Klan brethren that if God can keep me through this, the war is on, and I'm here for the duration.'"

## Organizer who provoked the system

By surviving the attack, the Rev. Shuttlesworth inspired others to join the bus protest: 21 of the 250 who rode were arrested, convicted, and fined. He was arrested more than 30 times and was involved in filing 40 civil rights lawsuits.

The Rev. Shuttlesworth fired some of the first shots in Birmingham's civil rights war.

Called by the congregation to pastor 250-member Bethel Baptist in 1953 – his first pulpit was First Baptist Church in Selma, Alabama – he immediately took up any related cause.

His first battle was for voting rights, which were denied African-Americans until the Voting Rights Act of 1965.

Then it was city services, such as sanitation, and equal access to public accommodations, hospitals, and lunch counters.

The Rev. Shuttlesworth filled a leadership vacuum, says Odessa Woolfook, a teacher in an all-black Birmingham high school at the time that the Rev. Shuttlesworth came to prominence.

"There was a biracial group that was negotiating quietly, but he came in and forced the issue by confronting it," Ms. Woolfook says. Today, she is director of the Civil Rights Institute, a museum opened in 1992 to commemorate the civil rights movement in Birmingham and nationwide. An 8-foot bronze statue of the Rev. Shuttlesworth greets visitors.

At the time, many Birmingham blacks tolerated segregation and didn't like him provoking the system. The white power structure saw him as a threat and thought the movement would die if he could be done away with. Bethel Baptist was bombed again in 1958.

He provoked at every turn.

The Rev. Shuttlesworth was membership chairman of the Birmingham chapter of the NAACP, which, on June 1, 1956, was outlawed in Alabama by the state's attorney general, John Patterson.

The Rev. Shuttlesworth led the combative response. On June 5, he formed a replacement organization, the Alabama Christian Movement for Human Rights, and served as its president until 1969. The movement would lead efforts to desegregate Birmingham and its institutions.

The tighter city officials tried to squeeze segregation's noose around Birmingham's black community, the harder the Rev. Shuttlesworth fought.

"I was sure I wouldn't see 40," he says. He was just 34 the night the church parsonage was bombed.

## His mother's son

The toughness that helped the Rev. Shuttlesworth survive to see 40 and beyond can be traced to his mother.

Alberta Shuttlesworth, who died in 1995 at age 95, was not married to Fred's father. She later married William Shuttlesworth.

She disciplined her children with a switch. Fred was the oldest of nine and went to school and played in the Alabama backwoods before attending high school in segregated Homewood, today a Birmingham suburb.

"She knocked the stuffing out of the older ones," he says. "The idea was the younger ones fell in line."

It was a characteristic that defined the Rev. Shuttlesworth's own fatherhood.

"He'd whip us and tell us, 'Now don't even whimper,'" Ricky Bester says.

When he was a boy, Fred's family was poor and lived by a popular motto of the Depression: *Let Jesus lead you and Roosevelt feed you.*

"I don't remember having the luxury of not going to church," the Rev. Shuttlesworth says. "I remember getting most excited near revival time. I knew I'd be a preacher or a doctor."

Yet not before being sidetracked. He married at 19, in 1941, the year he was convicted of running a family still. Fred worked as a truck driver and for a cement company, built a home in Mobile, Alabama, from World War II scrap metal, and bought a cow to feed his young family.

A Methodist, he converted to the Baptist church when he received a calling to become a country preacher. That was 1944.

He was a tireless worker, preaching simultaneously at three country churches outside Selma. It was not uncommon for him to preach at five churches on a given Sunday. He had stamina and still cuts an athletic figure, although he doesn't exercise. His waist is narrow, his shoulders broad, even today at 74. His neatly trimmed mustache and hair are still more brown than gray, and he's always seen in public wearing a business suit.

## "Always put his body on the line"

The Rev. Shuttlesworth's second brush with death came in September 1957, the day he tried to enroll his two oldest daughters – Patricia and Ricky – in a previously all-white Birmingham high school.

A dozen men waited as the family drove up. Another minister was driving. When the Rev. Shuttlesworth got out of the car, he was hurled into a gauntlet of bicycle chains, brass knuckles, and baseball bats. His wife, Ruby, was stabbed in the hip. Their daughter, Ricky, tried to get out to help but was pushed back into the car and had her ankle slammed in the door.

"There were at least three or four cops there, but the intent was on me getting roughed up," the Rev. Shuttlesworth says.

The city's safety director, Eugene "Bull" Connor, enforced Birmingham's institutionalized segregation and was the Rev. Shuttlesworth's nemesis for many years.

With each threat and attempt on his life, the Rev. Shuttlesworth won admirers across the country.

Among them were an NAACP chapter president in New Jersey and a black lawyer in Youngstown.

"What always struck me most about Shuttlesworth was his personal courage," says Judge Nathaniel Jones of the 6th Circuit Court of Appeals, Cincinnati, who was general counsel to the NAACP in the late 1960s.

"Shuttlesworth always put his body on the line. He was always manning the barricades and fighting for justice against the most egregious and brutal forms of police and racial excesses."

Milton Hinton, president of the Cincinnati NAACP chapter, was also a freedom fighter.

"I was never physically in danger," says Mr. Hinton, former president of the Glassboro, New Jersey NAACP chapter. "My children were never threatened. I wonder if I were living in the South if I'd have been so courageous.

"I remember seeing pictures of him with his arm stuck in doors of buses as they were closing. This guy put life and limb on the line."

## Two conditions on coming to Cincinnati in 1961

The Rev. Fred Shuttlesworth came to Cincinnati in 1961 to pastor Revelation Baptist Church in the West End. He says God wanted him here to affect the civil rights movements in two cities. But there was an additional, more earthbound reason. He needed to make more money to support his family and college-bound children.

"He didn't make a lot of money," says Ms. Bester, a special education teacher at Princeton Junior High School. "Whatever honorariums he received for speaking, he had always put them right into the church." Each of his four children are teachers, the oldest three in the Tristate; the youngest, Carolyn Shuttlesworth-Davidson, is an English professor at Howard University, Washington, D.C.

When he came to Cincinnati, he already was known nationally for his civil rights work in Birmingham.

He accepted the invitation under two conditions: He had to have complete control of the church and the opportunity to continue his work in Birmingham and other cities.

The Rev. Shuttlesworth had an immediate impact on local civil rights issues. He found an ally in the non-violent resistance movement, the Rev. Otis Moss Jr., a Lockland pastor who led the Valley Christian Improvement Association.

The two ministers joined forces to battle what they saw as unfair hiring practices at Hamilton County's Drake Hospital, now Drake Center.

"I don't think that would have been settled if not for Fred and his organizational skills," says the Rev. Damon Lynch Jr., pastor of New Jerusalem Baptist Church and president of the Baptist Ministers Conference, then an Avondale barber.

The Rev. Shuttlesworth also organized and led pickets at Cincinnati Gas & Electric headquarters, downtown. The issue was what he and other African-Americans saw as unequal utility rates.

Organizing demonstrations is a Fred Shuttlesworth specialty.

"He can make 20 people look like 200," the Rev. Lynch says. "It's hard to get a crowd estimate when Fred's in charge."

That was the case in May 1995, when the Rev. Shuttlesworth lent his skill to an NAACP-led coalition protesting police-community relations in the wake of the videotaped arrest of a black teenager, Pharon Crosby, by Cincinnati Police officers.

Mr. Hinton, the coalition leader, surrendered the megaphone to the Rev. Shuttlesworth the day the coalition marched to Cincinnati City Hall to present its demands to City Manager John Shirey.

"He came down to join in, and I could see the old civil rights warrior coming out," Mr. Hinton says. "He made sure the line spacing was correct. He made sure there weren't too many people in a line. It was natural for him. He didn't have to try."

## Winning the battle of Birmingham

Birmingham safety director Bull Connor had tried blowing him up, Fred Shuttlesworth says. Mr. Connor tried having him beaten. Now it was time to turn the water cannons on him.

By May 1963, the Rev. Shuttlesworth had been in Cincinnati for two years but had never strayed far from Birmingham. He was back again at the helm of the Alabama Christian Movement for Human Rights to lead demonstrations and, this time, had invited the Rev. King and the SCLC.

The Rev. King commented that Birmingham had the "worst big-city race relations in the United States."

By May 7, a demonstration by blacks crippled Birmingham's white retail district. From Washington, President Kennedy and U.S. Attorney General Robert Kennedy kept tabs on Birmingham via phone. The president said there was no way out except for a settlement.

By 3 that afternoon, police canine units and firefighters with water hoses were dueling with rock-throwing demonstrators. When the Rev. Shuttlesworth appeared at 16th Street Baptist Church, leading a line of singing children to the demonstration, firefighters pinned him against a church wall with a violent stream of water until he collapsed.

"Those hoses could take bark off a tree at 75 feet," he says.

The Rev. Shuttlesworth could have been injured more severely than he was but says he heard the firefighters mention his name, which gave him time to cover his face and turn his body away.

He was taken in an ambulance to the hospital, at which Mr. Connor said, "I wish they had carried him away in a hearse."

Negotiations took place that night and into the morning at the home of a white businessman. By 4 a.m., white merchants agreed to the following points with the Rev. King and prominent local blacks: Dressing rooms in downtown stores would be desegregated. Lunch counters would be desegregated at the end of 60 days or upon the integration of public schools, whichever came first.

One of the Rev. King's SCLC aides, future Atlanta Mayor Andrew Young, visited the Rev. Shuttlesworth in the hospital and said his approval was needed. The Rev. Shuttlesworth, who wanted the protest to continue, was furious. Escorted by two supporters, he confronted Rev. King.

"I said, 'Martin, why'd I have to get out of my sick bed?'

"He said, 'Fred, we got to call the demonstration off.'

"I said, 'No, we ain't going to call anything off.'

"He said, 'Fred, we got to call the demonstration off.'

"I said, 'Dammit, Martin, why we got to call it off?'

"He said, 'The merchants said they can't negotiate.'

"I said, 'Well, they've been negotiating. And they wouldn't be negotiating if the demonstrations hadn't been going on. That's why we started demonstrating – because they weren't negotiating.'"

The two men finally reached a truce. There would be a one-day break in demonstrations to give the fledgling agreement a chance to take hold.

By Friday afternoon, May 10, the Revs. King, Abernathy, and Shuttlesworth appeared at the Gaston Motel to meet reporters.

The Rev. Shuttlesworth was exhausted. He said, "The city of Birmingham has reached accord with its conscience." Then he collapsed and was rushed to the hospital. The mainstream national and international media, not knowing who he was, waited to hear the news from the Rev. King.

The Rev. Shuttlesworth made no public appearances until May 15. By then, the Rev. King and the Southern Christian Leadership Conference had moved on to Cleveland. President Kennedy had ordered troops to Birmingham to enforce the pact.

When the Rev. Shuttlesworth made his way into New Pilgrim Baptist Church, he told an enthusiastic crowd: "I have just about de-bulled ol' Bull. I didn't know it would take me seven years."

## "Unearned suffering redemptive"

The Cincinnati years have not been without controversy for the Rev. Fred Shuttlesworth.

During the 1970s and 1980s, he owned more than 80 units of rental property. Beginning in 1984, court records show, the equal-housing agency Housing Opportunities Made Equal (HOME) received sexual harassment complaints from tenants and prospective renters, although no cases went to trial and all were resolved or dropped.

But in May 1992, a former tenant filed a $500,000 sexual harassment suit against him. Patricia Patterson claimed that when she refused to have a sexual relationship with him, the Rev. Shuttlesworth groped her and threatened to evict her and her children between 1990 and 1992. A U.S. District Court jury rejected the suit two years later.

One month after he was cleared, the Rev. Shuttlesworth filed a $2.25 million countersuit, alleging that his accuser conspired with HOME and others to ruin him. The agency and its co-defendants were exonerated when a federal judge ruled in May 1995 that there was "no evidence" anyone bribed women to accuse him of sexual harassment.

"I made a statement, even in losing the countersuit, and emerged with my self-respect and integrity intact," the Rev. Shuttlesworth says today, then repeating a long-held personal slogan: "Unearned suffering is redemptive."

Even at 74, the Rev. Shuttlesworth maintains a busy schedule. He returns often to Birmingham – his most regular of several dozen annual destinations – and delivered a speech there Jan. 1 to mark the anniversary of the Emancipation Proclamation in 1863.

Almost half of his time is spent traveling and speaking. The rest is filled with duties at his church, which he organized with some members of his first Cincinnati church, Revelation Baptist, in 1966.

What can Fred Shuttlesworth do for an encore?

"I believe Christ has a goal for us that we come to know only through faith," he says. "Until the job is finished [death], you stay on the job. I'm just as interested now in destroying segregation as I was then."

These days, he is troubled by what he calls the violent, self-destructive nature of some young African-Americans. He thinks the nonviolent approach would serve them well.

But his appeal has often fallen fallow, as it did during the Avondale riots of the late 1960s.

Still, he's hopeful and ever the preacher. "If people can hold on to their basic principles, this world will not fail before it's called to an end."

The last few years have brought increased recognition for his civil rights service.

In 1988, a four-mile stretch of Huntsville Road was renamed F. L. Shuttlesworth Drive by the order of Birmingham City Council.

In 1992, his statue was placed on the grounds of the Civil Rights Institute.

The inscription reads:

*With singular courage, he fired the imagination and raised the hopes of an oppressed people.*

Christmas night, 1956, was the defining moment.

A half an hour after the explosion rocked the church parsonage, Ricky saddled up beside her father in the back of a police cruiser.

"They can't kill us, can they, Dad?"

"No, baby," he said as he put his arm around her. "They can't kill hope."

*This story was updated from its original newspaper version to clarify the timing of the founding of the Alabama Christian Movement for Human Rights.*

---

# Civil rights' shining light

"I will do whatever I can to further education, economic opportunity and prosperity for all people"
—Rosa Parks

*September 25, 1998*

FARMINGTON HILLS, Mich. – Forty-three years after refusing to give up her seat to a white man on a Montgomery, Alabama, bus – the peaceful protest that ignited a national movement – Rosa Parks remains on the civil rights watch.

Mrs. Parks will receive the first International Freedom Conductor Award from the National Underground Railroad Freedom Center on Saturday in Cincinnati. The black-tie event at the Westin Hotel is sold out.

"We're trying to set a standard," Freedom Center President and CEO Ed Rigaud said. "Conductors on the Underground Railroad were courageous people, but they were common people. Not celebrities. Rosa Parks exemplifies that."

Mrs. Parks appreciates the many accolades and acknowledgement of her role in the civil rights movement. But she is a woman still eager to contribute. At age 85, frail and with pacemaker in place, she wants to be more current than her five-paragraph entry in the World Book Encyclopedia.

She stays in the public eye, even though she is intensely private and humble. The former seamstress is comfortable making quilts or attending Sunday service at St. Matthew AME Church in Detroit. She stands in line at the grocery store and waits her turn to talk on radio call-in shows.

But she also knows that the name Rosa Parks and her mere presence draws attention to social causes she supports.

"I will do whatever I can to further education, economic opportunity and prosperity for all people," Mrs. Parks said in an interview in a suburban Detroit nursing home, where she dedicated a computer learning center earlier this month. "I will do as much as I can for as long as I can."

These days, making a contribution means showing up, saying a few words, and meeting people. That was the case at Botsford Commons, the nursing home in Farmington Hills.

CHAPTER 11

Mrs. Parks wore a flowered-print dress and a white baseball cap over her full head of braided gray hair. She walked slowly, sometimes using a wheelchair to cover long distances.

Nursing home staff and residents waited in line to meet her. A food-service employee, James Beckom, 39, couldn't control his glee after his introduction.

"She inspired me when I was a kid and she still inspires me today," said Mr. Beckom, a Mississippi native. "Our people pay homage to her for what she has done for us. Meeting her is like touching a piece of history."

Mrs. Parks will always have a place in history. She's the mother of the movement, civil rights activists say, an example that common people can accomplish the uncommon.

"The importance of Rosa Parks in American culture is almost singular in that it's not just what she did, but God's use of her in the fullness of time," the Rev. Jesse Jackson said. "There's something divine about her."

Even an attack in 1994 couldn't stop her. She was beaten in her house and robbed of $53. The assailant, a black man and a drug abuser, reportedly recognized her but hit her in the face anyway.

"I'm a little bruised. I believe I can go on with what I planned to do," Mrs. Parks said at the time.

She now lives in a secured apartment building in downtown Detroit.

That response, short and to the point, is typical of Mrs. Parks these days. Her voice comes out softly but evenly, and she sometimes defers to her assistant, Elaine Eason Steele, to elaborate.

A fiercely loyal staff of six and dozens of volunteers organize Mrs. Parks's more than 100 carefully selected public appearances a year. She approves each one.

"It's much better to be friendly and not be selfish," Mrs. Parks said. "I just like to see people happy and be as happy as I can myself. Life is what you make it."

She no longer makes speeches. She prefers settings in which she answers children's questions or dedicates programs or buildings that bear her name.

The Farmington Hills event was the dedication of the Rosa L. Parks Learning Center of Michigan. Come Oct. 5, high school students will teach seniors there how to use computers and, in turn, learn life lessons. Mrs. Parks, who enrolled in swimming classes for the first time three years ago, will be one of the senior computer students.

The program is the model that Mrs. Parks and her staff plan to expand nationwide; a similar program bearing Mrs. Parks's name is under way in Los Angeles.

In 1997, Mrs. Parks received more than 2,000 requests for speeches, appearances, and endorsements, including one from an author who was writing a book about celebrity feet and wanted a photograph of Mrs. Parks's toes. (Her staff didn't respond to that one.)

She has never cashed in on her celebrity by endorsing a product, although she has filmed public service announcements to promote voter registration.

Mrs. Steele and Mrs. Parks are co-founders of the Rosa and Raymond Parks Institute for Self-Development. The Detroit-based organization honors Mrs. Parks's late husband, promotes human development programs, and coordinates Mrs. Parks' schedule.

Mrs. Parks's lawyer, Gregory Reed, co-founded the Parks Legacy with Mrs. Parks to maintain the history and lessons of the civil rights movement.

Mr. Reed and Mrs. Steele work to ensure that Mrs. Parks is remembered. They negotiated with Troy State University in Montgomery for more than a year before reaching an agreement on a building that will house Mrs. Parks's artifacts and writings.

Mrs. Parks is "a living example of what individuals can do if they put their minds to it," Troy State board member Lamar Higgins said at the dedication.

Ground was broken in April on the $7.5 million Rosa Louise Parks Library-Museum near the site where Mrs. Parks was arrested for refusing to give up her bus seat. The 40,000-square-foot library (which opened in 2004) includes a 7,000-square-foot museum honoring Mrs. Parks and other civil rights pioneers.

There are hundreds of other roadways, elementary schools, parks, and youth programs around the country that bear her name. Among them:

- Interstate 475, which rings Toledo, is known as Rosa Parks Highway. Her likeness hangs on a plaque in a Los Angeles bus station.

- Her adopted hometown, Detroit, has a Rosa Parks elementary school and boulevard.

- She is featured prominently in displays at the National Civil Rights Museum in Memphis, Tennessee, and the Civil Rights Institute in Birmingham, Alabama.

\* \* \*

Mrs. Parks's peaceful defiance on the bus is immortalized now – in April, *Time* magazine, citing Mrs. Parks's heroism, selected her as one of the 100 most influential people of the twentieth century – but the act caused her and her husband immediate harm. Raymond and Rosa Parks, who had no children, left Montgomery to escape threats and harassing telephone calls related to the bus boycott.

Mrs. Parks was a seamstress at a Montgomery department store at the time of her arrest. The store soon eliminated its tailoring service, and Mrs. Parks lost her job. With Raymond Parks in poor health, the couple moved to Detroit, where Mrs. Park's brother, Sylvester McCauley, lived, in 1957.

In 1965, she went to work as the receptionist for Rep. John Conyers, D-Michigan, in his Detroit office. When she retired in 1988, she was office manager.

Mrs. Steele worked in the same building in the federal courts office. Mrs. Parks often gave the younger woman a ride home. It was during those commutes that they discovered a shared concern for young people.

Mrs. Parks considers Mrs. Steele the daughter she never had. No elderly parent ever had a more protective adult child.

As Mrs. Parks neared retirement, Mrs. Steele came up with a way to focus her remaining years.

They co-founded the Parks Institute to fulfill their ambition to help children excel and become productive members of society. In 13 years, the institute's programs have attempted to improve the self-esteem of more than 5,000 children of all races, ages 11–17.

Mrs. Parks's favorite program is "Pathways to Freedom," a two-week summer educational and historical research activity for 70 students who trace American history from the

Underground Railroad to the civil rights movement. It takes the form of a summer freedom ride on a bus and stops at several Underground Railroad sites.

But on that warm September afternoon at a Michigan nursing home, Mrs. Parks's attention turned to her primary interest: breaking down barriers that keep people apart. And attention, of course, is turned on her.

Mrs. Parks, surrounded by a half-dozen assistants, arrived at the nursing home at noon. Her entourage consisted of Mrs. Steele and the four employees of the Parks Institute, one of whom is a registered nurse, an institute volunteer, the volunteer computer specialist who designed the Botsford program, a makeup artist, and a photographer. Mrs. Parks's every move was choreographed by Mrs. Steele.

A standing ovation greeted Mrs. Parks. She acknowledged it with a wave and smile. Many of the 200 guests at the dedication wore blue buttons that read "I ♥ Rosa Parks," which Mrs. Parks's staff members distribute before each of her public appearances.

"We never seem to have enough," one of her assistants said.

Smiling, Mrs. Parks sat and listened to several speeches before being helped to the podium: "My late husband and I had always been concerned about freedom and equality for all people," she said. "We suffered a lot in the South."

The Botsford learning center open house was held in a dining room. Six computer stations ringed the area.

After speaking at a short news conference and meeting visitors, Mrs. Parks and her staff ate lunch in a private room.

Seventy-five minutes later, she came out to work on a computer and pose for more photographs.

Mrs. Parks spent 15 minutes at a Botsford computer with her tutor, Thiajuan Williamson, 13, a freshman at Detroit's Cooley High School.

First, Thiajuan showed Mrs. Parks a video golf game.

"Oh, my," she said as she watched a tee shot fly toward a virtual green.

Next was solitaire. Children gathered behind her chair. Photographers snapped the moment.

"It felt good. It's sort of like giving back," Thiajuan said. "She did something for me. So it was like I was able to do something for her."

Mrs. Parks said, "I want young people to get an education, take care of their bodies and have a good life."

Her public time ended with the receiving line of nursing home residents and staff.

Mrs. Steele arranged 20 Pathways to Freedom students behind Mrs. Parks. They wore white-and-blue T-shirts and blue baseball caps and were told to stand quietly and smile. Their presence made for a better picture.

No one seemed to mind the sometimes awkward staging.

After all, this is Rosa Parks. People of all races and many nationalities are drawn to her.

Baseball players Juan Gonzalez and Ivan Rodriguez, both all-stars with the Texas Rangers, had driven out to the suburbs from downtown Detroit, where they had played the night before against the Tigers. They wanted to meet the woman they studied in school in Puerto Rico.

Mrs. Parks didn't know who they were, and the fact they are celebrity athletes meant nothing to her. She treated them respectfully, as she does all people.

The ballplayers, however, were in awe.

"It is a dream come true to see her," said Mr. Gonzalez, 28, the 1996 American League Most Valuable Player and a candidate to win the award this season.

Added Mr. Rodriguez, 26, a catcher, "It is an honor to meet her."

With that, they tucked in behind Mrs. Parks, one off each of her shoulders, and asked to have their picture taken with her.

# Book helps Judge Jones cope with wife's death

"Managing to strike just that right balance of grieving and perseverance"

*January 7, 2012*

Nathaniel Jones started work on his memoir after retiring from the federal bench in March 2002.

"I wanted to regain my First Amendment right to free speech," he said of leaving the U.S. Court of Appeals for the 6th Circuit in Cincinnati.

Jones and his editor, Howard Wells, hope that the first volume of an expected three-volume story will be published by the end of this year.

Jones's wife, Lillian, shared the wish of seeing the story in print. She'd occasionally interrupt lengthy conversations her husband would be holding with Wells by asking, "When is this book going to be done?"

There's no shortage of material. Jones, now 85, served on President Lyndon Johnson's National Advisory Commission on Civil Disorders (the Kerner Commission) and as national general counsel for the NAACP for 10 years beginning in 1969. During that pivotal decade, he directed all NAACP litigation, argued several cases in the U.S. Supreme Court, and coordinated all of the civil rights organization's efforts to end school segregation, defend challenges to affirmative action, and investigate discrimination against black servicemen in the U.S. military.

A years-long process of professional recollection is now joined with a new one of personal reflection. Lil Jones, as she was known, died November 9. She was 77. They'd married in midlife in 1975. He was 49. She was 41. They'd both been married previously but, as a couple, were described by friends and associates as "inseparable soul mates."

The year begins for Jones in a new place.

Grief is not linear. No law provides relief. Even the ceaseless, mind-numbing number of details required to rewrite and index a manuscript don't equate to the number of empty hours that he now faces as a widower. Any attempt to relate the two, at least for now, would be forced.

"In due time, perhaps I will see that her passing makes it more important that this story is told so others will see the value of pressing forward [and] mastering the art of coping," he said.

Stephanie Jones, who has a consulting and public affairs firm in Washington, D.C., sees her father struggling, yet overcoming just the same.

"But he always has been very balanced – emotionally, spiritually," she said.

"What I see now is Dad managing to strike just that right balance of grieving and perseverance."

## The "new normal," familiar message

For now, life's steps are smaller for Nathaniel Jones, intensely personal, less grand in scale than the heights of oratory he can reach.

"I have to move to the 'new normal,' as it has been described to me," he said.

"The normal is no more. I keep reaching for a normal that no longer exists."

The day started in his old normal by rising to make coffee for Lil and bring her the newspaper. The new normal requires no coffee because he doesn't drink it.

There is no one at home with whom to discuss current events or the day ahead.

No one stands beside him at the twin sink in the master bath of the East Walnut Hills condominium they shared. Lil's toothbrush and clean towels remain in place. A piece of her jewelry went to each of their five granddaughters for Christmas, as she had wanted. Her suits must be sorted and cleaned before he donates to Dress for Success. Lil served as a founding board member of the nonprofit that provides professional clothing to low-income and other at-risk women making their way into the work force.

His voice faltered for a moment when ticking off the list of now-empty spaces. Jones regained his verbal composure, though his eyes remained damp with tears that he willed not to fall.

Finally, he said, "In due course, the writing and rewriting of this memoir will be a major part of the new normal. I am looking forward to building on it. What I see others taking from it will provide a lot of what I'm missing now."

What readers will get is Jones's aggressive repudiation of what he says is the effort to eliminate or revise historical fact detailing the effort to win basic human and civil rights for African-Americans.

"The book is polemic in the finest sense," said editor Wells, of Madisonville. "This is a political book."

An "appropriate" publisher is in place, Wells added.

Jones and Wells excerpted the manuscript to produce a 500-copy edition in 2009 to celebrate the 100th anniversary of the National Association for the Advancement of Colored People.

*Answering the Call: From a Child of the NAACP to the Federal Bench and Beyond* was less confrontational – touching on Jones's Depression-era youth in Youngstown and involvement in South Africa's struggle to dismantle apartheid – than the upcoming book.

The full memoir, which will carry the same title, is more in line with the commencement address Jones gave in June 2010 at the University of Cincinnati. That day Jones took critical aim at what he says is the broad attempt to "restore the discarded doctrine of states' rights."

He vigorously defended how "the national government, in keeping with its obligation to promote the general welfare, has stepped forward to meet the economic and social anguish of all citizens." Jones challenged UC graduates to ask hard questions of calls to "take America back."

"Back to what? To when?" Jones asked in his speech. "To a time when there were no child labor laws or minimum wages? When it was legal to segregate schools? Or to discriminate in the hiring and firing of racial minorities and women?"

Criticism of the speech surprised Jones but did not cause him to shrink from his position.

In a letter to the editor published June 20, 2010, an *Enquirer* reader wrote, "Judge Nathaniel Jones espoused socialism, denied the rights of the states, denounced God, mocked the Tea Party movement, and generally thumbed his nose at parents. I can only hope that the students were smart enough to realize the nonsense being spewed."

Jones's defense of civil rights – with legal remedy provided by the federal courts – is a primary theme of his memoir.

"I see an erosion taking place, and unless people are made aware of that erosion they will be like the person who didn't know their throat had been cut until they tried to turn their head," he said.

## "Busiest person I know"

A planned two-hour meeting in Jones's Fifth Street office at the Blank Rome law firm moved past five hours. He is senior counsel, having recently relinquished the position as the chief diversity and inclusion officer.

As is the case with his memoir, there was too much material to cover. Jones, ever the lawyer, prepared meticulously. He started with a display of influential books, including *A Man Called White: The Autobiography of Walter White*, the story first published in 1948 of the civil rights activist who served as the NAACP's executive secretary from 1931 through his death in 1955.

Several volumes of speeches Jones had made crowded the table in the conference room. He read from a letter from Nelson Mandela, president of South Africa, thanking him for his "important contribution . . . to the preservation and protection of human rights in South Africa." Jones borrowed from the collection of legal papers that he had donated to the University of Cincinnati College of Law.

"I had to sign them out," said Jones, laughing.

Former UC law school dean Joseph Tomain sought Jones's papers and encouraged him to write a memoir. So, too, did Chad Wick, founder and director of the downtown-based national education reform group KnowledgeWorks. Wick hired Wells to help Jones begin and shape his story. Jones and Tomain are members of KnowledgeWorks' board of directors.

"The education equity issue is close to his heart, as it is our heart, and his is a unique and important story of civil rights to tell," Wick said.

The writing process would continue for Jones upon returning from a holiday visit with his sister in Youngstown. This past week involved a two-day trip to Pittsburgh to preside over a mock appellate hearing at the request of attorneys preparing to go to court.

"He is the busiest person I know," Wells said.

Jones's book is his constant companion. Yet even more than his voluminous papers, the source of some of the latest rewrites and additions is his own heart. Lil is an integral part of his memoir. Her civil rights story sings in the narrative.

She'd come from Georgia at age 7 with her mother and brother. Her father, a tenant farmer, joined them later. He was on the run. A white landowner sought Lil's father because he had successfully applied for a grant from the U.S. Department of Agriculture. In that era, Jones said, some whites would tie a black man to a tree and whip him "to keep him in his place."

Lil's family had relatives in Youngstown. On the train ride north, even as a little girl in 1941, Lil would remember switching from the segregated, colored-only car to the integrated coach at Union Terminal in Cincinnati. In Youngstown, though schools were desegregated, Lil could not sing in glee clubs or be a cheerleader.

"There were just things black girls couldn't do in those times," said Jones, who knew Lil and her family in Youngstown's black community. He had taken her to a Negro League baseball game in the mid-1940s, some 30 years before their lives would intersect again.

A white teacher took Lil to white churches, where she gained an opportunity to perform in public. Her love of music lasted a lifetime. She brought it to Cincinnati in 1979 when her husband was appointed to the federal bench. She served on the board of Cincinnati Opera, which will dedicate its June 28 opening performance of *Porgy and Bess* to Mrs. Jones.

"She would not let people define her," said Nathaniel Jones, speaking of himself as much as his wife and his boyhood mentors and civil rights colleagues.

"The key to prevailing as a minority in a segregated, oppressive society is to not let the prevailing stereotypes define who you are."

# THE NFL BEAT

*By the time I had the opportunity to start the Bengals/NFL beat in July 2000, I was glad I was 38 years old, had been in the business 16 years, and had spent considerable time covering urban affairs. I wasn't awestruck by players' celebrity but was comfortable in a locker room that was two-thirds African-American. I embraced the chance to link football with civil rights, such as the late 2002 stories about efforts to increase the number of minority coaches.*

# Minority hiring in the NFL

The front-office power spots, coaching, and
top coordinators are void of blacks

*December 1, 2002*

The Baltimore Ravens will play their first game today, at Paul Brown Stadium against the Bengals, since naming Ozzie Newsome the first black general manager in NFL history.

Newsome and his Ravens come to town just six days after his promotion and at a time when the NFL again is making a big issue of minority hiring on coaching staffs and in front offices.

The Bengals have four African-Americans on their sixteen-coach staff, which is roughly in line with the 27 percent league rate.

The Bengals have never had a black head coach in their 35-year franchise history. Nor have they had a black offensive or defensive coordinator, the top two assistant coaching positions on a football staff. The Bengals never even have interviewed a candidate of color for one of their top three coaching jobs.

"We've talked about [black prospects for] those jobs [coordinators] and the head-coaching job, but it just didn't end up that way," Bengals president Mike Brown said. "I don't know that we interview very many people anyway."

In the Bengals' front office, where Brown and four members of his family hold the most powerful positions, there are even fewer African-Americans than on the coaching staff.

The Bengals staff directory lists 65 employees and team support positions. Two of the 65 are African-American.

"How do we stack up? Compared to what? Compared to the business norm? Probably, we look good," Brown said. "Compared to an ideal situation? Maybe we could do better. There is a conscious effort to do better in this league in that area."

On October 31, NFL commissioner Paul Tagliabue announced the formation of a committee to address the NFL's minority-hiring practices. Pittsburgh Steelers owner Dan Rooney will chair the ten-person committee of team owners and executives, a panel that doesn't include any Bengals representatives.

Tagliabue's announcement came a little more than a week after prominent civil rights attorney Cyrus Mehri met with NFL officials in New York to determine if the league is serious about hiring minority candidates as head coaches.

Of 32 NFL teams, there are just two minority head coaches – Indianapolis's Tony Dungy and the New York Jets' Herman Edwards – and 12 coordinators.

Mehri, working with attorney Johnnie Cochran, has backed off threats to sue the league in hopes of a positive resolution that it will hire more minorities as general managers, head coaches, and coordinators.

Mehri is familiar with the Bengals.

"They are the poster child. Their decision-making process has excluded African-Americans from competing," he said. "The Bengals have never had an African-American in a position of real authority in their front office or on the team."

Mehri and Cochran are pushing a diverse candidate slate, which would penalize teams by taking away a draft pick if they failed to interview minority candidates for top organizational vacancies in the front office and on the coaching staff. Their plan also would reward an organization – such as the Ravens for promoting Newsome – that shows leadership in this area.

The pool of prospective black coaches and executives is well-stocked. Almost 70 percent of NFL players are African-American, which also is the case with the Bengals' roster.

## Glass walls

The NFL, the United States' most popular sports league, is concerned about diversity throughout its member organizations.

But the Bengals buck the trend in their front office. The two African-American employees in the Bengals' front office are former running back Eric Ball and Jason Williams, who is one of four ticket-office employees.

Ball is the director of player relations, and he oversees players' off-field conduct and appearances.

"There are glass walls," Mehri said. "Eric Ball is in player relations, not player selection. He has no power."

Several NFL teams have African-Americans in their personnel/scouting departments. The Ravens, for example, have four blacks among the twelve members of their personnel department – including pro personnel director James Harris and director of player development Earnest Byner. They, along with Newsome, are all former NFL players.

The six members of the Bengals' player personnel department – headed by Pete Brown and Paul H. Brown, Mike Brown's brother and son – all are white.

The other two Brown family members in the administration are executive vice president Katie Blackburn, Mike Brown's daughter and heir apparent, and business development director Troy Blackburn, husband of Katie Blackburn.

"NFL teams all want to win, and the overriding thing in their mind when they go to hire somebody is, who is going to help them win. Regardless of anything else," Mike Brown said.

Bengals teams haven't won in a long time. They have a league-worst 54–133 composite record since Brown assumed control of the franchise in August 1991 from his late father, Paul Brown.

The Bengals' twelve-year playoff dry spell is twice as long as any other NFL team. They have had five consecutive seasons of double-digit losses and nine of the past twelve.

## Four titles, Green fired

The three coaches in the Bengals' twelve-year futility streak all have been white. Dave Shula, like Dick LeBeau, had no previous NFL head-coaching experience. Bruce Coslet, now the offensive coordinator for the Dallas Cowboys, had been the Jets' head coach but had never had a winning record.

Dennis Green, an African-American who coached the Minnesota Vikings from 1992–2001, was fired after compiling a 97–62 record with four division titles.

"Dave Shula was unproven, and they've never even considered the likes of [former Los Angeles/Oakland Raiders coach] Art Shell or [Washington Redskins defensive coordinator] Marvin Lewis," Mehri said.

"Black coaches are proven to win more than white coaches in the NFL," he said.

Dungy, in his first year with the Colts, led Tampa Bay to four playoff appearances in six years. Edwards, in his second year with the Jets and a former Dungy assistant with the Buccaneers, took New York to the playoffs in his rookie season as coach.

There have been three other African-American head coaches in the last fifteen years: Shell, Green, and Ray Rhodes (Green Bay Packers).

The five black coaches have averaged 1.1 more wins than the white coaches and led their teams to the playoffs 67 percent of the time, compared to 39 percent of the time for white coaches.

A look at current league statistics also speaks to the success of black coordinators. There are eleven black defensive coordinators in the NFL and five of those teams are ranked in the top ten of league defenses. There is one black offensive coordinator, Maurice Carthon, of the Detroit Lions.

The league insists it has made progress. In 1980, 14 black coaches were assistants, not one of them a coordinator. In 1997, 103 black assistant coaches were working in the NFL. There are now 154 black assistant coaches, including the 12 coordinators – up from five coordinators in 1997.

Said Mehri: "We've been watching [Tagliabue] try to move the chains, but his playbook isn't getting it done. Cincinnati fans want the best hire, regardless of race, and the Bengals have ignored an entire talent pool."

# Bengals coach Jim Anderson thankful for opportunity to be assistant

*December 1, 2002*

The dean of the Bengals' coaching staff is running backs coach Jim Anderson.

He is an African-American who interviewed for the head-coaching position at Stanford University in January but never has been asked to interview for the offensive coordinator's job with the Bengals.

Anderson, 54, has been the Bengals' running backs coach since 1984. One measure of his success is the number of Pro Bowl seasons achieved by Bengals running backs – eight – far more than any other of the team's position coaches.

The Bengals' running backs under Anderson, including current featured back Corey Dillon, are its most productive players.

Another measure of Anderson's success: 10 times in his tenure, the Bengals have finished in the top 10 in rushing, including consecutive No. 1 rankings in 1988 and 1989.

"We've been involved in one [offensive] system, and I knew people wanted to change," Anderson said when asked if he ever pursued the offensive coordinator's job. "I knew the system had to be changed, and maybe that's what we should have done a good while ago, change the system. They brought in the right man [Bob Bratkowski, who is white] to do the job. I have no problems with that."

Anderson maintains a positive attitude about his role.

"I've been given the opportunity to coach," he said. "And some places, you coach, but you don't. You know what I mean? I've been given the opportunity to coach here and have input and to be an integral part of the staff and the organization. I certainly do appreciate that."

The other three black coaches on the team's staff are special teams coach Al Roberts, assistant strength and conditioning coach Rodney Holman, and safeties coach Darren Perry.

Anderson is encouraged by the current efforts to promote the hiring of minority coaches, but he is skeptical about the prospects for success.

"It's a good thing, but let's be honest: You're not going to pressure the NFL," he said. "It's only words. People do what they want to do. They hire who they want to hire."

---

# Marvin Lewis brings discipline he learned on and off the field to revive Bengals

*January 16, 2003*

MOBILE – As a child growing up in McDonald, Pennsylvania, Marvin Roland Lewis, Jr. never left the house without first making his bed and straightening up his room.

Vanetta Lewis, mother of the Cincinnati Bengals' new head coach, can't remember her son ever being unprepared for anything in his life.

"He always did his homework," Mrs. Lewis says from her Pennsylvania home. "He always did his chores without a reminder."

Mr. Lewis always knew his responsibilities, as well as everyone else's in the household.

And that's the way he will run the Bengals. Signed Tuesday to a five-year contract believed to be worth $1.5 million a season – not including incentives – Mr. Lewis inherits a team that has not been to the playoffs since 1990 and is coming off a franchise record 14-loss season.

He will approach the job the same way he has every challenge in his 44 years. He'll work hard and intelligently. He already has a plan and, apparently, more control than Bengals' fans believe team president Mike Brown would ever yield.

Mr. Lewis went to work Tuesday night. He called quarterback Jon Kitna roughly one hour after his news conference. Mr. Lewis talked to prospective assistant coaches in the hotel lobby later that night.

In his first 18 hours as Bengals coach, Mr. Lewis seems to have centralized power. He was the only team official talking to the media Wednesday. Mr. Brown and the rest of his family, including daughter Katie Blackburn, the team's executive vice president, refused media requests for interviews.

Mr. Lewis, on the other hand, was talking but not allowing any detail regarding the team's minicamp schedule and off-season conditioning program.

He was evasive of questions about the coaching staff he was piecing together.

"We're going to attend to that all at once," Mr. Lewis says. "We'll have some guys coming in this weekend to talk to."

But it's not power for power's sake that Lewis appears to crave. His organizational skills seem born from a heightened sense of personal responsibility.

"He thrives on discipline, and I think he will bring that to Cincinnati," says one of his former defensive stars, Baltimore Ravens cornerback Chris McAlister. "He knows his personnel and always puts people in the right situation to succeed. He will make sure his players know their strengths and weaknesses."

Mr. Lewis was the Ravens' defensive coordinator for six seasons, a run highlighted by the team's Super Bowl victory after the 2000 season. Mr. Lewis's defense allowed an NFL-low 165 points in a 16-game schedule.

Success was the standard from the beginning in the Lewis household. His mother went back to school to become a nurse practitioner. His father was a supervisor and spent 28 years working in a western Pennsylvania steel mill. His youngest sister, Andrea, now 38, is an Allegheny County police officer. His other sibling, Carol Joy, has a degree in electrical engineering and lives outside Akron.

Young Marvin was a success in school and in football. He started playing at age 9 and immediately put his brain to work to make up for his lack of brawn.

"The coaches always said he was like a little coach on the field," Vanetta Lewis says. "He knew all the plays and where everybody else on his team was supposed to be."

He carried his academic and athletic success to Fort Cherry High School.

He played baseball in the summer and worked for his neighbor's garbage-collecting company.

He'd work all day and would have just enough time to change in the truck on the way to practice or a game. There was no chance to shower.

His teammates' greeting was always the same: "Oh, Marvin, you stink, man."

He wasn't just a jock, though. He was a good student and a leader. He was the first youth Sunday school superintendent in the history of McDonald's First Baptist Church.

Mr. Lewis played quarterback out of necessity at Fort Cherry. He was not the classic, strong-armed, future NFL quarterback such as Dan Marino, Joe Montana, Jim Kelly, and Joe Namath, all of whom came out of western Pennsylvania.

Mr. Lewis was a good safety, and his knowledge of the game made up for his lack of size.

Jim Garry was Marvin's football coach at Fort Cherry, which also produced another NFL head coach, San Diego's Marty Schottenheimer.

"Marvin gave you everything he had," Mr. Garry says.

The budding coach would go to Mr. Garry's office throughout the week during study hall and watch film of the upcoming opponent.

"He wanted to make sure he knew what was coming up," Mr. Garry says.

Math was his favorite subject, and his analytical ability led him to a decision to walk on as a football player at Purdue University, where he planned to study engineering.

Before Mr. Lewis left for West Lafayette, Indiana, a family friend found out that Idaho State University had a football scholarship left and wanted to fill it with a top student.

Mr. Lewis leapt at the opportunity. The reason: "My parents wouldn't have to pay for anything," he says.

When Mr. Lewis arrived on the Pocatello campus, Idaho State officials – not knowing he was African-American – apologized for giving him a white roommate. His reaction: "It doesn't matter. A lot of my friends are white."

"He could assimilate with all kinds of people," says Phil Luckey, head athletic trainer at Idaho State since 1967.

"It was his destiny to come here. Part of his life experience, his diversity skills, if he had missed this experience, he might not be where he is now."

Mr. Lewis played linebacker at Idaho State. He earned all-Big Sky Conference honors three consecutive years, and his coach as a senior, Dave Kragthorpe, says the only things that kept Mr. Lewis from an NFL playing career were "about 3 or 4 inches and 50 pounds."

Mr. Kragthorpe took over a program with a long history of losing, a skid that started to turn during Mr. Lewis's senior season.

"I remember one specific game that he played a huge part in: Our first conference road win was at the University of Nevada. Marvin blocked a punt late in the game. We scored and won that game. I thought that was the major turning point in our season. It wasn't something called from the bench. It wasn't the coaching staff that saw a weakness and put in this punt block. It was Marvin on his own who decided he could do that based on previous punts.

"It was getting down toward the end of the game, and he realized we had to do something significant to win."

The coach didn't want to lose Mr. Lewis's leadership ability and hired him as a graduate assistant before the 1981 season.

The Bengals went 12–1 and won the Division I-AA national championship. (That season also was a good one for another Bengals team, in Cincinnati, which went 12–4 and played in its first Super Bowl.)

Before he earned his master's degree in athletic administration, Mr. Lewis was promoted to linebackers coach – which lifted his salary to $10,000.

After the 1984 season, Mr. Lewis and his wife, Peggy, packed their Trans Am and headed for Long Beach State. (They have two children: daughter, Whitney, 17, a high school senior; and son, Marcus, 12, a seventh-grader and devoted lacrosse player.)

The next coaching stop was New Mexico. Then it was home to coach linebackers at the University of Pittsburgh in 1990–91. Then rookie Pittsburgh Steelers coach Bill Cowher made Mr. Lewis one of his first hires as linebackers coach.

Mr. Lewis is aware of his position as just the third African-American head coach in the NFL and just the eighth in league history. But, when introduced Tuesday night as the Bengals ninth coach, he said he "represented all the coaches who came up the way I did."

That night, civil rights leaders and black ministers welcomed Mr. Lewis to Cincinnati and said they hoped he would get involved in helping heal the city's racial wounds.

He will.

"I think that's important for the head coach of the Bengals to do," he says. "We'll be judged (how we do) as a football team on the field, but, as we bring quality people to Cincinnati, hopefully, we all need to be involved in the community."

---

# Brown did it right, Cochran, Mehri say

Civil rights lawyers applaud coaching search

*January 23, 2003*

SAN DIEGO – The Bengals' head coaching interview process was hailed Wednesday as exemplary in meeting NFL minority hiring guidelines.

"We believe the Bengals have created a superb model for carrying out [a coaching search]," civil rights attorney Johnnie L. Cochran Jr. said Wednesday.

Lewis, hired January 14, is one of three African-American coaches in the league and the eighth in NFL history.

The NFL's minority hiring plan, announced December 20 by a committee headed by Steelers president Dan Rooney, calls for teams to interview at least one minority candidate before hiring a head coach.

The Bengals interviewed five candidates, two of whom are African-Americans.

Bengals president Mike Brown declined to comment Wednesday.

Cochran and fellow attorney Cyrus Mehri have worked with the NFL to improve opportunities for minority coaches. Tagliabue created a league workplace diversity committee October 31 and appointed Rooney as chair.

While praising the Bengals, Cochran and Mehri criticized coaching searches conducted by the Jacksonville Jaguars and Dallas Cowboys. They said Jacksonville owner Wayne Weaver violated the Rooney plan by interviewing just one candidate, Jack Del Rio, before hiring Del Rio last week. They also said Dallas owner Jerry Jones violated the spirit of the plan by interviewing Bill Parcells – whom he hired January 2 – in person and interviewing former Vikings coach Dennis Green by phone.

"There will be no compromise on face-to-face interviews," Mehri said.

Mehri and Cochran were joined at the news conference by former NFL stars Warren Moon and Kellen Winslow, both of whom are African-American.

"We're not talking about quotas or affirmative action," said Winslow. "We're talking about equal opportunity."

The 49ers head-coaching job, vacant since the firing of Steve Mariucci on January 15, is the only job open in the league.

"We hope San Francisco will follow the process like Cincinnati," Mehri said.

# Big brother has it covered

Madieu Williams, a Bengals safety, also has another
position – role model to his younger sibling

*April 23, 2006*

It's no wonder the Bengals feel confident with Madieu Williams at safety.

Who would a team rather have as its last line of defense than a man who changed colleges to help his recently divorced mother care for her young son, who used much of his $1.2 million rookie signing bonus to pay medical bills incurred by his mother's deteriorating health, and who now is his teenaged brother's guardian?

In a sport in which players routinely regret the big-dollar contracts they signed a year before, the 24-year-old Williams regrets that he couldn't buy his mom a house before she died.

"She didn't get to enjoy the fruits of her labor," he said.

It was two years ago this week that Williams became a Bengal. With the NFL draft just days away, teams have conducted countless tests and interviews trying to find the sort of mettle Williams has. And he can play, too.

"He brings a lot of ability and character to our football team," Bengals coach Marvin Lewis said.

In just two seasons, Bengals fans have learned what the Williams family has known for years: Madieu is a good guy to have on your side, and you miss him a lot when he's not there.

A shoulder injury that required surgery forced Williams to miss all but four games in 2005.

Without him in the lineup, the Bengals' defense struggled down the stretch. Williams was fourth on the team in total tackles (95) and third in solos (71) as a rookie in 2004, and he started a total of 13 games at three positions.

Like most athletes, his initial reaction to sitting out while injured was one of anger and disappointment.

"It was like, 'This isn't fair. Why me?'" said Hugh McDonough, Williams' friend and real estate agent.

Then the answer came. His little brother was the reason. The injury would give Madieu more time with Mike.

Madieu became Mike Williams's guardian after the death of their mother, Abigail Butscher, in April 2005. She was 45. She suffered a stroke late in 2003 and spent much of the last year of her life in a Maryland hospital.

Madieu spent much of his rookie season, 2004, flying to Maryland Monday afternoons and returning late Tuesday to be ready for meetings and practice Wednesday.

Mike moved to Cincinnati in June 2005 after finishing sixth grade. Madieu hired a sitter, and he plans to hire a cook and a housekeeper/driver for the next school year.

"Mike is the center of his universe," McDonough said. "When he brought Mike here, his whole life focus changed. Everything he does focuses on 'What does Mike need to be doing?' and 'Where does he need to be?'"

While their mother was ill, Mike lived with the boys' father, Mohamed Forna, 54. But Forna often traveled on business between Maryland and the family's native Sierra Leone, so Mike went to live with Madieu.

"It was never a question," Madieu said of his brother's living arrangement. "[His father] just kind of figured it was the best thing, because I'm here and I'm more stable. Mike wasn't getting the supervision he was accustomed to, the attention he had received from my mom."

Madieu started babysitting Mike when the boy was 4 months old. When their parents divorced, Madieu was a sophomore at Towson State University. He drove an hour home to watch Mike at night so their mother, who was a registered nurse, could go to work; she didn't trust Mike with anyone except Madieu.

Madieu transferred to the University of Maryland because the school was closer to their Lanham, Maryland, home, though it meant sitting out a year and starting all over again as a walk-on junior in a larger, more competitive football program.

There was no resentment.

"She was everything to me," Madieu said of his mother. "She was always there for me."

So Madieu is there for Mike.

"There was never a thought, 'Should I do it?' Or, 'Was it the right thing?'" Madieu said. "It was something that had to be done, and it came natural. And it's been a blessing, a true blessing."

Their father declined to be interviewed.

\* \* \*

After undergoing surgery October 24 to repair a torn labrum, Madieu was more available for Mike. After driving him from their home near downtown to school at Cincinnati Country Day, Madieu would head to the stadium for rehabilitation. His workdays were shorter than his teammates' – he'd be home by 1 p.m., leaving plenty of time to start dinner and head back to Indian Hill to pick up Mike.

"It was a blessing in disguise, because [Mike] didn't have to go through it alone after the first four games," Madieu said of his injury. "After the first four games, I was there. Things just kind of happened. Everything just clicked.

"Granted, I was devastated being hurt and not being out there helping the team. But then I took a look at the big picture, and I realized there was a 12-year-old kid here who just lost his mom, and he's going through so much that for me to be able to be with him was more important."

Their bond was always there. As soon as he learned to walk, Mike wanted to sleep with Madieu. If Madieu went out with friends, he'd come home to find Mike in his bed.

Henry Brady coached Madieu in football and track at Duval High School in Lanham. Brady also made sure Madieu – and Mike – had a ride if they needed one.

"I wasn't surprised Mike ended up living with Madieu," Brady said. "Madieu always has acted much older than he is."

As a high school athlete in football and track, Madieu always took Mike with him to off-season workouts with friends.

"If you saw Madieu, you saw Mike," said J. B. Gerald, a high school football teammate of Williams's who is an offensive graduate assistant at Penn State. "Mike is such a great kid; their mom did a great job with him. We all love Mike. We're happy he's with Madieu and we're proud of him. Mike is a testament to his mother. So is Madieu."

\* \* \*

Mike, like Madieu, is mature for his age. He gets up at 5:45 on school mornings and often makes breakfast for Madieu – pancakes or scrambled eggs.

"He knows his bedtime; I don't have to say anything," Madieu said. "It's 'Dieu, see you in the morning.' I'm proud of him. He doesn't realize how far that self-discipline will carry him in life."

Mike does much of his own laundry and irons his school uniform shirts.

"He pushes me a lot. That's what keeps me going," Mike said of his big brother. "I like when he pushes me. It shows me I can do anything I put my mind to."

The push comes in schoolwork, not sports. Though Madieu is a professional football player, academics come first in his household. He has a bachelor's degree in family studies from Maryland.

Mike must meet Madieu's tough academic requirements in order to participate in football, basketball, and track during the school year. Madieu checks Mike's homework every night.

Madieu hired a tutor to help Mike keep up at CCD, which has an advanced curriculum compared to the public school he had attended in Maryland.

"One of the things Madieu emphasizes is, 'I will provide you with anything you need, but you have to get [the education] for yourself,'" said Sheryl McClung Garner of Envision Learning Center in Roselawn, where Mike receives 8–10 hours of tutoring a week.

"Michael knows that all it will take is one phone call to Madieu. Michael does not want to disappoint Madieu."

Madieu doesn't want to disappoint Mike.

He attends as many of his brother's athletic events as he can. On an early April afternoon, Madieu sat through one of Mike's four-hour track meets.

About halfway through the meet, Madieu said, "Man, now I know how my mom felt."

She used to bring a bag of snacks and do crossword puzzles while waiting for her son's events.

Madieu kills time on his cell phone and drinks bottled water. Mike finished second in the 200-meter dash and the long jump. Mike, who also was seventh in the 100-meter dash, walked into the stands to talk with his brother between his events.

"You did better today," Madieu said softly to Mike. "You didn't look around."

They discussed arm movement and "turnover" – how quickly a runner gets his feet up and down in a sprint. Madieu ran the 110-meter high hurdles in high school and qualified for the Maryland state meet.

Madieu sat in his regular spot at the finish line – the same place his mother would sit when he ran.

Earlier, the brothers talked about the importance of hydration and warming up with sweat clothes on, even though the day was warm.

"Please don't be drinking Kool-Aid," Madieu told Mike via cell phone en route to the meet.

\* \* \*

For Madieu, no detail is too small when it comes to Mike.

Madieu, as a pro football player, eats carefully – pasta, chicken, and fish are his staples. He has shown Mike the importance of improving his own diet.

"Mike was a typical kid, eating McDonald's and things like that," Madieu said. "One of the things when he moved in, I said, 'I don't eat McDonald's, and you're not going to eat McDonald's. We're going to try to eat healthy, because it's important that you get a good foundation now so we can live healthier lives later on.'"

Mike has bought in to that philosophy. There's an atypical introspection about him for a teen-ager.

"I was way different," he said of how he has changed since living with his older brother. "I changed my eating habits, my discipline, the way I think, some of my reactions during sports and other stuff. I think things through and am calmer. It's his influence."

Madieu doesn't just talk it, Mike said. He sees his big brother live it.

But this relationship is a two-way street. And Madieu might even benefit more from it than Mike.

Mike makes Madieu laugh. Mike floods Madieu's cell phone with messages during a game.

"He knows the ins and outs of football as well as I do, and he can articulate them, and that's a problem," Madieu said. "When I played my rookie year and he's back in Maryland watching on TV, every mistake I made he let me know.

"It was, 'All right, 'Dieu, that tackle, you got to keep your head up.'

"Then it's, 'Aw, man, you didn't bring your hips. You're not even trying to wrap.'

"I come out and the game's over and I have 30 messages, and 25 are from my brother while he's watching the game. He was in the stands [for Bengals games] at Washington and Baltimore in my rookie year and calling me.

"At Chicago last year, you should have seen what I got on my phone. He critiqued the game so critically, some of the things he told me after the game were what the coaches were telling me I needed to work on."

CHAPTER 12

* * *

The brothers also helped each other get through the past year and the aftermath of their mother's death. At the end, she no longer could feed herself. She died of pulmonary edema – fluid in the lungs.

She had to sell her house when she got sick and no longer could work. She lost her medical insurance as a result.

Said Madieu of Mike: "We cried together. When he cried, I was crying. When I was crying, he would cry. We were holding each other and telling each other, 'Hey, it's going to be OK.'

"And to be able to look at each other and know exactly the pain, it was great, because nobody else knew but us. Having him there, we were able to grieve together, and it helped us move forward.

"It would have been more difficult if he hadn't been here. He was only 12. That's a lot for a 12-year-old to deal with. It made us both stronger. The adjustment he had to make – moving to a new city, a new school, losing your mom – I applaud him a lot. I tell him a lot, 'I'm very proud of you because of the way you've handled yourself through this whole ordeal, and believe me, you'll be a better person than you would have been if you had not gone through this. You're going to be able to handle adversity better than you could have.'"

Madieu is aware that his responsibilities with Mike, while opening doors in their relationship, have closed others.

"Being a 24-year-old, there are times you want to go out. I want to go back to Maryland right after the season and work out with guys who are in the NFL now that I went to school with. It's my time to bond with those guys," Madieu said.

"But [not going is] a sacrifice I have to make. But I don't see them as a downside. I see them as sacrifices I have to make for him; that's something my mom did for me. That's something she wanted me to do for Mike, and Mike knows it. He will say, 'Man, 'Dieu, I know you really want to do this, but I really appreciate it.' It makes me feel good. He knows I'm putting things on hold for him."

Mike said simply of his brother: "He's a great man."

* * *

The Bengals know all about Madieu and Mike. From the team's cook to its head coach, everyone is impressed with the relationship. Mike comes around from time to time during the offseason, and he helped out at training camp in 2005.

"It's almost incredible when you see the depth of the commitment Madieu has made at this point in his own life," Lewis said. "He's a young guy in the peak, early years of his own football career, and that gives you a lot to focus on.

"But he still has the time and the focus to take the responsibility for his brother having a secure life and good opportunities [and] just being a real part of his life."

Teammate T. J. Houshmandzadeh recently asked Madieu to go to a Reds game.

"He said, 'Can't – it's a school night,'" Houshmandzadeh said. "Even though he's not the going-out type, there are times he wants to go get out of the house. He's given up a lot to show [Mike] what family is all about."

After the track meet, because Mike placed in two events, he received a rare dinner out as a treat. He chose La Rosa's carryout. Mike ordered two calzones. Madieu, who has increased his weight to 205 pounds to try to improve his durability without losing speed, got a pasta dish with chicken. During a 10-minute wait for their food, Mike stood proudly beside his big brother. They continued the conversation they started at the track meet.

"You know what helped you in the 200, don't you?" Madieu asked, "It was running next to that fast dude from [North College Hill]."

At one point, Mike leaned into Madieu and placed his head on his brother's shoulder. Madieu put one arm around the boy's neck and hugged him tightly to his chest.

# A world apart

T. J. Houshmandzadeh was OK with finally talking
to the father he never knew and who lives in Iran.
But make no mistake: the Bengals wide receiver
and devoted dad is his own man

*September 9, 2007*

About a week after Father's Day, Bengals wide receiver T. J. Houshmandzadeh picked up the phone in his Los Angeles home, dialed overseas to Iran, and spoke for the first time to his own dad.

"I called him and said, 'Can I speak to Touraj?'

"He said, 'This is him.'

"I said, 'This is T. J.'

"He said, 'Oh, my God.' And he just started crying."

T. J. Houshmandzadeh did not weep, though nearing 30 years of age, he had not heard his father's voice before.

The conversation was guarded, formal. There were moments of awkward silence. Touraj said he had looked for T. J. since 1990. He explained that the political situation in Iran, coupled with his inability to find T. J.'s mother, prevented him from contacting his son sooner. He told T. J. that he was married and working as a mechanical engineer, and that T. J. had a half-brother and half-sister in Tehran. T. J. said he was married and had two young daughters and that he and his mother, Deborah Johnson, harbored no hard feelings toward him.

"He asked if he could continue to call me, and I said, 'It doesn't matter. If that's what you like, it doesn't bother me either way,'" T. J. said.

They have talked two more times on the phone, each time for about fifteen minutes.

There are no immediate plans for them to meet in person. Logistics are a problem. Touraj Houshmandzadeh lives in Tehran and his work takes him throughout the country. T. J. lives part of the year in Los Angeles and spends the football season in Cincinnati. He is in his seventh year as a Bengals wide receiver.

In late May, Touraj Houshmandzadeh contacted the *Enquirer* via e-mail, and it was forwarded by a reporter to T. J. The e-mail included three phone numbers in Iran and attachments of photographs – Touraj and his children: son Ali Houshmandzadeh, 26; and daughter Ati Houshmandzadeh, 24.

Curiosity, T. J. said, not anger or longing for a father–son relationship, was his motivation for calling.

First, he asked his wife and his mother what he should do.

"Yes? No?" he said. "I didn't care at all. But I was curious. So then I told my mamma, and she was like, 'Curious, boy?'"

"So I forwarded [the e-mail] to her, and she looked at the picture and said, 'That's him.'"

## Love and revolution

Touraj Houshmandzadeh was a foreign-exchange student who met Deborah Johnson in the mid-1970s in California. He earned a bachelor's degree (1977) and then a master's (1979) in engineering from San Diego State University. Their relationship lasted two years but ended before the birth of their son on September 26, 1977.

She named her son after his father because "I wanted to," Deborah, 51, said from her home in Victorville, California.

He is Touraj, Jr. From it, Deborah came up with the nickname T. J.

Touraj was living just down the West Coast in San Diego, yet he never contacted Deborah or sent money while he was there.

"I really don't know why he didn't try to come see him," she said.

Almost 30 years after the fact, she will admit she was upset then. "But time does heal wounds," she said.

Touraj said he was called home to Iran by his parents. He wanted to return to California, but the Iranian Revolution began to unfold in 1978 and hit its stride in 1979. U.S.–Iranian relations, once friendly, turned volatile and remain tense to this day. On November 4, 1979, Islamic students stormed the U.S. embassy in Tehran and took 66 hostages, most of them Americans; 14 would be released by the end of that month, but 52 would be held until January 1981.

"I was not allowed to leave," Touraj Houshmandzadeh said by phone from the western Iranian city of Ilam, where he was on a job site. He is now 58 and works for a privately owned petroleum-chemical company.

"I could not send money for six or seven years," he said. "I promised Deborah I would send money. After the revolution, I wasn't able to keep my promises. I want T. J. to understand that I was not able to do my duties."

Touraj, his wife, Nasrin, and their two children are aware of T. J.'s athletic success. Ali is a fan of American football, Touraj said, and was the one who found out via the Internet that his half-brother was a college football star at Oregon State and would go on to play professionally in Cincinnati. He follows T. J.'s football career on the computer.

"Unfortunately," Ali said, "we don't have sports on television."

Touraj played soccer.

"I understand what American football is; I don't know the rules," he said. "When I see that he is a good football player, I feel very good inside. I am very proud of him."

## Single mom

For whatever the reasons – political or personal – T. J. grew up without his father.

As a teenager in Barstow, California, T. J. got into some trouble. Neither he nor his mother would elaborate.

"All teenagers get in trouble," Deborah said. "We were always close; we went through it together. But he was no angel at times. He came back down to earth."

T. J. never connected any of his problems growing up to the fact he did not have a father in his life.

"A lot of people growing up in my generation didn't have fathers," he said.

T. J.'s grandmother would tell him about his father and say he was a good man. Deborah would answer any question T. J. had about Touraj, but he didn't ask many.

When T. J. called her about receiving the e-mail from his father and forwarded it to her, Deborah did not discourage him from contacting Touraj. The decision was her son's to make.

Although T. J. decided to call Touraj, he's not ready to view him as a family member.

"I mean, he is my biological father, but I don't want to be associated with him," T. J. said.

Deborah is African-American, and in the past T. J. has said he considers himself part of that culture. He identifies with his mother religiously as well – they are Christian; Touraj is Muslim.

Deborah said T. J. does resemble his father. He has the same physical build and intelligence.

Thinking back to her struggles to support a family as a single mother, Deborah said determination got her through. She moved to San Antonio, Texas, for some time. She wasn't hiding from Touraj, who said he would try to contact her.

"He probably couldn't find us even if he tried," she said.

She said T. J. has the same type of determination. It is what has lifted him to an NFL career.

"He has come a mighty long way," she said.

## T. J. and Chad

T. J. graduated from Barstow High School. His senior season, he played running back and rushed for 868 yards, with a whopping 10.1-yard average per carry, and led his team to a 10-1 record.

But his grades prevented him from attending an NCAA Division I school. He attended Cerritos Junior College in California for two years and played wide receiver. Then he played two seasons at Oregon State, where, in fall 2000, he played opposite fellow Bengals wide receiver Chad Johnson.

Johnson said he never heard Houshmandzadeh complain about not knowing his father. Johnson understood: Raised by his grandmother in Miami, Johnson would not meet his father until 2005.

"He is very strong," Johnson said of Houshmandzadeh. "At the point where you haven't had a certain individual in your life for that amount of time, you really aren't worried about it. But you are curious."

Johnson's grandmother did not like that Chad met his father.

"Her favorite line was, 'He didn't give you a quarter your whole life. Now that you are successful, here they come.'"

Touraj Houshmandzadeh knows the stereotype of the long-lost father appearing when his son makes good.

T. J. is in the third year of a four-year contract with the Bengals that's worth more than $12.5 million. Touraj said money is not his motivation for wanting a relationship with his son.

"No father can take from his son," Touraj said. "I am doing fine. I do not want anything I do not have. I want to know him."

## Son now a father

The man who grew up without a father is himself an attentive one to daughters Karrington, 7, and Kennedi, 5.

"He is the world's greatest dad," Kaci Houshmandzadeh said of her husband. "He is really into our kids."

T. J. has given his children their baths. He has changed their diapers. T. J. would get up overnight to give the babies a bottle so his wife could sleep.

Now he and the girls wrestle in the house. They play ball outside and ride bikes.

"I do appreciate it," Kaci said. "I know a lot of women who have to do everything by themselves. I look at T. J. and see the joy in his eyes when he's with the girls. But I don't know if it's because he didn't have a father."

T. J. does wonder what effect not having a father has on his own parenting style, but he doesn't pause long on that question. No reason to. It's not as if he can change his past.

"I discipline them," he said of his daughters. "I don't like to be mean to my kids, but I have and I will because I need them to know right from wrong and that not everything is going to be given to you, things of that nature. I do the best I can. I'm not perfect."

Kaci grew up without a father. But she was brought up by her grandparents, so she had a father figure.

T. J. said he had no adult male role models, except for one or two of his mother's brothers. Still, his contact with his uncles was limited because they did not live nearby.

"I was my own father figure, if you ask me," T. J. said. "I grew up fast. My mom would tell you that. Everybody in the house, when I was 13 or 14, came to me for money. I was never angry."

Any frustration he had was a result of growing up in a low-income family in Barstow. Deborah would have two more sons with another man a few years after T. J. was born, but that man died, T. J. said.

"It never bothered me," he said. "If it did, it might have been when I was younger, before my teenage years: 'I wish I could get these shoes or those shoes or go eat here.' But that's how it was."

## Father and son talk

During one of their phone calls, Touraj invited T. J. and his family to visit him in Tehran.

"I wanted him to come to see his family," Touraj said.

T. J. declined.

"My brothers are my mom's kids," T. J. said.

Besides, there was the matter of taking his wife and daughters with him on the trip.

"I couldn't put my wife and kids in a situation where I was going to be nervous because if I'm nervous, I know they're going to be nervous," he said.

T. J. did say he would meet Touraj if he came to the United States.

"I will try to do that in the next one or two years," said Touraj, who fervently wants to meet his son and establish a relationship.

T. J. has indifference regarding all things other than his family and job, his wife said. Such an attitude was displayed when T. J. was asked whether he felt sad or happy about speaking to Touraj.

"I don't think it made me feel either way," T. J. said. "My wife tells me all the time that I have no emotions. My emotional side, when it comes to softer things, it's nonexistent. It's like I don't have it in my body, unless it's my kids."

Where the fledgling father–son relationship goes from here is up to T. J.

"He said, 'Deborah knew how much you meant to me. I don't understand why she didn't try to find me,'" T. J. said when asked what they discussed. "But when you [his mother] don't have any money, you can't do anything. So it was just one of those [situations where he said], 'I'm sorry,' and I said, 'I'm cool.'"

The two did not talk about football.

"I don't know what we would have in common," T. J. said. "When I was talking to him, my wife said, she caught me: 'You're talking to him like he's one of your friends.' I had to stop saying it's OK. He was crying. I was just trying to be nice to him."

In Iran, Touraj Houshmandzadeh, now that he has established communication with his American son, has one fear.

"I don't think he wants to pursue this," Touraj said. "This is a new situation for T. J. That is why I will not try [to contact T. J.] again. He can call me if he wants to know me. This is something I hated, that some people would say I want his money. I do not care anything about his money. All I want is to know him."

# She lost her son but found a cause

Chris Henry's mother is the soul of the organ donor movement

*September 25, 2011*

Carolyn Henry Glaspy stocked shelves and helped unload a truck during her shift Tuesday at the Warsaw Avenue Family Dollar Store.

On Wednesday morning, she took a flight to Tampa, Florida, where she sat for TV interviews that afternoon and was a featured speaker Thursday at the 19th annual national convention of the Association of Multicultural Affairs in Transplantation. The Richmond, Virginia-based organization works to increase organ donation among African-Americans and other minority groups.

Glaspy was back at work at the store Friday before driving to Mason to participate at a fundraiser for LifeCenter Organ Donor Network – Greater Cincinnati's organ and tissue procurement organization, for which she's made 25 appearances in the past year.

Glaspy, 46, the mother of former Bengals wide receiver Chris Henry, says her life changed the morning of December 17, 2009, when in a Charlotte, North Carolina, hospital she made the decision to donate her son's organs and tissue.

Eleven months later, on Thanksgiving, CBS Sports in its NFL pregame show featured a seven-minute film of Glaspy's reunion with the four people who received her son's organs. That's when her star was born.

Today she is much more than the face and voice of the movement promoting organ donation. She is its soul.

She lost a son. A vocation found her.

The Tampa event was the eighth Glaspy has done nationally in conjunction with Life-Share Of The Carolinas. She'll be back in Florida in October to tell her story again. Glaspy accepts no honorarium or fees from any organ procurement group, just her expenses. She tells them to put the money back into the organizations.

"I don't ask for anything," she said while sitting in her sparsely furnished, wood-frame house on Minion Avenue. "I didn't ask God to take my son so I could make money doing this. It gives me joy in my heart to try to help."

She made an immediate difference in the hours after her story aired Thanksgiving Day. That day alone, there were 1,927 hits on the donatelife.net site. The television coverage spawned 205 stories about Glaspy and organ donation, according to LifeShare.

"When people hear her story, they realize it could be them making the same decision she had to," said Debbie Gibbs, LifeShare public relations manager who was with Glaspy last week in Tampa. "Luckily for us, she is willing to tell her story over and over, and to my knowledge she has never turned anyone down."

In the past ten months, she's spoken twice each in Florida, Kentucky, and West Virginia and once in Colorado and Virginia.

Closer to home, Glaspy is always available to LifeCenter. Andi Johnson, LifeCenter's director of public relations, has driven with her to a speaking engagement in Dayton and accompanied her last month to the Midwest Black Family Reunion. Everywhere she goes she carries with her a tapestry bearing a lifelike image of Chris in his Bengals helmet and No. 15 jersey.

"There is something beautifully organic and genuine about her," Johnson said. "No event we call her about is too big or too small."

Family Dollar is another of Glaspy's healing grounds. Her store manager, Robert Wade, has seen customers reach for Glaspy's hand, contact that often leads to tears and an embrace. They recognize her from the CBS Sports report, which is available on YouTube.

"People are asking her how she coped with her loss and kept living her life," said Wade, who has offered her a promotion from associate to assistant manager because of her outstanding job performance.

"She won't take it because she doesn't want to lose the flexibility in her schedule," he said.

Glaspy recommends counseling to people who ask her advice, or a grief support group, which she attended. Telling her story, in public or privately, has helped her heal.

"All I can say is, 'One day at a time God will deliver you.' God can deliver us from anything. I have nothing to hide," said Glaspy, a native of Belle Chasse, Louisiana. "God delivered me from [Hurricane] Katrina. The God I serve is helping me every day."

In her grieving group, she wrote a letter to Chris and asked him what heaven was like. She told him about the people who received his organs. She envisioned him telling her that he was happy that other people received a second chance at life and that he was playing a lot of football in heaven.

"He said he was a first-round draft pick in heaven and scoring on a lot of long touchdown catches," she said.

Henry, the Bengals' third-round draft pick in 2005 out of West Virginia, had 119 catches and scored 21 touchdowns in 55 NFL games, a career shortened by five arrests over 28 months that led to three NFL suspensions totaling 14 games. He was often injured, including a broken arm that ended his 2009 season.

He was in Charlotte, North Carolina, with the family of his fiancée, Loleini Tonga, to make plans for their March 2010 wedding.

He jumped in the bed of a pickup driven by Tonga during what police described as a "domestic situation." Henry, police said, "came out of the back" of the truck and sustained fatal head injuries. He was on life support when his mother made the decision to donate.

That led to her appearance on the former CBS network daytime show *The Talk* in May. As a "Mom Who Moves Us," she was presented with a $25,000 check from Publisher's Clearinghouse and $7,500 worth of furniture from Havertys.

The money is in the bank. She wants to spend about half of it on underprivileged, inner-city youths, "food and clothing, maybe I can work with a nonprofit."

She received a new couch. A couple of new beds are upstairs in the home she shares with one of her two other sons and husband, Willie Glaspy, 56. He is a Christian storefront church minister and appliance repairman she met during a house call to fix Chris's dishwasher a few years ago. They married two weeks before Chris's death.

Otherwise, the house is bare, save the back room where Glaspy stores photos, jerseys, and mementos of Chris's life and football career.

Their modest life is a good life, they say.

"We got clean carpet and clean dishes and food to eat," Willie Glaspy said.

Some people are surprised to see the mother of a former NFL player living in a low-income neighborhood.

Sitting beside her husband on the new couch, Carolyn Glaspy brushed hair from her forehead with her right hand, on her wrist a wooden bracelet bearing Chris's image and the words "R.I.P. Slim." The date – December 17, 2009 – is encircled in a heart. The bracelet was the gift of Bengals players' family members.

"Chris didn't want me to work when he played," she said. "I wanted to work. He said he wanted to take care of me the way I took care of him and his two [younger] brothers when they were little."

Chris' NFL benefits went to his three children in a trust fund.

"That's where they belong," she said.

She appreciates everything the Bengals organization and the NFL have done for her son and family. They chartered a flight for the funeral in Westwego, Louisiana.

"They didn't turn their back, ever," she said. "I love them for that, Mr. [coach Marvin] Lewis and Mr. [owner Mike] Brown. They always will be part of my family."

She'll be off Sunday when the Bengals play their home opener against San Francisco, which is blacked out on local TV. She'll listen at home on the radio, which is what she does when she has to work on game days.

Just as she hasn't forgotten the support the Bengals showed her family, Glaspy has not forgotten where she came from – a small Louisiana town.

"I am not uppity, and I'm not riding in a Lexus or living in a gated community," Glaspy said. "That's not me. When Chris made it big, I stayed humble. Chris died. So if I had gotten all uppity, who would be left to pay my uppity bills?"

She is at peace, but there are dark moments that come when she's alone. Reality is her oldest child died at 26, at the point where all the people closest to him say he'd turned his life around. "From the bad-boy thug to a family man," she said. "He made his mistakes and learned from them."

Though Glaspy is giving away several pairs of Chris' size 14 football cleats – "I clean them all up real nice," she said – she has hung on to some of his clothes, especially shirts she won't wash.

"I hold them close to my face," she said, "and I can still smell him."

The memory of one sound haunts as much as it comforts: The *thump, thump, thump* of her son's strong, athletic heart she heard when she placed her head on his chest in the last minutes of his life.

# CHAPTER 13

# BASEBALL

*I saw him walking north on Burnet Avenue in Avondale in spring 2015. I'd stopped at the post office after a doctor's appointment. Former Cincinnati Red Eddie Milner was 59 and still looked like he could run down a fly ball in center field. He didn't recognize me. I introduced myself and said I had profiled him in 1998, during his battle with drug addiction. He said he remembered. We shook hands, and he gave me a crumpled business card for his services as a professional baseball instructor. A few months later, he was dead at 60. The cause of death was not made public.*

# Musings on baseball and beyond from a boy of summer

Twenty-five years later, Roger Kahn's book still resonates

*April 1, 1997*

The book had pictures of baseball players in it. Didn't matter that I didn't know who most of them were. And it had cuss words. Strung together to form phrases I'd never heard.

For me, at age 10, that combination was irresistible.

*The Boys of Summer* (HarperCollins; $14) was a Christmas gift to my dad from my older brother the year it was published in 1972. But I took ownership of the book, and it has since become a constant companion.

Roger Kahn's look at the Jackie Robinson Brooklyn Dodgers turns 25 this year. It has sold 2.5 million copies. But I can't imagine one that has had more effect on a reader than the original hardback I swiped from Dad. Somewhere in my teens, I started reading *Boys of Summer* every spring. Through the years, these annual readings revealed several books in one. Least among them, I can see now, was a book about baseball.

*Boys of Summer* helped shape my views on race relations. It showed me the pain and joy of aging. You could actually get too old to play baseball? It introduced me to poetry and the possibilities of a newspaper career.

Even as a fifth-grader, I suspected my days in organized baseball were limited. My arm wouldn't take me to the Bigs, but maybe I could make it – like Mr. Kahn – as a writer. Since then, I have tried to pattern my writing style after his. On my best days, I fancy myself writing as well about people as he does.

*The Boys of Summer* was born in 1952, the first of two seasons that Mr. Kahn covered the Brooklyn Dodgers for the New York *Herald Tribune*. He was 24. The first half of the book recounts those seasons, his upbringing in Brooklyn, and the baseball-based relationship he shared with his father.

In *Summer's* second half, Mr. Kahn revisits key Dodgers almost 20 years later. The biggest and strongest Dodger, Gil Hodges, suffered a heart attack while managing the New York Mets. A traffic accident sentenced Roy Campanella to a wheelchair. Carl Erskine returned to Anderson, Indiana, and raised a son who has Down's syndrome.

The chapter on Mr. Robinson, "The Lion at Dusk," is widely considered one of the most telling and intimate looks at the man who broke baseball's color barrier in 1947. This year's baseball season, which marks the fiftieth anniversary of baseball's desegregation, is dedicated to him.

Mr. Kahn became a family friend, and his tender portrait ends with the ferocious ballplayer slumped in tears at the funeral of his oldest son, Jackie Jr.

Before I read the book, I knew who Jackie Robinson was and could say – like my 7-year-old son Peter told me the other night – that Jackie Robinson was "the first man with brown skin to play in the major leagues."

As I read and reread *The Boys of Summer*, I learned exactly what that meant. It was a frightening first look at racism.

In the Robinson era, members of other teams ate watermelon in the dugout during games. Pitchers tried to bean him when he was batting. In the field, he was the target of spikes and base runners' barrel rolls. The verbal attacks were just as vicious. And, because he was the first African-American in the game, he couldn't fight back.

I went to Dad in tears one night after reading that chapter. Then, as now, bigotry made no sense.

Another lesson I learned was about Vietnam. My two older brothers, 21 and 19 in 1972, had college deferments. Another guy on the block went to Canada to avoid the draft.

In *Boys of Summer* I met Clem and Jay Labine. Clem was a Dodger pitcher. Jay was his son, who enlisted in the Marines against his father's wishes and lost a leg in Vietnam.

Mr. Kahn cites poet Emily Dickinson to note the change in Clem Labine: "After great pain a formal feeling comes."

I took an American literature class at Miami University during the fall semester of my senior year in 1983. One possible topic was to examine Ms. Dickinson's poems by subject matter. I chose her pain poems and told Mr. Labine's story through them. I even tried to reach him at his Rhode Island clothing business to update his story. He didn't return my calls.

Because it was in a baseball book, poetry was now cool in the mind of a 10-year-old. It was a hall-of-fame lineup: Robert Frost, Langston Hughes, Ezra Pound, and Dylan Thomas, from whose work Mr. Kahn took his title.

> *I see the boys of summer in their ruin*
> *Lay the gold tithings barren,*
> *Setting no store by harvest, freeze the soils.*

Until I read *The Boys of Summer*, baseball was all I cared about. Roger Kahn showed me the beauty of the written word. And he showed me the many vicarious lives a writer could live.

❖

# Faith helps former Reds outfielder Eddie Milner fight his addiction

*September 10, 1998*

The service begins with praise and worship. Former Cincinnati Reds outfielder Eddie Milner is the featured speaker. He joins in with three dozen juvenile offenders.

"I will rejoice," they sing, "for he has made me glad."

These days, Mr. Milner is glad. And clean.

Sunday marks nine months of sobriety for Mr. Milner, who says he hasn't used cocaine since completing a rehab stint December 13. The stretch is the longest he has stayed clean on his own in 14 years. He started using in 1984 while playing for the Reds.

As a result, his life – and the lives of his wife, Retha, and daughters Elisha, 12, and Erin, 6 –have been a series of ups and downs. Trust won. Trust lost. Trust regained, only to be lost again. As is the case with many families that deal with drug and alcohol addictions, the Milners are trying to make trust permanent. Repeated relapses and six rehab stays in ten years estranged him from his family for months at a time. His first rehab came in 1987 while he played for the San Francisco Giants.

The family deals with his addiction by leaning on their Christian faith. Mr. Milner clings to his faith. It's the guard he raises against temptation. When his faith wavers, his shield falls, and he finds himself first in a drug house. Then a rehab center, far away from the family's Blue Ash condo. But when his faith is strong – as it has been these past nine months – Mr. Milner is the man he aspires to be: Involved father. Devoted husband. Entrepreneur. Evangelist.

When he feels good about himself, he fervently shares his story of drug abuse in the hope it will help others avoid the same mistakes. Many other times, he emotionally retreats deep inside himself. Tonight, though, in the chapel of the Hillcrest Training School, he's talking.

"Being a former major leaguer ain't my claim to fame," Mr. Milner tells Hillcrest residents. At 43, he's still in big-league shape: 5-foot-11, a trim, muscular 170 pounds.

"My claim to fame," he says with a pause, "is being a son of God. And I'm on a mission to share with you how Christ has saved my life. I had one brother killed. He was hooked on drugs, like I was. I lost my career to cocaine."

Hillcrest is a faith-based juvenile correctional center in Springfield Township. The chapel is still. Only Mr. Milner is in motion. He prowls the aisle in search of lost souls. It's the same relentlessness he showed – his nickname was Greyhound – chasing down baseballs in center field for the Reds from 1980 through 1986 and again briefly in 1988. Teens in the audience hang on his words.

"But I have a new career today," Mr. Milner says. "I'm here to help you find the peace that only Christ can give."

He speaks from experience. Mr. Milner knows peace with Jesus because, he says, he knows torment without him.

Peace. Daughter Elisha turned 12 on August 24, the day before she started seventh grade. The Milners took the girls to Paramount's Kings Island. The family was all smiles. Two days later, Erin turned 6. The family celebrated at home. Mrs. Milner made Erin's favorite dessert, strawberry shortcake.

Torment. A year ago, Mr. Milner missed his girls' birthdays. He was a month into what he now hopes will have been his last rehab, at the Good Samaritan Inn in Hamilton, a Christian-based center. He lived there almost five months.

"Did Ed try to make up for last year? I don't know," his wife, Retha, says. "He's just taking things a day at a time."

Being married to a drug abuser and having to hold the family together in his absence has taken a toll on Mrs. Milner. She always has been shy, she says. Now she is even more guarded.

Emily Dickinson wrote, "After great pain a formal feeling comes." That is Retha Milner.

She fiercely guards her and her children's privacy. She had doubts about her husband going public with his story. Her primary concern is the teasing Elisha and Erin might have to endure at school. Mrs. Milner declined to let them be interviewed for this story. She agreed to be interviewed only after repeated requests.

She agrees with her husband. If an addiction can be beaten, it will be only with God's help. Like her husband, she leans on God in good times and bad. And she's trying to teach her daughters to do the same.

"It's my faith in Christ that allows me to stay in this marriage," says Mrs. Milner, who owns a nail salon, A Polished Touch, in Silverton. "God helps me to see Christ in Ed, the new man in him. It comes back to my commitment in the Lord. If he says he will see me though, he will. Many times, I have said, 'I don't want to do this anymore.' I've said to myself, 'Heck with this.' I had to ask the Lord to help me see beyond."

## God, family, job

These days, Mr. Milner is asking the Lord for help. He's trying to rebuild his most important relationships and find balance in his life. He's trying to let up on his perfectionist ways. His goal is to be a dependable God-family-job man.

He has held a variety of jobs since leaving baseball. He has a finance degree and has sold insurance. Before his last relapse in 1997, he had worked himself from the loading dock to the finance department of an Oakley company. He has started two new businesses: A Christian-based financial planning firm and another that raises money for religious organizations. Wherever his work takes him, he checks in with Retha by phone at least twice a day. But when he's gone and the girls don't know where he is, they note his absence.

"My youngest girl will say, 'Daddy, where was you at?' I tell her, 'I've been at a basketball game.' I tell her the truth," Mr. Milner says. "As she sees me doing what I'm supposed to, coming back consistently, she can [increasingly] count on me."

The relationship is more complex with Elisha because of her age. "There's hurt there," he says. "I can remember her crying a couple of times and asking me why I did this. I told her I was having problems. 'I was sick. I made the wrong choices.'"

His last relapse started on June 21, 1997. He recalls the night in great detail. He'd gone to a bachelor party with a group of Christian friends. He stopped at a crack house downtown on his way home. He can't explain why.

"I learned how quick I could change from focusing on God to doing drugs," he says. "When temptation hit, I didn't run to the Lord."

His family didn't hear from him for two weeks. Finally, the phone rang. "I said, 'I'm struggling. You know I'm struggling. I've put you through this before, and I'm sorry,'" he says. "I asked [Retha's] forgiveness. I think she forgave me."

She says she forgives him because her faith calls her to forgive.

He last smoked crack on July 17, 1997, the same day he found a bed in a West End detox center. On July 24, he went to Good Samaritan Inn, where he cooked for other residents. He stayed until December 13.

"Eddie is very determined to stay clean this time," says the Rev. Josh Willis, Good Samaritan founder.

Mrs. Milner's reaction is more reserved. "Is Ed solid this time? I'm very careful when I venture into that," she says. "I can't say I have total trust in Ed. That would be a lie. When a relationship has suffered the turmoil and stress ours has, it might take the rest of our lives to get to a point where we can trust each other."

## "He was Deion"

They married in 1984, the same year Mr. Milner used cocaine for the first time. He was upset by his reduced playing time (117 games) with the Reds. He had played in 146 games in 1983, batting .261 with 41 stolen bases.

"Then my mother [Evangeline Milner] passed," he says. "I was injured. All those feelings were there, and I didn't address them. I kept beating them down with drugs and partying."

He went to rehab the first time as a member of the San Francisco Giants in 1987. He relapsed again in March 1988, this time as a member of the Reds, and was suspended for one year. He served 81 days after completing rehab at the former Emerson North Hospital in College Hill. Mr. Milner came back to play in 23 games for Cincinnati in 1988 but retired before the season was over. He had signed for $250,000.

Drug use brought his baseball career to a premature end, says the scout who had signed the Columbus native in 1976. Gene Bennett is today the special assistant to Reds General Manager Jim Bowden.

"His problems might have cost Eddie about $10 million," Mr. Bennett says. "He was Deion [Sanders] before Deion. He was that good."

Mr. Milner realizes what he lost – professionally and personally – to drugs. And he held onto the bitterness after his playing days.

"Every spring would come along, and I'd say, 'I should be out there,'" he says. "And then I'd get high to deal with the pain."

Every time he relapsed, shame and guilt overwhelmed him. That's why he separated from his family. Those are the times, he explains, his faith wasn't as strong as his addiction. The cycle is familiar: Relapse, rehab, reconciliation.

He has worked a series of temporary jobs to support himself. One, in June 1996, found him back in what had become Cinergy Field, home of the Reds, where he spent the majority of his playing career. But this time, he was pushing a broom as part of a post-game cleaning crew.

## Keeping promises

His sobriety has been the result of several positive steps in faith, in spite of the previous missteps.

A Christian since 1985, he is involved in the Christian men's movement Promise Keepers and attended its Cincinnati rally in May 1997. On February 1, Mr. Milner was ordained an evangelist by his pastor, the Rev. Ray McMillian of Faith Christian Center, Forest Park. Mr. Milner can now counsel prison inmates and hospital patients but has yet to do that.

His public testimonials garner invitations. The activities further insulate him in his faith. He is held accountable for his actions. He wants, he says, to take what was bad for him and turn it into something good – prevention – for other people.

In July, Mr. Milner spoke at the Ninth Street United Methodist Church in Hamilton. He later worked with children attending the church's sports camp. It drew participants from Hamilton's impoverished Fourth Ward. "You catch his fire," the Rev. Georgiana Salyers, Ninth Street's pastor, says.

Today, in his burgeoning evangelical role, Mr. Milner is most comfortable in settings that combine athletics and spirituality. He was successful as a volunteer assistant varsity baseball coach at Cincinnati Hills Christian Academy, says Bob Gardner, team manager and the Sycamore Township school's athletic director.

Mr. Milner knows everything he has could be lost if he relapses. He says he's found balance and inner peace in his deepening relationship with Jesus. One day at a time.

"The glory belongs to the Lord," says Mr. Milner, high-stepping around his living room in joy. He claps his hands and raises his arms. "God has taken the desire for drugs from me. I'm ready to be a soldier in the Lord's army. It's always going to be a battle. I've accepted the responsibility of being a Christian.

"It's better than any home run I ever hit."

# Junior's effect: Baseball superstar takes bite out of basketball

Urban kids return to the diamonds

*May 11, 2000*

Joshua Harp has three words to explain why he's out for baseball this season after a two-year layoff:

Ken Griffey Jr.

"When he came to the Reds, I felt happy," said Joshua, 8, of Avondale. "Thinking about Griffey made me want to play. He's cool."

There are a lot of Joshua Harps out there.

When Mr. Griffey was traded to the Cincinnati Reds on February 10, organizers of youth baseball programs in urban neighborhoods said they hoped his homecoming would help to revive the game among young African-Americans.

Their wish, it appears, is coming true.

While regional registration numbers are not yet available for the 2000 season, youth baseball districts within Cincinnati have experienced significant increases in the number of black youths playing on organized teams.

Baseball, which hasn't lagged as much among suburban kids, used to be the game in the city. But flashy, high-speed sports like basketball – especially during the Michael Jordan era – captured kids' imaginations and interest.

"Michael Jordan almost killed baseball in the black community," said Fred Carnes, coordinator of youth baseball leagues in the West End and a youth baseball coach in his eleventh season.

But that is beginning to change.

In the Knothole district that covers downtown, Avondale, and Bond Hill, participation is up 50 percent from this past year among children under 10 and about 25 percent in leagues for boys and girls in the middle grades and middle school, said Vince Ward, volunteer coach of four youth teams and manager of the Woodward High School squad.

The Knothole Club of Greater Cincinnati, Inc., is a youth baseball organization for boys and girls ages 7–17.

In Mr. Ward's neighborhoods, some 80 children ages 8 and 9 played baseball in 1998 and 1999. This year, there are 120 children playing in that age group.

"We are having a revitalization, without a doubt," said Mr. Ward, 38.

Woodward's participation has doubled in one year. It has 26 boys out for baseball this season and can field both varsity and reserve teams for the first time in years, Mr. Ward said.

Santoro Hill, 15, a Woodward freshman from Mount Auburn, is playing organized baseball this season for the first time. The appeal of Mr. Griffey – he grew up in the Tristate and played high school baseball at Moeller – helped to lead Santoro to the diamond.

"I've been kind of following him," he said after practice last week. "I like how he goes all out for everything."

Errick Daniels, 15, a Woodward sophomore from Bond Hill, has played baseball since he was 5. He's more enthused about the game because Mr. Griffey came home to play for the Reds.

"He has boosted me up," said Errick, who plays center field, the same position as Mr. Griffey. "I think about him when I play. I ask myself what would Griffey do if the ball was hit to him."

Errick also watches more Reds games on television. He records them on tape and studies Mr. Griffey.

"I watch everything Junior does," he said. "I watch his feet. I watch how he throws."

Mr. Griffey's baseball drawing power in Cincinnati's black neighborhoods complements efforts that have been under way for the past few years.

The Cincinnati Recreation Commission has built two full-size fields and two youth fields at Roselawn Park, a few blocks away from Woodward High School on Seymour Avenue.

In 1999, Cincinnati started a program instituted in the late 1980s by Major League Baseball called RBI (Reviving Baseball in the Inner Cities). The Reds and civic groups have funded new leagues and playing opportunities for young people.

"We've been busting our butts in the West End, Avondale, and Bond Hill, and here comes one person to town and takes it to another level. That's good," said Jack Violand, baseball supervisor and a recreation coordinator for the Cincinnati Recreation Commission. "Just his presence in town has made a difference."

Chris Nelms, 45, a former Reds minor leaguer, oversees Cincinnati's RBI program.

"We have not noticed a massive increase, but the kids who are playing are more enthusiastic about the game because of Griffey," said Mr. Nelms, of Evanston. This includes children such as Joshua Harp, whose interest in baseball has been reborn because of Ken Griffey Jr. Joshua has a Griffey Jr. pennant that his grandfather bought him at the Opening Day parade.

"I like how he jumps to get the balls that are hit over the fence. I love how he hits home runs. I try to copy what he does," said Joshua, a Kilgour Elementary third-grader who plays catcher and third base. "I know his daddy played for the Reds. I know he wanted to come home and play for the Reds."

He's not the only one who's excited. "My friends are the same," Joshua said. "Everybody wants to be like him."

—◆——◆——◆—

# His ongoing quest? Teach them how to live.

Once upon a time, they were stars on a champion baseball squad. Now many of these black youths are dead. As their coach tells the tale, their violent deaths are simply a sad reflection of the community in which they were born.

*May 5, 2013*

Vince Ward spoke in March at the memorial service of aspiring University of Akron pitcher Jordan Smith – the eighteenth time in 10 years he has done that for one of his former youth baseball players.

Ward's experience trying to help young black males in his native Avondale is a microcosm of the dangers of growing up in the inner city. At the same time, despite the pain of his players' untimely deaths, his continuing work as a coach exemplifies the determination Ward and others have to help young men escape those threats.

"I am teaching dignity, character, respect – how to survive in this world," said Ward, 51, a security officer for Cincinnati Public Schools and baseball coach at Riverview East Academy. "The problem is they get older, leave you and fall under the influence of other people. They do things you don't know about. It's just the environment."

Two decades of coaching in some of Cincinnati's highest-crime and lowest-income neighborhoods has left Ward with this stark calculation: "A third are locked up, a third succeed and get out, a third die," he said.

Ten young baseball players, including Smith, 21, who was killed when he fought back March 9 while being robbed by two men in Colerain Township, died of gunshot wounds. One died in a fight. Another drowned. Six of Ward's former players, including his own stepson, Daryle Jackson, died in auto crashes.

His eulogies, deeply appreciated by relatives and friends, take an emotional and physical toll on Ward. He was hospitalized briefly for heart palpitations and other complications related to high blood pressure after Smith's memorial service in March at Withrow High School.

"He talked about how Jordan was a very mature young man and was able at 13 and 14 years old to communicate with adults," said Ed Smith Jr., Jordan's father. "He said Jordan always had a smile on his face and played hard in all sports."

Jordan Smith is an anomaly among the players. He had two parents active in his life.

"Vince is the only father figure some of these boys have, so he tries to be a dad to them all," said Marie Ward, his wife. "He takes it so hard. He is very compassionate. Jordan was at our house for a grill out last year on the Fourth of July."

Ward's empathy is rooted in Avondale's streets and parks. He grew up on Rockdale Avenue.

The 1970s were a different time, with fewer guns and more jobs in the black community. For Ward, a power-hitting third baseman and speedy defensive back all the way through Hughes High School, sports kept him busy, out of trouble, and motivated in school. After his 1981 graduation, he went to college and turned an associate's degree into a series of IT jobs that led him to Dallas before he was laid off.

He came back to the same block on Rockdale with his young family and noticed how life had changed: more guns, fewer jobs, for sure, and fewer opportunities for boys to play sports. Along with two of his brothers, Ward secured donations from ministers, politicians, and doctors, and the Avondale Indians – along with football and basketball teams – were born.

They won and won big. In 1999, players from Ward's 13- to 15-year-old Indians teams formed the core of Cincinnati's junior RBI team (Major League Baseball's Reviving Baseball in the Inner City program), which played in the regional championship game at the former Tiger Stadium in Detroit. In 2000, the 16- to 17-year-old RBI team played in the national tournament in Orlando, Florida, after defeating Detroit in the regional championship at Cincinnati's Cinergy Field. They also played and won in Chicago and Cleveland.

Yet violence and death closed in like shorter daylight at the end of a baseball season. A boyhood friend, Vincent "Tubby" Berry, was shot dead in front of a West End car wash in 1997. Vince Berry Jr., Tubby's son, played center field and batted leadoff for Ward's Indians.

Then came the first wave of Ward's former players' deaths, boys who were 8, 9, and 10 years old when he coached them:

Jeff Wise, just 18, a criminology major and former Avondale Indians second baseman, died after being hit in the throat in a fight on the Central State University campus in May 2003. Wise, a three-sport start at Woodward, turned down a full football scholarship to Indiana University because he wanted to attend an all-black college.

Folando Allen, a top-of-the-order hitter who could run, was shot in the spine on an Avondale street in August 2003 and paralyzed. Allen died of a brain hemorrhage in January 2007.

Anthony Buck, "an all-around great athlete," Ward said, was shot in the head and killed while sitting in a car near Vine Street and Mitchell Avenue in June 2004.

Then in July 2005 a mentor of Ward's, Cleveland "Pepi" Parker, 57, a youth coach and baseball lover, was killed when a stray bullet blasted through the front window of his Ridgeway Avenue home and into his chest.

"It was safer here when we were younger," Ward said. "The older we got the worse it got for us, too."

In any given year in Cincinnati, about 70 percent of homicide victims are African-American males, almost half of them in their teens and 20s. On Wednesday night, two more black males, ages 17 and 24, were shot and killed in Evanston and Millvale.

## Eight (young) men out
*May 5, 2013*

In the 23 years Vince Ward has coached youth baseball and football in leagues and Cincinnati Public Schools, 28 of his former players have died, more than half by guns. Eighteen of Ward's former players for the Avondale Indians youth baseball program have died in the past 10 years. He co-founded the youth baseball program, as well as basketball and football teams for boys in the neighborhood, in 1992.

However, a greater concentration of deaths has touched a single Indians team from 2006 through 2008. Eight young African-American men who played together as 16-, 17- or 18-year-olds in that span have died – six from gunshot wounds. Their stories:

**Denino Harris**, 17, died July 31, 2008, a gunshot victim of a friend who said he had shot Harris accidentally and pleaded guilty to involuntary manslaughter. Ward describes Harris as "a little chunky, but he could cover ground in the outfield. He was kind of quiet on the team, but when a girl came around he would talk."

**Josh Sanders**, 19, died June 4, 2010, from multiple gunshot wounds on Peabody Avenue in Madisonville. He attended Woodward High School and played shortstop, catcher, and pitcher for Ward, who said Sanders "had to grow up fast. He was streetwise. He had a lot of raw talent but had to be slowed down and taught to play the game."

**Chris Billingsley**, 17, died October 31, 2004, a passenger in a single-car crash

A couple thousand mourners attended Parker's funeral back in 2005, among them boys dressed in baseball uniforms or holding baseball caps on their laps, because Coach Parker wouldn't approve of wearing them indoors.

One boy, Denino Harris, then 14, an Avondale Indians outfielder from Golf Manor, said that night, "It shouldn't have happened to him."

## A youth in mourning becomes shooting victim

Three years later, it would happen to Denino Harris.

On the evening of July 31, 2008, Denino, just 17, sat in the Roselawn apartment of family friend Anthony Thompson, then 27. They talked about the pain they would inflict on anyone who harmed their families. To illustrate, Thompson pulled what he believed to be an unloaded handgun from beneath the couch, pointed it at Denino and pulled the trigger.

Thompson pleaded guilty to involuntary manslaughter and is serving a six-year term. Denino's mother, Tonya Harris, forgave Thompson in court. The former manager of the Ponderosa restaurant in Roselawn, she moved back to her native Lexington after Denino's death.

"'Nino wasn't a great baseball player, but he loved being on the teams. He looked forward to every game and practice," said Tonya Harris, 48. "The coaches would pick him up and take him home or back to Ponderosa if I was still here. Baseball kept my guy focused and out of trouble. Those coaches were so good to him and so good for him."

Several Indians players and coaches arrived as a large group at Denino's funeral. They wore T-shirts bearing their on Martin Luther King Drive in Corryville. He would have played in 2006 with the Avondale Indians AA team. An outfielder, catcher, and pitcher, though only 5 feet 7 inches tall, Billingsley "could play anywhere," Ward said. "He was stockier, but he loved to hit the ball and run."

**Daryle Jackson**, 21, died November 4, 2010, in a single-vehicle crash on Ronald Reagan Highway in Colerain Township. He was thrown from the car and bled to death. Jackson was Ward's stepson, a natural baseball player who played shortstop and could "do it all," Ward said. On the bench, Jackson would crack jokes with teammates, "but they took their game seriously."

**Michael Johnson**, 22, died May 5, 2011, from a gunshot wound to the chest at the corner of Reading Road and Blair Avenue in Avondale. He attended Woodward High School and was a power pitcher, Ward said of his nephew. Johnson, "a comedian who loved being with his teammates," was big – growing to 6 feet, 3 inches and a solid 200-plus pounds. "He always batted fourth or fifth and could hit the ball."

**Dion Thomas**, 18, died June 26, 2011, from two gunshot wounds to the head at Grant Playground on Back Street in Over-the-Rhine. He played baseball at Aiken his first two years of high school as an infielder and pitcher but played outfield for the Indians. Coaches recall him as "a really good kid" who nonetheless got into trouble in school and "couldn't

first Indians team picture. They were 7 years old.

## Coach to players: "Can't straddle the fence"

Even the young black men who live and avoid a criminal record walk a fine line between safety and danger.

Marsalis Charles, 25, a 2006 graduate of the former Shroder Paideia High School, pitched and played outfield for Ward and the Indians for three seasons, 2004–06. Using a 35 percent scholarship to play baseball at Alcorn State University in Mississippi, Charles earned a degree in electrical engineering and is closing in on a second bachelor's in industrial engineering from Mercer University in Macon, Georgia.

One night, though, when he was 16, Charles, who grew up in Silverton, lied to his dad about his plans and ended up at a party in Roselawn. Afterward, he was part of a large group walking south on Reading Road toward Bond Hill when a car circled and its occupants starting firing bullets into the crowd.

Charles was unharmed but shaken. Another night, because he was hanging out with friends from Kennedy Heights, he was attacked.

"I was putting myself in danger because I just wanted to fit in," said Charles, a for-

decide which way he wanted to go in life."

**Steven Derden**, 23, died November 5, 2012, shot by a known drug dealer and associate in East Price Hill. A natural second baseman, Derden played several seasons with Daryle Jackson at shortstop. "A great second baseman and fundamentally perfect," Ward said of Derden. "He knew how to position himself defensively and had a perfect hitting trigger."

**Jordan Smith**, 21, died March 9, shot in the torso as he fought against two men who were robbing him on Jonrose Avenue in Colerain Township. "Jordan spent a lot of time in this house," said Ward, sitting in his Colerain Township home. "He played short and third and was an ace pitcher." He graduated third in his class in 2009 from Lockland High School after attending Withrow and Aiken. Smith, who threw more than 90 miles an hour, first played at Berea College in Kentucky before transferring to the University of Akron. He was in his first year at Akron, his parents' hometown, and was interested in a career in sports medicine.

mer intern at the U.S. Department of Defense Naval Surface Warfare Center in Virginia. "Just thinking about it now scares me. Just thinking about my former teammates who are dead scares me. It hurts, but I use it as motivation. If I don't make it, how can I give back to my community? I want to pull some young guys through the way Coach Ward pulled me through."

Yet Charles almost fell prey to what Ward calls his players' attempts to "straddle the fence."

"We're all good on the team, but in our black families, we have somebody who is doing the family business," Ward said. "I tell my players, 'Don't be hanging with that cousin or uncle you know is doing no good. Stay out of the cars. That's how you end up in the wrong place at the wrong time.'"

Errick Daniels, 28, played for Ward at Woodward and as an Avondale Indians outfielder in 2000 before graduating the next year. His passion for music, as a high school musician and disc jockey, saved him.

"There were just so many guns and stupid drugs everywhere when I was coming up," said Daniels, better known today by his professional moniker DJ Easy. "We don't even have high school reunions because so many people are just gone."

Another Ward warning: "If something sounds too good to be true – like $2,000 cash in your pocket and a car – it is."

Geno Ward, 27, Vince Ward's son, is a 2004 Woodward graduate and former Avondale Indians player. He said he can count on one hand the number of teammates who are dead but doesn't have enough fingers and toes to account for all of his teammates and friends who are in prison.

"It is heartbreaking," said Geno Ward, who last year completed a job-readiness program at the Urban League of Greater Cincinnati and is now working in construction. He would like to teach and coach.

"For you to have a role model at a young age," he said, "it's harder for the devil to reach you."

Yet the efforts of Vince Ward and others, like Al Shumar, a math teacher and baseball coach at Aiken High School, just aren't enough sometimes.

A former Avondale Indians catcher, Charles Carter, now 26, is serving a life sentence with no chance of parole for 30 years for aggravated murder and aggravated robbery in the death of Phil Bates, husband of Cincinnati Public Schools board member Melanie Bates. Carter admitted to shooting Bates in August 2006 at Bates's North Avondale home.

A recklessness can take over the psyche of the brightest young man.

The Rev. Peterson Mingo, pastor of Christ Temple Full Gospel Baptist Church, Evanston, said many think they won't live to 25, "so they rush through life, not worrying about who they hang out with, trying to fit it all in before they die."

## An island of peace in a sea of violence

At Aiken, Shumar has coached seven of Ward's Avondale Indians who've died. With each young man's death, he said, the pain multiplies.

"We've gone to enough funerals," said Shumar, who has lost at least two other players whom he hadn't sent to Ward for summer baseball.

They both coached Jordan Smith.

"I'll never forget Vince getting up there and talking about Jordan," Shumar said. "All of these kids are like his sons. You feel the love and care that Vince gives them. Sometimes, I really don't know how he goes on."

Ward finds peace in baseball. If his wife, a nurse, is at work, Ward seeks out a game to watch.

"It keeps my mind off thoughts of kids from the past, not just the ones who passed away – the ones who are in prison, on the street or strung out," he said. "I always wonder if they are safe. So instead of worrying about the past, I try to help these younger guys make it."

Usually, though, Ward is coaching. On Tuesday night, his Riverview East Academy team improved to 10–5 by holding onto a 10–9 victory at Hughes. On one perfect hop, center fielder

Damon Payne threw out a Hughes runner at home to end the game. Catcher Derek Law blocked the plate.

"I knew that kid wasn't even going to touch it," said Ward.

"Coach," Law said, "I just dropped my knee like you taught me."

# CHAPTER 14

# THE NEWEST BLACK CINCINNATIANS

*Most of my immigration stories originate in Greater Cincinnati's burgeoning Hispanic communities. Yet groups of refugees continue to arrive here from several African nations. The cohesion and self-discipline of the Fulani people from West Africa struck me; they occupied an entire apartment building in suburban Lockland. I won't soon forget the joy in the voices and faces of the Congolese Sumuni brothers when they talked about their love of soccer and how it helped them endure growing up in the world's most overcrowded refugee camp.*

# Fulani develop strength in unity

Immigrants use community living to keep culture alive

*August 28, 2011*

LOCKLAND – The smell of cooking – rice with a brown sauce flavored with onions and peanut butter – fills the hallways of the three-story apartment building.

A third-floor unit, rented collectively by a community of West African immigrants, is the mosque. A dozen pairs of shoes are scattered in the hallway outside the door.

Downstairs, another rented apartment serves as a school, where the Pulaar language and Fulani culture are taught to young people.

The other 68 units in Mulberry Court Apartments are homes to one of the region's most cohesive and distinctive immigrant groups, the Fulani people – primarily from the African nations of Mauritania, Senegal, and Guinea. The community began forming in the early 1990s and has grown to about 1,200, households clustered in other apartment houses in Springdale, the West End, and Florence, Kentucky.

The Fulani have largely kept to themselves, working and living with each other, otherwise blending into American culture as dark-skinned Africans, often indistinguishable from black Americans.

Proud and protective of their culture – adhering to an elaborate code of conduct emphasizing modesty, common sense, and patience – the Fulani now want to share that culture with Greater Cincinnati.

The first African cultural day, known as Nyaldi Pinal, will be next weekend in the West End.

"The reason is to bridge the gap and share our culture," said community leader Abda Tall, 52, an asylee from Senegal who works as an interpreter at the Lincoln Heights Health Center, where many Fulani and other African immigrants receive medical care. "We know there is a fence between us and the other guys, especially black Americans."

The goal is to assimilate into American culture while maintaining Fulani culture, primarily Muslim teachings.

"We want to become part of America," said Cheikh Sao, 36. He and his wife are permanent U.S. residents and live in Lockland, not far from Mulberry Court. He has a master's degree in French from a Mauritanian university. He is studying computer programming at Cincinnati State Technical and Community College and works at Wornick Foods in Blue Ash.

Immigrants often live near their work. Fulani people worked at Club Chef when it was in the West End, giving rise to concentrations of Fulani living at the Park Town and Ezzard Charles apartments. Another community of Fulani is growing in and around Cross Creek Village Apartments in Florence.

"We are good people," Sao said. "We want to use our knowledge. We want to live in peace and freedom."

Historically, peace and freedom have been elusive.

Living as nomadic black Muslim herdsmen in Africa, the Fulani endured discrimination to the point of slavery in Mauritania, especially where the lighter-skinned Arab-Berber class has ruled for 800 years.

A dispute over grazing rights on the Mauritania-Senegal border in April 1989 ignited a two-year war and the forced exile into Senegal of 70,000 black Mauritanians. In all, a quarter-million Fulani in both countries fled their homes to escape persecution, many ending up in refugee camps in Mali.

It was in 1989, too, that the Pulaar Speaking Association formed in Brooklyn, N.Y. The nonprofit promotes volunteerism to create a stronger community of African immigrants that contributes to the larger American society. The Ohio Pulaar chapter is one of 21 nationally.

The refugee resettlement program in the Archdiocese of Cincinnati brought in 15 Mauritanians in the early 2000s.

Regardless of their country of origin, or what reason the U.S. government let them in – asylee or refugee – members of the local community follow the traditional ways of immigrants: They are stronger in a group than as individuals.

Pulaar members will pool their financial resources to send the body of a person who dies in the United States back to Africa for burial if family members there choose. It costs about $1,300.

There are multiple examples of community.

A women's group met on a recent Saturday in the Forest Park apartment of Aminata Sall, 34, a permanent U.S. resident from Senegal and the married mother of five.

Fifteen women, part of a larger group that contributes up to $100 a month into a common pool, gave $3,700 to Sall to go toward the cost of dentures. She and her husband work for a food company that does not offer dental benefits.

Many of the Fulani immigrants in Greater Cincinnati and Northern Kentucky are men whose wives and children remain in Africa.

As many as four men will share a single apartment at Mulberry Court. A newcomer is given a grace period of four paychecks before he must contribute to the collective budget.

Mamadou Sow, 60, a Mauritanian with one wife and eight children living in Senegal, works at Club Chef in Covington.

"Some good things happen because of my Fulani family," said Sow, who came to the United States in 1997 and lived first in Memphis and Colorado.

He spoke through a Pulaar-speaking interpreter, Tall.

"Life is very expensive here. We split rent. We split food. I forbid myself any luxury."

As he was interviewed, one of his roommates prayed near the sliding glass patio door. Down the hall, several men prayed. It was Ramadan, the holiest month in Islam.

The mosque is being expanded to include another apartment, said landlord Clara Harkavy. She is paying to take out a wall and gives the Fulani a deep discount on the mosque rent.

"These are very honorable people," said Harkavy, better known to many Cincinnatians for her paintings.

Her tenants pay in full and on time. Turnover is low. The community is stable.

Downstairs, in the school, professional men wearing flowing, colorful kaftans teach Pulaar language and Fulani culture to children. Aminata Diallo, 13, who lived in her native Mauritania until age 9, wore a traditional Muslim hijab scarf on her head while studying her lessons.

The room was crowded with four or five teachers and about 20 students of many ages.

"When I go back, I don't want to be embarrassed if I didn't know the language," Aminata said in English.

Education is stressed for children and adults. Habsa Sileymane, 42, who lives at Cross Creek Village in Florence with her husband and niece, is working toward her MBA at Indiana Wesleyan University.

"Our first immigrants here, many were illiterate and had to take whatever work they could find," Sileymane, a Mauritian who moved from New York, said in proper English. "Education gives us more choice."

She works as an accounting analyst at Sun Chemical in St. Bernard. Many Fulani women work and raise children.

The women help each other with child care. They pool resources to help some families pay bills. "We share everything," she said. "Our strength is community."

# How the Beautiful Game reconnects Cincinnati's African refugees

*June 3, 2016*

It may be the world's most overcrowded refugee camp, built in western Tanzania for 50,000 people but now teeming with 160,000 Congolese and Burundians.

It was there the Sumuni brothers of Westwood once passed many hours playing soccer barefooted on a dirt field with a makeshift ball.

They'd find discarded latex medical gloves – two were ideal – blow them up and tie them off. They'd encase the inflated gloves in fabric salvaged from 110-pound rice bags. They would wrap the core in strips cut from a plastic garbage bag, which they would tie in small knots.

And then they'd kick the homemade ball through goals that stretched from a tree to a pile of rocks.

"You would have a nice ball that would last a long time," said Chance Sumuni, 22, the oldest of the family's seven children, five of them sons. "You could kick it far."

On Saturday, three of the Sumunis will be wearing cleats and kicking a regulation ball for the Congo 2 team in the World Refugee Day Cup tournament at Withrow High School. Sponsored by the Junior League of Cincinnati's RefugeeConnect program, the soccer tournament will consist of 15 national squads – most of them African – and illustrate the slow-growing but increasing international quality of Greater Cincinnati.

Other national teams of refugees and immigrants will represent Zimbabwe, Senegal, Mauritania, Burundi, Myanmar (Burma), and Bhutan. The Hispanic Chamber Cincinnati USA also will field a team.

The soccer tournament and family day, which includes health screenings and a community resource fair, comes two weeks before United Nations World Refugee Day on June 20. The event Saturday mirrors the international refugee day in that it encourages people to recognize the resilience of refugees, a number estimated at 50 million worldwide, and works to build tolerance, organizers say.

Refugee groups are being resettled in Greater Cincinnati by Catholic Charities Southwestern Ohio – primarily but not limited to Iraqis, Bhutanese, and Somalis. Of these groups, Congolese are projected to be the fastest-growing this year and next. People from the Democratic Republic of the Congo represent about a quarter of the 216 refugees brought here in the past 11 months.

The local arrival of Congolese reflects an international priority to resettle 50,000 people from the civil war–torn Central African nation during the next few years. The majority are headed to the United States, according to the United Nations refugee agency.

## One Congolese family's story of escape, survival, resilience

The Sumuni family fled its home in eastern Congo for Tanzania in 1997, among the 150,000 Congolese who tried to escape political and ethnic violence over a two-year period. They lived in the Nyarugusa refugee camp in western Tanzania for 15 years. The family feared for its members' safety if they returned to their homeland, where millions have died in a civil war begun in 1993.

The family of Yembe Sumuni and his wife Avijawa Neema came to the United States in December 2012. Sponsored by Catholic Charities Southwestern Ohio's Refugee Resettlement Program, the family first was at home in an apartment on Moosewood Avenue in Millvale.

The family's nine members are among the 1,200 refugees from around the world who've come to Greater Cincinnati through the Catholic Charities resettlement program since 2009. Since bringing about 10,000 Vietnamese refugees here in the years immediately following the fall of Saigon in 1975, the local Catholic Church has sponsored the arrivals of another 12,000 refugees from around the globe.

Yembe works at Club Chef in Covington. Avijawa works as a housekeeper at a downtown hotel. Their older sons work the overnight shift – 6 p.m. to 4:30 a.m. – at the Amazon warehouse in Hebron. Hard work and education are their priorities. They pool resources and in February bought a four-bedroom house on a tree-lined Westwood street, a far cry from the canvas tent and cinder-block hut they called home in the Tanzanian refugee camp.

Life here is far simpler, full of promise, and meets all of their basic needs, especially food and clean water. The older children speak up to five languages, among them French, English, and the regional Congolese dialect Kifulero. The family communicates in Swahili in the house.

The sons remember coming home from the refugee camp school and having nothing to eat or to do, except play soccer with one of those 3-pound makeshift balls. Each day, they had one meal, consisting of beans and corn, sometimes rice.

Soccer was their joy and escape, an international language that allowed children from multiple countries – Burundi and Uganda, say – to play together.

"We could play barefoot without a problem, as long as no one was wearing shoes," said Daniel Dumuni, 19, who is finishing coursework in summer school at Withrow and plans to attend the University of Cincinnati Blue Ash in the fall. "Our feet never hurt until we stopped playing."

But national pride is at stake on the soccer field. The Sumuni brothers say their homeland is always a strong contender in the African Cup soccer championships.

Babu Sumuni, 21, wears his brother Daniel's Withrow soccer jersey on a recent afternoon. Sitting in a rocking chair in the shade on his family's front porch, he said, "We just love to play soccer. Everyone in Congo plays. It reminds us of home."

## Soccer links experiences of refugees across continents

Resurrecting some of those soccer-based memories of home, whether it be in Africa, Asia, or Central America, is among the ideas behind the one-day tournament sponsored by the Junior League of Cincinnati. So is providing an environment in which groups of people from disparate parts of the world can meet through their shared love of the so-called Beautiful Game.

In one of its frequent community surveys, the local Junior League learned refugees living here need ongoing services beyond initial settlement, said Erin Rolfes, incoming co-chair of RefugeeConnect.

"While the official resettlement agencies help a great deal in the first 90 days, those organizations can only do so much," Rolfes said.

The Junior League, which in its history has served as an incubator for nonprofits or assisted in their creation, hopes to build RefugeeConnect into an independent nonprofit that would provide long-term help to members of refugee communities.

This will be its third annual refugee soccer tournament.

Some of the African teams scheduled to play in the refugee tournament Saturday play in a regular grouping called the African Premier League of Cincinnati. National teams made up of refugees, immigrants, and persons granted asylum from Ghana, Nigeria, Ethiopia, Senegal, and Mauritania play games at Winton Woods High School and on fields throughout Forest Park, home to concentrations of West African refugees.

Two teams of Mauritanians will play in the Junior League tournament Saturday.

On Sunday night in Forest Park, a team called Mauritania Players 1 had a league game against Cameroon.

Amadou Dia, a 46-year-old asylum recipient and new U.S. citizen, is the Mauritanian coach. He retired as a player to concentrate on furthering his education and pursuing political participation. He moved to the United States in 2001, is the married father of four children, and works in information technology for a local company.

He looked out on the field, where his yellow-shirted players warmed up before the game. His team had players simultaneously working and going to school, where many of them are studying to become engineers.

"We were oppressed by our governments, so when we get here we work very hard," Dia said. "The opportunity is here. The door is opened to the sky."

His thoughts turned back to the game about to begin.

"This younger generation loves soccer," he said. "Soccer is how we reconnect as Africans. It is not one country. Africa is a continent with 52 countries. And many of its people have been scattered. This is how we reconnect."

CHAPTER 15

# MARTIN LUTHER KING JR. DAY

*The second public swearing-in ceremony of President Barack Obama, January 21, 2013, coincided with the celebration of the Martin Luther King Jr. Day national holiday. It might have been a high point because, even then, the number of anti-black hate groups was on the rise. Of course, white supremacy would explode into the mainstream in Charlottesville, Virginia, in August 2017. There was joy that January day, when African-Americans and other people looked back at King's life and forward to Obama's second term. There also was palpable concern regarding renewed backlash. I felt it as I walked along with marchers that winter morning through downtown Cincinnati.*

# Memorial experience adds to local MLK reflections

*January 16, 2012*

One of the most powerful sights 14-year-old Ennis Tait experienced in October at the dedication of the Martin Luther King Jr. National Memorial was that of older African-Americans weeping or cheering.

At first, he didn't understand. "Then I realized, with what they lived through they thought it would never happen," said the Cincinnati Hills Christian Academy freshman from St. Bernard.

Cathi Alexander experienced that range of emotions on October 16 in Washington, D.C. The 33-year Cincinnati Public Schools teacher remembers when an assassin's bullet killed King in April 1968 in Memphis. She was a senior at Withrow High School. Her past met her present that day.

"We cried first; then I was in shock; we talked, then fear set in, fear that it could be anybody; then something else rose up in me, that I couldn't stop fighting for justice," Alexander said of her reaction to news of King's death. "I thought of all that at the dedication, the day he was killed. I was caught between emotions: I couldn't believe [the memorial] had been built. Then I said, 'Yes, dreams can become reality.'"

Today is the 26th anniversary of the first observation of the federal holiday honoring King, the Baptist minister from a Montgomery, Alabama, church and leader of the modern civil rights movement to end legal discrimination against African-Americans. It's the first Martin Luther King Jr. Day since the King monument dedication – an event still relevant and immediate in the minds of a sampling of Greater Cincinnatians who were there that day on the National Mall.

A sense of peace and harmony filled the air, they said. Races and generations blended, just like the America that King envisioned.

President Obama, who credited King and other civil rights leaders for paving his way to the White House, dedicated the memorial. Stevie Wonder and Aretha Franklin sang. About 50,000 people attended the dedication of the 30-foot-tall statue of King and the granite walls in which 14 of his quotations are carved.

Months later, the highlighted King quote that sticks in the mind of young Ennis Tait is this one: "Darkness cannot drive out darkness, only light can do that. Hate cannot drive out hate, only love can do that."

He rode a bus with members of the Avondale congregation of the Church of the Living God, of which his father, also named Ennis Tait, is pastor.

"It made me feel grateful for the things I didn't have to go through," the son said.

Young people were not forgotten.

Alexander went, in part, so she could bring her experience, photographs, and souvenirs back to share with students. She teaches fifth grade at Midway School in Westwood. She made the memorial dedication a class project. On Friday, using King's famed "I Have a Dream" speech as the framework, Alexander had her students give oral presentations on their dreams. She will use them in a documentary she is preparing about her trip to Washington.

"I want to know what their contribution will be and what they can do," Alexander said. "They've come to understand that the dreamer can't accomplish their dreams by themselves."

She is applying the lesson she's teaching to her own life.

"I was there that day thinking about how this man [King], this human being, lived a life of service to others," Alexander said. "It made me question myself: 'What is it I can do to provide more service?'"

Service is one of the specific themes of the King holiday. Martin Luther King Day of Service, the federal legislation challenging Americans to turn the holiday into a day of citizen action, was signed into law by President Bill Clinton in 1994.

Michael Little, 46, of Fairfield Township, lives a life of service. He worked previously as prison chaplain at Lebanon Correctional Institution. Now he is a chemical dependency counselor at Talbert House. He heard about the rescheduled October 16 dedication on the radio. Organizers postponed the initial dedication ceremony, scheduled for August 28, because of Hurricane Irene. It swept through the nation's capital that weekend with high winds and rain.

"I wanted to be able to come back and talk to men in my [treatment] groups about it," Little said.

His message: "It was good to see a large African-American community present. It was good to see people of other races there. I expected to see protests and violence. There were none. Not everyone accepted [King's] view of things or methods when he was alive, and they don't now."

He had driven to the Million Man March, also held on October 16, in 1995, and to Obama's inauguration in 2009. He rode one of two buses that left from Swifton Commons Mall in Bond Hill to the King dedication.

He bought T-shirts at the dedication for himself and family members. He purchased two copies – one in color and the other black-and-white – of a photoshopped image of King and Obama sitting in conversation at a table. One hangs on a wall of his home; the other rests on his fireplace mantle.

The King memorial dedication and Obama's inauguration – like the men themselves – are linked in the minds of some African-Americans.

Like Little, Josephine Hardy, 51, of Colerain Township, attended both events. She rode buses both times and felt connected to events during the civil rights movement, primarily the 1963 March on Washington at which King delivered his "I Have a Dream" speech. Thousands of African-Americans rode buses from across the country that August.

"Both times, I wanted to see history being made and to be a part of it," she said. "It was an honor."

She traveled with her older sister, Vanessa Haggard, 54, of Paddock Hills.

Hardy rattled off the names of the famous people she saw: Stevie Wonder, Aretha Franklin, Cicely Tyson, Andrew Young, the president and the first family.

"It was so exciting when the president walked through the space in the monument," Hardy said. "We were in tears. We all shed tears of joy, tears of excitement, tears of awe."

The monument to King, which opened to the public August 22 on the banks of the Tidal Basin, is the first major memorial on the National Mall for a non-U.S. president and for a person of color.

"I want to say we have arrived and that we have finally overcome," Hardy said, "but I know we haven't totally arrived."

A machine operator, Hardy's employer of 14 years, laid her off in September. She recently found work with another company.

The dedication weekend became a rallying point for the growing disparity in white and black incomes across the country, conditions reflected locally. U.S. Census Bureau estimates released in September show that the median household income for blacks in Greater Cincinnati in 2010 was $29,705 compared with $55,277 for whites (not including white Hispanics). Nationally, the median household income was $54,168 for whites and $33,578 for African-Americans.

Hardy came home inspired to stay positive.

"It was one of the best things, the most exciting things, to ever happen to me," she said of the King memorial dedication. "It brought back all of the feelings of what it stands for to stand up for justice for all people. The weekend was about unity and peace. I want to believe in those possibilities."

## Holiday history

Efforts to create a national holiday on the Rev. Martin Luther King Jr.'s birthday, Jan. 15, started soon after his assassination in April 1968.

The Southern Christian Leadership Conference, which King founded, presented Congress with 3 million signatures in 1971 seeking a King holiday. Another 6 million signatures were presented to Congress in 1980 by King's widow, Coretta Scott King, and singer Stevie Wonder. The holiday's path to reality was steeped in partisan politics and racism.

President Ronald Reagan signed a bill into law in November 1983 to create Martin Luther King Jr. Day. The first official holiday was observed on the third Monday of January 1986.

At that time, only 27 states and the District of Columbia honored the holiday. Arizona and South Carolina were especially contentious. The NFL moved Super Bowl XXVII from Tempe, Arizona, to Pasadena, California – played in January 1993 – because of Arizona's refusal to recognize the federal holiday. South Carolina became the last state to sign a bill creating Martin Luther King Jr. Day as a paid holiday in 2000, the same year it pulled the Confederate flag down from the Capitol dome in Columbia.

---

# On MLK Day, second Obama inauguration sign of progress

The race divide may be wider, but "we would not go backward"

*January 19, 2013*

To Mitchel Livingston, whose career in higher education reaches back to the 1960s and the height of the civil rights movement, Barack Obama's re-election is more important than Obama's election to a first term in 2008.

"With the ugliest voices in politics and billions of dollars working systematically against him, America – black, white, Hispanic, women – spoke clearly and said we would not backward," said Livingston, 68, of Cleves.

He is among the millions of African-Americans for whom this weekend will long be remembered.

Obama, though he will be formally and privately sworn in on Sunday, will take the oath of office in public on Monday. The ceremony at the U.S. Capitol will coincide with celebrations across the country of the Martin Luther King Jr. holiday.

"I don't look at this presidency as an end point; it's a new beginning," said Livingston, who will return to the University of Cincinnati in 2014 to help build a doctoral program in higher education administration. "There are forces at work that want to undo 30 years of civil rights legislation. This is a clarion call."

Obama's second term may indeed be a sign of continued progress for African-Americans, but the country can hardly be called color-blind. In fact, some surveys suggest the country has lost ground on the civil rights front – ironically, in just four years, since Obama first took office.

A majority of Americans now express prejudice toward African-Americans, even if they don't recognize those attitudes, according to an Associated Press survey released in October 2012. Conducted with researchers from Stanford University, the University of Michigan, and University of Chicago, the survey showed that the number of Americans with anti-black sentiments increased to 56 percent in 2012, up from 49 percent in 2008, when measured by an implicit racial attitudes test.

The widening gap in household income between whites and African-Americans nationally is even wider in Greater Cincinnati. U.S. Census Bureau estimates released in September 2011 showed that median household income for blacks in 2010 was $29,705, compared to $55,277 for whites in 15 counties covering Southwest Ohio, Northern Kentucky, and southeast Indiana. That's down 12.2 percent for blacks and 10.1 percent for whites since 1999.

The U.S. prison population comprises 40 percent African-American males, though they make up just 14 percent of the overall population. In Hamilton County, 70 percent of the jail population is black men, even though the overall black population – male and female – is 26 percent.

The number of hate groups – which includes neo-Nazis, the Ku Klux Klan, skinheads, black separatists, and others – has increased 69 percent since 2000 and now has reached 1,018 nationally, according to the Southern Poverty Law Center, a nonprofit civil rights organization based in Montgomery, Alabama. Since the end of 2008, the number of anti-government groups, including armed militias, grew 755 percent, from 149 to 1,274 in 2011.

Obama's election and re-election, say the law center's staff, fuels the underlying anger and fear related to the country's sluggish economy, increase in numbers of non-white immigrants from Central and South America and Africa, and the diminishing white majority.

"These attitudes don't surprise me," said Ericka King-Betts, 36, executive director of the Cincinnati Human Relations Commission. "With the economic downturn, a lot of people feel like their piece of the pie is shrinking.

"And they look at the 'other' and think that their piece is getting bigger. Without contact outside of their own communities, people sometimes fall back on negative stereotypes and experiences."

Despite advances in workforce integration, Cincinnati remains one of the nation's most racially segregated cities. Cincinnati ranked eighth in residential segregation of the nation's 22 most racially divided cities, according to an analysis of 2010 census results by the University of Michigan Institute for Social Research. It reports that 66.9 percent of one racial group would have to move to other census tracts to integrate Cincinnati.

## Does unity on King Day mask underlying division?

Yet even as many Americans remain separated by race in their neighborhoods and churches, King holiday celebrations appear to be gaining in popularity and acceptance by whites.

For retired federal judge Nathaniel Jones, though, racial harmony on the holiday masks hardening racial attitudes, fervent attempts to turn back the clock on civil and voting rights, and attempts to weaken the federal government.

"We celebrate by performing community service, we attend the program, join hands, and sing 'We Shall Overcome,' yet some of these same legislators then vote against programs and initiatives that Dr. King supported," said Jones, 86, general counsel of the National Association for the Advancement of Colored People in New York from 1969 through 1979, when he appeared frequently before the U.S. Supreme Court to argue for school desegregation.

Another regional civil rights leader with national NAACP experience is John J. Johnson, executive director of the Kentucky Commission on Human Rights, which has a regional office in Covington. To Johnson, 67, the convergence of Obama's second inauguration and the King holiday is a sign of great progress over the past 50 years.

With 22 years of experience in the NAACP national office in Baltimore, where he worked for the King Federal Holiday Commission (which pushed for the legislation to create the holiday), Johnson is now most concerned about the racial climate in his home state. "We don't want to see Kentucky become the breeding ground for social conservatism across the nation," said Johnson, whose service to the NAACP started as president of the Franklin, Kentucky, chapter when he was 18 years old. "Those forces play to the worst fears in people."

## Education, faith, talk are ways to close gap

A positive response is to increase educational opportunities for black students, said Dannie Moore, associate dean and director for African-American Student Affairs at Northern Kentucky University. Black student enrollment has grown to about 8 percent of the total student population of 16,000 on the Highland Heights campus.

To Moore, progress of any kind most often brings a negative response, whether the issue is Obama's election and re-election, King's effective anti-violence organization and leadership of the civil rights movement, or increases in educational attainment for blacks. "There is backlash to the progress, but backlash is not going to stop progress," he said. "We have come so far."

LeighAndria Young, 18, of Over-the-Rhine, is the first person in her family to attend college. A 2012 creative writing graduate of the School for the Creative and Performing Arts, she is a freshman communications major at the University of Cincinnati. For her, Monday's celebration of Obama's second inauguration and the King holiday reminds her of King's lesson: that it would be whites and blacks working together to force progress.

"There has been this struggle and racial tension because he was president, and it was more evident when he ran the second time," Young said. "The country came together and said that we trust him to lead us in a second term."

Obama has been the lightning rod for more overt expressions of racism since he took office. Bumper stickers, cartoons, and protest posters portray Obama as a monkey or lion. He has been lynched in effigy.

"If a woman [Hillary Clinton] had been elected in 2008, we'd be talking now about gender," said Rodney Coates, professor of sociology and interim director of Black World Studies at Miami University, Oxford. The nation's awkwardness around issues of race and its unwillingness to discuss it honestly – "A problem on both sides," Coates said – make race an even more explosive topic when events such as having a black man in the White House bring it to the surface.

For Lesley E. Jones, founder and senior pastor of Truth and Destiny Ministries, Mount Airy, the negative racial attitudes and tension are obvious in American society. An antidote to the poison might be to pause and reflect, she said, on the country's blessings.

"This America; it belongs to all of us," she said. "This is not Republican America or Democrat America. In spite of our challenges, this is the greatest country on earth. Dr. King worked for all of America. That is what I hope we try to remember Monday."

# Getting to know the "militant" King

*January 19, 2016*

Much of Cincinnati's commemoration of the Martin Luther King Jr. holiday has become tradition: A march from the National Underground Railroad Freedom Center to Fountain Square, where an interfaith prayer is said, with participants then continuing on to Cincinnati Music Hall for a program featuring an address by the city's mayor.

So it was Monday, when several hundred people bundled up against single-digit temperatures to pay homage to the slain civil rights leader and the movement that popular culture recalls him as almost single-handedly creating and leading.

The civil rights group Black Lives Matter Cincinnati sponsored a new event this year, an educational forum at the Public Library of Cincinnati & Hamilton County. "MLK Day: Dream But Stay Woke" attempted to give fuller dimension to King's life and work. It focused especially on his evolving positions on militarism and economic justice, otherwise known as the "Militant King" – and connected King and the movement's other leaders to the ongoing struggle for racial justice today.

"For me, to participate in the march and to see so much of his legacy co-opted and whitewashed is frustration," said Ashley Harrington, 24, one of three members of the Black Lives Matter steering committee. "There were no references to Tamir Rice or Sandra Bland and economic exploitation in this country."

Rice, 12, was shot and killed by police outside a Cleveland recreation center in November 2014. Bland, 28, was found hanged in July in her jail cell in Waller County, Texas, after her arrest on a minor traffic violation. Actually, Black Lives Matter members – carrying signs bearing Rice's, Bland's, and Samuel DuBose's names – did chant on the march from the Freedom Center to the library.

"Justice for Tamir!" It led to the rallying cry, "Back up, back up, we want freedom, freedom, racist cops, we don't need 'em, need 'em."

About 90 people – half of them white – attended the three-hour program at the library's main branch downtown. Event organizers did reference the $4.85 million settlement announced earlier Monday by the University of Cincinnati with the family of DuBose, shot and killed July 19 in Mount Auburn following a traffic stop by former university police officer Ray Tensing.

The King Day event was indicative of the Black Lives Matter's approach to building a focused and sustainable movement. With meticulous footnoting and citation, the forum's two formal presentations focused on King's texts – among them "All Labor Has Dignity," "Beyond Vietnam / A Time to Break the Silence," and "Where Do We Go from Here?" – and featured video of speech snippets. The entire presentation was available to audience members on their electronic devices via peardeck.com.

Those writings and speeches show how King "made the connection between poor black folks and poor white folks," Harrington said during her presentation. A series of recent books, including a collection of his labor speeches titled "All Labor Has Dignity" (2011) and "The Radical King" (2015) by Cornel West, give full treatment to King's late texts and reveal him to be as radical as Malcolm X and a democratic socialist who sided with the poor and working people.

"What does it profit a man to be able to eat at an integrated lunch counter if he doesn't earn enough money to buy a hamburger and a cup of coffee?" King said in April 1967, just a year before his death, at Riverside Church in New York.

The program's second half, led by another of Black Lives Matter's steering committee members, Brian Taylor, 41, looked at King's role as one of the leaders of the movement – not its sole leader.

"It had tons of people – [gays], women, and him," Taylor said of King. "People might say, 'You're dissing King.' No, we're trying to explain how someone becomes a leader. King had gifts, but he was an ordinary man – just like the people in this room – who was swept into an extraordinary situation."

In great detail, Taylor then told the story of E. D. Nixon, who led the Montgomery, Alabama, NAACP and Brotherhood of Sleeping Car Porters organizations. Nixon's work to end discriminatory seating practices on Montgomery's municipal buses predated Rosa Parks's refusal to give up her bus seat to a white man, which sparked a movement.

Taylor emphasized that the movement of black liberation comes first, and out of that movement leaders emerge. He said King's speeches on labor, living wages, and economic justice expanded well beyond the black struggle of the 1960s and apply today to movements such as the $15 minimum wage, police brutality, organized labor, immigration reform, universal health care, and women's reproductive rights.

In fact, audience members reflected Black Lives Matter's inclusive nature. Audience members participating in the public forum included people who self-identified as members of the Public Allies community service and leadership program as well as groups advocating for the GLBT, immigrant, and homeless communities.

"We want you to be involved in the immigrant rights movement and the women's rights movements," Taylor said. "It makes you stronger."

Philip Argyres, white and a University of Cincinnati physics professor, is a member. Asked what motivated him to join, he said, "the news."

CHAPTER 16

# THE STREETS

*"That's as close as I want you to get, no closer," my* Enquirer *editor, Randy Essex, said when I explained that two hours after I'd interviewed her a young drug dealer was shot in the face. Our story about revenge shootings unfolded in real time. The two years I spent working the streets in Avondale through 2012 and 2013, up until my cancer diagnosis and start of treatment, were the most fulfilling and interesting of my career.*

# Return to workforce not an easy road

A returning citizen accepts obstacles as
consequences of his choices

*June 10, 2012*

The one-mile walk on Hawaiian Terrace in Mount Airy is an appropriate symbol to Marcus Bell of his road back to productivity.

"It's a long way uphill," said Bell, 29, who served two years in a Kentucky prison after being convicted in 2005 of felony firearm possession in Covington.

These days he splits time between Mount Airy and his mother's house in Avondale. He graduated from the SOAR job-readiness program at the Urban League of Greater Cincinnati in November and still wears the dress clothes he received.

Except for the black dress shoes. "Hurt my feet too much with all this walking," he said.

On a Friday morning in April, Bell hiked from his fiancee's apartment at the bottom of the Hawaiian Terrace hill to wait for a Metro bus on Hamilton Avenue. He can't afford a car.

He carried his resume and an application in a blue Nike bag. He finished his GED while in prison.

His destination was a car wash in Paddock Hills that gives ex-offenders a chance to work. Bell wore his tie, dress shirt, and dark pants and red Nike high-top sneakers.

The bus cost him $2.25 to get downtown to Government Square and transfer to another route out Reading Road. The trip took him one hour and 24 minutes, from Mount Airy to Paddock Hills. His buses made a total of 37 stops before he got off near Howdy Car Wash to drop off his resume. The car wash, fully staffed, was not hiring. Bell thanked co-owner Marchelle Donald, and shook her hand before leaving to retrace his steps.

Six weeks later, a restaurant in Colerain Township would hire Bell as a grill cook.

"You got to stay after it," said Bell, who did odd jobs such as yard work and light construction and repairs to help pay bills. He has had a seasonal warehouse job. "I have four kids. There's no dropping my rap [sheet]. I got to deal with it."

# Culture of revenge

Breaking the cycle of inner-city retribution
will help save lives and create a safer Cincinnati

*October 8, 2012*

At 7:30 on a Monday evening, Donshae Stokes walked up to LeShanna Wilson while she stood on the sidewalk with friends and her 7-year-old daughter.

What was about to happen is part of a culture of revenge that drives many of the city's shootings and homicides, say police and street outreach workers battling to interrupt the cycle.

"It's urgent because getting in the middle of this is a way we can save a life, actually two," said Cincinnati Police Chief James Craig, who believes at least half of all shootings in the city are motivated by revenge.

It's a critical issue in building a safer region, too, from struggling and rebounding core neighborhoods to suburbs. "We're one," Craig said. "If we don't wrap our arms around these men, there will be more bloodshed."

That's what happened when Stokes, 18, approached Wilson, 22, a drug dealer known on the streets as "Bucket" or "Buckwheat."

"Why you running your mouth to my peoples?" Stokes demanded. Not waiting for an answer, he hit her in the back of the head with his gun and started shooting, according to a Cincinnati police statement filed in Hamilton County Municipal Court. One bullet tore through her nose and out her cheek. Luckily, she survived.

Six days earlier, Stokes had robbed Wilson at gunpoint, of $10 and her cellular phone, threatening to kill her if she talked to police – or his mother.

After the robbery, Stokes heard that one of Wilson's friends had asked Stokes's sister where he could be found. Known on the street as "pushing down," asking too many questions about somebody is an affront. So, Wilson and authorities say, Stokes came back and shot her. Street code said he had to. In the metaphor of the streets, he couldn't come across as a sheep in a land of wolves.

Retribution is part of a larger, more complicated mindset involving respect, perceived personal weakness and a need to get even. At this culture's root is the lack of structure in the home, where a distorted image of masculinity can take shape before later hardening on the streets. Violence is common. Survival requires swift and sure response to any affront.

Acute sensitivity to slights and insensitivity to violence, both learned young, are underpinnings to the culture of revenge.

Christopher Godby of Walnut Hills, now 34 and working as a reformer, once was referred to by police and federal investigators as being among Cincinnati's most notorious black-market gun dealers. He started in the drug business at age 5 as a runner. By 13, he was selling crack cocaine in Avondale. At 16, he was bound over as an adult and served a year and a half in prison.

At 18, he was trying to live clean but was shot in the back in a robbery in the West End. Forced to use a wheelchair, he said taunts by other drug and gun dealers that he could no longer thrive on the streets drew him back in. They challenged his manhood.

"You flaunt yourself, you flaunt your money, you flaunt your respect," Godby said of the lifestyle. "I was in it for the respect. If someone pushed up on your female or your prized possessions – the streets where you did your businesses – you were going to show your muscle."

That preoccupation with respect is often mistakenly associated with drug-related turf wars, said Robin Engel, a University of Cincinnati criminologist, co-founder of the Cincinnati Initiative to Reduce Violence (CIRV) and an internationally known anti-violence expert.

She returned a week ago from Scotland, where she consulted in the creation of an anti-violence program. The players are younger in Glasgow than Cincinnati, 10 or 11, and they fight with knives, not guns.

"There are similarities," Engel said of antisocial responses to confrontation and intense poverty that create a sense of being respected and valued. "It's about individuals who are profoundly marginalized. They have had constant exposure to violence – domestic violence and child abuse."

Communities are increasingly trying to set a new norm. In Avondale, a combination of increased police patrols and the CIRV Moral Voice program since early spring have helped prevent any homicides so far in 2012 in a neighborhood that tied for most in the city in 2011 with 11.

Godby knows Avondale, the West End, and Bond Hill. Those were places he got into shootouts and sold drugs.

In 2001, a judge sentenced Godby to 10 years in federal prison as an illegal gun dealer who used women to make the initial purchases at suburban gun shows. Now a full-time college student and anti-crime motivational speaker, Godby can recognize his flawed logic.

"It's immature, and you get so caught up in the peer pressure. You grow up, look back, and realize you were the scum of the earth. What I was doing was tearing down communities, hurting people, and causing senseless deaths.

"I know now I can save one kid, and, if I can save one kid, I can save a thousand."

## "The street code says I'm supposed to kill him"

Another ex-felon, Torrance Jones, 41, is as evangelical as Godby about saving souls from the streets and their culture of revenge. His effort – based in an Avondale barbershop and surrounding streets – is among an increasing number of local efforts, large and small, pushing back.

Jones, who served six years in Ohio prisons for dealing drugs and felonious assault, uses his life experience to motivate younger people involved in the drug-and-gun culture. He often tells them about standing at a crossroads just three years ago.

"I was on my way out," his story goes. "I was engaged to be married. My daughter was in high school. And a friend robbed me at gunpoint in my own house."

The gunman tied Jones up in a chair and demanded jewelry and money, but Jones's trappings of his old life were gone. So the gunman left empty-handed yet left Jones with a decision.

"The street code says I'm supposed to kill him because, if I don't, I'm a sheep, not a wolf," he said.

Jones called his uncle and his fiancée.

"I'll never forget it," he said. "I had the devil on one shoulder telling me to go kill him. I had an angel on the other showing me a better life."

He followed his uncle's advice and called police. The assailant is now serving a prison sentence but has sent death threats to Jones through released inmates. Jones now has an associate's degree in social work and is working on a bachelor's degree in sociology at Northern Kentucky University.

## Mass incarceration by the numbers

*February 21, 2015*

The United States leads the world with 2.2 million people now in its prisons and jails, meaning that 1 of every 100 Americans are behind bars.

National incarceration rates have dropped in the past three years, but the overall incarceration rate increased 500 percent in the past 30 years.

65 million Americans have a criminal record, 19.8 million with felony convictions.

51,729 is the Ohio state prison inmate population.

12,111is the Kentucky state prison inmate population.

1 in 28 American children has an incarcerated parent.

1 in 4 African-American children has a parent in prison or jail.

1 in 3 African-American males born today will go to prison at some point in their lives, if trends continue.

1 in 100 African-American women are incarcerated.

Though they make up only 25 percent of the U.S. population, African-Americans and Hispanics comprise 58 percent of all prisoners.

In September 2012, Ohio passed the Collateral Sanctions Reform Bill, which removed or revised 675 statutes that blocked former offenders from getting jobs in some of the

Jones's passion and teamwork with De'Angelo Boynton, owner of Stag's Barber Shop on Burnet Avondale, are paying off.

Their support has helped Randel Riley, 21, stay in junior college and on the job at a grocery store. A second-year student at Cincinnati State Technical and Community College, Riley is frustrated at times by the long road he faces. Going back to the streets is tempting.

"I did bad stuff; I had to fight a lot to prove I was a wolf," said Riley, who tried out but was cut this year from Cincinnati State's basketball team.

He is studying sports medicine and wants to work as a rehabilitation therapist with injured athletes.

One of his motivations to stay in school is the sight of people in their 30s and 40s still hustling on the streets.

"And they don't have any bigger pack [money] than they ever had," Riley said.

> state's largest employment sectors, such as health care and education.
>
> Ohio's rate of repeat offenders – recidivism rate – continues to drop: from 34 percent in 2011, to 28.7 percent to 27.1 in fiscal year 2014.
>
> *Sources: U.S. Conference of Catholic Bishops, the Pew Charitable Trust, NAACP, Ohio Department of Rehabilitation and Correction*

## "You will either be killed or end up back in prison"

Craig took his personal anti-revenge message in August to 75 inmates within months of release from prison, urging them to think of becoming the father, husband, or citizen the community needs.

Cincinnati's police chief sees the population of ex-offenders as the most dangerous to the community. An average of 2,100 ex-offenders returned to Hamilton County in 2010 and 2011.

"There are two guarantees if you entertain this mindset of revenge: You will either be killed yourself, or you will end up back in prison for the rest of your life," Craig told inmates.

Harold Croft, 36, could face life in prison without chance of parole after his indictment for aggravated murder in the June 18 shooting death of 15-year-old Africa Hope in Over-the-Rhine. Croft, who had served 10 years for manslaughter, had been out for only two months and was aiming for someone else when his gunfire struck Africa. The chief said it was a revenge shooting.

Attacking the same challenge as Craig in a different environment is Mitchell Morris, recruiter for the Phoenix Program at Cincinnati Works. Phoenix is a job-readiness and training program for people involved in group violence.

Morris, 62, who once worked for CIRV as a street outreach worker, sees the younger criminal who has never been in prison as the most likely to seek revenge over even the most minor affront – stepping on a foot, touching a car, making eye contact, dancing with a girlfriend.

"These are 13- and 14-year-olds up to 25 or so, who haven't been locked up and don't understand the consequences of pulling the trigger," he said.

With Phoenix, Morris – who also is a former felony offender from Avondale – shows up at the scenes of shootings and homicides. If he knows the victim's relatives or friends, he goes looking for them.

"I talk to brothers, cousins, uncles to try to stop any retaliation," said Morris, who estimates that nine of every ten shootings in Cincinnati involves a revenge motive or domestic violence.

He offers a new path that can begin at Cincinnati Works or several other local agencies – Cincinnati–Hamilton County Community Action Agency, Talbert House, or the Urban League. Hamilton County is working to coordinate existing services in its re-entry office, said director DeAnna Hoskins.

Mental health or addiction services might be needed before a person is ready to work every day.

Existing programs boast of success stories and positive numbers. They are also a source of hope. Since Cincinnati Works started its Phoenix program in May 2011, for example, 104 people completed job-readiness training; 65 found jobs.

## Thought a sheep, "I used to get bit"

The streets remain dangerous and tempting places. As the story of LeShanna Wilson and Donshae Stokes proves, the culture of revenge is alive there.

Beneath the tragedy of a revenge shooting motivated by nothing more than the perceived affront of Wilson's "running her mouth" to Stokes' affiliates, there is some good news: Wilson, though wounded, was released from the hospital within hours of the shooting. Rumor that a relative had taken her and her daughter out of state proved false.

Most important, the shooting didn't provoke another one.

On that Monday afternoon, just hours before Stokes shot Wilson, a friend of hers talked about the need to respond violently to her robbery the week before. His street name is Dale. He's 23 and says he served time in prison for illegal gun possession. He also says he has been stabbed once and shot twice.

"I used to get bit [attacked] all the time because people thought I was a sheep," Dale said that afternoon, as he and Wilson recounted her robbery. "No more."

Because Dale and Bucket are members of the same loosely organized and informal group – "affiliated" on the street – Dale said he might have to retaliate.

Police didn't arrest Stokes until Thursday. Dale had time to act. He didn't. Was his talk bravado? Maybe he already knew better. Or did a couple of people get to him and make sure?

They might have reminded him that he'd done well in the construction management program at Woodward Career Technical High School. They could have told Dale to remember how he liked working in a Colerain Township restaurant, and how he loves to cook and work in landscaping. They probably warned him that, if he gave in to vengeance, his prison sentence would be longer.

They could have repeated to Dale what he had told an *Enquirer* reporter just two hours before Bucket was shot: "I'm just trying to get a job and get out of Cincinnati."

# Where ex-offenders clean the fenders

Two Cincinnati police officers buy a car wash
to employ workers whose criminal records
had kept them jobless

*November 5, 2012*

As they make regular patrols through the Cincinnati police district covering Avondale, Bond Hill, Roselawn, and seven other neighborhoods, officers Michael Donald and Charles Utley always hear the same answer when they ask, "Why'd you do it?"

"I can't get a job because of my record," the offenders answer.

Looking two years ago to start a side business as a hedge against possible police layoffs – Donald and Utley were among 250 police officers let go in Cleveland in 2004 – they focused their idea on helping former criminals who'd been jailed.

On patrol one day, they noticed that Howdy Car Wash, which had been open since 1950 on Reading Road in Paddock Hills, had closed and was for sale. They bought the property in late July 2011, made $22,000 in improvements and opened a month later. Back in business for a little more than a year, Howdy has 12 employees making $8 an hour and is about to hire its thirteenth worker.

"This is our way of giving back," said Utley, 42, originally from Toledo and now living in Golf Manor. "We thought about what we could do to reduce crime."

Utley, Donald, and Donald's wife, Marchelle, who runs the business, have not made any money from the car wash. "Our first goal," added Donald, 47, of Colerain Township, "is pretty simple: Get them off the street, give them a job, and help them become more productive citizens."

Need is great for jobs for people with felony records. Ohio prisons release an average of 2,100 inmates back to Hamilton County each year, mixing with the county's roster of about 5,000 felony probationers – criminals convicted of serious crimes but sentenced to probation instead of prison.

Anthony White, 41, unemployed since 2003, has worked at Howdy since February and says he has never been more productive.

He'd filled out countless job applications, but prospective employers couldn't get around his multiple felony convictions that included grand theft auto and drug trafficking. Off and on, he'd go back to the streets to sell drugs but didn't get caught.

Then White applied for a job at Howdy Car Wash. He'd heard the owners give ex-cons a chance. "They've helped me get on the right track," White said.

The ride hasn't been smooth, for either White or his employers. "I was leery of working for cops," White said. "Then I realized they are just people, good people."

"I fired him and kicked him off the property in the beginning," Michael Donald said.

"I brought him back," Marchelle Donald, 42, said. "I had a long talk with him."

"I wasn't listening and wasn't being part of the team," White said. "I wanted to do everything my own way."

Marchelle Donald's nurturing tough love is something White hadn't ever experienced. "I do feel like their mother," she said. "They all have my cell number. They all know they have to call me if they're going to be late. They're all learning how to work."

They're seeing the benefits.

"I'd never had a job this long," said White, who recently rented an apartment nearby for himself, his two young children and their mother. He works 15 to 25 hours a week and likes how it feels to pay his bills legally: "I look forward to going to work."

Burl McLachlan, 38, of Norwood likes the sense of self-worth that comes with honest work. He gets 30 hours a week at Howdy and can pay his rent and utility bills and otherwise support himself and his two young daughters. He served 10 years at Mansfield Correctional Institution for assaulting a police officer when he was 18.

"It's a rush to do a good job," said McLachlan, whose own work history is spotted with stops and starts related to his criminal record. "Our bosses respect us here and get that respect back. If you do something wrong, they let you know, but it's not out of line."

Rules are listed on a sheet inside the car wash. Customers are to be called "sir" or "ma'am." Tips can be accepted, but, if as much as a nickel comes up missing from a car, "We will fire you, and we will press charges," Michael Donald said.

"Attrition is high," Utley said.

The owners take pride in the successes of their employees, especially that of a man convicted of rape 13 years ago who today is among their longest-running and most productive employees.

"We believe people can change for the better," said Marchelle Donald, who had to be okay with hiring a sex offender.

Word on the street is Howdy is a good place to work. The owners recently hired a woman and two men without criminal records referred from a job fair.

Cincinnati police chief James Craig likes what two of his officers are doing. "It's noble on their part," he said. "They see a need and are addressing it. It's what community policing is all about. They're giving people a second chance who need a second chance."

---

# Returning citizen "perfect for job"
Former prisoner leads a re-entry program for convicted felons
*February 21, 2015*

Dominic Duren remembers October 28, 2008, as the scariest day of his life, more frightening than the day he received a 12-year prison sentence as a convicted felon.

That October morning he walked out of Allen Correctional Institution in Lima, Ohio, and into an uncertain future. His girlfriend drove him back home.

"All I knew until then was hustling in the streets," said Duren, now 42. "I was setting out to rebuild my life, and I didn't know how."

His experience in overcoming the barriers a returning citizen faces is one of the reasons Duren was hired to coordinate a national pilot re-entry program housed in Cincinnati's St. Vincent de Paul Society. Among the goals of the program – which will hold a public information meeting Monday night, Feb. 23 – is to inform and engage Catholics about mass incarceration and re-entry issues.

Duren will tell his story: He started selling crack cocaine at age 12 in his native Los Angeles. He managed to do well in school, so well, in fact, he skipped two grades and graduated from high school at 16. A friend in Columbus told him central Ohio had become a lucrative market, so Duren eventually moved east.

Business was good, until the night rival dealers robbed Duren's partner. They plotted revenge, finally retaliating. Duren did not fire his gun, but his friend did, killing one of the opposing dealers.

Duren pled guilty in court to involuntary manslaughter and aggravated robbery, both felonies. "I took a deal," he said. "The public defender couldn't remember my name."

In prison, he learned data entry and earned an associate's degree in business administration.

"I did everything I could to make myself employable when I got out," Duren said. "I stayed busy, but in prison you have to deal with yourself. I did a lot of self-reflection."

## Effort seeks to cut poverty

There are a lot of Dominic Durens in Ohio.

The Ohio Department of Rehabilitation and Correction released more than 21,000 prisoners in calendar year 2012, not counting inmates still under local transitional control.

That year, 1,940 prisoners who had been committed from Hamilton County were released – 566 from Butler County, 376 from Clermont, and 261 from Warren.

Hamilton County created a re-entry office to help former prisoners find housing and work, get a driver's license and clear up problems such as overdue child support payments. Cincinnati Works started its Phoenix Program with many of the same goals and to prepare former convicts for the workplace. The Urban League of Greater Cincinnati's SOAR job-readiness program – the acronym stands for Solid Opportunities for Advancement and Retention – is not designed for returning citizens but attracts many of them. The HELP Program at St.

Francis de Sales Church, Walnut Hills, where Duren first received help in 2009, is faith-based and run by a religious Marianist Brother, Mike Murphy.

St. Vincent de Paul's program – Duren is its coordinator – is different. It grew out of a partnership between the Cincinnati Archdiocese and the Amos Project, a West End–based coalition of 30 congregations committed to social justice. They were successful in leading the effort around Ohio to remove the box on job applications that asked if the applicant had a felony record.

Paid for by the Catholic Campaign for Human Development, an anti-poverty program of the US Conference of Catholic Bishops, the St. Vincent de Paul Reentry Program takes aim at poverty. Up to 20 percent of the nation's poverty is caused by its mass incarceration system and the laws and stigma that follow ex-offenders when they try to get jobs, places to live, and loans – and even when they try to vote, according to a 2014 National Academy of Sciences report requested by the U.S. Department of Justice and other organizations.

The cost of housing prisoners is another drain on society. It costs Ohio taxpayers $24,784 to care for a prisoner in the state's prisons. Locally, the care of an inmate at the Hamilton County Justice Center costs $65 a day – or $23,725 a year. The justice center has an average daily inmate population of 1,424.

Cincinnati is just one of four Catholic dioceses nationwide chosen to start the pilot program, along with Milwaukee, Boston, and Orlando. The former director of Cincinnati's AMOS Project, Paul Graham, heads the national St. Vincent de Paul–based re-entry efforts.

"We are trying to end poverty through systematic change," Graham said. "Home visits (a staple of St. Vincent de Paul's efforts in the past) aren't enough. We need to be involved more deeply. We're bringing Catholics into a new understanding of criminal justice alternatives for drug addiction."

In 2009, Duren had contact with Cincinnati's St. Vincent de Paul office on Bank Street in the West End – as a client.

"I stood in line out on the street for a winter coat," he said. "I couldn't even afford my own jacket."

His girlfriend, whom he would later marry, was living on student loans and finishing a nursing degree at Northern Kentucky University. With two felonies, Duren could not find work. Construction jobs never materialized. He said he gave in to despair in 2009 and returned to the streets of Cincinnati to sell drugs, all in the name of trying to support his family.

The couple's son was born prematurely and spent 10 weeks in the neonatal intensive care unit. (The boy is now 5 and healthy; Duren and his wife also have a 2-year-old daughter.)

"I had needs – right now," Duren said of his life in 2009.

He had met Brother Mike at the HELP Program. He fell away from the process twice. The third time he stuck.

"I never had experienced so much compassion; I didn't feel worthy," Duren said. "They did so much for me and my family. They gave me a chance when nobody else would."

Before long, Murphy hired Duren and promoted him to run the program.

Duren's strengths are evident in his first year there.

"He's humble, honest, and caring," said Don Meyer, a deacon and coordinating chaplain for Catholic ministries at the Hamilton County Justice Center.

"He recognizes the mistakes in his past and so clearly identifies with people's struggles. He is the perfect person for this job."

Said Tony Stieritz, director of Catholic Social Action in the Cincinnati Archdiocese, "In one word, because of who he is and the network of solidarity that surrounds him, what Dominic uniquely brings [to] this whole effort is hope."

# CHAPTER 17

# ISSUES

*My life and work experiences make me wonder how anyone can not see the truth in the title of sociologist Andrew Hacker's 1992 book,* Two Nations: Black and White, Separate, Hostile, Unequal. *From disparities in life expectancy, health outcomes, law enforcement, and the legal system, African-Americans nationwide continue to live as second-class citizens. Here, I examine local applications of these disparities.*

## Africa Hope's blood marks dividing line

The 15-year-old was shot in Over-the-Rhine, providing a stark contrast between street violence and community rebirth

*June 20, 2012*

By the noon hour Tuesday, Africa Hope's blood had been washed off the sidewalk at 1710 Vine St. and replaced with three teddy bears, a candle, a bouquet of wrapped flowers, and a half-inflated Serenity Prayer balloon.

The 15-year-old West End girl died after being shot there at 11 p.m. Monday. Africa was not involved in any criminal activity at the time of the shooting, and no arrest had been made by Tuesday evening, said Cincinnati Police Chief James Craig.

A police officer sitting in an idling cruiser kept watch on the scene a couple of doors down. Passersby slowed but didn't stop at the makeshift memorial.

Meanwhile, about six blocks away, south of Liberty Street in a different part of the neighborhood, construction workers driving Bobcats and wielding leaf blowers put finishing touches on renovated Washington Park.

It will open July 6 as the centerpiece of the development driven by business and government that has swept the southern half of the one-time German enclave and former home to two generations of the city's poorest residents.

Visible signs of change have yet to reach the part of Over-the-Rhine (OTR) where a bullet pierced Africa's neck, though the proposed Cincinnati streetcar route will pass just a block to the west on Race Street at Findlay Market.

At this point in its redevelopment – a painful process not uncommon to U.S. cities trying to reclaim charming historic neighborhoods adjacent to downtown and attract new residents; critics call the process "gentrification" – Over-the-Rhine looks and feels like two distinct communities.

The shooting death of a teenage girl who'd struggled early in her life just brings that contrast into sharper focus.

"It's a black eye on the city," Shawn Richard, 32, an Over-the-Rhine native, said Tuesday morning near the shooting scene. "It seems like they are building new buildings and doing renovations for economic redevelopment, but the crime is still down here," Richard added.

"They need to come clean the blood up. It is just another unsolved murder, man. She was so young, ain't even begin to live her life."

Crime is down in Over-the-Rhine in the past year, Craig said: shootings, not homicides, have decreased 52 percent, and there has been a 31 percent dip in violent crime. In all of police District 1, of which Over-the-Rhine is a part, homicide is down 88 percent.

Yet, Craig said, "We do see violence more in the undeveloped area" north of Liberty Street.

An *Enquirer* analysis of homicide data since 2007, the year Cincinnati Center City Development Corp. (3CDC) established itself in Over-the-Rhine, illustrates the divide north and south of Liberty. Including Africa's homicide, 31 killings have been recorded north of Liberty since the start of 2007, compared with 10 to the south.

The police are there, though, working behind the scenes. The Vine Street corridor north of Liberty is an area of intense focus, said District 1 Capt. Gary Lee. He said police completed a yearlong investigation that led to the arrests of 19 or 20 of the neighborhood's "big-time felony criminals."

More than half of them were convicted and are serving long sentences. "They were responsible for the majority of the crime," Lee said.

## Business "hopping" in Gateway Quarter

Going south from the shooting scene, several social service agencies cluster near the intersection of Vine and Liberty. That area is home to the Jobs Plus agency, Over-the-Rhine Kitchen (at 35 years, the region's oldest soup kitchen), St. Francis Seraph Catholic School, St. Francis Church and Friary, and the Crossroad Health Center. A block to the east is the Freestore Foodbank.

A few more blocks to the south on Vine is 3CDC's Gateway Quarter. It's the main artery of a 110-square-block redevelopment area that is bounded on the north and east by Central Parkway and which is south of Liberty.

News of Africa's death reached Tuesday into the bars, restaurants, art galleries, and upscale shops lining Vine Street.

At Bakersfield OTR, a restaurant opened in February 2011 at 1213 Vine, general manager Lauren Altman said of the shooting, "Our hearts go out to everybody involved."

Crime is down, she said, and the commitment of the city, residents, and business community is too strong to be curtailed.

"The force behind the movement is not going to be easily broken, and I don't feel this will have a negative impact on us at all," Altman said. "In fact, I think it will only make us stronger. . . . My business is hopping."

Next door, at the 1215 Wine Bar & Coffee Lab, business has been robust, too, since its February opening, said coffee manager Alex Stahler.

"There's enough momentum that something like this shouldn't scare people away from the neighborhood," he said.

Developer 3CDC has restored or is in process of restoring 74 historic buildings and has created 186 new and rehabbed home ownership condos and 56 market-rate apartments in Over-the-Rhine.

Spokeswoman Anastasia Mileham did not return two phone messages or an email message Tuesday seeking comment.

Two blocks west on 12th Street from Vine is the southeast corner of Washington Park, where a row of new trees – their roots still wrapped in dirt inside burlap bags – stand in a row awaiting planting.

On the park's southwest corner stands the Drop Inn Center, the region's largest homeless shelter. Unlike other shelters and related agencies in the southern part of Over-the-Rhine, such as City Gospel Mission, the Drop does not yet have a new destination. It is the temporary home for up to 180 men and 42 women.

The irony of Africa's last name was not lost on Josh Spring, executive director of the Greater Cincinnati Homeless Coalition.

"Instead of investing in the lives of so many people in our community that are experiencing such need, we are choosing to spend millions of dollars on development for a few people," he said. "We must instead invest in the systematic support of life. This young girl with such a powerful last name – Hope – was too important not to."

Mary Burke Rivers, a long-time advocate for the poor, is executive director of Over-the-Rhine Community Housing, which has 380 units of affordable housing.

"It's heartbreaking," she said of Africa's death. "You just wonder what it's going to take to stop it and when people will stop thinking it's OK to carry and use guns."

*The Enquirer's Jennifer Edwards Baker, Angela Travillian, Mark Wert, Jason Williams contributed.*

—✦———◆———✦—

# "Beautiful girl with the beautiful name"Pastor challenges Africa Hope's mourners to change

*June 29, 2012*

Mourners recalled Africa Hope at her funeral on Thursday in Over-the-Rhine as a girl who excelled at math and science and planned a career as a biologist and model with the brains and beauty to do both.

"That little girl was brilliant," said Lisa Hamm, president of the Cincinnati College Preparatory Program, West End, which Africa attended from fourth to seventh grade. "She always was smiling. She always was polite. She always visited my office to give me a big hug."

The sanctuary of New Prospect Baptist Church, about a quarter of a mile from the 1700 block of Vine Street where Africa was shot and killed June 18, was filled to standing room for her visitation and funeral.

Corline Stone, 74, of the West End, the grandmother who cared for Africa since she was 2 months old, sat in the front row, a few feet from the open casket in which Africa's body lay, dressed in a white blouse and holding a flower.

Stone raised Africa because her mother, Vanessa Hope, 50, was addicted to drugs.

One by one, relatives spoke during the 90-minute funeral, forgiving Vanessa Hope, praising Stone for her selflessness and pledging to unify the family in the wake of Africa's death.

Harold W. Croft, 36, is being held on $500,000 bond after his arrest last Friday on the charge of felony murder in connection with Africa's death.

And while speakers expressed their faith that Africa was now in heaven, New Prospect Pastor Damon Lynch III criticized the thinking that God called Africa home. Instead, Lynch anguished over the loss of her limitless potential and challenged the congregation of African-American mourners to turn their own lives around.

"God didn't say, 'I need another rose in heaven.' Stop putting that stuff on God," Lynch said in his eulogy, which started with the display of the rap video "Self Destruction" from the Stop the Violence Movement.

"That's a message for our people: We're headed to self-destruction," said Lynch, referring both to Croft's race as an African-American and how Africa, though gifted, couldn't resist the lure of the streets.

From the start of 2005 through April 22 of this year, 86.1 percent of homicides in Cincinnati in which an arrest was made are cases of black-on-black violence, up from 75.1 percent from 2000 through 2004. Those numbers are reflected nationally.

Africa, a ninth-grade student at Taft Information Technology High School, near her home, had a juvenile record that included curfew violation, running away, and disorderly conduct.

Lynch compared Africa and other struggling African-Americans to the Biblical prodigal son. They go away. Some straighten themselves out, learning hard lessons, and come home. Others, like Africa, don't live long enough to learn how gifted, lovable, and valuable they are.

"It's in you, beautiful black people; there is all kinds of greatness in this room. Ain't no quitting in this life," said Lynch, who then looked down from the pulpit to Africa's grandmother. "Miss Corline, job well done. You gave all."

And then to the congregation, he said, "This beautiful young girl with the beautiful name has gone to find peace and rest. If you love Africa, you owe it to her to do something with yourself."

# Mourners pay respects to woman killed in park

*August 7, 2010*

For the first hour of Joann Burton's funeral Friday morning a few blocks from where a police cruiser killed her as she rested on the Washington Park grass, mourners and family members said all the traditional things people say at funerals.

She is in a better place, in the loving arms of God.

Her pain and struggle are gone.

It was her time.

Then, the Rev. Damon Lynch III, pastor of New Prospect Baptist Church – the sanctuary filled with about 300 mourners – delivered the eulogy and challenged family, friends, and the larger community not to let Burton's death be in vain.

"Joann should not be dead," Lynch said to shouts of "amen" from the pews. "They [the police car] should not have been on the grass, and Joann should not be gone."

Lynch placed her death July 27 in context of the effort of the quasi-public development group Cincinnati Center City Development Corp. (3CDC) to – in his words – take over the entire Over-the-Rhine neighborhood south of Liberty Street and drive out the suffering and homeless.

"When things like this happen, God has purpose for Joann's life," Lynch said. "There is a land-grab going on. There are folks who don't want the folks who are here to be here anymore."

3CDC officials declined to comment.

Development of Washington Park is scheduled to begin this month.

"Joann represents all of us, all of us who are tired and just want to lay down in the grass and rest," Lynch said. "Of all things to have a car drive up on the grass, that's the truth and reality."

Burton, 48, died of her noon-hour injuries after being taken to University Hospital. She was resting beneath a blanket between two large trees when a Cincinnati police cruiser driven by veteran park Officer Marty Polk ran over her.

"Joann died almost as a martyr in the larger struggle," Lynch said.

The 90-minute funeral ended with Lynch leading family and friends to the spot of Burton's death on the Elm Street side of the park.

Lynch said from the pulpit at the end of his eulogy that he saw no politicians or city officials in the congregation. There were almost a dozen ministers in attendance.

Visitation ran from 9:30 a.m. past the scheduled 10:30 start of the funeral. Burton's body rested in an open casket. She wore a red dress.

Mourners and family members recalled her life. She liked to dance and enjoyed listening to "old school" soul music. She played cards and Nintendo 64. She graduated from the former Greenhills High School and is survived by her husband, Thomas, five children, three sisters and two brothers.

Her son, Kenneth Burton, 22, read an open letter to his mother. He recalled his mother's love, how she comforted him with kisses to his forehead.

He recalled how one time, as a teenager, he ignored his mother when he passed her on the street with his friends. He said he cried over the denial, and the next time he saw her he ran across the street, kissed her and told all of his friends that she was indeed his mother.

"I love you, I miss you and know you did your best to raise us," Kenneth Burton said.

Fourteen people lined up and shared memories of Burton during the funeral.

Pallbearers removed her casket from the church and carried it to the hearse. Burial was at Baltimore Pike Cemetery.

The family insisted that Burton was not homeless but lived that way by choice.

Josh Spring, executive director of the Greater Cincinnati Coalition for the Homeless – who attended the funeral – said the family still needs help with funeral expenses. An account had been established at PNC Bank locations.

Lynch envisioned the new Washington Park in five or 10 years and how it should memorialize how and why Burton died.

"There won't be any people in pain there, or any homeless people," he said. "But it won't be because we ended pain and homelessness. It will be because they moved us out of the way."

# 50 years after "Dream," loose ends are left untied

## Advocates are trying to reduce the gap in health disparities between African-Americans and white Americans

*August 25, 2013*

This is one new front in the civil rights movement:

Walking groups are forming and health education classes are planned in Mount Auburn. At a Cincinnati festival, Bennie Lundy had his first prostate cancer test at age 55.

And in Colerain Township, when Jocelyn Storr turned 40, she looked at her scale and her father's deteriorating health from a stroke and heart attack and decided to make a change.

As an African-American, she had resigned herself to a life of hypertension and weight struggles. Then she realized that she controlled her own health. So she started walking regularly, closely monitoring her portion sizes and sugar intake as well as that of her children and grandchildren. She has lost 30 pounds and gained energy to put into her event planning business.

"I didn't want to end up like my dad, and I know how hard it is to change, so I wanted to give my kids and grandkids a head start," said Storr, 43.

These actions embody the type of change that health advocates want more people of color to experience. The effort to reduce critical health disparities between African-Americans and white Americans is expanding locally and nationally and – on this, the 50th anniversary of the March on Washington for Jobs and Freedom – is increasingly seen as some of the unfinished business in the fight for racial equality.

The 1963 event stands as the pivotal moment of the civil rights movement, the day 50 years ago Wednesday that Martin Luther King delivered his "I Have a Dream" speech on racial harmony. Other speakers that day called for jobs and a living wage for low-income people, particularly African-Americans.

As the anniversary renews attention on economic inequality, health disparity moves to the fore as well. African-Americans on average don't live as long as whites. They have less access to private health care and healthy foods and are significantly more likely to suffer from an array of diseases and conditions, ranging from cancer and diabetes to high blood pressure and obesity.

"Health disparities certainly are a civil rights issue, and while each person has the responsibility to care for themselves by eating right and exercising, it is clear that African-Americans do not have equal access to health care," said Bobby Hilton, senior pastor of Word of Deliverance, Forest Park, and president of the Greater Cincinnati Chapter of the National Action Network, a civil rights group founded in 1991 by Al Sharpton and sponsor of the daylong march held Saturday in Washington.

The local National Action Network, along with the Baptist Ministers Conference and the Black Nurses Association of Greater Cincinnati, are among organizations supporting the local movement to narrow health disparities, led by the non-profit Center for Closing the Health Gap.

"Everything else has been addressed –

## Health disparities by the numbers

*August 25, 2013*

- Life expectancy for black males is 71.8 years, compared with 76.5 years for white men.
- 88 percent of white Americans have health insurance, compared with 79 percent of African-Americans.
- In Hamilton County, the infant mortality rate for African-Americans is 16.9, compared to 9.8 for Hispanics and 6.4 for whites per 1,000 live births.
- African-Americans had a 41 percent higher rate of death from all causes than whites. Age-adjusted death rates for African-Americans exceeded those for whites by 77 percent in stroke, 47 percent in heart disease, 34 percent in cancer, and 655 percent in HIV.
- Black men in the United States have the highest prostate cancer incidence, and mortality rates in the world.
- In Ohio, the black rate of diabetes is more than 2.5 times greater than the rate for whites.

*Sources: U.S. Centers for Disease Control, National Health Interview Survey 2010, Cincinnati Children's Hospital Medical Center, National Urban League Policy Institute "State of Urban Health."*

education, housing, jobs, voting rights – even though they're not all figured out," said Dwight Tillery, Health Gap's founder and president and a former Cincinnati mayor and councilman.

Health and economics are closely linked and, to some civil rights activists, inseparable.

"Social justice is what drives us," said Noble Maseru, Cincinnati health commissioner. "If you start with food, shelter, and clothing, you have greater distribution of health."

The disparity between blacks and whites is greater in Cincinnati than it is nationally. Several government and health industry reports quantify the disparities.

In 2002, the Institute of Medicine, part of the National Academy of Sciences, in its report "Unequal Treatment," said, "some evidence suggests that bias, prejudice, and stereotype on the part of health care providers may contribute to differences in care."

In 2011, the U.S. Centers for Disease Control and Prevention released its "Health Disparities and Inequalities Report" that, in part, used data to show how people living in "lower socioeconomic circumstances are at increased risk" for serious disease and premature death, have reduced access to health care, and receive an inadequate quality of care.

Advocates say the Affordable Care Act, by making health insurance available to millions of currently uninsured Americans, provides part of the solution.

Nationally, the New Jersey-based Robert Wood Johnson Foundation is one of the strongest voices working to close health disparities. Another involved group is the American Public Health Association, whose president, Adewale Troutman, spoke June 1 at Woodward High School as a guest of the Center for Closing the Health Gap.

"A basic part of the problem is there is still a 'them' and an 'us,'" said Troutman, a physician. "I say when an African-American baby dies in the first year of life, it affects us all. We are connected."

In his Woodward speech, attended by about 275 people, Troutman said, "In order for all members of the community to know that there is an injustice in the health of African-Americans, we must teach them about health disparities."

Greater Cincinnati's Center for Closing the Health Gap is one of the leading organizations nationally in creating awareness, Troutman said.

## Individual lives change to change communities

The center's latest program is the Mount Auburn Block by Block model, a resident-led education program that has gone door-to-door in the hilltop neighborhood of 6,700 residents with information on diet and exercise. Besides the new walking groups, cooking classes and other education sessions are planned.

Howard Martin, 40, an unemployed diabetic who lives with his elderly parents, earned a stipend by walking the neighborhood to deliver pamphlets. The money was enough to buy medicine to treat his diabetes.

"I got involved to save myself," Martin said. "I don't get the splitting headaches any more. I'm jogging now. I feel better."

On Aug. 10, the Health Gap and local National Action Network chapter sponsored a screening of the documentary "Soul Food Junkies" at Hirsch Recreation Center as part of the Avondale Health Fair. The film examines soul food, such as fried chicken and barbecued pork, as part of black cultural identity and measures its often negative effects on African-American health.

Joyce Edwards, 68, of North Avondale spoke during a post-screening discussion, saying how she changed to a vegetarian diet 10 years ago when she started having to take medicine to treat high blood pressure.

"I was always a little chunky thing," said Edwards, who now makes and drinks carrot juice, "but I lost 20, 25 pounds by changing my diet and starting to walk at least three times a week."

She now looks more optimistically at a longer and better-quality life and no longer has to take blood pressure medicine.

The Center for Closing the Health Gap had an information table at the Midwest Black Family Reunion last weekend at Sawyer Point, where event planner Storr and many others received free information on diet, exercise, and other prevention programs and medical assistance.

Nearby, Lundy of Walnut Hills had blood drawn for a prostate cancer screening. Herschel Chalk, 67, a two-time prostate cancer survivor and advocate for screening, waved down Lundy and persuaded him to have the free screening provided by the Barrett Cancer Center at the University of Cincinnati Medical Center.

"I hope I'm good," said Lundy, on disability after getting hurt on his manufacturing job. "I am scared of the results. This is the first time I have had this test. I've been walking more and trying to not eat things like fried chicken."

"Economics," said Chalk, of Roselawn. "People say they don't get checked because they don't have insurance. We try to take away any excuse. It's free and we will go anywhere, a church or an organization. By any means necessary will I get men tested."

Chalk is one of the major organizers of a black men's health conference planned for Nov. 9 at Drake Center.

## Hospitals, churches are key players in movement

Hospitals and predominantly black churches play vital roles in increasing awareness and decreasing disparities.

Overall, 112 black churches regionally have expanded their health ministries in recent years with the help of the Center for Closing the Health Gap. Of them, 22 churches in Hamilton County created community gardens that reach 60,000 people, 25 percent of whom live below the federal poverty levels.

Produce markets at churches, schools, and the Gabriel's Place food ministry in Avondale are temporary solutions, advocates say, while grants from the Greater Cincinnati Foundation and American Heart Association are being used in efforts to bring grocery stores to urban neighborhoods that lack them.

Three Avondale-based corner stores have improved display and in-store location of fresh produce and whole-grain foods. Still, buying habits are largely unchanged. The Lexington Market, at the corner of Lexington Avenue in Reading Road, stocks a produce cooler every Monday but is forced to either throw away or discount much of it by week's end.

The 33 member hospitals or health organizations in the 14-county region that are members of the Greater Cincinnati Health Council also are working to do more to close the gap, said Colleen O'Toole, council president.

She said emergency departments, where many low-income people go for primary care, are now connecting patients to primary care physicians, nurse practitioners, and specific clinics for underserved people inside their hospitals.

Increasing attention is being paid to transportation or other social issues, and referrals are being made to social agencies that can address environmental or other causes of poor health.

Interpreter services are increasing for the growing number of Spanish-speaking residents. Data collectors and doctors are trying to get more race- and income-specific information from patients that can help hospitals better understand underlying causes.

Four hospital systems – the Christ Hospital, Mercy Health, TriHealth, and UC Medical Center – provide the Center for Closing the Health Gap with most of its budget, a total of $700,000. Another $200,000 from the city of Cincinnati is pending, though some in City Hall are critical of Tillery and the center for receiving money when some direct health services for the poor have seen their funding cut or reduced in previous city budgets.

## Health disparities are costly to society in many ways

Progress is being made, advocates say, and the stakes are high.

"In black history, people often felt there was nothing they could do about their health," Tillery said. "They accepted diabetes as a little sugar or high blood pressure as just part of life or the way things are. But we have seen people realize that they do control their own health. This movement, like any movement, will have to rise up from the people who demand better health care."

Said O'Toole, "It's not just an individual tragedy. They affect the quality of life and our competitiveness in the global economy. It's that big when you're talking about inclusion and diversity."

Steve Schwalbe, senior vice president of strategy and communications at TriHealth, is a Health Gap board member. "I think about low birth weight and how we have such great hospitals and doctors in this region," he said. "Then I think of the disconnect. It's the space in between them that isn't working. It severely undermines the overall strength of the community."

Health disparities exact a high price. Nationally in 2009, they cost the U.S. economy $82.2 billion – $60 billion in health care spending and $22.2 billion in lost productivity – according to "The State of Urban Health," a study released in December by the National Urban League Policy Institute in Washington, D.C.

And as he had crystallized the modern civil rights movement 50 years ago, King provided watchwords for the movement working to close health gaps.

"Of all forms of inequality," King said at the 1966 convention of the Medical Committee for Human Rights, a group of health care professions that supported the civil rights movement, "injustice in health care is the most shocking and the most inhumane."

---

# Residence, race might send you to early grave

People live longer in city's wealthier neighborhoods

*November 26, 2013*

Where you live in Cincinnati and your race help to determine how long you will live – by a difference of as much as 20 years.

If you live in South Fairmount, Avondale, or a handful of other lower-income or predominantly black or urban Appalachian neighborhoods, your life expectancy is 66.4 to 68.2 years.

Yet if you live in Mount Lookout, Columbia Tusculum, Hyde Park, or one of the city's other wealthier and largely white communities, your life expectancy is 83.2 to 87.8 years.

The new data come from the Cincinnati Health Department, which will release the information Tuesday. A larger, community-wide discussion is planned for Jan. 10.

The top four causes of death in the city are cardiovascular disease, cancer, stroke, and lower-respiratory disease, such as asthma and lung cancer related to smoking.

Homicide is listed as one of the top 10 causes of death. The annual record for the city is 88 homicides in 2006. The number dropped to 53 in 2012, but stood at 69 through the weekend.

Researchers analyzed every death record in Cincinnati from 2001 through 2009 to create the data set. They measured death in U.S. Census tracts and fitted them to neighborhood boundaries. Health department officials hope this analysis can be used to create base knowledge of health disparities within the city and spur work on how they can be reduced.

"Our objective is to develop some level of intervention to have greater equity in our community," said Cincinnati Health Commissioner Noble Maseru.

The average life expectancy in the United States is 78.6 years. Of the 47 Cincinnati neighborhood groups measured, only 14 had rates that were better than the national average. Cincinnati's average for 2001–09 was 76.7 years.

Such dramatic variations in life expectancy are not uncommon in many large American cities. New Orleans, Kansas City, and Minneapolis are three cities where a Robert Wood Johnson Foundation study found large discrepancies. Urban areas have higher death rates because, generally, their populations are older, poorer, and sicker with chronic diseases such as heart disease, diabetes, and obesity.

Maseru and Camille Jones, a physician and assistant health commissioner, said the department wants to work with community councils to create or support wellness committees, possibly like health ministries in many predominantly African-American churches.

In an interview with the *Enquirer*, they said they would like to work within city government to create positive effects on the "built environment," issues that range from the placement of industry and grocery stores to helping improve how safely residents can walk or ride bicycles within their communities.

"It goes to governance and policy and appropriation of resources," Maseru said.

Ultimately, they said, they want to work with civic organizations and academicians to help improve health for residents across the city.

The new data also show that the life expectancy in Cincinnati for African-American men is 10 years less than white men, 63.8 years to 73.8 years. The life expectancy for black women is 72.4 years, compared with 79 years for white women.

The gap in life expectancy for black men and white men in Cincinnati is wider than the national numbers, 70.8 years for African-Americans and 76.2 for white men.

In August, the *Enquirer* reported on local and national efforts to reduce critical health disparities between African-Americans and white Americans.

Infant mortality rates are higher for women of color, who are at greater risk to have their babies die before age 1. In Hamilton County, the rate for African-Americans is 16.9 deaths for every 1,000 live births and is 9.8 for Hispanic women. For whites, it is 6.4.

Death from respiratory disease is a major factor in shorter life expectancies in some near-West Side Cincinnati neighborhoods: Lower Price Hill, Sedamsville, Riverside, and Camp Washington.

"It's air quality and smoking," Jones said.

Drug-related deaths, caused primarily by heroin and abuse of prescription opioids, such as OxyContin and Percocet, are an increasing reason for premature death, Maseru said.

The five neighborhoods with the highest life expectancies are Mount Lookout/Columbia Tusculum (87.8 years), North Avondale/Paddock Hills (87.1), Mount Adams (86.4), Mount Lookout (85.9), and Hyde Park (83.2).

The difference between North Avondale/Paddock Hills and adjacent Avondale to the south is dramatic, 18.9 years.

"There is no one reason for the differences," Maseru said.

"Poverty would be the [catchall]. The World Health Organization takes into account poverty, income, and education."

---

# Black community holds fast to Collaborative Agreement

*November 17, 2017*

Flyers started to circulate on social media Nov. 9.

The day before, the story had broken that the Cincinnati police union president was trying to prevent two officers accused of racial profiling and using excessive force from being interviewed by the city's Citizen Complaint Authority.

"Collaborative Agreement Refresh Emergency," the flyers read. "Community Mobilization Meeting. November 15th."

Iris Roley of the Cincinnati Black United Front organized the meeting.

"It is an emergency," she said Wednesday night, midway through the meeting at Roselawn's New Prospect Baptist Church.

"It was a dangerous precedent to try to get around that part of the Collaborative Agreement."

The city's groundbreaking Collaborative Agreement of 2002, which is still hailed nationally as a model, changed how the Cincinnati Police Department did its job. Changes in use of force, accountability, data collection, bias-free policing, and community-oriented policing became department policies. The agreement's main goal was to increase trust between the department and the city's black community.

Fraternal Order of Police President Dan Hils's efforts to delay a Citizen Complaint Authority investigation shocked the community and moved Roley and others to action.

Here's why. The Collaborative Agreement is important on its face, and the Authority – empowered to probe citizens' complaints against officers – is a critical part of it. Police brutality and misconduct, say many African-Americans, have been a part of their daily life.

Yet the Collaborative Agreement means even more, many people say, because its adoption marked the first time city government listened to the voices of its black citizens and made a change that benefited them.

"There have been so few victories over the years," Police Chief Eliot Isaac, who is African-American, said Wednesday after answering audience questions.

"The Collaborative is a victory, a major victory."

That's why several dozen people attended a Tuesday night Collaborative Refresh meeting sponsored by the city at the Cincinnati–Hamilton County Community Action Agency. About the same number attended the Wednesday night emergency meeting. More meetings are planned.

Saul Green, the monitor who supervised the Collaborative, is coming back with a new report on what has worked and what has been allowed to slide in the past 15 years. It's complicated, difficult material. That's why Roley and New Prospect Baptist pastor the Rev. Damon Lynch III, who've led the Black United Front since its founding in 2000, want to make sure community members understand the material and can act on it.

"This is our baby," Roley said. "It came from us."

Eileen Cooper Reed, a former Cincinnati Public Schools board president, was at the church meeting Wednesday night.

"It's the one time our voices were heard and mattered in the decision-making process," she said.

In a time of racial fissures, when black Cincinnati sees gentrification continuing to displace it from neighborhoods, the community holds fast to the Collaborative. It's a piece of validation at a point when people say they feel threatened that other neighborhoods, such as Avondale, will change like Over-the-Rhine and Corryville have — with lower-income African-Americans pushed out.

It's a reassurance amid a time of national challenges, as well. The economic recovery has been slow to reach the black community. White supremacist groups have moved into the mainstream.

Cincinnati's black community has the Collaborative, almost as a beacon that their lives matter.

"D.C. is the only other city that has evaluated this type of agreement," said Monique Dixon, deputy director of policy and senior counsel at the NAACP Legal Defense and Educational Fund.

She was at the meeting Wednesday. She spoke to the audience and said the community must approach the Refresh with urgency and energy.

"The federal government is not your friend anymore," Dixon said. "The president has encouraged police to beat and brutalize people. The attorney general has made it clear he has no intention to make sure police departments comply with civil rights laws."

The best path, she concluded, was to work through local government. Mayor John Cranley, City Manager Harry Black, and Isaac all support the Collaborative Refresh.

Progress has been made, say Roley, Lynch, and other community leaders. More work remains, they say: A disproportionate number of African-Americans are involved in traffic stops; the Citizen Complaint Authority must remain fully funded and fully staffed; elected officials need to understand and support the Collaborative.

Distrust remains. A nonscientific Community Perception survey of 1,253 people — 511 African-Americans, 742 white people — showed that whites have a more favorable opinion about Cincinnati police. For example, 48 percent of whites say they trust the police "a lot." Only 10 percent of African-Americans do.

The Sentinel Police Association, a group made up almost exclusively of African-American officers, pushed for reforms even before April 2001. That's when the police shooting of Timothy Thomas, an unarmed black man, in Over-the-Rhine sparked days of rioting, violence, and a declaration of martial law. It also created the momentum that led to the Collaborative.

Sentinel members Isaac and Police Spc. Scotty Johnson, a former Sentinel president wearing a Sentinel jacket, were at the Wednesday meeting. So was the current president, Officer Eddie Hawkins, who leads the organization of roughly 230 officers.

Hawkins grew up in Avondale and looked up to the police and firefighters he knew.

"When you come from the community, you understand," he said.

# LIVES REMEMBERED

*The featured obituary is a foundational element of daily newspapers. The Enquirer used to run at least one if not two or three a day. We then had a reporter dedicated to stories we labeled Lives Remembered. For my part, instead of searching the paid obituaries, which were almost exclusively white people, I called black-owned funeral homes, which handled arrangements for many African-American families, when it was my turn in the rotation. In December 2012, I wrote about the life of the Rev. Clarence Wallace, a Presbyterian church pastor in Avondale whom I deeply respected. Four years later, I wrote the obit of his wife, Jackie.*

# Bennett Cooper Sr., 91, was director of Ohio prisons

*March 10, 2013*

AMBERLEY VILLAGE — African-Americans who defeated Jim Crow before the modern civil rights movement sometimes found themselves as "the first."

Bennett Cooper Sr., one such person, was the first African-American to become a prison superintendent in a state government system in 1966 and the first African-American director of a state prison system in 1972.

Mr. Cooper, 91, died of natural causes March 3 at his home in Amberley Village.

"Daddy taught us two major things: We were no better or worse than any other human being, and he always said what became of us is up to us," said his daughter, Eileen Cooper Reed, 66, of Avondale.

Born June 3, 1921, in Cleveland, twin of a brother, the late Emmett Cooper, Bennett Cooper Sr. attended Xavier University in New Orleans, where he met his wife of 70 years, the former Zelda Mohr.

Emmett Cooper married Zelda's twin sister, Ermelda Mohr, in a double wedding ceremony in Cleveland on November 19, 1941.

Inducted into the Army, Bennett Cooper served during World War II in the Pacific theater and was in Okinawa when atomic bombs were dropped on Japan in August 1945 to end the war.

He returned to Cleveland, where he and Emmett and their wives and children would share the same house for 12 years.

The brothers both attended Case Western Reserve University and both earned master's degrees in psychology in 1957. Within a few months, Bennett Cooper moved his wife and three children to Mansfield, where he became chief psychologist at Mansfield Correctional Institution.

In 1966, Ohio Gov. James Rhodes appointed Mr. Cooper superintendent of the Ohio State Reformatory, making him the first African-American to hold that position in any state penal system. In 1972, Ohio Gov. Jack Gilligan appointed Mr. Cooper as the first director of the Ohio Department of Rehabilitation and Correction, another national first for an African-American. He held that position until 1975.

Emmett Cooper moved to Chicago and became postmaster general of the Chicago Regional office.

In 1974, Bennett Cooper was one of the founders of the National Association of Blacks in Criminal Justice, a nonprofit created to promote the interests of blacks and other minorities in the justice system.

"One of my cousins said of Daddy, 'I don't know of anyone who lived a better life,'" Cooper Reed said. "He was a kind gentleman who made a difference in the lives of many people, and he was greatly loved."

In addition to his wife, now 92, of Avondale, and oldest daughter, Mr. Cooper is survived by a son, Bennett Cooper Jr. of Walnut Hills; daughter Bernice Cooper of Avondale; 13 grandchildren; and 18 great-grandchildren.

Mass of Christian Burial will be 2 p.m. today at St. Francis de Sales Catholic Church, Walnut Hills. Interment will be at Gate of Heaven Cemetery, Montgomery.

Memorials: National Association of Blacks in Criminal Justice, 1801 Fayetteville St., 106 Whiting Criminal Justice Building, P.O. Box 20011-C, Durham, NC 27707.

# Marcia Caulton, 53, sang to the end

*August 13, 2012*

SPRINGFIELD TWP. — Marcia Caulton's last public singing performance might have been her best.

On June 24 at Cintas Center, she sang "I Hope You Dance" during the Cincinnati State Technical and Community College graduation ceremony. The song was one of her signatures and had become the unofficial school song.

Even as her three-year battle with cancer was nearing an end, and though she had begun to use a wheelchair, Miss Caulton belted out the song in clear, strong tones, receiving a standing ovation and moving many to tears.

"She made an incredible statement by living up to a commitment she had made to be there," Cincinnati State President O'Dell Owens said.

Miss Caulton, 53, died Wednesday, August 8, at Hospice of Cincinnati, Blue Ash. What had been initially diagnosed in July 2009 as ovarian cancer had spread to her lungs, lymph nodes, hip, and skull.

The June 24 graduation performance was one of her sister's favorites. Administrators said that if Miss Caulton couldn't sing, they'd have to use a recorded version to maintain tradition and to meet student demand.

"Marcia wouldn't have that," said Julia Caulton, 61, her sister with whom she lived for the past seven years in the Pleasant Run Farms neighborhood in northern Springfield Township.

Though she never married or had her own children, Miss Caulton reached thousands in her 27 years at Cincinnati State. She worked for the past 17 in the Student Affairs department. Students called her "Smiley." She always had a smile on her face, no matter what she was going through, Owens said.

Miss Caulton knew the value of education. After graduating from Hughes High School in 1977, she attended Ohio University, where she earned a communications degree in 1981.

"She loved those students, and they loved her," Julia Caulton said.

Miss Caulton began her long career as a well-known local vocalist in the church, first as a child in Mt. Sinai Baptist Church in the West End and Silverton before moving to Christ Emmanuel Christian Fellowship in Walnut Hills and then for the final six years of her life at Vineyard Community Church in Springdale.

As a younger woman, when Miss Caulton might have pursued a singing career, she instead lived in the family home in Corryville to care for her seriously ill mother, Rosie Caulton, who died in 1999.

Miss Caulton performed frequently at Cincinnati State – she sang "God Bless America" at its annual naturalization ceremony and other events, including Owens's inauguration as college president. Church music was her favorite.

"She loved singing and praising, but she didn't like to hear her own self singing," Julia Caulton said. "I would always say to her, 'Don't you see that when people hear you sing that they feel what God put into you?'"

Worshippers at Vineyard would frequently use their smartphones to record Miss Caulton's performances and approach her in tears afterward to thank her, her sister and friends said.

In the end, music gave Miss Caulton comfort. During stays at Mercy Fairfield and then Good Samaritan hospitals, Miss Caulton sang. She sang hymns, including "I'm Amazed by You," from her hospital bed. Even though her speech had become garbled, Miss Caulton could still sing.

The last song Julia Caulton heard her sister sing, as she was wheeled on a gurney into Good Samaritan Hospital earlier this month, was "It's Not Over (Til God Says It's Over)."

Visitation will be from 10 a.m. to 1 p.m. Tuesday at Vineyard Community Church, 11340 Century Circle East, Springdale. Her funeral service will begin at 1 p.m.

In addition to her sister, Marcia Caulton is survived by a brother, Ronald Caulton, 63, of Corryville.

Memorial: I Hope You Dream Scholarship Fund in Memory of Marcia Caulton, Cincinnati State Foundation, 3520 Central Parkway, Cincinnati, OH 45223. Call 569-1706.

---

# Rev. Clarence Wallace, 63, led Avondale's Carmel Presbyterian

*December 19, 2012*

Through the worst of times, the Rev. Clarence Wallace and his church stayed in the heart of Avondale.

In 1983, members of Carmel Presbyterian Church voted to remodel their sanctuary at the corner of Reading Road and Rockdale Avenue instead of moving to suburban Forest Park.

"He always said that church was put on that corner and should stay there to serve the people in the community," Jacqueline Wallace said of her husband of 33 years.

The Rev. Wallace, 63, died Sunday night at his home in Mount Airy of complications from prostate cancer. He had been ill for more than two years.

He was 29 years old when he came to Cincinnati in 1978 to become pastor at Carmel. Already ordained, he was working as an alcohol and substance abuse counselor in Charleston, S.C., a sensitivity that would show up later in his Carmel ministry with the creation of a long-standing, vibrant Alcoholics Anonymous meeting.

"Anything that had to do with lifting up that community," Jacqueline Wallace said.

Wallace did not seek the limelight – "he ran from it," his wife said – yet he played a pivotal role in Avondale's current rebirth.

One of his most visible roles was accepting in 1996 the presidency of the Avondale Coalition of Churches, which owns the Avondale Town Center strip mall that shares a parking lot with Carmel. Wallace replaced the Rev. James Milton, pastor of Avondale's Southern Baptist Church, who, like Wallace, died of prostate cancer at 63.

Patricia Milton, James Milton's daughter, became Avondale Community Council president in 2005.

"He was the most faithful pastor who helped us consistently with anything to do with Avondale," she said of Wallace. "He understood how the neighborhood had to come up with solutions."

The need for food assistance in Avondale turned Sunday breakfasts for church members into community meals attracting 75 children. That meal morphed into the fellowship dinner that has been a Carmel tradition since 2004 after the 11 o'clock service.

More than 2 in 5 of Avondale's 12,500 residents live below federal poverty levels. Almost 90 percent of its residents are African-American.

Carmel sponsored summer academic enrichment programs and community health fairs. Since 2006, Carmel has housed the Every Child Succeeds program for at-risk, first-time mothers.

Regular meetings for mothers and fathers are held in space donated by Carmel. The church in 2007 opened the Avondale Caring Network Pantry in conjunction with Every Child Succeeds. It provides free formula, diapers and wipes, and other supplies.

"He was low-key but quite effective as a community leader," said Dwight Tillery, former Cincinnati mayor and council member who now is executive director of the nonprofit Center for Closing the Health Gap.

Tillery said Wallace was ahead of his time in understanding the personal health challenges faced by people in low-income, minority communities.

Even as his health deteriorated, Wallace stayed engaged, attending meetings that led to the formation late in 2011 of the Avondale Comprehensive Development Corp. "I don't have many heroes. He was one of them," said Ozie Davis, corporation executive director.

"You stay involved," Wallace told the *Enquirer* in a February interview about his social action.

"People need to know that Jesus is not just preaching on Sunday. Jesus embraces, loves, cares, and supports."

Wallace, born in Charlotte, N.C., earned a master's degree in divinity from Johnson C. Smith Theological Seminary, Atlanta, the only historically black theological seminary of the Presbyterian Church.

Besides his wife, he is survived by daughters Angela Sroufe, of Tampa, Florida, and Allison Wallace, of Atlanta, four grandchildren, and one great-grandchild.

Visitation will be from 10 a.m. to noon Saturday at Carmel Presbyterian, 3549 Reading Road, Avondale, followed by the funeral service at noon.

Memorial: The Rev. Clarence Wallace Memorial Fund at Carmel Presbyterian Church, 3549 Reading Road, Cincinnati, OH 45229.

---

# Nannie Hinkston, 91, tiny woman, strong voice for poor

*March 12, 2013*

In March 1994, as president of the Over-the-Rhine Community Council, Nannie Hinkston was asked what she thought of a judge's decision to throw out a lawsuit brought by a group of business owners who said the concentration of poor people in Over-the-Rhine was too dense.

She said she feared the "integration" of higher income people into the neighborhood would force out the poor.

"It's kind of like she saw the future," said fellow affordable housing advocate Bonnie Neumeier, who, to this day, is among those who refers to Hinkston as "the Rosa Parks of Over-the-Rhine."

Ms. Hinkston, who lived in Over-the-Rhine for almost 60 years, died Feb. 27 at the Harmony Court assisted living home in Bond Hill. She was 91.

Born in Covington on May 4, 1921, the youngest of 13 children, Ms. Hinkston moved to Over-the-Rhine in the early 1950s.

Ms. Hinkston was preceded in death by her only child, a son, Lewis, and one of her six grandchildren.

She raised her grandchildren in a small apartment on Race Street, not far from the former Washington Park School, which was torn down in 2007.

"She was a lady with great wisdom," said one of her grandchildren, Jo Ann Whitehead, 46, of Avondale. "She was a straight shooter. She spoke her mind and never backed down."

Ms. Hinkston was involved with the Over-the-Rhine Community Council as a neighborhood resident and later served for 12 years as its president. She befriended a young white advocate for the poor, Buddy Gray, who moved to Over-the-Rhine from Anderson Township and in 1973 opened what would grow to become the region's largest homeless shelter, the Drop Inn Center.

Often, Ms. Hinkston, Gray, and the Rev. Maurice McCrackin spoke together at Cincinnati City Council or committee meetings on behalf of the poor and minorities in Over-the-Rhine and the West End.

From 1980 to 1985, Ms. Hinkston participated in the creation of the Over-the-Rhine Comprehensive Plan, also known as the 5520 Plan. Its goal was to preserve the 5,520 affordable housing units in Over-the-Rhine at that time.

She watched with a keen eye what she perceived as attempts by outside forces, politicians and developers, to bring wholesale change to Over-the-Rhine.

"I want to see development, but don't want to be pushed out of my neighborhood," she frequently said.

Not even 5 feet tall or 100 pounds, Ms. Hinkston walked everywhere, often pushing or pulling her wheeled grocery cart. The strength of her voice belied her petite frame.

Past residents of Over-the-Rhine, and those of her friends who remain, remember her as a consistent, strong voice unafraid to speak up for others like her – the poor.

"Nannie understood the challenges of living on little," Neumeier said, "but she shared everything she had."

Ms. Hinkston's family doesn't have enough money for her burial. Contributions to the Nannie Hinkston Memorial Fund may be made at any Fifth Third Bank location.

Visitation will be from 11 a.m. to 1 p.m. Tuesday at St. Francis Seraph Catholic Church, 1615 Vine St., Over-the-Rhine. Mass of Christian Burial will follow at 1 p.m.

Burial will be in Vine Street Cemetery, Clifton. A reception will be held at 3 p.m. at the Peaslee Neighborhood Center, 215 E. 14th St., Over-the-Rhine.

# Jackie Wallace: Teacher, Freedom Center educator

*March 24, 2016*

Jackie Wallace, the great-granddaughter of a white Kentucky slave owner, had an inborn understanding of the National Underground Railroad Freedom Center.

A retired Cincinnati Public Schools teacher, Mrs. Wallace developed and oversaw the Freedom Center's student tours, designed its curriculum, and was its manager of educational initiatives.

Mrs. Wallace died March 19. A blood clot broke loose and traveled to her heart, causing her death, family members said. The Mount Airy resident was 67.

"More than any other staff member with whom I worked in almost 20 years I have been associated with the Freedom Center, Jackie was the foundation for my hope and my confidence that we would be able to make a difference in the learning and lives of young people," said John Pepper, honorary co-chair of the Freedom Center. "She was a beacon of integrity, warmth and caring."

About 40,000 students a year tour the Freedom Center.

"The loss of Mrs. Jackie Wallace, a master educator, has greatly impacted the National Underground Railroad Freedom Center family," said Clarence Newsome, center president. "She was deeply loved, and her love for us will continue to inspire and energize our team to live up to the highest standards possible for many years to come."

The eighth of nine children, she was born Jacqueline "Jackie" Kay Sroufe in Ripley, Ohio. Ripley is home of the Rankin House, which overlooks the Ohio River into Kentucky and was one of the better-known sites on the Underground Railroad that helped black slaves escape bondage in the South.

"She knew the story, she lived it," said Allison Wallace, of Atlanta, one of Mrs. Wallace's two surviving daughters.

In her three-decade teaching career, Mrs. Wallace taught at Cummins, North Avondale, Cheviot, and Mount Airy elementary schools.

Family and friends say Mrs. Wallace, who earned an education degree from the University of Cincinnati, was accomplished in her own right. Yet many people in the city's black community knew her as the first lady of Carmel Presbyterian Church in Avondale. Already a parishioner, she married the church pastor, the Rev. Clarence Wallace, in 1980. He preceded her in death in 2012.

"She took her role at Carmel very seriously, and it was not easy on her," Allison Wallace said.

Mrs. Wallace helped to develop the church pantry, known as the Avondale Caring Network Pantry, which opened in 2007 to provide neighborhood families with free baby formula, diapers, diaper wipes, and other supplies. The church's outreach pantry grew out of the early childhood program Every Child Succeeds, which has been housed in donated space in the church's undercroft since 2006.

During her husband's pastorate at Carmel, Mrs. Wallace also taught in its summer enrichment program, served on the usher board, sang in the Inspirational Choir, and was an elder.

Family and friends remember her love of shopping, especially for purses, and how she enjoyed trips to the Ohio River gaming boats in Indiana, where she liked to play the slot machines.

"My mother lived life to the fullest," Allison Wallace said. "No matter the tough times she was going through, she managed always to keep a positive attitude."

She is survived by another daughter, Angela Sroufe, of Tampa, Florida, four granddaughters and two great-grandchildren. The Rev. and Mrs. Wallace reared one of their granddaughters, Jordan Kilgore (Mandel) as their own, family members said.

Visitation will be 4 p.m. to 6 p.m. Friday at Carmel Presbyterian Church, 3549 Reading Road, Avondale. The funeral service will be at 6 p.m. Internment will be at 9:30 a.m. Saturday at Spring Grove Cemetery.

The family had yet to decide on a memorial.

# Anna Fields, 101, pioneering black Army nurse

*April 9, 2016*

Anna Belle Covington Fields did not consider herself a trailblazer.

Yet she was one of just an estimated 500 African-American nurses in two all-black U.S. Women's Army Corps (WAC) units during World War II. Mrs. Fields served two years at Thomas M. England General Hospital, converted hotels on the Atlantic City, New Jersey, Boardwalk that became the world's largest amputee hospital.

Mrs. Fields died Sunday of pneumonia at Daniel Drake Center, Hartwell, where she had been admitted 24 hours earlier. The Bond Hill resident was 101.

"We didn't know all she had done until the Army found her when she was 98," said one of her two surviving daughters, Paula Fields, 58, who lived with and cared for her mother in recent years.

A Columbus native, the late Mrs. Fields attended nursing school in Chicago and took her first job at a hospital there.

In January 1941, just as Mrs. Fields had turned 26, the U.S. Army opened its nursing corps to African-Americans. Wanting to serve her country, Mrs. Fields responded to a recruitment call and went through training at Fort Des Moines, Iowa. She and other black nurses were known as "ten-percenters," because WAC recruitment of African-Americans was limited to 10 percent – the corresponding national black population percentage at the time.

Such potential distractions did not deter Mrs. Fields. As a member of the 31st WAC Division, she volunteered to go to Atlantic City, otherwise known as Camp Boardwalk.

From June 1942 through November 1945, 5,000 American war casualties from Europe and North Africa received care at the England General Hospital. Mrs. Fields worked in the amputation ward, as a surgical technician, and with troops who had been blinded by explosions.

In an interview with the U.S. Department of Veterans Affairs just three years ago, Mrs. Fields recalled her work, saying, "We conditioned their stubs and fit them with artificial limbs."

Mrs. Fields did talk to her family about the troops for whom she cared.

She had turned 30 in January 1945 and was about 10 years older than many of the men in her care.

"She said that a lot of those young guys were without hope when they got there that they could go on and live a 'normal' life," Paula Fields said. "She nurtured them. She became a surrogate mother to them. She encouraged them."

Later in life, Paula Fields said, her mother continued to nurture and care for the people around her. She would stand on the front porch of her Bond Hill home in the morning to make sure neighborhood children boarded the school bus. She would visit neighbors who called if a family member were sick. She insisted that her grandchildren and subsequent generations of family were brought up in the church.

After the war, Mrs. Fields returned to her native Columbus. She married Karl William Fields Sr., an African-American soldier who'd been wounded in Italy.

Honorably discharged from the service, Mrs. Fields went to work in the maternity ward in the Lockbourne Air Force Base hospital near Columbus. She worked there until the mid-1950s when her husband, a truck driver, took a job in Cincinnati. They lived for nine years in Avondale, where she attended the former St. Michael's and All Saints Episcopal Church, before buying a house in Bond Hill in the mid-1960s. Her church connection led to a nursing job at what is now the Marjorie P. Lee Nursing Home, an Episcopal Retirement Homes facility in Fairfax.

She worked into her 80s. She loved hats and had more than 300, one for every occasion.

At the time of her death, Mrs. Fields was a member of Harac Parech Ministries for the World, Bond Hill, which she had served on the missionary and mother's board ministries.

In addition to her husband, who died in 1995, Mrs. Fields is preceded in death by a son, Karl William Fields Jr.

In addition to Paula Fields, she is survived by a son, William Karl Fields, of Northside; a daughter, Pamela Dock, of Roselawn; and 18 grandchildren, 42 great-grandchildren, and 26 great-great-grandchildren.

"She had a sharp mind and was talking until her last day," Paula Fields said. "She woke up on Sunday afternoon and started laughing. She said, 'Today?' And then she went to sleep. She told us the angels would come for her on a Sunday."

Visitation will be from 9:30 a.m. to 11 a.m. Saturday at Word of Life Ministry Christian Center, 10555 Hamilton Ave., Springfield Township. Service will be at 11 a.m. Interment will be at Crown Hill Memorial Park and Mausoleum, Colerain Township.

---

# Retired Bishop Lewis Hilton Sr., wife Sarah, married 71 years, die four days apart

*December 4, 2017*

In almost 72 years of marriage, Lewis and Sarah Hilton together operated a farm in Bulloch County, Georgia, started a large family, and nurtured a small Avondale church into what is now a suburban Forest Park megachurch.

Their children say Lewis and Sarah were inseparable and a dynamic team. Mr. Hilton, especially, was unhappy when serious health problems forced them to live apart during the past few months.

Surrounded by family members and with his wife at his side, Mr. Hilton died November 23, Thanksgiving Day, at Maple Knoll Village Rehabilitation Center in Springdale. He had suffered a stroke several years ago and had been hospitalized with complications since August. He had celebrated his ninety-second birthday the previous day.

Then, on Sunday morning, November 26, three days after her husband's death, Mrs. Hilton drove with her daughter and granddaughter to church. Mrs. Hilton had been alert and said she was feeling good. Then she had a heart attack and lost consciousness. She had suffered her first heart attack August 22, just 11 days after her husband had been hospitalized.

At the church, CPR was administered. She was placed on life support but died the next day, November 27, at Mercy Health Hospital in Fairfield. She was 90.

"We are so proud of our parents," said their oldest son, Lewis Hilton Jr., better known as Bishop Bobby Hilton, senior pastor of Word of Deliverance Ministries for the World in Forest Park.

"We are sad they left us together. But after almost 72 years of marriage, we are grateful."

A joint funeral will be held Monday, December 4, at 6 p.m. at Word of Deliverance. The Hiltons will be buried at 11 a.m. Tuesday at Landmark Memorial Gardens, Springdale.

Bishop Hilton Jr. will not preside. "I am their pastor," he said. "This week, I only want to be their son."

In 1990, Bishop Hilton Jr. became senior pastor of Apostolic Church of Deliverance.

His father and mother had founded the church in a house on Hearne Avenue in Avondale in 1970. Elder Hilton Sr. soon was ordained a bishop and served as Northwest Diocese Bishop of the Born Again Church of Jesus Christ.

Bishop Hilton Sr. and his wife first met shortly after the Hilton family moved from South Carolina to Statesboro, Georgia. He had to quit school before graduating to help his father farm.

He married Mrs. Hilton, a Statesboro native, January 12, 1946.

They operated a farm and grew tobacco and cotton. In 1956, they moved their family, which at that time included two daughters, to the Cincinnati area. The Hiltons soon settled in Lincoln Heights and later moved to Silverton before settling in Forest Park. They had five children.

Before entering the ministry, Mr. Hilton started what would be a 28-year career at Cincinnati Milling Machine, which would later be named Cincinnati Milacron, in Oakley.

Their children remember Mr. Hilton as "a faithful and hard-working man who took excellent care of his family. There was never a day he was not working full time until he retired from Cincinnati Milacron."

Their mother ran the household. They cared for foster children. "She made sure home-cooked meals were hot and ready every evening by the time her husband would arrive from work," her children recall. The consistency and their parents' loving marriage and togetherness created a strong sense of security, they said.

Even as their lives came to an end, Lewis and Sarah were together.

After he was released from the hospital, Lewis Sr. was sent to Maple Knoll. After her release, Sarah also was sent to Maple Knoll. They had adjacent private rooms. Soon, Mrs. Hilton was discharged and went home. She would visit her husband as often as her strength would allow.

His mood lifted considerably when she entered the room. "Here comes my baby," he would say. "How are you doing, baby?"

A few months later, just four days apart, they would die.

"We believe Mother had made up her mind," Bobby Hilton said. "She was ready to see Jesus and knew her husband would be waiting for her there."

The Hiltons are survived by daughters Martha Mae Dillingham and Angela Hilton of Pleasant Run and LeBertha Southall of Forest Park, sons Lewis "Bobby" Hilton of Amberley Village and John Hilton of Pleasant Ridge, 16 grandchildren, 26 great-grandchildren, and eight great-great-grandchildren.

Visitation will be 2–6 p.m. Monday, December 4, at Word of Deliverance Family Life Center, 693 Fresno Drive, Forest Park. The funeral will follow at 6 p.m.

The American Heart Association and some researchers say it is not uncommon for elderly married couples to die within hours or days of each other. "Broken heart syndrome" is known medically as stress-induced cardiomyopathy, or an abnormal heart muscle that makes it more difficult for the heart to pump and deliver blood to the rest of the body.

"Women are more likely than men to experience the sudden, intense chest pain — the reaction to a surge of stress hormones — that can be caused by an emotionally stressful event."

# 'Cincinnati's Redeemer'

## Marian Spencer led battles to integrate schools, pools

*July 11, 2019*

Somewhere, a former slave named Henry Washington Walker Alexander has to be pleased with how his granddaughter listened to his morning lectures back home in Gallipolis, Ohio.

Not only did she hear them, Marian Regelia Alexander Spencer carried out her grandfather's words. "Every morning, he preached that we should never fail to vote, we should get our education, and speak up when we saw wrong being do:ne," she said.

Spencer, who led the battle to desegregate Coney Island's swimming pools in the 1950s and became the first African American woman elected to Cincinnati City Council in 1983, died Tuesday. She was 99.

Spencer, who lived in Avondale, died at 9:55 p.m. at Hospice of Cincinnati at Twin Towers, in College Hill. She had suffered a stroke on her 99th birthday, June 28, said her niece, Camille Haamid, of Clifton. Spencer was hospitalized fo    three days at University of Cincinnati Medical Center and then returned to her room at Twin Towers.

"I simply would say I am lucky to have had two mothers," said Haamid, who is the daughter of Marian's twin sister, Mildred, who is in hospice iin Washington, District of Columbia.

"What happened to one- even a cold- seemed to happen to the other. Aunt Marian was one of the nicest people. She was gracious all the time. Some people act that way in public. Aunt Mari.an was gracious and kind when she was making breakfast."

By any measure, as an individual or in partnership with her late husband, Donald Spencer Sr., Mari.an Spencer lived a life of consequence and purpose. Friends and admirers referred to her as "Ms. Civil Rights."

"She was Cincinnati's redeemer," said retired federal judge Nathaniel Jones, who met the Spencers in the early 1970s when they traveled to New York to meet with him. He was general counsel of the national NAACP at the time. The Spencers, leaders of the local NAACP branch, wanted Jones' help in desegregating Cincinnati Public Schools.

The Spencers had raised $30,000 as a sign of good faith, Jones said.

"Marian made it possible for people to realize they were better than they thought they were," Jones said. "To that extent, she assisted people in realizing their potential goodness."

Cincinnati Mayor John Cranley is among Spencer's admirers.

"Small in stature, but a giant in impact, Marian Spencer led by example to build a more integrated city, and we are all trying to live up to her example," Cranley said. "We mourn this loss but we are so grateful our city is better for her life."

In March 2016, the city of Cincinnati named a portion of Walnut Street Downtown in her honor. Marian Spencer Way runs between Theodore Berry Way and Second Street at The Banks.

"One of my greatest joys as mayor was driving her to City Hall the day we named a street in her honor, during which she shared with me that as a granddaughter of a slave she has seen a lot of change for the better," Cranley said. "She was that change."

Cranley on Wednesday said he has asked that city flags be flown at half-staff in her honor.

Though biracial, with a mix of African American, Cherokee and Scottish immigrant ancestors, she identified as African American. "If one drop of black blood is so precious, I was going to claim it," Spencer said.

In fact, in an interview with The Enquirer a few weeks before her 98th birthday in 2018, Spencer ranked the Coney Island campaign as her top achievement in a life filled with them.

One day in 1952, her sons – Donald Jr., 10, and Edward 8 – were watching a popular local children's TV program, "The Uncle Al Show," and saw a commercial for the park: "Everyone comes to Coney Island."

"When my kids said they wanted to go, I waited until they weren't around and called," Spencer said. "I talked to the girl who answered. I said, `We're Negroes, can we get in?' She was very quiet and said, `No, but I don't make the rules.'

"I said, `I know you don't, sweetheart, but I am going to find out who does.' I got 25 mothers and grandmothers together in Walnut Hills, and that's where I started the fight."

She built the foundation of her coalition with women because black men were afraid of losing their jobs at that time. Other supporters came from the Woman's City Club of Greater Cincinnati, where Spencer was one of the first African American members.

Spencer also was head of the NAACP's Legislative Committee then and found a young black lawyer, Michael Turpeau, to take the case. On the Fourth of July 1952, an armed guard chased Spencer and other women protestors away from the park gate.

She didn't give up even in the face of stubborn segregationists. The park was desegregated in 1955, but the whites-only rule for Coney's main attraction, Sunlite Pool, held on until 1961.

"I never felt I had to accept anything I didn't want to," Spencer said. "I didn't accept a 'no' when it was wrong. It has been my responsibility to change things."

She was valedictorian of her graduating class at Gallia Academy High School. She moved to Cincinnati with her twin in 1938 to attend the University of Cincinnati.

She married Donald Spencer on Aug. 12, 1940, and gave birth to Donald Jr. on Jan. 12, 1942. Later that spring, she earned her undergraduate degree in English from UC. She was prohibited as an African American from living on campus, but in December 2017 the university named its newest residence building after her, Marian Spencer Hall. She had served on the UC Board of Trustees from 1975 to 1980.

"Marian Spencer was a persistent and mighty agent of change who dedicated her life to justice and breaking down barriers that restrict the lives and opportunities of Americans of color," UC President Neville Pinto said. "We have lost a true trailblazer. Her example will inspire generations to come."

Spencer sat in the living room of the house that she and her husband, a teacher who also worked in real estate, had built at the end of Lexington Avenue in Avondale in the early 1950s.

Her friend and biographer, Dorothy Christenson, who wrote "Keep on Fighting: The Life and Civil Rights Legacy of Marian A. Spencer," joined Spencer for the interview. The book was published in 2015 by Ohio University Press.

"She never demanded a spotlight for herself," said Christenson, who moved with her late husband to Cincinnati in 1971 and met Spencer through the fair-housing group Housing Opportunities Made Equal (HOME), the nonprofit Spencer had helped to create in 1969.

"Through it all, she knew she was dealing with big egos," Christenson added. "She said she would never get anywhere if she wasn't polite. She was polite. She smiled. She was tenacious. She is such a fine role model for anyone, particularly young African-American woman."

Though she lost, Spencer considered her failed run for the Cincinnati Board of Education in 1973 another accomplishment. She supported busing and school integration and had been instrumental in the NAACP's legal efforts to desegregate Cincinnati Public Schools in 1972. She chaired the education committee of the Cincinnati NAACP branch for 20 years and was elected the chapter's first female president in 1981.

"You don't win them all," she said in retrospect of her school board loss. "You learn from it and move on. That's what I always told my sons."

Spencer lived by those words.

As NAACP chapter president in the early 1980s, she teamed with famed civil rights preacher the Rev. Fred Shuttlesworth to clean up a polluted site in Lower Price Hill. Their work led to a city ordinance, which was later adapted into national Superfund legislation.

Leaders of the Charter Committee asked her to run for city council as a Charterite.

"They asked me, and I ran," Spencer said. Her election, she added, "meant a few people thought I was right."

Hers was a life filled with public service and firsts.

Including Cincinnati City Council.

"I was in tears this morning when I heard the news," said councilwoman Tamaya Dennard, who is African American. "I think about what I am up against in 2019, but the fight I have is nothing compared to what she faced.

"I wouldn't be there if not for her taking the darts and insults. She paved the way for me. I stand on her shoulders."

Spencer served on boards or worked in other capacities with the U.S. Civil Rights Commission Ohio Advisory Board, Planned Parenthood, the Cincinnati Human Services Task Force, American Civil Liberties Union, Cincinnati Woman's City Club and the National Underground Railroad Freedom Center.

She represented the Ohio Democratic Party at the party's national conventions in 1984 and 1988.

A list of her awards covers more than three pages in her biography. Her honors include Cincinnati Enquirer Woman of the Year in 1972, Great Living Cincinnatian in 1998, the Ohio Civil Rights Hall of Fame in 2010 and YWCA Racial Justice Award in 2011. In 2015, the Cincinnatus Association created the Donald and Marian Spencer "Spirit of America" Awards to recognize advocates of inclusion.

Spencer is survived by her two sons, Donald Spencer Jr. of Avondale and Edward Spencer of Richmond, California; three grandchildren; and one great-grandchild. Her husband, Donald Spencer Sr., preceded her in death in 2010 at age 95.

A private ceremony for family and close friends will precede cremation. Her ashes will go to Fox Lake, Indiana, where she summered and swam. A public memorial celebration of her life will be held at 3 p.m. on Aug. 10 in the Fifth Third Arena at the University of Cincinnati.

# METRICS, CUTS TO BUDGET, AND STAFFING ALTER NEWSROOM LANDSCAPE, STORY CHOICES

Eleven television screens or monitors hang from the walls or rest on file cabinets in the middle of the newsroom.

They are sleeker in design than their predecessors, with sharper pictures and clearer sound, of course, and they've changed locations – slightly – since I first went to work at the Cincinnati *Enquirer* in May 1993. Their presence and prominence in the room are unchanged.

The major difference is the screens' primary purpose, a change that symbolizes the industry's evolution in the 25 years since I first walked into the nineteenth-floor newsroom at Third and Elm streets, downtown Cincinnati. The transformation of print journalism in the past quarter of a century has been dramatic, and to be in the middle of the changes has been personally dizzying and frustrating and frightening and exhilarating and satisfying. (I remember the widespread introduction of the plain-paper fax machine in the late 1980s.)

I wish budgets were larger and would allow for more investigative and watchdog reporting. I wish staffs were larger. I lament the loss of the traditional copy desk. That final layer of checks, that final set of eyes, that safety net, it's all gone. I miss the 9:30 p.m. call to the landline at my house in 1995 from a copy editor who would say, "I have a couple of questions on your story. Sorry to bug you so late." I never minded. I welcomed the calls, and my standard response to my colleague was, "Thanks for helping make the story better." Knowing that a copy editor had scoured the story one final time reduced the incidence and intensity of the 2 a.m. panic attack that you'd spelled a name wrong or had made a mistake in your math.

Yet I am not here to complain. We do enough of that internally at times. Besides, no one cares or should care about our challenges as professional news gatherers, save the increased appreciation we've been shown collectively across our polarized society by supporters who understand our vital role as an independent voice in a democracy. The boost comes in the face of "fake news" attacks on the truth-telling mainstream media.

As I wrote earlier, the ride as a reporter is an exciting one, even as the demands and inherent deadline stresses have multiplied. I know I've had a front-row seat for life. I'm grateful.

* * *

Back to those monitors in the center of our newsroom. A couple are tuned to national cable news channels. The ones we pay closest attention to are those measuring our readership: pageviews, unique viewers, concurrent readers, what kinds of stories might convince a visitor to subscribe digitally, where readers are exiting a story, how long they're reading, what kinds of stories are most popular with our readership base, and how successful we are at attracting readers to our homepage, Cincinnati.com.

The most intimidating, heartbreaking, or euphoric tool – depending how your story is performing – is called Chartbeat, a real-time dashboard that shows several story measures. It lists recirculation, engaged time, and pageviews. It also reveals from which type of device a reader is accessing the story: mobile, desktop, or tablet.

Collectively, metrics.

The weekly roundup of top stories sent out each Friday by our editor lists pageviews.

With few exceptions, the priorities and methods of digital delivery and measure are the same in every daily newspaper newsroom across the country.

What these changes mean in the context of this book is that a number of these 80 *Enquirer* stories reported from Cincinnati's black community and about African-Americans would likely not have been pursued or published – primarily those dated in the 1990s. Print journalism and its methods for survival have changed that dramatically and that fast, and the change just continues to accelerate.

In my experience, stories of isolated importance to African-Americans don't produce the metrics. I walked away from a metrics screen early in August 2018, frustrated, mumbling to myself that a story about a significant investment by the Greater Cincinnati Urban League and Cincinnati Children's Hospital Medical Center in an innovation center in the heart of the black community "only did 1,200." And most of them likely came from a reposting of the link on the Urban League's website.

A reporter can have a few stories a month that fail to perform well, like the Urban League story that was timed to the organization's national conference and tied to its stated national priority to close "the digital divide" in black communities across the country. In the old days, there'd be no second-guessing. Now, we're all about second-guessing in the name of analysis and audience growth.

I am reminded of what a former *Enquirer* marketing colleague told me in 2013, at the height of my reporting from the city's largest black neighborhood, Avondale, and how it was poised – after decades of neglect and blight – for redevelopment.

"No other community in the region has been covered as thoroughly as Avondale for the past two years," I said. "Why don't we do more to promote it?"

"I understand your frustration," she said, before pausing and then referring to Avondale's zip code. "We just don't market to 45229."

That isn't to say that some African-Americans don't read the *Enquirer* or that part of our predominantly white readership doesn't care about what happens in Avondale or other parts of the black community. What it says is that more of them, tens of thousands more of them, care significantly more about what happens in their predominantly white parts of the city and region. Like their local Catholic high school football team and real estate development. We now have an empirical measure that helps management direct where we invest our precious and ever-diminishing resources.

No official minimums exist in our newsroom, but reporters have been told that a collective 80,000 pageviews a month are expected, and that 5,000 pageviews is a solid showing for an individual story. A threshold for major success is 10,000. (My personal best is about 160,000 pageviews in early 2018 for a deportation story about a man who was caregiver – and would later marry the mother – of a paraplegic boy. It went viral on Twitter, thanks in part to a retweet from actor/social activist Alyssa Milano.)

Our traditional strong performers are sports stories, especially about the hometown NFL team, the Cincinnati Bengals. Other traditional hot spots are breaking news, government scandal, high school sports, and quirky pieces – including video – involving food or animals. Have I mentioned Fiona the hippo at the Cincinnati Zoo and Botanical Garden? Or Harambe, the Western lowland gorilla shot by a zoo worker after a 3-year-old boy climbed into the gorilla enclosure in 2016?

When our staff project "Seven Days of Heroin" was announced in April 2018 as winner of the Pulitzer Prize for local reporting, it immediately zoomed into the high three-digits in concurrent views. The *Enquirer* is part of the USA Today Network and getting play on the *USA Today* website is a boon for any local story because it's then introduced to a national audience.

"Page views are impressions, and impressions are dollars," a corporate news trainer told our staff.

That session summarized the change over time in how newspapers cover their communities.

"We don't serve all the people anymore," the trainer said. "We have to super-serve people. We don't have the numbers of people we used to."

The *Enquirer*'s managing editor had a newsroom yearbook compiled in 1999. We had more than 200 people on the news staff then: reporters, editors, photographers, clerks. Newsroom personnel hovered around 80 for most of 2018, according to the staff directory published at Cincinnati.com. That number dropped by about another ten in early 2019 through layoffs and elimination of positions that had not been filled throughout the previous year.

Gone are national and local display advertising accounts that fed the news-gathering machine. The Internet, social media such as Twitter and Facebook, and the 24-hour cable news cycle are among the forces that changed how we collect and present the news.

\* \* \*

When I arrived at the *Enquirer* in 1993, the televisions in the middle of the newsroom were tuned to the four local television stations – our competitors – in the Cincinnati media market: ABC, CBS, Fox, and NBC. A couple of reporters, a news aide, and an assistant local news editor monitored the TV newscasts that started at 4 each weekday afternoon and ran until the national network news came on at 6:30 p.m. A couple of people – always a reporter with a pocket-sized notebook or legal pad and pen in hand – monitored the news broadcasts when they started up at 9 at night and ran until 11:30 p.m.

We watched to make sure we didn't miss something. After all, in Cincinnati, as I wrote earlier, the *Enquirer* was the paper of record.

At 11:01 p.m., the most important responsibility for the person charged with watching those four TV screens in the still-crowded *Enquirer* newsroom was to know what we had so we could tell if one of the stations had a story we didn't or something else late and breaking, such as a shooting, an auto crash, or a fire that we might not have caught on the police scanners.

For all the attention we paid to the four television stations, they weren't our primary competitor. Our chief competitor was the city's afternoon paper, the *Cincinnati Post*, for many years the flagship of Scripps-Howard Newspapers. Shortly before lunch, *Enquirer* clerks would bring up a bundle of the early *Post* edition, which was followed around 2 p.m. by its final. The competition was most often collegial but fierce. An *Enquirer* reporter with a specific core news beat – city hall, county government, courts, police, or one of the major Cincinnati-based companies, especially Procter & Gamble – had better not get beaten too frequently on a story by their *Post* counterpart.

That industry is the one I entered as a college graduate in 1984, first as a sports reporting intern at the *Enquirer* before being farmed out for professional development at a smaller Gannett Co. newspaper in Lafayette, Indiana, the *Journal & Courier*. I'd work there four years. I'd make my way back to the *Enquirer* after additional stops at the Rockford (Illinois) *Register Star* and the then-family-owned *News & Observer* in Raleigh, North Carolina.

In all, as I write this essay in October 2018, I have 33 years in daily newspapers – not counting the three summers I worked full-time in the newsroom of my hometown paper, the Dixon (Illinois) *Evening Telegraph,* as a college student. My first professional byline published in the *Telegraph* in 1978. I was 16 and a high school junior and earned $5 for covering my high school wrestling team's annual invitational. I will always remember the intoxicating scent of ink rising from the basement-level press when I first walked in the *Telegraph* office on Peoria Avenue. Back then, I wrote in black pen on college-ruled notebook paper, following the handful of Associated Press and pencil-editing style points I knew at the time. I marked the end of each sentence with an X.

Six years later I was an *Enquirer* sports intern, filing my final story on a bulky portable computer that you had to carry like a suitcase. It required jamming the earpiece and mouthpiece of a landline phone into round receptacles. The machine squealed a high-pitched buzz as the story transmitted to the office. Nine years later, I would be back at the *Enquirer* as a general assignment news reporter.

I break my time at the *Enquirer* into three major blocks. The first spans May 1993–July 2000, when I worked in news and features. The series I reported then on race relations in Cincinnati, "A Polite Silence," published in November 1993.

Block 2 is the nine seasons I spent as Bengals/NFL beat writer, July 2000–January 2009.

Block 3 began when I went back to news that January. I've been there for almost 10 years, minus the 14 months I was away on medical leave and to work as a vice president at the local Urban League affiliate.

Change was a constant in this industry, but it has sped up since early 2013. That February, reporters were given iPhones and underwent extensive video training.

The newsroom I left at the end of November 2014 when I took a corporate buyout and the one I returned to in January 2016 were jarringly different. The staff was significantly smaller in number of people, and younger.

I came of age in newspapers at a time when the expectation for a reporter was to marry quality with quantity. My approach: How much can I do well? I came back to the newsroom in 2016 to a philosophy that first clanged in my ear: "Fewer things better."

That motto was reinforced as recently as December 2018 by another corporate trainer.

I asked a few of my fellow veteran *Enquirer* reporter colleagues to summarize the changes in our newsroom in the past 25 years.

- Metrics: Just a little more about them. They influence our story choices. We worry about falling behind in our monthly pageviews if we invest time into projects as opposed to stories that are sure-fire winners with readers.

- Time: We have less of it. We grew up and into a cycle focused on one deadline, whether for a morning (a.m.) or afternoon (p.m.) paper. We work now in a relentless 24-hour cycle. If we are on a breaking story, we're reporting, writing, shooting iPhone photos and maybe even video as it's developing. An older colleague calls the new process, "Making sausage in public." At times, not a pretty sight.

- Workload: Technology and staff reductions have made reporters jacks of all trades. Reporters commonly report a story, write it, proofread it (or proof for a colleague), write the headline, write the subheads, take photos or pull them from the electronic library and write or rewrite those captions (we call them cutlines), optimize the story with links to previous or related stories, and post it to social media, such as Facebook, Twitter, and Instagram. Those posts must intentionally link to interested organizations or sources so that the story can get maximum social media exposure. The additional roles are done without copy editors, who caught typos, misspellings, and style inconsistencies. Reporting and writing without copy editors compares to driving a car on an ice-covered roadway without a seatbelt or a motorcycle without a helmet.

By 2016, the language of the newsroom had changed, too. Stories were now "content." Reporters were content creators. Editors were producers. We had a social media producer on staff.

Painstaking attention is now paid to SEO, otherwise known as search engine optimization. Headlines are written only after checking Google Trends for hot keywords. We do Facebook Live. Page 1 on Sunday in print is no longer the prime real estate for a story. The *Enquirer* posts its most compelling enterprise content on Cincinnati.com for the "wake-up" slot on Monday through Thursday morning. Timing is everything. We're now about building audience segments in areas called "Family Forward" and "Know the Score."

"The audience is looking for great journalism," our corporate news trainer told us.

Conflict is a timeless element in newspaper stories. It's even more important today to attract readers who have multiple media choices, including social media and those outlets whose coverage is known to align closely with their political opinions. Never mind the government agencies, private companies, and even sports teams and colleges that dress up public relations copy and often try to pass it off as unbiased news.

Finding the right balance of ignoring the chaos and paying the right amount of attention to the other media is challenging. We can easily drown in information. At times, it's nearly impossible to concentrate. Inefficiency sets in.

I've managed to hit the sweet spot a few times since my return in January 2016. I followed several leads to find and then report on a high school student named Tywon Thomas. He was 3 months old in April 2001 when his father, Timothy Thomas, an unarmed black man, was shot and killed by a white Cincinnati Police officer, touching off social unrest and rioting and leading to a declaration of martial law. I placed into historical context the attempt to force a soccer stadium into a black neighborhood that had been torn by interstate construction, slum clearance, and the demolition of several hundred units of public housing. As the 2016 NAACP national convention arrived in Cincinnati, I wrote an analytical piece about how the rise of white supremacy and incidents of police brutality elevated the civil rights organization to vital relevancy.

On one level, those stories transcended metrics, yet, at the same time, I was disappointed that they didn't reach more readers. I didn't face that potential downside 20 years ago.

I'll never stop trying to do the most I can with every story within the allotted reporting and writing time.

* * *

Still, as I wrote earlier in this story's nut graf – the paragraph high up, following the lede, that contains the kernel, or essential aspects, of the story – I am not complaining. I am not whining. Conversely, looking back, I am grateful. Deeply appreciative for every day I've had in the newspaper business and for each day I may still have. I could have made that my lede. (I hope I didn't bury the lede, which is a sin for a reporter.) "Lede" is a word I'd better explain: an alternative and now archaic spelling of the word "lead," used these days exclusively, I suppose, by newspaper journalists to specify the opening or top of a story. "Burying the lede" is putting the essential information too far down, which also is known as "backing into" a story.

So, I have now come to my ending, which is the second most important part of a story, second only in importance to the ... lede. Excellent job. You're catching on.

Those of us left standing who started when newspapers were still king and before we knew the end of the golden age of the industry was fast approaching or actually had begun, we're thankful. We have all seen too many talented and dedicated colleagues laid off, or leaving on their own terms, too often for lesser work. We thought we were slim on resources and people 20 years ago. Looking back, those were the halcyon days.

Today, no matter our experience level, two years or 20, we're doing our best to skillfully juggle the many facets of the job. *Mark, can you tell this as a video-only story? Wochit has some new features that can help you. Maybe Instagram?*

So, that ending I promised you. I want to end with a beloved newspaper symbol that clearly needs explanation. It's a designation I used when I hand-wrote my stories as a high school student working as a $5-an-assignment stringer for my hometown paper in Illinois, and the same symbol I pounded out at the end of in-class deadline writing assignments on a manual typewriter at Miami University.

–30–

What does that mean? Some theories trace its use to the era when newspaper stories were transmitted by telegraph, and -30- in Morse code denoted "the end." Others assign its use to filing of stories in longhand: X meant the end of a sentence. XX was the end of a paragraph, and XXX symbolized the end of a story. In Roman numerals, of course, XXX is 30.

So, there you have it. And now I can write, with certainty that you understand:

–30–

# AFTERWORD

In the summer of 2009 Mark Curnutte stopped me in the middle of the *Cincinnati Enquirer* newsroom.

He looked concerned. He had recently given up what for many would be a coveted beat covering the Cincinnati Bengals to a newly created assignment focused on race and social issues. While Mark said that he had burned out covering the Bengals for nine seasons, he worried about his status as the news industry – and the *Enquirer* – dealt with a recession that resulted in layoffs and buyouts on the staff.

"I'll go back to the Bengals beat if you want me to," he said.

My response: "No, Mark, what you're doing now is more important than football."

When I arrived in Cincinnati as editor of the *Enquirer* in 2002, the wounds of 2001 were fresh, as Mark notes in this book.

"The April 2001 shooting of Timothy Thomas, an unarmed black man, in Over-The-Rhine had led to a boycott of Downtown Cincinnati. Bill Cosby and other national entertainment acts refused to perform in Cincinnati, and the National Urban League was one of several organizations to move its conventions from Cincinnati to other cities."

In the following year, the *Enquirer* embarked on an investigative reporting campaign on a pattern of police shootings and bad behavior by officers. An analysis of a database of 5,500 use-of-force records that revealed hundreds of citizens' complaints from 1997 to 2000 discovered that police had been routinely exonerated of misconduct nine times out of ten. The result: a Department of Justice Collaborative Agreement order that police reform policies and form partnerships to improve community relations.

But no plan on paper would soon ease the tension and polarization of the black community, police, and certainly white suburbanites reluctant to travel downtown to Over-the-Rhine. Over time, the visible tensions in the streets eased, but polarization and disparities simmered under the headlines.

While the stories of conflict needed to be covered, we needed to focus as well on stories – and the people behind them – that provided context to a deeper understanding of problems, solutions, hope, and healing.

Mark's reporting centered on the effects of the recession on the poor, how the Ohio welfare system was being cut, and additional weight to help people being put on nonprofits like the FreeStore/Foodbank and Urban League. Hunger/food insecurity and youth homelessness were big topics, all intensified because of the recession. Sadly, one of the reasons the recession was such big news was it was hitting white people in ways that African-Americans had been dealing with for generations. It was akin today to how heroin is such big news because it's affecting mainly white people.

Mark produced several stories about homelessness and the effects of the economic changes in Over-the-Rhine on the poor, largely African-American community that had lived there for two generations and now felt as if they were being pushed out. He broke a number of stories about the efforts, plans, and ultimate success of moving the homeless shelters away from the Washington Park area.

He inherited the coverage responsibilities of the Freedom Center and reported on its ongoing economic struggles and challenges to find peace with the city's black community and define its mission more sharply with a traveling exhibit on lynching and a permanent exhibit on contemporary slavery.

In 2010, Mark traveled to Haiti with photographer Carrie Cochran to cover Cincinnati-area groups on the ground there trying to help in the aftermath of the deadly earthquake. They produced a major daily story and a sophisticated special section.

Later in 2010, Mark focused increasingly on immigration issues. He wrote about wage theft involving a high-end vet/animal hospital and three of its undocumented Mexican laborers. He broke the story of a young Dreamer, Bernard Pastor, who was arrested after a traffic accident in suburban Springdale. Over almost two months, the *Enquirer* followed every move of the story, which ended with his release and receipt of deferred action. In 2012, he was one of the first DACA recipients.

I retired at the end of 2010 after a 35-year career in the news business, and I am encouraged that the newspaper continued to value Mark's expertise – and the voices of the communities he has established relationships with.

My years as an editor (1975–2010) were of a post-civil rights era and a time when newspapers worked to increase newsroom diversity and to do a better job of covering communities of color. Over those years I witnessed the soul-searching and awakening of a media industry that did not look much like America. They were dominated from top to bottom by white men.

Indeed, in 1978 minorities made up 0.4 percent of top editors – while people of color represented 17 percent of the nation's population. (There remains work to be done. An American Society of News Editors survey in 2017 found that racial minorities make up just 17 percent of online and print newsroom employees; in the U.S., racial minorities account for 39 percent of the population.)

Early in my career, I was introduced to another Gannett editor, Robert C. Maynard of the Oakland, California, *Tribune*, who was a leader in an industrywide effort to change that imbalance in numbers and improve the quality of coverage – beyond conflict and stereotypes – of diverse communities.

"We will not let you off the hook," he declared to a gathering of American Society of Newspaper Editors in 1978. "We must desegregate this business." The declaration symbolized his willpower as well as the vision and determination that have marked the journalism training institute that bears his name: the Robert C. Maynard Institute for Journalism Education.

In the 1980s, I was editor of the Lansing (Michigan) *State Journal*, and was invited to serve on the faculty of the Maynard Institute's Summer Program for Minority Journalists at the University of California, Berkeley.

I was the only Anglo on that faculty, but was welcomed to the table. Our discussions that summer centered on improving diversity in newsrooms. That would take time (and years later the challenge continues). But a parallel commitment should be to immediately change the way all journalists portray all segments of society with sensitivity and accuracy.

AFTERWORD

The Maynard Institute's position was that "the media plays a pivotal role in shaping our perceptions of each other. The distorted image of communities of color influences public policy and the decisions we make in our personal lives."

Editors needed to take personal responsibility for changing their newsrooms – the way they looked and the way they thought about coverage of minority communities.

While Gannett, the company I worked for, has endured (often deserved) ridicule for its tight budgets, often shallow journalism, and "click-bait" mentality in recent years, its commitment to diversity it its newsrooms and coverage in the 1970s, 1980s, and 1990s was alive when I arrived in Cincinnati in 2002.

One of its programs was "mainstreaming" – an expectation that its reporters and editors would go beyond stereotypical sources and find names, faces, and voices of minorities and women in its communities who may not be represented in stories that spun on an axis of conflict and polarization. Because hiring, retention, and coverage were monitored and measured by the corporate headquarters, the program was viewed with cynicism in the industry and often in its newsrooms.

Certainly, in smaller, rural Gannett newspaper communities, reporters were scrambling to put together minority source lists and to insert mainstream minority voices into their coverage (not always well – in South Carolina a Gannett newspaper was found to have quoted the same Asian woman three times in 13 weeks: about a new area jogging path, the need to change area rugs, and an Elton John concert coming to town).

An often-heard phrase in the news industry then was "diversity fatigue" – it was just too hard for the too-white news operations to keep up with the need to change the colors of its newsrooms and the quality of its coverage of diversity issues.

If finding Latino, black, and Asian journalists was difficult, finding white reporters who could tell the true stories was equally challenging. But the cause was important, especially in Cincinnati. And Cincinnati was fortunate to have Mark Curnutte.

Mark's reporting focused on the historical perspectives of places like Over-the-Rhine and Avondale and introduced readers to everyday heroes in their community – church leaders, war veterans, media personalities, small business owners. One of my favorite Curnutte feature stories was about the reunion of Pullman porters on National Train Day in Philadelphia.

Mark's reporting is rich because his source list is not just a shallow listing of names. It's replete with relationships he has nurtured as the core of his life.

One of the most telling moments in Mark's book is in his "Into the Marvelous Light" introduction, talking about his experiences at the Church of The Resurrection as a white man embraced and trusted in the African-American community.

Indeed, he is doing important work. Mark Curnutte is the right reporter at the right time to tell important stories, the right way: "Across the Color Line."

**Tom Callinan**
Former Editor and Vice President, Enquirer Media
Scottsdale, Arizona
August 10, 2018

# EPILOGUES

*A key element of narrative storytelling is answering the question, "What happened next?" With this collection of newspaper stories compiled from a 25-year period, plenty of opportunities exist to respond, "This is what happened next." At the end of almost every calendar year at the Enquirer, we revisit some of the people who we introduced readers to in the previous 12 months. Here then, are updates on some of the people whose stories are contained in this book.*

## Chapter 2: Bond Hill on verge of urban rebound

Gardenia and Jesse Roper are still in business on California Avenue in Bond Hill. Their Ropers Southern Cooking Restaurant is open four days a week, and Chef Jesse's sweet potato pie is available at several local grocers, including Kroger.

Corinthian Baptist Church, under the leadership of the Rev. K.Z. Smith, successfully redeveloped what was known as the Showcase site. Mercy Health, Ohio's largest health system, moved 1,500 workers into its new headquarters in 2016. The new church home of Corinthian Baptist, as of September 2018, had taken form on the site.

Farther north, the former Jordan Crossing site, renamed MidPointe Crossing, remained a vacant 27 acres five years after the demolition of the outdoor shopping mall that had fallen into decay. A little to the east down Seymour Avenue, Cincinnati Gardens – the former home of the NBA's Cincinnati Royals (now the Sacramento Kings) was demolished in spring 2018.

## Chapter 2: History makes West End residents wary of FC Cincinnati stadium plan

FC Cincinnati received its official invitation to join Major League Soccer (MLS) in an announcement May 29, 2018. Its stadium will be built on property behind Taft IT High School in the West End. The effort received substantial support from Mark Mallory, the former two-term Cincinnati mayor whose family has deep roots on Dayton Street in the neighborhood.

## Chapter 3: Saving Avondale

Ozie Davis III, former executive director of the nonprofit Avondale Comprehensive Development Corp., in May 2018 was voted to a seat on the Cincinnati Public Schools Board of Education. He had finished eleventh for nine seats in the election for Cincinnati City Council in November 2017.

## Chapter 4: Eye on life lessons

As he turned 87, Chester Pryor – Cincinnati's first African-American ophthalmologist – was selected in November 2017 as one of four of the newest Great Living Cincinnatians. When he was installed at a banquet in February 2018, the *Enquirer's* 1998 profile was displayed on a large screen.

## Chapter 4: The children came first

Margaret "Nanny" Andrews died January 29, 2006, at age 93. She was survived by two daughters, eight grandchildren, 14 great grandchildren, 13 great-great grandchildren and one grateful community. Nanny's is still operating at the corner of Reading and Rockdale, Avondale.

## Chapter 5: For some black students, failing is safer

Carrie Lucas, who had gone to court to escape her birth home, where she was expected to clean and care for younger children, graduated from Taft High School in 1999. She went on to Northern Kentucky University, earning degrees in English and philosophy with a minor in political science. Now 37 and the mother of a son, 17, she lives in Covington, Kentucky, and works as a legal assistant in a Cincinnati law firm.

## Chapter 5: For some black students, failing is safer

Kitalena Mason celebrated 10 years of marketing and public relations work with IKEA in 2017. She had worked previously as a news producer at television station WCPO (Channel 9) in Cincinnati after earning her bachelor's degree in mass communications from Miami University.

## Chapter 6: America's Forgotten Heroes

John Leahr died in March 2015 at age 94. In 2012, he talked about his experiences with reporters at a screening of the movie *Red Tails*, a story about the famed African-American Tuskegee Airmen. His friendship and public appearances with a former schoolmate, a white bomber pilot named Herb Heilbrun, became the subject of a children's book published in 2007, *Black and White Airmen: Their True Story.*

## Chapter 6: Clinging to a glimmer of hope

Mary Moore died October 4, 2012, at age 83. The name of her son, Sgt. Raymond Gregory Moore, is inscribed at the Honolulu Memorial in Hawaii, otherwise known as the Court of the Missing. He was declared dead October 9, 1969, and presumed drowned. His remains were not recovered.

## Chapter 7: Faith in action

The Rev. Michael Dantley is in his forty-fifth year as senior pastor at Christ Emmanuel Christian Fellowship in Walnut Hills. He also since 2015 is Dean of the College of Education, Health and Society at Miami University in Oxford, Ohio.

## Chapter 7: The *Cincinnati Herald* at 40

The weekly newspaper is now in its sixty-fourth year. It was sold in 1996 to Sesh Communications by Marjorie Parham, widow of founder Gerald Porter. Jan-Michele Lemon Kearney is *Herald* publisher, and its officers are on Burnet Avenue in Avondale.

## Chapter 9: Father's Day for a non-traditional father

After their story appeared in the *Enquirer*, Jackie and Robert Humphries were chosen as family of the year for the 2013 Midwest Black Family Reunion. They have led the effort to get a pardon for one of her relatives, Zachary Pettus, a native Cincinnatian, who was sentenced to life in prison in 1985 in California for first-degree murder. The Humphries say Pettus is not guilty.

## Chapter 10: Black men's march inspires and divides

The local Nation of Islam community, organized in Mosque No. 5, continues to be a polarizing organization and a challenge to cover yet one worth the effort. It maintains a low profile in Cincinnati. In 2016, after the death of Muhammad Ali, the local leader, Donald Shabazz, talked about what Ali meant to his faith community. "The short answer to that question [how Cassius Clay became Muhammad Ali] is he heard the teachings of the Honorable Elijah Muhammad and believed them and put them into action," Shabazz said.

## Chapter 11: Book helps Judge Jones cope with wife's death

Nathaniel Jones endured the grief of his wife's death and moved forward, even in his late 80s, to achieve. In 2016, the year he turned 90, Jones received the NAACP's highest honor, the Spingarn Medal, and published his memoir, *Answering the Call*. He also received the International Freedom Conductor Award – the greatest honor bestowed by the National Underground Railroad Freedom Center, an institution in Jones's adopted hometown of Cincinnati, which he helped to create.

## Chapter 12: Marvin Lewis brings discipline to revive Bengals

Hired in January 2003, at a time of intense national interest in minority hiring in the NFL, Marvin Lewis parted ways with the Bengals in January 2019, after sixteen seasons as the team's head coach. Lewis's 131 coaching victories are the most in franchise history, yet he was 0–7 in postseason games. He was NFL coach of the year in 2009 and has led his teams to four AFC North division titles in sixteen seasons.

## Chapter 12: Big brother has it covered

Defensive back Madieu Williams went on to play nine NFL seasons for four teams and was named NFL Walter Payton Man of the Year in 2010 for his charitable work in urban communities and the West African nation of Sierra Leone, his homeland. Williams's foundation has built schools in Sierra Leone and provided free medical services to students and community members. Michael Williams was on the track team and also played cornerback at the University of Tennessee football team for 10 games during the 2014 season. He was once projected to be an NFL draft pick. He and Tennessee teammate A. J. Johnson were each charged with two counts of aggravated rape following an alleged incident that took place in November 2014. In July 2018, Johnson and Michael Williams were acquitted of all changes by a jury.

## Chapter 15: On MLK Day, second Obama inauguration sign of progress

The profile of Lesley E. Jones, founder and senior pastor of Truth and Destiny Ministries, Mount Airy, has continued to grow. She leads her diverse faith community, is a sought-after public speaker, and ran a long-shot campaign for Cincinnati City Council in 2017. She received the Democratic Party endorsement for that race and finished twelfth for nine seats. She has promised to run again for political office.

## Chapter 16: Where ex-offenders clean the fenders

Howdy Car Wash in Paddock Hills marked its sixth anniversary in August 2018. It continues to operate as an entry-level employment program for citizens returning to the community from prison. Marchelle Donald, the wife of one of the two Cincinnati Police officers who had the idea for the business, is listed as its owners and manages the car wash's daily operations. In 2016, owners reported that one of their employees, whom had worked there for a year and had been promoted to assistant manager, stole from the cash register and payroll. The owners said they were undeterred in their mission.

# SELECTED BIBLIOGRAPHY

Coates, Ta-Nehisi (2015). *Between the World and Me*. New York: Spiegel & Grau.

Cone, James H (1969). *Black Theology & Black Power*. New York: The Seabury Press.

Dabney, Wendell P (1926). *Cincinnati's Colored Citizens: Historical, Sociological and Biographical*. Cincinnati: The Dabney Publishing Company.

Griffin, John Howard (1961). *Black Like Me*. Boston: Houghton Mifflin.

Hacker, Andrew (1993). Two Nations: Black and White, Separate, Unequal, Hostile. New York: Ballantine Books.

Jones, Nathaniel (2016). *Answering the Call: An Autobiography of the Modern Struggle to End Racial Discrimination in America*. New York: The New Press.

Kahn, Roger (1972). *The Boys of Summer*. New York: Harper & Row.

King, Martin Luther Jr (1967). *Where Do We Go from Here: Chaos or Community?* New York: Harper & Row.

Manis, Andrew (1999). *A Fire You Can't Put Out: The Civil Rights Life of Birmingham's Reverend Fred Shuttlesworth*. Tuscaloosa: University of Alabama Press.

Rankine, Claudia (2001). *Plot*. New York: Grove Press.

# INDEX